BROADCAST JOURNALISM

A GUIDE
FOR THE PRESENTATION
OF RADIO
AND TELEVISION NEWS

DAVID KEITH COHLER

Prentice-Hall, Inc., Englewood Cliffs, New Jersey 07632

Library of Congress Cataloging in Publication Data

Cohler, David Keith.
  Broadcast journalism.

  Bibliography: p.
  Includes index.
  1. Broadcast journalism. I. Title.
PN4784.B75C63 1985   070.1′9   84-24865
ISBN 0-13-083155-7

**For my father,
Charles Ezra Cohler,
in loving memory.**

Editorial/production supervision and
  interior design: Virginia L. McCarthy
Cover design: Wanda Lubelska Design
Manufacturing buyer: Harry P. Baisley
Page layout: Jill S. Packer

Printed in the United States of America

10 9 8 7 6 5 4 3 2 1

ISBN 0-13-083155-7 01

Prentice-Hall International, Inc., *London*
Prentice-Hall of Australia Pty. Limited, *Sydney*
Editora Prentice-Hall do Brasil, Ltda., *Rio de Janeiro*
Prentice-Hall Canada Inc., *Toronto*
Prentice-Hall Hispanoamericana, S.A., *Mexico*
Prentice-Hall of India Private Limited, *New Delhi*
PrenticeHall of Japan, Inc., *Tokyo*
Prentice-Hall of Southeast Asia Pte. Ltd., *Singapore*
Whitehall Books Limited, *Wellington, New Zealand*

CONTENTS

PART II: RADIO NEWS

PART III: TELEVISION NEWS

PART IV: THE FUTURE AND THE JOB MARKET

PREFACE

This book is about the techniques—verbal, mechanical, and electronic—that broadcasters use to gather and present the news.

The text is aimed primarily at students already familiar with the fundamentals of journalism who are now ready to tackle the specialized techniques of broadcast news, either as preparation for a career in the field or as part of a study sequence. The book may also prove helpful for employees of corporate audiovisual departments, community television systems, public relations firms, print journalists contemplating a career change, and enterprises or individuals who must deal with the media.

This book is *not* about specific technology in the sense of being an instruction manual. While it treats videotape as the standard tool of TV news production, it does not list instructions for operating a Sony model this or an RCA model that. Any such button-pusher's guide would risk instant obsolescence at today's rate of technological change.

However, the book *is* specific in its instructions and suggestions for the *journalistic* use of technology. For, regardless of what technological marvels lie ahead, the ability to arrange live and recorded words, sounds, and pictures in a coherent manner is a function of human brain power, not electronic circuitry, protoplasm not silicon.

In short, this book accepts the adage, "In the Beginning was the Word."

Some broadcasters are fond of saying there's nothing you can do with a newspaper that you can't do with television, except wrap fish. The remark is usually made defensively, in response to charges that broadcasters do an inadequate job of presenting news and information.

Both the claim and the response are overstated. That broadcasting is *capable* of presenting news with the same depth, detail, and analysis as print is, at this late date, beyond question. That broadcasting has only rarely *chosen* to do so is quite another matter.

The trouble with sweeping generalizations about the broadcast news business is that, like the news itself, the industry is so multi-faceted as to defy strict categorizing. Just as the *New York Times* shares rack space with the *New York Post,* and *Newsweek* with the *National Enquirer,* so "Nightline" shares the air waves with "Eyewitness News." Ultimately, the choice of what to read or watch is up to the consumer.

Journalists, too, make a choice. Insofar as individual talents and job opportunities coincide, journalists in all media choose the type of journalism they will practice, ranging from the high-minded to the sleazy. While the author of a textbook should not attempt to dictate that choice to students and interested readers, he can try to influence them to recognize and uphold high standards of news presentation and responsibility.

So while this book is about news relayed by oral and electronic means, it is first and foremost about journalism. The technology of broadcast news creates something of the same atmosphere as the video game arcade for the teenager; sometimes, the fun of playing in it comes at the expense of one's homework. Thus, the thrust of this book is toward the main job of journalism, which is to inform and enlighten. The forest must not be lost for the trees.

Broadcasting—specifically television—is blamed for many things these days, from provoking imitative violence to lowering standards of education and public manners. It is also blamed for helping to put newspapers out of business. Only this last charge is demonstrably true. Wire service stories such as the following have become depressingly familiar:

> MEMPHIS, Tenn. (AP)—The final edition of the Memphis Press-Scimitar will appear Monday, ending a 102-year afternoon newspaper tradition and leaving dozens of journalists out of work.
> The end of the Press-Scimitar was announced Sept. 20 when Scripps-Howard Newspapers ended a five-year battle with the paper's slumping circulation....

Part of the "battle" was with television, which, combined with changing life styles, lured away customers and advertisers. The afternoon press, numbed by such foldings in recent years, has had good reason to regard TV news as the *Wehrmacht*, circa 1939-41.

One result is that the news business has been coming full circle. Broadcasters, who in the beginning aped the style and presentation of newspapers, and who eventually found their own ways of doing things, now see a growing number of newspapers aping *them* in order to survive. Color, brevity, variety—less analytical detail. Broadcasters have little to fear in this competition, and it is perhaps howling into the wind to wish that newspapers would stick to what they do best—providing a wealth of detail for which there are not enough hours on broadcasting's clock.

Unlike the evening newspaper business, the broadcast news business is in the pink of health. Overall, its profitability has remained high. While newspapers try a little of this drug and a little of that as a matter of survival, broadcasters use drugs only experimentally. A dose of color here, a tincture of graphic there, an injection of anchorman, a fresh dressing of news set—all of it not to ward off failure but rather to enhance success.

The effect of broadcasting's good health on the job market is as you'd expect: there *are* openings for newcomers. But there are also a lot of newcomers. The competition is stiff. Newcomers need to learn broadcasting's news-gathering techniques *before* entering the competition, to stand a fighting chance.

I have designed this book to give you just that—a fighting chance. In both radio and television, I have concentrated on writing and reporting, because those are the entry areas for newcomers, and also because they are the heart of journalism.

But a word of caution: just because you read this or any other book does not mean that you're ready to be hired. Preparation for the field requires constant supervision and practice. It requires patience and hard work. It requires faith in one's own abilities rather than in blind luck. In the words of the Greek moralist Plutarch,

> No man ever wetted clay and then left it, as if there would be bricks by chance and fortune.

ACKNOWLEDGMENTS

A number of extremely talented broadcast news veterans agreed to review all or parts of the manuscript of this book and to offer comments and suggestions. In many cases, their suggestions are reflected in these pages. I am deeply grateful for their assistance, and I consider it only fitting that I name them:

> Richard Brown, formerly of CBS News, now director of the graduate broadcast reporting sequence at Northwestern University's Medill School of Journalism;
>
> John Callaway, formerly of CBS Radio, now Senior Correspondent at WTTW-TV, Chicago, and director of the William Benton Fellowships in Broadcast Journalism at the University of Chicago;
>
> Doug Ramsey, former correspondent, anchor, and news director, now Vice President of the Los Angeles-based Foundation for American Communications (FACS);
>
> Jim Ruddle, formerly of NBC News, now an anchor/commentator at WMAQ-TV, Chicago;
>
> Bill Slatter, former anchor and news director, now a talent scout for NBC.

I am also grateful to Paul Davis, news director of WGN-TV, Chicago, for patiently explaining the workings of his computerized newsroom.

Among the many news organizations whose work appears in this book, my special thanks go to the entire managements and staffs of WMAQ AM and TV, Chicago, and of WBBM-TV, Chicago, for granting blanket permission to photograph personnel in the course of gathering and presenting the news. Inevitably, some of the staffers pictured here will have moved on to other positions at other stations. I wish them all well.

David Keith Cohler
Chicago

INTRODUCTION

ON BECOMING A NEWS JUNKIE

To make a career in broadcast news, you don't have to look like Robert Redford or Morgan Fairchild. It helps, but there's not much you can do about the face you were born with.

You don't have to sound like Orson Wells or Faye Dunaway. It helps, but there's a limit to the flexibility of your vocal cords.

You don't have to have a famous parent or marry the boss's daughter. It helps, but nepotism is comparatively rare in broadcasting.

You don't have to write like Charles Kuralt or Charles Osgood. But it helps. In fact, it helps so much that if you will concentrate on developing your writing skills, you will almost certainly be successful in radio/TV news.

Often, what you see and hear on your local news appears to contradict this. It's true that some stations rely on cosmetics over substance. It's also true that a great many more stations, perhaps most, stress the substance.

Make no mistake about it, though: except for Public Broadcasting, stations are in business to make money. The more viewers or listeners a station attracts, the more it can charge advertisers. Its choice of how to increase its news audience depends on the philosophy of its top management. If management believes that the news is just another form of entertainment, the station's newscasts are likely to be fast-paced and flashy, its coverage haphazard and superficial, its anchors and reporters uninformed and disorganized.

If, on the other hand, top management believes that the news is a forum for the transmission of ideas to an informed citizenry, the station's newscasts will be thought-provoking and deliberate, its coverage comprehensive and well-written, its anchors and reporters informed and inquisitive.

Notice, I did not say dull. The news is endlessly interesting. But it takes good writing to preserve that interest for the audience.

If you were to see or hear a newscast on, say, the BBC or West German television, you would probably find it informative but dreary. Its writers and producers, working in a state-supported, non-commercial environment, do not need to force viewers to stay tuned through a used car ad to learn the weather forecast. But in American commercial radio and television, there is the need to grab and hold viewers, and no amount of wishful thinking will make it go away.

In fact, wishing it away would be tantamount to wishing yourself out of a job. The used car dealer helps to pay your salary.

That is the reality of most news broadcasting in the United States. It is the same reality that governs newspapers and magazines—with one important difference. In print, you can skip the ads; you can be your own editor. In broadcasting, you don't have that option; if you tune out the commercial, you may also tune out the news.

Good broadcast journalists will not let that happen. They will try to make the viewer/listener say, "Hey, this stuff is just so darned interesting, I want to hear more." They will try to find a common ground between the often complicated details of a story and the simpler needs of the general audience. They will recognize that although the used car dealer is paying for the *time* in which the news is presented, he is not paying for its content. That duty is up to broadcast journalists, who will try their utmost to fill the allotted time with the clearest, most accurate, most well-written account of the news that their experience and professionalism can devise.

There's another reason for this no-nonsense approach to the news: it pays.

With rare exceptions, attempts to "enliven" newscasts through flashy visuals, faster pacing, expensive "high-tech" sets, color-coordinated wardrobes, inane banter among anchors and reporters, and weathergirls with prominent cleavages have failed to attract and hold larger audiences over the long run. In their heyday, the formats typically billed as "Eyewitness News" or "Action News" won high ratings for their stations, not to mention high fees for the "consultants" who conceived them. But, for the most part, good journalists shied away from these stations, and eventually so did intelligent viewers.

One reason is that when the news gets serious—as is its habit—most people just won't place their trust in a bunch of pretty faces in color-coordinated wardrobes.

If you go into broadcast news, especially television, it may not be long before you meet some of the "pretty faces." You'll probably find them primping in front of the mirror. This one may have had his face lifted, that one her teeth capped. Either or both may have been to a makeup expert or hired an acting coach. On the set, they may argue over who gets the more flattering camera angles or who gets to read more items and thus be on-camera longer. Off camera, they almost never discuss the news, except insofar as its presentation—the "packaging"—might affect the ratings. After the newscast, the question they are most likely to ask is, "How'd I look?"

Yes, Ted Baxter, the bumbling, egomaniacal anchorman in the 1970s Mary Tyler Moore situation comedy, is alive and well—although probably not in Minneapolis, where the people who run local TV generally take the news seriously.

While bona fide journalists (and intelligent viewers) may snicker at the Ted Baxters, there is something to be said in their defense: they did not hire themselves. They are filling some employer's desire to lure a news audience on the cheap. Thorough news coverage is expensive. It costs a fortune to buy cameras, recorders, editing gear, and microwave vans; to hire reporters, writers, producers, editors, camera crews, and studio personnel. A cheaper way is to hire one or two "personalities" and a group of writers to deliver the whole package.

That sort of news operation can be a graveyard for a good journalist if he or she stays too long—but a golden opportunity for someone just starting out. For if you are a good writer or reporter, it won't be long before one of the classier operations comes courting.

Almost every beginner goes through this process of starting small. After all, it's the smaller, feebler operations that are usually hiring new people, because they are constantly losing the talented veterans to bigger, classier newsrooms. At the same time, given the small total of entry-level job opportunities in broadcast news, your prospects for getting hired at even a small place depend on your ability to write and report well.

So how do you go about it?

Well, for starters, you become a news junkie.

More than a "news hound" or a "tiger," a news junkie is someone who must always know what's going on. Someone who can't wait to read the morning papers, and then the afternoon editions. Someone who listens to radio news in the morning and watches TV news at night, on several stations. Someone who pays attention to the different ways competing news organizations handled the same story—the way it appeared in the *Daily Bugle* as compared with the *Daily Blatt;* the way it was told on CBS as compared with NBC and Cable News Network; the way it was told locally at 6 o'clock, again at 11 o'clock, and again the next morning on all news radio, and the way the weekly and monthly magazines handled it. Someone who consistently asks himself, "How would *I* have handled that story?"

The obsession may be going too far if you find yourself installing a teleprompter in your shower, ordering salt and pepper shakers in the shape of microphones, or renaming your cat Edward R. Meow. But short of that, you must eat, sleep, and breathe the news.

Does such single-mindedness seem excessive to you? It had better not. Unlike a budding doctor or lawyer, you will not go through several years of formal advanced study. You will not stay up half the night, every night, memorizing the cellular structure of muscle tissue or the common law interpretation of easements. No one will give you a three-day examination and, if you pass, hand you a parchment granting you the right to set up practice.

You will be on your own. You will need to discipline yourself. Instead of an examination, you will be given an audition; instead of a parchment, a paycheck.

The purpose of what follows is to help you prepare for that audition. The emphasis will be on writing and reporting, because those are the areas most open to young journalists in radio and television news departments.

The thing to remember, once you arrive in the electronic playground that is today's radio or TV newsroom, is that all the cameras and microphones, all the flashing lights and digital readouts, all the fancy recording and transmission gear, are there *to serve your words,* not vice versa.

The main concern, then, is to know which words.

1

THE WAY PEOPLE TALK

WRITING FOR THE EAR

The first word man ever spoke probably wasn't even a word. More likely, it was an inflected grunt, perhaps a reaction to stepping on a sharp rock or to biting into a tasty hunk of zebra meat.

The comedy writer–director Mel Brooks, in a routine called "The 2,000-Year-Old Man," claims the first word was in "rock talk," as in, "Hey, you dere, don't throw dat rock!"

The point is, the first word was *spoken*, not chiseled in stone at Cave Man U. The chiseling—writing—came a lot later in our cultural awakening. What makes things hard for broadcast journalists is that the printing press was invented before radio and television. Journalists first learned to write for print. They must unlearn a few things to write well for broadcast.

News written for broadcast is meant to be *spoken*. It's a form of story-telling—informal, but not as informal as sitting around the old campfire. It needs to follow certain rules. Most of these rules are simply common sense. Others, though, are contrary to the way many young print journalists have learned to write.

The language of print journalism is artificial and convoluted. Deliberately so. Print style is designed to accommodate two main technical requirements: limited space and delay in publication. Limited space imposes on the writer a need to tell as many facts as possible *in the very first sentence;* after all, maybe that sentence (known as the *lead*) is all there'll be space for. Hence the "inverted pyramid" structure, enabling a copy editor to trim from the end.

The delay in publication—between writing and delivery to homes, newsstands, and vending machines—requires protective treatment of the "when" element to make clear that the facts, as related, refer to things that may have changed in the meantime.

The result, while clear to the reader's eye, is often incomprehensible to the listener's ear. In fact, the requirements of print style often result in an artificiality that would have the story of Little Red Riding Hood begin this way:

THE WOODS, OCT. 25—An eight-year-old girl narrowly missed serious injury when she was saved by a woodsman who snatched her from the claws of a transvestite wolf which had already devoured her grandmother, reliable sources reported Thursday.

A broadcast newswriter can relax a bit. He might begin

A remarkable rescue in The Woods today . . .

That's what's known as a "broadcast sentence." Grammatically, it's only a fragment. But it is perfectly clear when *read aloud.* It relates only a few facts at a time, in this case (journalistically speaking), the "what," "where," and "when" elements.

Of course, news stories aren't fairy tales. They're about a reality which is often ugly and complex. "Once upon a time there was a brutal murder" is not an acceptable way to start a news story. And yet,

A murder on the West Side today . . .

is an acceptable opening. In fact, a very good one. It orients us by telling "what," "when," and "where" in general terms. More detailed information will follow, and it, too, will be revealed gradually, not to tease us or keep us on the edge of our seats, but to avoid overloading our ability to comprehend. For, unlike readers of a print story, listeners of broadcast news *cannot go back and rehear what they may have missed.*

Listening is a very different experience from reading. The reader must focus his attention on the printed words. If he is momentarily distracted, he can go back and find his place. Not so the listener. Any distractions may cause him to lose irretrievably information essential to his understanding of the story.*

---

*The English language calls for using the masculine personal pronouns "he," "him," and "his" when the gender of the singular antecedent is unspecified. I explain this to avoid a charge of "sexism." In fact, these days women are entering newsrooms in roughly the same numbers as men. In some news departments, they outnumber men. The very top level of management was the *only* place where, at this writing, women were not yet present in significant numbers. However, they will no doubt be there shortly. Meanwhile, any book stressing correct English obviously must obey the rules of grammar. Thus, "news*men*" is the correct way to refer to journalists of both genders—*not* "news-

Broadcast journalists must take this into account. They must not try to tell too much, too fast. Instead, they must reveal story elements a few at a time, presenting them logically, and linking them in a clear, coherent manner. One way they do this is by using simpler language than print journalists.

The everyday vocabulary of print journalism is small—around 8,000 to 10,000 words. The vocabulary of broadcast journalism is smaller still—about 6,000 to 8,000 words—about the same as the average person's speaking vocabulary. This doesn't mean that the broadcast journalist loves words or language any less than the print journalist. But it does mean that the broadcaster makes a strong effort to keep his language conversational, phrasing sentences and thoughts in everyday wording whenever possible. Broadcast journalists strive for a middle ground between the simplistic "See Spot run" and the pretentious "Regard Spot hasten;" they say "Watch Spot go."

To choose more relevant examples, broadcasters rely heavily on the verbs *say, tell,* and *explain* rather than on verbs such as *declare, state, aver, avow, expound, opine, recount, elucidate,* and so on. When's the last time you heard anyone "declare" or "state" that he was tired or hungry? Or "make a statement" or "issue a declaration" to that effect? Chances are the person simply *said* it.

When people talk, they use informal language. They don't pause to diagram a sentence in their heads before speaking it. The trouble with writing the way people talk is that all too many people talk improperly. They often get the facts wrong, garble their syntax, say "lay down" when they mean "lie down," mistake "infer" for "imply," and so on.

So let's put it this way: broadcast newswriting is writing the way people *would* talk if they used language correctly and got the facts straight.

So far, so easy—right? Well, maybe. If informality were the only difference between print and broadcast styles, you could have saved yourself the price of this book. There are, however, several other differences, some of them so far-reaching as to require nothing short of a totally fresh approach, an ability to organize a story in a way that, to a print journalist, often seems very strange indeed.

If the print journalist's enemy is space, the broadcaster faces a far more implacable foe, *time.* Everything in broadcasting is measured by the clock: the length of a newscast, when it goes on the air, when it goes off, the length of each story, and, within each story, the length of each and every taped component. So pervasive, so fundamental to broadcast writing is the clock that a stopwatch comes under the heading of required equipment. If you do not own a stopwatch, and your school or business does not provide one, buy one as soon as you can. (Digital wristwatches with a stopwatch—or "chronograph"—function cost only a few dollars these days. However, if you intend to work in a professional broadcast newsroom, you should buy a better stopwatch as a necesssary investment; you'll want one with a large, clear readout and a cord to hang around

---

person," "newspeople," or "newshen." "Newswomen" is correct when it refers to female journalists *only*. Similarly, "spokesman" and "spokeswoman," "chairman" and "chairwoman," but never "spokesperson" or "chairperson."

Some writers and speakers try to get around the "sexism" problem by using the plural "they" or "their" to refer to a singular antecedent (e.g., "The buyer is getting *their* money's worth."). This is not only incorrect, it's silly, and newswriters must stick to correct English ("The buyer is getting *his* money's worth.").

your neck, leaving your hands free to make notes or operate equipment.)

But the clock comes into play long before it is used to time a story. In many cases, it virtually dictates a story's organization and structure—in short, how it must be written.

The writer almost always knows in advance, to within 5 seconds either way, how much time he is allotted for a given story. He thus knows how long he's got to get from point A to point Z, point Z being the listener's understanding. If the writer is allotted 45 seconds or 1 minute to tell a story, he can present the facts slowly, strive for stylistic effect, and make the story's details compelling and relevant to the audience. But if the writer is allotted only 15 or 20 seconds, he literally hasn't a second to waste; each second may spell the difference between clarity and ambiguity.

The combination of the time allotted to a story and the need to tell it clearly and conversationally imposes a structure on the broadcast version which is vastly different from the print version. Broadcast story structure is often a difficult matter for journalists accustomed to print style. For one thing, there are no "roundups" in broadcasting—no combinations of stories in which the writer jumps back and forth from one story to another. Instead, broadcasting calls for "straight-line" writing, in which each story, although possibly related to the stories preceding and following it, is written separately from beginning to end. In broadcasting, the linking of related stories is done by *order of presentation* rather than by selective interweaving.

These and other matters are best demonstrated by taking a "typical" print story and seeing how it might be transformed for broadcast. The following story, which opened on the front page of a major daily newspaper, was rewritten from wire service reports:

WASHINGTON—In a gloomy warning not to take the economy's resurgence for granted, President Reagan's top economic adviser told a group of business executives Monday that enormous federal budget deficits could dampen the still-young recovery and lead to a pickup in unemployment as early as next year.

Addressing the same group later, House Speaker Thomas P. O'Neill, Jr. (D-Mass.) issued a major political challenge to Reagan, disclosing plans to rush a bill through the House this month to trim the scheduled July 1 tax cut for upper-income Americans.

"It is time the rich started to accept their fair share of the (tax) burden," O'Neill declared.

In his comments to executives assembled by the American Stock Exchange, Martin S. Feldstein, chairman of the president's Council of Economic Advisers, said huge federal budget deficits looming in the future will contribute to a "lopsided recovery" during the next three to five years.

The deficits, he said, will keep interest rates high and that will prevent interest-sensitive industries, like housing, from "sharing in the over-all recovery."

"The lopsided character of the recovery carries with it the danger that the recovery may lose momentum," he said.

Later, answering reporters' questions, Feldstein depicted an economic recovery distorted by high interest rates.

"I do think there is a risk," he said. "Maybe it's one chance in three that if we don't provide clear evidence that we're getting deficits under control, the recovery will peter out.

"It's not that the deficits in themselves produce the 1-in-3 risk. But they clearly have raised the risk to a higher level than I would like to see."

As for unemployment, Feldstein said there is "some good risk" it will go back up next year, although he described the chance of increased joblessness as "less likely (rather) than more likely."

For the time being, the recovery "does seem very sound," he said, although the rapid growth of the money supply recently is "a cause of serious concern" in threatening a revival of inflation.

The basic money supply, known as M-1, composed of currency and checking account deposits, has risen at an annual rate of 11.9 percent in the six-month period ending in April. Over the last 13 weeks it has been rising at an annualized rate of 13.2 percent.

Both increases have brought the supply about $15 billion above the level consistent with the Federal Reserve System's 1983 growth range of 4 percent to 8 percent. Part of the rise stems from the inflow into checking accounts of the unusually large federal tax refunds.

Feldstein said the money supply "must not be allowed to go on expanding at its recent pace." The Federal Reserve Board would have to act to lower money supply growth, he said, unless it declined automatically "over an extended period of time" to fall within the Fed's targets.

As for taxes, Feldstein's speech reiterated Reagan's commitment to new taxes beginning in 1985.

The president, he said, "has been falsely accused of being stubbornly opposed to all additional tax revenue" because he has pledged to veto any changes in the 1983 tax cut.

"If the Democrats are serious about wanting to reduce . . . the deficits, the time has come to stop arguing about the inevitable and to start seeking a solution along the lines suggested in the administration's budget," Feldstein said, alluding to Reagan's all-but-forgotten proposal to raise taxes on a standby basis starting Oct. 1, 1985, if deficits do not drop sharply by then.

O'Neill, in his comments to the business group, charged that Reagan was following a course of confrontation with Congress over budget deficits that could jeopardize recovery.

He said his proposal—to limit the 1983 tax reduction to $700 instead of providing a 10 percent across-the-board reduction for all taxpayers without any ceiling—would lower red-ink spending by nearly $7 billion this year. The cap would reduce tax cuts for those making more than $47,000 a year.

Democrats in the House are expected to approve O'Neill's plan at a party caucus Tuesday. But few believe the tax cap will be approved by the Republican-controlled Senate.

Still, O'Neill issued a statement saying that considerations of fairness justified the last-minute legislation to modify the third year of the tax cut enacted in 1981 at Reagan's request.

Noting that lower- and middle-income Americans had been affected adversely by Reagan's cuts in social and domestic programs ranging from food stamps to student loans, the House speaker said, "It is time that the burden of Reaganomics is shared by those in the upper income groups. For two years, this group has benefited mightily from the Reagan tax program. This has been a program of the rich, by the rich, and for the rich."

Still awake? I ask because some beginning journalists find economic stories boring or confusing. That's too bad, since, if there's anything like a "typical" story in the news business, it's the economic one. Week in, week out, rain or shine, hell or high water, you can count on writing economic news. Which is as it should be—because if you stop to think about it, economic news is just a generic term for stories that affect people you know, how they live, what they eat and wear, and if they can afford to exchange gifts at Christmas.

But back to the matter at hand. The story you just read contains about 750 words. By modern newspaper standards, it offers a rather full account of Feldstein's and O'Neill's remarks, supported where appropriate by direct quotes. If you read at an average rate, it took you about $2\frac{1}{2}$ minutes to complete the article.

Reading silently, however, is not the way to test for the pitfalls of broadcast news, which, obviously, is read aloud. So read that story again, this time *out loud*.

I'm not kidding about this. The sooner you get in the habit of reading copy aloud, the quicker you'll learn broadcast style. Reading aloud is the best way, sometimes the *only* way, to tell if the copy will be clearly understandable on the air. If you've ever visited a radio or TV newsroom, you're bound to have heard reporters and writers reading their copy aloud—"talking to the typewriter" it's called—proofreading it not only for factual content but also for its *sound*. If it doesn't sound clear to the person who wrote it, it emphatically will not sound clear to the listener.

Since you are probably not in the habit of reading news copy aloud, it's natural for you to feel self-conscious at first. The feeling will quickly pass. Shyness, on the other hand, is more difficult to overcome; it's a definite hindrance not only to reading aloud, but also to your chances for success in *any* branch of journalism. Reporting is not a pursuit for shrinking violets. On the contrary, it often requires a boldness bordering on aggression.

So swallow that lump in your throat—and start talking.

Okay, you can give the pipes a rest now.

If you read the entire article, and if you speak ("announce") at a normal rate, this little exercise took you around $4\frac{1}{2}$ minutes, nearly twice as long as reading the same words silently.

Remember, the print story is of *average* length. But the *average* time allotted to a similar story in U.S. commercial radio would be from a minimum of about 20 seconds to a maximum of 1 minute and in television from the same minimum to a maximum of 2 minutes. That is a bear of a problem for broadcasters, for they must condense the story radically, without losing its essence. They need to organize their thoughts much more sharply and clearly than do print writers. Thus, to succeed, they must be more disciplined writers.

Now take another look at the newspaper story's lead sentence. It is 47 words long. That's a mouthful. You probably ran out of breath before you came to the period, with the likely result that both you and any listeners lost the thread. So broadcast news sentences must be *short*. They must allow time for the newscaster to breathe and for the listener to comprehend *at once*:

> The Reagan administration's top economist says the recession is not over yet.   He
>
> warns there might even be a rise in unemployment next year.

Skip now to the print story's fifth-from-last paragraph, beginning, "O'Neill, in his comments . . ." The print writer has been able to reidentify his protagonist simply by using his last name; a forgetful reader could glance back to the story's second paragraph for O'Neill's full identification. But the listener doesn't have that luxury. He can't glance back at anything. The broadcast writer might add a word of reidentification, *Speaker* O'Neill," but that doesn't really solve the problem. The problem really is that a certain amount of *time has elapsed* not only between the first identification and the second, but also between subject matters. This jumping back and forth, while acceptable in print, is jarring and disorienting in broadcasting. The broadcast version thus demands a different story structure.

Although there are no hard and fast rules, the broadcast version should deal with one subject or protagonist *completely* before moving on to the next. For example, the print story used here starts with Feldstein, goes on to O'Neill, goes back to Feldstein, then returns once again to O'Neill. The broadcast version should open with one man's remarks, then move on to the other's. Period, end of story. This is a more natural way of telling a story. The print writer used the unnatural inverted pyramid structure—just one of the things you'll have to unlearn in broadcast writing.

Paragraph 3 of the print story presents double trouble for the broadcaster:

> "It is time the rich started to accept their fair share of the (tax) burden," O'Neill declared.

First, print style often identifies the speaker of a direct quotation, or the source of information (the attribution), at the end of a sentence, preceded by a comma. But as you read aloud, you probably noticed that such sentence structure sounds unnatural. The natural speech rhythm would end the sentence after the word "burden." Adding the words "O'Neill declared" forces the speaker to raise his or her inflection unnaturally.

Broadcasters thus *change the sentence structure to conform to natural speech patterns*. Identification or attribution comes most often *at the start* of the sentence:

> O'Neill said "it is time the rich started to accept their fair share of the tax burden."

But wait. *Listeners can't see the quotation marks.* How are they to know if the remark is O'Neill's opinion or the writer's? It's clearly not the newswriter's role to decide what's "fair" and what isn't. So for the listeners' benefit, the writer must make absolutely clear that the words belong exclusively to O'Neill. Therefore, in a rare departure from natural speech, the broadcaster must add a few words to make the source of the quote clear:

> O'Neill said -- *and these are his words* -- "it's time the rich started to accept their
>
> fair share of the tax burden."

or

O'Neill said it's time the rich started to accept *what he called* "their fair share" of the tax burden.

Further examples from the print story illustrate cases in which broadcast writers must add words that do not actually appear in the printed text—for example, the figure "$15 billion." Reading aloud, you didn't say "dollar sign 15 billion." You said "fifteen billion *dollars.*" And that is the way you'd write your copy as well. The figure "13.2%" becomes "thirteen-point-two percent." In other words, you *write exactly what is to be said.*

Broadcast copy, while meant for the ears of the listener, is meant in the first instance for an intermediary, the eyes of the newscaster, who is trained to speak the words as they appear in the script. Newscasters can't pronounce short-hand, copyediting, symbols, or names like Myschklyczevskinov without help. Broadcast writers must help them by making it "Mizz-kluh-SHEFFS-kin-off."

PROFESSIONAL AIMS AND RESPONSIBILITIES

Although I've begun the newswriting section of this book by stressing the dif-ferences between print and broadcast styles, attention must also be paid to the similarities of news coverage in the different media.

Most broadcast writing is either original, as in the case of a reporter covering events at the scene, or is based on writing meant for print, as from wire service copy, government or industry handouts, and so on. A basic job of the broadcast newswriter is to translate this eye-oriented writing into ear-oriented writing.

However, the *content* of the writing, as opposed to its *form,* must meet the same *journalistic* criteria in broadcasting as in print. Newsmen in all media share certain aims:

To inform and enlighten
To dig for the truth
To witness and chronicle events great and small
To render understandable a complex reality
To expose wrongdoing harmful to society at large
To scoop the competition whenever possible

Since the goals are the same and only the methods differ, broadcast journalists and their print colleagues also share the same professional respon-sibilities:

To be accurate
To be fair
To be first

Although no book can teach you what questions to ask, where and how to dig for facts and answers—in short, how to *be* a great writer or a great reporter—it can urge you to develop habits in small things that will help you later to handle the big things. I am talking about all journalists' duty to use words and grammar correctly and to check facts.

READY REFERENCE MATERIALS

Most broadcast newsrooms contain essential reference materials—dictionaries, atlases, telephone books, government directories, street guides, maps, ward and precinct diagrams, and so on. However, many of these materials, especially dictionaries, have a way of disappearing as they are borrowed and not returned. Career journalists will usually assemble their own personal reference materials and lock them in their desks upon leaving the newsroom for the night.

Most ready reference materials serve equally well for print or broadcast use. But broadcasters need certain "extras" that print writers do not, even when it comes to that most basic of reference books, the dictionary.

Dictionaries

Since his words will be spoken aloud, any broadcast writer's dictionary must contain word-by-word pronunciations. It should also indicate which pronunciation is preferred where more than one is permissible.

The standard, ultimate-definition dictionary in American newsrooms is *Webster's Unabridged.* But if you happen to drop it on your foot, you'll be laid up for a while—and it's expensive as well as heavy. For everyday, quick-reference use, there are a number of inexpensive paperback dictionaries, including the *Scribner-Bantam* and the *Oxford American,* both available at most bookstores. (Forget the 75-cent paperback dictionary you find at the supermarket checkout counter; it isn't for anyone over age 11.)

For broadcast newsroom use, your dictionary should

1. Be up-to-date. It should contain words having come into common use in the preceding decade.
2. Contain clear pronunciations as already noted.
3. Contain alphabetized historical names and places.
4. Contain brief usage guidelines, also alphabetized.

Grammar and Usage Guides

When may you split an infinitive? Does "presently" mean "soon" or "now"? Does one "flout" the law or "flaunt" it? Should you write "The man *who* was going" or "The man *that* was going?" A good writer needs to find the answers to those questions, and the answers are not always in dictionaries. That's where grammer and usage guides come in handy.

Until recently, the standard reference was H. W. Fowler's *A Dictionary of Modern English Usage* (revised 1983 by Sir Ernest Gowers, Oxford University Press), usually known just as "Fowler" for short. Although Fowler remains the standard in many parts of the English-speaking world, its advice, apart from being somewhat long-winded, is keyed to British standards, not American. All of which is fine if you are writing for the BBC. American audiences, however, prefer Americanisms because that's the way they speak. (It's been said that Britain and America are "two countries divided by a common language." For example, the statement, "I'm mad about my flat," means in America, "I'm angry about my flat tire," whereas in Britain in means, "I just love my apartment.")

There are two American-oriented language guides in widespread use: Wilson Follett's *Modern American Usage* (paperback, Warner Books, 1966, $2.50) and Theodore Bernstein's *The Careful Writer* (paperback, Atheneum, 1965, $9.95). Both list things alphabetically (as other guides do not), enabling the broadcast writer to resolve language problems quickly. Of the two, Bernstein is the more complete and more entertaining.*

Serious writers and students of language will, over time, refine their skills by reading works by authors such as William Safire, Edwin Newman, Richard Mitchell, and John Simon, to name but a few. They will also follow magazine columns such as William Safire's "On Language" in the Sunday *New York Times Magazine.*

Atlases and Almanacs

Where is Maracaibo? What is the capital of Angola? Who won the heavyweight boxing crown in 1947? What movie won the Oscar for Best Picture in 1933? What does the U.S. Constitution say about the private ownership of firearms? Is a train from Prague to Budapest going east or west? Who was Speaker of the House before the present one?

These are the kinds of questions, ranging from the important to the trivial, that pop up every day in the news business. If you're like most of us, your first impulse will be to shout around the newsroom in hopes that someone will know the answer. The answer you usually get is, "The train would be going east—*I think.*" So you end up looking up the information anyway, which is what you should have done in the first place. For some reason, that short trip across the newsroom to the reference shelf seems like a major undertaking.

Save yourself the trip by buying a world almanac. There are several published each year, each selling for around $5. The publishers change frequently; past almanacs have been issued by CBS News, *The New York Times,* the *Washington Post,* and the Associated Press, among others. They all provide the same basic facts and figures. Just be sure the one you buy includes world maps of sufficient detail to enable you to tell listeners which way that train was going.

Computer Data Systems

(That's da*ta,* not da*ting.*) More and more these days, newsrooms are subscribing to computer information systems—such as "Nexis," "Compu-Serve," etc.—to enable staffers to do modest research without having to visit a library. While no staff broadcast journalist can be expected to purchase his or her own computer terminal, such computerized retrieval systems are clearly the wave of

---

*Some standard works on writing and usage, while excellent guides for print writers, are of comparatively little practical value for broadcast writers. That's because they deal largely with print punctuation, paragraph structure, and other matters of no concern for spoken English.

WMAQ-TV News researcher Chris Kehoe checks background information via the "Nexis" computer data service. More and more, computer systems such as this are supplanting hard-copy "morgues."

the future. At the very least, writers or reporters should know how to use ("access") any computer system acquired by their employers. Computer information systems are in growing use at universities and businesses, and students should take the trouble to visit such installations to learn their operation.

NEWS JUNKIE (CONT.)

Trust me on this: the quicker you become a news junkie—the quicker you get in the habit of keeping up on the news, day in, day out—the less you will need to consult reference materials. If you know the background of a story, chances are that you will be prepared to write knowledgeably about any new developments without spending precious time in research.

WHEN IN DOUBT, ASK!

Okay, now you're armed with a dictionary, a usage guide, and an almanac. You know how to use the company computers, and you're well on your way to news junkie-hood. Does this make you an authority on every story that breaks? Unfortunately, no.

Almost every day, you are likely to come upon a story you don't quite understand and be expected to write it in broadcast style. No journalist, no matter how long his or her experience, can be expected to understand everything. The world is too complex. And yet, the job requires explaining that complexity to a mass audience.

The solution is, ask someone for help. It is not stupid not to know something. It *is* stupid not to seek help.

Occasionally, under the pressure of the clock, there may not be time to ask for help. In a later chapter (in the part on radio news), you will learn what you can do in such a situation. But for now, and as a general rule, **do not write a story you do not understand!**

If *you* don't understand it, chances are the *audience* won't understand it either. In that case, you will have done something worse than fail to inform: you will have *mis*informed.

2
SHAPE, STRUCTURE, AND SYNTAX

COPY APPEARANCE

Despite the electronic wizardry at their command and the technological marvels just around the corner (see Chapter 22, The Future), most broadcast news departments are old-fashioned in one respect: they use typewriters and paper instead of video display terminals (VDTs). *Lots* of paper.

And because the words written and edited on that paper must be read easily and fluently by newscasters and production personnel, the typing must be neat and the pages clean. The dreaded words "Neatness counts" are strictly applied to broadcast news copy. Dirty copy causes newscasters to fumble and engineers to push the wrong buttons, resulting in errors of both form and content.

So before we dig into the meat and potatoes of broadcast style, we must pause to set the table properly. The following is an irreducible list of hard rules for typing broadcast copy:

1. **Triple space.** There must be adequate space between lines for corrections. Use $8\frac{1}{2}'' \times 11''$ script or copy paper.
2. Use a **70-space line for radio,** a **35-space line for TV.** Pica typeface is preferable to Elite because it is larger and easier to read.

3. **Upper/lower-case** is preferable to all caps or all lower because it allows the greatest flexibility in punctuation, phonetics, and technical instructions.

4. Leave a **top margin** of 1½ to 2 inches. This allows room for identifications, slugs, and timings.

5. Type only **one story per page,** no matter how short the item. Paper is the cheapest commodity in the newsroom. If a story must be continued onto a second page, **draw an arrow** in the lower right-hand corner.

This is broadcasting's way of saying "more" or "continued." Since the lack of an arrow means the end of a story, it is *not* necessary to type "30" or "-0-" or any other print symbol.

6. **Do not split words between lines.** Split words can throw the newscaster.

7. **Do not split sentences between pages.** Same reason.

8. **Do not use copyediting symbols.** Correct errors by striking out the entire word containing the error, then **retype or print the entire correction** just above the strikeover.

No: The brown quick fox jumped over the lazy dog.

Yes: The ~~brown quick~~ fox jumped ~~ovre~~ the lazy ~~dig~~.
        quick brown   over   dog.

9. If a sentence or page contains so many corrections that a newscaster can't read it aloud fluently, **retype the entire sentence or entire page.**

Yes, strict adherence to these rules can be tedious at times. So can a lot of things: football practice, playing the scales, studying for final exams, and so on. The point is, the rules are designed to maximize clarity and minimize errors on the air.

When we get to the specifics of preparing radio news copy, and then television copy, there will be some additional guidelines for where to put slugs, IDs, timings, right/left margins, and so on. These additional guidelines vary slightly from newsroom to newsroom. But you may rely on the nine rules just given to be universally understood.

(If you enter broadcast news in an on-air capacity, in other words, writing copy you yourself will deliver, you will probably evolve your own set of rules, designed exclusively for your own use. However, when writing for someone else, you must not endanger the air product by sloppy copy preparation.)

Now for the meat and potatoes.

SHORT, DIRECT SENTENCES

Most of us speak in short sentences. Sometimes, when we try to utter a long sentence, we lose the thread, get hopelessly confused, and have to begin over. Listeners, too, are accustomed to receiving information the same way—in short takes. So, because we want the news to be understood, it makes sense to write in short sentences.

Although many daily newspapers are now adopting a style favoring shorter sentences, the traditional print sentence, especially the lead sentence, is too long to *say* comfortably:

> WARSAW, Poland—Lech Walesa, the mustachioed Polish electrician whose personal charisma and negotiating skills propelled him to leadership of the Soviet Bloc's first independent trade union, Wednesday was awarded the 1983 Nobel Peace Prize for his struggle on behalf of worker rights.

(Dan Fisher, Los Angeles Times, reprinted by permission)

That sentence, 40 words long, leaves us panting for breath. And it contains so much information that it risks overloading listeners' capacity to comprehend.

Reduced to its essence, the story is this:

Lech Walesa won the Nobel Peace Prize today.

Those eight words, the story's barest bones, are direct and to the point. We don't get lost in excess verbiage, subsidiary clauses, and descriptive prose. In the *next* sentence we can put flesh on the bones:

The Polish Solidarity union leader got the award for his fight for workers' rights.

That's another 13 words, for a total so far of 21—still 19 words shorter than the print example's single sentence. Of course, we've lost the mustache, the personal charisma, the negotiating skills, and the reference to the Soviet Bloc. So be it. Obviously, when you shorten things, some details have to be omitted or postponed. In broadcasting, what usually gets omitted are the adjectives and much of the background. There simply isn't time to get it all in. The trade-off is greater flexibility in how to begin and how to follow up. Here are a few ways:

The 1983 Nobel Peace Prize was announced today. It went to Lech Walesa (Lek Vah-WEN-sah), leader of the banned Polish labor union Solidarity . . .

-0-

Polish Solidarity union leader Lech Walesa (Lek Vah-WEN-sah) is the winner of this year's Nobel Peace Prize. He won it, the Nobel committee said, for his struggle on behalf of workers' rights . . .

-0-

Lech Walesa's (Lek Vah-WEN-sah's) long struggle for the rights of Polish workers paid off today in an unexpected way. Walesa (Vah-WEN-sah) has won the 1983 Nobel Peace Prize.

Naturally, there were many more details to this story, but I've deliberately withheld them to make the point that even without details, short sentences are the rule in broadcasting. It's impossible to make a rule establishing the exact number of words in each sentence. But generally speaking, if you find yourself writing a sentence that exceeds 20 to 25 words, start over and make a deliberate effort to write two sentences instead of one.

This applies to *all* broadcast writing, not just opening sentences. Forget about complex, comprehensive sentences. Don't use them as leads, don't use them as follow-ups, don't use them for direct quotes.

Here's a somewhat harder example:

MOSCOW—The Soviet Union moved Wednesday to dispel suggestions in the West that it may make concessions in the talks on limiting nuclear weapons in Europe to regain the political initiative after the furor over the downing of a South Korean airliner.

Deputy Foreign Minister Georgy Kornienko insisted at a press conference there is no connection between the intermediate-range missile talks and the Sept. 1 downing by the Soviets of the airliner. All 269 people aboard, at least 61 of them from the United States, were killed.

Kornienko described as "wishful thinking" West German Foreign Minister Hans-Dietrich Genscher's remark that the Kremlin may be ready to compromise on the issue of whether British and French missile systems should be included in the talks in Geneva, Switzerland.

(Michael Dobbs, *Washington Post*)

Two transformations are required here to achieve broadcast style: shorter sentences and *simpler* (less convoluted) *language*. Examples:

Moscow says its shooting down of that Korean jetliner will not lead to Soviet concessions on arms control. A Soviet deputy foreign minister says there's no connection between the jetliner incident and the talks in Geneva on limiting nuclear arms in Europe.

-0-

The Soviets say they won't bend in arms control talks, despite their downing of that Korean jetliner. A Soviet deputy foreign minister says the two matters are not related. He says Moscow will still insist that British and French missiles be included in any agreement to limit arms in Europe.

-0-

Some Western leaders have speculated that the downing of that Korean jetliner may force the Soviets to make concessions in the Geneva arms control talks.   But today, a Soviet official said that won't happen.   Deputy Foreign Minister Georgy Kornienko (Ĝay-OR-ghee Kor-nee-EN-ko) said the jetliner is one thing, the arms talks another.

-0-

A Soviet official today described as "wishful thinking" speculation that the Korean jetliner incident will lead to Soviet concessions in arms control. . .

-0-

"Wishful thinking" -- That's what a Soviet official is calling speculation about Soviet arms control concessions because of the Korean jetliner incident.

In a couple of these examples, the language varies considerably from the print version. But the meaning, the essence, remains the same. Broadcast editors and producers *want* you to use different language from print. It's what you're being paid for.

LEADS

By and large, a print lead seeks to impart the most information in the fewest words. The result is a ministory that stands on its own.

By and large, a broadcast lead seeks to impart only as much information as can be easily grasped. It can stand on its own—but just as often it can't.

Except for the word "tonight," the following lead would serve either print or broadcast:

A bullet-proof vest saved a policeman's life in the Kenmore District tonight, stopping a handgun bullet fired by a teenage assailant.

But the following leads lend themselves to broadcasting only:

There's a lucky cop in the Kenmore District tonight. . .

-0-

A Kenmore District patrolman is alive and well tonight, thanks to his bullet-proof vest. . .

Such leads, which require follow-up sentences to complete the essential information, serve the double function of piquing the listener's interest while telling only part of the story. The same result can be achieved in even fewer words:

> A shooting in the Kenmore District. . .
>
> -0-
>
> A lucky cop in the Kenmore District. . .

Such use of the incomplete sentence, amounting to a sort of "lead fragment," sets up a direction, a guidepost for the listener. The listener knows full well that you have merely provided a context and that you will tell the details without further delay.

Still another type of broadcast lead, one that requires sufficient air time to bring off well, is the chronological approach. You begin with old information (background) as a means of setting the stage for new information (the news):

> Last month, after years of indecision, beat cops finally agreed to start wearing those
>
> new bulletproof vests -- even though many officers still consider them a nuisance.
>
> Well, tonight, one of those nuisances saved a cop's life. . .

The flexibility of leads in broadcasting takes some getting used to for people who have first been trained in print. Their tendency is to compose a self-sufficient lead sentence for every story. Since the news is presented in broadcasting as a *series* of stories, this approach results in stodginess and lack of variety and pacing.

Perhaps it will help to think of the broadcast lead in non-newspaper terms. A lead in broadcasting means nothing more than a *beginning*, a way of getting into a story. It need not be a capsule version of the story, but rather just an attention-getter or scene-setter.

The flexibility of broadcast leads can also stimulate the creative juices. In print, an editor may tell you, "Here, give me this story in 500 words," both of you knowing that eventually there may be space for only the first 100 or 200 of those words, and therefore you had better write a comprehensive lead. In broadcasting, you or a producer will decide in advance how long the story is to run—whether 20 seconds or 1 minute and 20 seconds—and that is indeed how long it will run. You know how long you have to get to point Z, so you can play around with point A, writing the lead you *wish* to write, not the lead you *have* to write. That's why many journalists prefer writing for broadcast: it's more fun.

FOLLOWS

Unlike print, follow-up sentences ("follows" or "folos") in broadcasting must reinforce the lead *immediately*. A broadcast story has a "story line," and the line must not be broken. Any breaks or delays in the form of secondary issues, sidebars, or events of equal importance elsewhere can confuse listeners and cause them to lose the thread. You can't play oral hopscotch and be understood clearly.

Obviously, when you lead a story this way

> There's a lucky cop in the Kenmore District tonight. . .

you must go on to explain *why* he's lucky. You can't suddenly change gears and write about the weather.

But here's a less obvious example, showing how print structure must be radically changed for broadcast:

> WAKKANAI, Japan—A Soviet search vessel on Sunday lowered a small yellow submarine into international waters where the downed South Korean airliner is believed to have crashed, and warned a Japanese patrol boat to stay away from the sea, the Japanese navy said.
>
> In Edinburgh, Scotland, the editor in chief of the Soviet Communist Party newspaper Pravda criticized his nation's military for the six-day Soviet delay in acknowledging that one of its jet fighters shot down the airliner.
>
> However, the editor, Victor Afanasyev, insisted the attack was justified, and that the Soviet Union would never apologize nor compensate the victims' families.
>
> "Any apology or compensation would amount to an admission of guilt on our part, and we do not regard ourselves as guilty," he said.
>
> In the Sea of Japan, the 15,000-ton Georgi Kozumin opened a hatch near the bow and lowered a sub into the waters, said Rear Adm. Masayusho Kato of the Japanese Maritime Safety Agency. Three men boarded the underwater craft before it submerged, he said.
>
> The zone is dominated by at least 23 Soviet vessels, including the 8,200-ton guided missile cruiser Petropavlovsk. At least four U.S. ships and four South Korean trawlers also were seen in the area Sunday, Kato said.
>
> Pravda editor Afanasyev, who was in Scotland for private talks with foreign affairs and military experts, was asked why it took Soviet leaders six days to acknowledge it shot down the airliner.
>
> "I think in this respect our military people are guilty," he said.
>
> "Probably they let some inaccuracies slip by," Afanasyev said through an interpreter. "Perhaps they weren't certain what had happened, and when there were close investigations into what happened, it was established that (the airliner's) flight had been stopped, in other words it had been shot down.... I wouldn't say I was very pleased with our first reports."
>
> (AP/UPI)

What the print writer has done is to combine two related but different stories, interweaving portions of each. He has devoted a lead paragraph to one story and a subsidiary lead paragraph to the second.

In broadcasting, there is *no subsidiary lead.** The writer makes a choice

---

*Broadcasters do make occasional use of so-called "umbrella" leads on days when there is no clear choice of how to lead a newscast, in other words, on days when there are either a lot of stories competing for attention (a "good news day") or very few stories altogether (a "slow news day").
A typical umbrella lead might go like this:

> Good evening. In the Middle East tonight, the stage is set for another clash of Israeli and Syrian forces. And in Latin America, the Nicaraguan and Honduran armies are poised along their common border. First the Middle East. . . .

For the umbrella lead to work, the stories "under the umbrella" must be connected logically in some manner. And, remember, the technique applies only to the *lead stories* of a *newscast*, not the leads of separate stories within the newscast.

of which story to do first—in this case either the search efforts or the *Pravda* editor—does it *completely* (in the allotted time), then does the other story completely. Two stories. Two separate copy pages. The progression is lead—follow(s)—end of story; lead—follow(s)—end of story.

(PRAVDA EDITOR)

The editor of the Soviet Communist Party newspaper Pravda says his country made one mistake in shooting down that Korean jetliner: waiting six days before admitting it.   Victor Afanasyev (Ah-fah-nah-SEYE-yeff), on a visit to Scotland, said in all other respects his country behaved correctly.   He said the Soviet military probably released some false information and probably should've spoken up sooner.   But, the Pravda editor went on, the Soviet Union will never apologize for shooting the plane down.   To do so, he said, would be to admit guilt, and -- in his words -- "we do not regard ourselves as guilty."

(AIRLINER SEARCH)

In the Sea of Japan today, the Soviet and Japanese navies pressed their search for debris from the downed (Korean) jetliner.   A Japanese naval spokesman said the Soviets lowered a small yellow submarine into international waters.   A crew of three entered the sub before it submerged.

Writing related stories this way, each story standing on its own, allows maximum flexibility in assembling a newscast. In radio, the usual practice is to decide story order shortly before air time. And in television, where story order is decided much earlier than in radio, pages must still be inserted or deleted on short notice. Stories written, timed, and paged separately permit newscasters, editors, and producers to organize and *re*organize a newscast at will.

VERBS

By far the most important component of the broadcast sentence is the verb. Although I'm trying my best in this book to give common sense reasons for doing things "the broadcasting way," I find I have to resort to grammatical explanations when it comes to verbs. That's because broadcasters use verbs in special ways to express voice, person, and tense.

Voice

Voice refers to the function of a verb as it relates to its subject. When the verb shows the subject to be doing the action,

He **sees** the ball

the verb is said to be in the *active voice*. When the verb shows the subject being acted upon,

> The ball **is seen** by him

the verb is said to be in the *passive voice*.

Far and away, broadcasters prefer the *active* voice:

> The Supreme Court today **handed down** a ruling on civil rights. . .
>
> (instead of: A ruling on civil rights **was handed down** today by the Supreme Court . . .)

-0-

> Governor Clements **has announced** his stand on the proposed highway tax. . .
>
> (instead of: A stand on the highway tax **was announced** today by Governor Clements . . .)

-0-

> Observers **saw** the action as a thinly veiled response to. . .
>
> (instead of: The action **was seen** by observers as a thinly veiled response to. . .)

Why the active voice? Because most of the time it is

1. Clearer
2. More concise
3. More natural to the rhythms of spoken English.

On this last point, try a modest experiment: think of a joke you've heard recently and tell it to anyone who happens to be present (unless, of course, it's too dirty for present company). Chances are, in telling the joke naturally, you didn't put a single verb in the passive voice.

Or read a newspaper story and then retell it aloud without looking back at it, sort of ad-libbing it. Again, you probably found the active voice coming naturally; the passive, if you used it, sounded artificial and stodgy.

That said, using the active voice is not an ironclad rule. Sometimes the passive voice works better, especially if the subject of the sentence is a well-known person:

> Comedian Richard Pryor **was released** from the hospital today. . .
>
> (instead of: The hospital **released** comedian Richard Pryor today . . .)

-0-

> Carmaker John De Lorean **was arrested** by federal agents this morning on a cocaine smuggling charge. . .
>
> (as good as: Federal agents **arrested** carmaker John De Lorean this morning on a cocaine smuggling charge . . .)

If you should happen to find yourself in a dilemma over which voice to use, try rephrasing the story altogether. The flexibility of broadcast writing allows great freedom:

Richard Pryor went home today.　The comedian left the hospital nearly two

months after critically burning himself. . .

-0-

Carmaker John De Lorean is in jail this morning.　Federal agents charge him with

cocaine smuggling. . .

Person

In the strictest grammatical sense, *person* refers to the subject or person being addressed. But *person* is meaningless without an attendant verb. Thus, in writing of any kind, the two go together.

In print newswriting (as opposed to feature columns), the third person prevails: *he, she, it, they* are the pronouns. There might be an occasional "eye-witness" piece written in the first person (*I, we*), but otherwise print news reaches us in the third-person singular or plural.

Broadcasting, however, enjoys more freedom of expression, and although most broadcast newswriting also is in the third person, much is in the *second person*—**you.**

The audience, after all, is not some amorphous mass of flesh. It is composed of individuals, each with a name, address, and personal history. In conversation, people pepper their remarks with "you":

> You know that rock pile down by the river? Well, I heard on the radio some kids found a body there last night. Imagine. You can't even go skinny-dipping any more without tripping over something gruesome.

The first "you" in that little chunk of dialogue is directed at the speaker's immediate listeners, making it a "personal second person." The second "you" is meant impersonally to mean "people" or "one," in the sense of the French *on* or the German *man;* we'll call it the "impersonal second person." Both uses of the second person are effective in communicating the news in broadcasting, where one person (the newscaster or anchor) is speaking directly to other people (the audience):

PERSONAL "YOU"

You'll be paying more for gas next month.　Mobil and Shell both announced

wholesale increases of two cents a gallon.　Other suppliers are expected to follow

suit.　And gas station owners say they'll tack the increase onto the price **you** pay

at the pump.

-0-

IMPERSONAL "YOU"

It seems **you** can't get ahead these days.   The Labor Department reports that

Americans earned more last year than ever before.   But it also reports that

inflation ate away more than ever before in real buying power.   Net result: on

average, people are a little bit poorer.

The trick to using the second person effectively is not to overdo it. Use it sparingly, just one or two times per newscast, wherever you feel it will best serve clarity of communication.

In broadcasting, there's also a special use of the third person plural *they*. "They" may be used like the impersonal second person "you" as a substitute for "people," "authorities," "officials," or "observers."

In conversation people often say such things as, "They say it'll rain over the weekend." "They" in this case refers to an indefinite source, possibly the weather bureau, but also possibly something overheard in a parking lot. Although broadcasters have a duty to specify sources, they also have the freedom to use "they" informally from time to time:

They came from all over the Southwest -- young people packing a fair grounds

near San Bernardino for what's being billed as the largest rock music festival since

Woodstock. . .

-0-

They're calling it the largest stock swindle in U-S history.   The Justice Department

has charged two Wall Street firms with bilking thousands of retired people of their

life savings. . .

Again, the effectiveness of "they" depends on using it sparingly, and only where the exact source is either inconsequential or is spelled out elsewhere in the story.

Tenses

It would be a simple matter to be dictatorial in the matter of verb tenses. I could command you to use the present tense here, the past tense there, and the present perfect tense somewhere else. But you wouldn't understand *why* I was laying out the law in that way—and, if you're anything like I am, you don't like to follow orders blindly. So I'll try reasoning with you.

Since broadcasters are ruled by the clock, it's only natural that they do their best to make time work for them instead of against them. Obviously, broadcasting's biggest advantage over print is speed; broadcasters, especially in radio, bring the news to the public hours before newspapers can. Broadcasters call this built-in advantage *immediacy*—and they do everything they can to exploit it in the ways they cover and present the news.

You've already seen some of this in the examples given so far. The print style of naming the date or day of the week is changed to **today, this morning, this evening, tonight, yesterday, tomorrow, day before yesterday, day after tomorrow, last month, a month from now, next year, in a few days, by the end of the week, next Sunday, a week from Thursday,** and on and on. In short, wherever possible, you should state the "when" element informally, in relation to *now*, the moment you are on the air. If the date is November 1, and a professor tells his students that an assignment is due "by noon, November 2," it may take the students a few seconds to realize that the assignment is due *tomorrow*, less than 24 hours from *now*. Since we don't want the broadcast news audience pausing a few seconds in mental recalculation, and possibly losing the thread of the story, we do the recalculation for them in immediately understandable terms.

So far, so good; we're using language that emphasizes immediacy. Unfortunately, it's impossible to be immediate all the time. And yet, since broadcast news is highly competitive—you are competing with other stations as well as with other media—broadcast executives want their stations' news to *sound* immediate even when it's not.

Let's take a typical situation: A fire burns down a warehouse at 10 A.M., and the fire is put out by 10:30 A.M. Only once, on the 10 A.M. News, can we properly use the present tense.

Firemen **are fighting** a warehouse fire on West Eighth Street.

or

Firemen **at this hour are fighting** a warehouse fire on West Eighth Street.

By 11 A.M., the fire having been extinguished, we must switch (obviously) to the past tense for the 11 A.M. News and the Noon News. But we can still show immediacy by saying "this morning."

A fire **destroyed** a warehouse on West Eighth Street **this morning.**

or

A fire **destroyed** a warehouse on West Eighth Street **a little while ago.**

For the 1 P.M. and 2 P.M. News, we can still say "this morning." After all, it happened only a few hours ago. We will still sound fresh and immediate.

But by 3:00 P.M., we risk sounding stale if we retain "this morning." (In the news business, staleness sets in *very* quickly.) We have two options. We can switch to "today":

Fire **today destroyed** a warehouse on West Eighth Street.

or

Fire **destroyed** a warehouse **today** on West Eighth Street.

or we can switch to the *present perfect* tense:

> Fire **has destroyed** a warehouse on West Eighth Street.

What we have done in each case is to slightly de-emphasize the time lag between the event and our reporting of it. And in so doing, we have preserved our *sound* (or "image") of immediacy.

While this may not seem important in absolute terms, believe me, it is extremely important in competitive terms. No broadcast newsman works in a vacuum. He works for a station that is trying to attract and hold an audience by building, over time, a reputation for accuracy and speed in reporting the news. An integral part of that effort is, at all times, to appear "on top of things." And the best way to do that—along with actually *being* on top of the news—is to choose the right words and verb tenses.

To show you how far this goes, let's continue with the present example. The word "today" or use of the present perfect tense will carry us through the Evening News (radio or TV). But by the Late News (10:00 P.M. or 11:00 P.M.), not only will the story be stale, it will also be very close to ancient history. (In broadcasting, ancient history is hot on the heels of staleness.) So once again, we must find a way to preserve our immediacy. By Late News time, we want very much to be able to say "tonight." So we must find a legitimate way, both in news gathering and in language, to remain on top of the news.

> Investigators **tonight are ruling out** arson in a fire that **destroyed** a warehouse on West Eighth Street.

> or

> Fire investigators **tonight are probing** the cause of the blaze that **leveled** a warehouse on West Eighth Street **today.**

This way, we have not only found a way to get "tonight" into the lead, we have been able to return to the present tense as well.

And to push the example a step farther, let's say it's now the next morning—nearly 24 hours after the event (which, for the record, is fast receding into prehistoric times). If we report the story at all, it must only be in terms of a fresh and immediate angle.

> Fire investigators **are** still **puzzled this morning** over the cause of that warehouse fire on West Eighth Street.

Okay, I grant you, that's not all that fresh. The point is, that's the kind of wording and approach you must use if you decide to use the story at all. It emphasizes what is happening *now* and treats what happened yesterday as common knowledge.

Rule: Always use wording that emphasizes immediacy.

To sum up: in broadcasting, the "when" element and verb tenses are expressed according to two related factors:

1. The time an event occurs
2. The air time of the newscast

Now we can proceed with a more dictatorial approach:

1. Use the present tense whenever possible.

   The school board **is meeting (at this hour)** to consider the teachers' request for a pay increase.

   -0-

   A fifth hook-and-ladder company **is on its way** to a three-alarm fire on the South Side.

   -0-

   Mayor Conroy **is** the guest of honor at **this evening's** fund-raising dinner at the Hilton Hotel.

   -0-

   Mayor Conroy **tonight is getting** the guest-of-honor treatment at the Hilton.

2. Use the present tense for statements or conditions that are still true at air time.

   Mayor Conroy **says** he won't attend tomorrow's fund-raising dinner at the Hilton Hotel.
   (instead of: Mayor Conroy **said today** . . ., etc.)

   -0-

   Senator Piltdown **says** under no circumstances will he run again for president.

   -0-

   The Soviet Union **is demanding** that the United Nations move out of New York.

   -0-

   The indictment **alleges** Alderman Piltdown took forty thousand dollars in kickbacks.

   -0-

   Three Ridgewood businessmen **are** under indictment **this evening** for alleged bidrigging at Westwood Mall.

3. Use the simple past tense for one-time events that took place shortly before air time.

Fire **destroyed** a warehouse **this morning** on West Eighth Street.

-0-

A bridge over the Lackawanna River **collapsed a short time ago.** First reports **say** no one **was** hurt.

4. Switch to the present perfect tense as the time lag widens between event and air time.

Fire **has destroyed** a warehouse on West Eighth Street.

-0-

A bridge **has collapsed** over the Lackawanna River.

-0-

Three Ridgewood businessmen **have been indicted** on bid-rigging charges.

Many fledgling newswriters get confused on the wording of past tense and present perfect tense sentences. Here's a guideline: *include* the specific "when" element with the simple past tense, and *omit* the specific "when" with the present perfect.

A one-armed man **swam** the English Channel **today,** in both directions. (past)

-0-

A one-armed man **has swum** the English Channel, in both directions. (present perfect)

-0-

Peru **this morning warned** foreign fishermen to stay out of its territorial waters. (past)

-0-

Peru **has warned** foreign fisherman to stay out of its territorial waters. (present perfect)

or

Peru **is warning** foreign fishermen. . . (present)

Again, consider the flexibility of *spoken* English, allowing broadcasters to break the grammatical constraints of written English:

It's never been done before -- a one-armed man swimming round-trip across the English Channel.

-0-

A warning from Peru to foreign fishermen: Stay out!

5. In compound sentences, use present–future tenses instead of the print-style past–conditional.

print: Mayor Conroy **said** he **would visit** the area Wednesday. (past conditional)

broadcast: Mayor Conroy **says** he **will visit** the area tomorrow. (present future)

Similarly,

Peru **is warning** its navy **will shoot** at foreign fishing ships entering its territorial waters.

-0-

The White House **predicts** the inflation rate **will decrease** by late summer.

-0-

Senator Piltdown **says** under no circumstances **will** he **run** again for president.

PLACEMENT OF "WHEN"

While we're on the subject, a few words about where to put the "today," "tonight," and so on, in the sentence. Take the sentence, "The White House announced President Jones will visit Mexico today." The meaning of such wording is that the *trip* begins today. That's probably not what the writer meant. If the meaning is the *announcement* came today, the sentence should read, "The White House announced today that President Jones will visit Mexico."

That was a rather obvious example. Even so, it illustrates the general rule that in broadcasting, *the "when" should be placed close to the verb it modifies.*

No: A bomb **exploded** at the El Al ticket office in Manhattan, wounding 12 people **this morning.**

-0-

Yes: A bomb **exploded this morning** at the El Al ticket office in Manhattan, wounding 12 people.

-0-

No: **Today** a truck **collided** with a school bus on Interstate-80, injuring six children and the bus driver.

-0-

Yes: A truck **collided today** with a school bus...

or

Yes: A truck **ran into** a school bus **today** on Interstate-80, injuring...

As with so many things concerning writing, there are exceptions, especially when we wish to maintain informality or to achieve stylistic effect:

> **Last month,** President Jones **said** he did not intend to visit Mexico in the near future. **Today** he **changed** his mind. The White House announced the president **will** go to Mexico City and Cancun next Friday and Saturday. . .

Storytelling.

3
IN WHOSE WORDS?

Whenever possible, journalists serve as the eyes and ears of the public. But even with the aid of cameras and microphones, broadcasters often find themselves at the same disadvantage as their print colleagues in not being present to witness events directly, and having instead to rely on information supplied by other, possibly interested parties. Such second- or third-hand information may be completely true. Then again, it may be completely false. Although reporters and newswriters must make every effort to check facts and thus ascertain what is true and what is false, this is not always possible, especially in broadcasting with its hourly or half-hourly deadlines. So how do broadcasters protect themselves and their audiences from serious and possibly libelous inaccuracies? They do it by making crystal clear who said what, and by knowing the law. Let's look first at the law.

AVOIDING LIBEL

In the news business, libel may occur when *you* convict someone before a court does or when *you* accuse someone of wrongdoing without proof. The result may be a lawsuit against you, your employer, or both—possibly leading to a fine large enough to leave you both in the poorhouse.

In short, libel is to be strenuously avoided.

Any lawyer will tell you that libel is an especially tricky legal issue. First, it's not always called libel. Some states call it slander. Second, other states define libel as *written* defamation and slander as *oral* (hence broadcast) defamation. Whatever it's called, though, to commit libel is to hurt someone unjustly, to rob him of his good name. You wouldn't want to do that to anybody, just as you wouldn't want it to happen to you.

Broadly speaking, broadcasters are open to two kinds of libel charges. The first, *direct libel,* occurs when you yourself report that So-and-So is a gangster, child-abuser, or other undesirable type, and So-and-So can show that it's not true, either demonstrably or by court decision.

The second, *libel by propagation,* occurs when you *repeat* something nasty that *someone else* says about a person or group, without giving that person or group a chance to respond. In other words, if John Doe calls Richard Roe a child-beater, and you report John Doe's charge—with the result that large numbers of people will hear what otherwise would have remained a private remark—you must give Richard Roe a chance to deny the charge. And even then, because it may be too late to repair the damage, a libel-by-propagation charge could be made to stick, either to be upheld or overturned by a higher court.

So what we have here is serious business. However, now that I've sufficiently scared you, let me add that successful libel suits against the media are about as rare as penguins in Arizona. With few exceptions, the federal courts have given the news media wide latitude in investigative reporting (original findings of possible wrongdoing) and in general reporting (repeating the allegations of executive and investigative agencies), especially where public officials are involved. Indeed, the federal courts have held that *malice* is the only real test by which you can be sued successfully by a public official; the official would have to prove beyond a reasonable doubt that your newspaper, magazine, or radio or TV station deliberately set out to do him in. And even then, if what you printed or broadcast is *true,* the suer gets thrown out of court.

Well, of course I'm simplifying things somewhat. If I didn't, this could turn into a lawbook. Still, the crux of what I'm saying is undeniably accurate, and that is,

> *The best defense against libel is truth.*

Now pay attention. That's "truth" with a small "t." Truth with a capital "T" is, obviously, an ultimate defense. But journalists, only some of whom have ready access to legal advice, are rarely in the business of deciding Ultimate Truth. They are in the business of reporting the news, and reporting it swiftly, especially in broadcasting. So if they use the right language, they're on safe ground.

For example, if I report

John Doe robbed a bank

it may or may not be "True," capital "T." If it's not "True," John's lawyer will probably come after me. But if I report

Police said John Doe robbed a bank

that most certainly is true, as long as the police did say it. In other words, I've put the accusation into the mouth of an executive agency, a recognized authority. Even if a court finds John not guilty, I was still reporting the "truth," small "t."

Those of you with experience in print reporting are probably aware of the journalistic lingo in such matters, consisting in such words as *alleged, accused, charged,* and *reputed.* Those words, which serve to protect the rights of the accused even as they protect the company against libel suits, signify, in broadcasting as well as print, "What I'm reporting may or may not be True. I'm simply repeating what someone else *claims*—someone else who's usually reliable."

By far the most frequent use of antilibel wording comes in stories involving criminal offenses (oops, make that *alleged* criminal offenses). The trouble with such words as "alleged," "allegations," "reputed," and so on is that they *sound* stilted. Sometimes, there is no way to avoid using them, but very often broadcasters can simply substitute the word "say" or "said," which sounds more informal but which carries equal antilibel protection. At the same time, the source of the allegation should be named in every sentence:

> **Police arrested** a suspect **they identified** as 41-year-old John Doe.   **Police say**
>
> Doe was picked up a block from the bank with the loot in a laundry bag slung
>
> over his shoulder.   **They say** he tried to run, but two officers chased him down.

Admittedly, to a creative writer this constant use of "say" and mention of "police" can seem boring and repetitious. However, it *sounds* natural and makes the story accurate, clear, and non-libelous—just in case John Doe turns out to have innocently picked up the laundry bag dropped by the real culprit.

Indictments are a bit trickier. An indictment is merely an *accusation* of wrongdoing, not proof. Anyone under indictment has a right to a trial in a courtroom, not in the news media. But since public perception of this elementary legal point is somewhat shaky (to say the least), broadcasters are better advised to use the more stilted wording:

> A Nelson County grand jury today **indicted** two Ridgewood building contractors in
>
> an **alleged** bid-rigging scheme.   Contractors John Doe and Richard Roe **are**
>
> **accused** of conspiring to drive up the price of county garage-building projects.
>
> **The indictment charges** that Doe and Roe overbilled county taxpayers to the tune
>
> of nearly four million dollars.

An extra degree of caution is also advisable in reporting crime details, especially when the accused has had a preliminary say. In such cases, "say" and "said" may be too weak, whereas "alleged" and "charged" may be too strong. In broadcasting, the middle ground lies in the verbs *claim* and, to a lesser degree, *assert:*

> The suspect denies the accusation. He **claims** he found the laundry bag lying in the street.
>
> -0-
>
> The man arrested in the case **is claiming** police brutality. He **says** four officers punched him in the face and stomach on the way to the lockup. Police deny the charge, **asserting** the suspect tripped and fell.

You should *not,* repeat *not,* use such newspaper words as "affirm," "avow," "aver," "maintain," or "declare." These words sound pretentious and do not convey shades of meaning to clarify things for the listener.

ATTRIBUTION (SOURCING)

The effect of simple cautionary words, like "say," moderate cautionary words, like "claim," and strong cautionary words, like "charge" and "accuse," is to raise doubt in the listener's mind about the Ultimate Truth. As I've said, newswriters themselves cannot always discover the Truth for the listener. But they must always raise doubt where the facts are not clear-cut.

Raising doubt on behalf of listeners is a main reason for attributing stories about events not witnessed by absolutely trustworthy people—which means *most* stories. If I report,

> The bridge collapsed at ten-thirty this morning.

either I or some absolutely trustworthy, firsthand source must have seen it happen. Otherwise, I must make sure that listeners know that what I'm reporting is secondhand information.

> Nearby residents say the bridge collapsed at ten-thirty this morning.

Actually, the example of a bridge collapse is overly simple, the exact time of occurrence being a relatively minor matter. In the news business, things are usually more complicated. First word of events often comes from sources that are only moderately trustworthy (untrained witnesses and some government officials), or rarely trustworthy (chronic drunks and some other government officials), or completely *un*trustworthy (pathological liars and still other government officials). Such stories *must* be attributed for both print and broadcast.

However, the print writer's perceived need to include the attribution in the lead usually results in a convoluted, unwieldy sentence. The print lead usually ends in a clause such as, "according to a Commerce Department study released Wednesday," or "Governor Smith announced at a press conference here Wednesday."

Broadcasting solves the problem by

1. Changing the order of the sentence to eliminate the cumbersome clause, or by
2. Delaying the attribution to a later sentence.

print: The population of the earth will exceed 5 billion by the year 2000,
according to a United Nations study released Wednesday.

broadcast: **A United Nations study says** world population will top five billion by the year
two thousand.

or

There'll be over five billion of us by the end of the century.   **A U-N study**
released today **says** world population is growing at an alarming rate.

To attribute in broadcast style, get rid of the print comma and move the attribution from the end of the sentence to the start of the sentence. Or delay the attribution to the start of a later sentence. And once again I call your attention to the possibilities of spoken English:

You think it's crowded now, just wait till the year two thousand.   That's when the
U-N says world population will top five billion.

Okay, let's move on to something more complicated:

WARSAW (UPI)—Communist Party bosses Monday told Poles, struggling with the worst financial crisis since World War II, that they face 30 percent to 40 percent increases in food prices and reported hoarding already has begun.

In the past, such increases have sparked riots and the downfall of party leaders.

A senior party official, Manfred Gorywoda, told a meeting of economic experts at a Central Committee headquarters in Warsaw that workers face a drop in living standards of 4 percent when the food price increases take effect in January, 1984, the official PAP news agency reported.

Gorywoda described the economic plight of the debt-ridden nation as "very complicated," the agency said.

He then confirmed reports that panic buying and hoarding of basic foods already had started in some Polish provinces as a result of persistent rumors that increases would be dramatic.

"We are getting signals from the provinces about the buying up of some foodstuffs," Gorywoda said. "Common sense and avoidance of the madness of hoarding lie in the interest of all of us."

You have to read to the end of paragraph 3 to learn the source of this story: PAP, short for the Polish words for "Polish Press Agency." The writer of this print-style story was not present to hear the reported remarks and thus attributed to identify the source.

PAP, like its Soviet counterpart TASS (an acronym for the Russian words for "Telegraph Agency of the Soviet Union"), is a government-run agency. It is not independent as are most Western news agencies. Being an agency of a Communist government, it rarely, if ever, reports anything unfavorable to the government or to Communism anywhere. It is therefore not very trustworthy, and its accuracy is suspect. Thus it *must* be identified as the source in any print or broadcast story for U.S. news media.

UPI's writer has taken some justifiable liberties in interpreting the significance of PAP's account in order to put the story in context. For instance, it's hardly likely that PAP would have mentioned that past food price increases led to "riots and the downfall of party leaders." No, that was the UPI reporter calling upon his knowledge of his beat.

Broadcasters are entitled to the same freedom of responsible, informed interpretation, at the same time as they make the story more "speakable":

> Poles, already struggling to make ends meet, may soon find the going even tougher.   A high Polish Communist official says Poles can expect food prices to go up 30 or 40 percent next January.   The official, **as quoted by the official Polish news agency P-A-P,** said people have already begun to hoard food.   He said such hoarding will only make matters worse.

In broadcasting, attribution can be made *anywhere,* as long as it is made *somewhere,* even as a separate sentence:

> . . .The official's remarks were carried by the Polish news agency P-A-P.

What I'm saying is that in broadcasting, while the language and structure are very different from those in print, the journalistic responsibilities are identical. (Unfortunately, radio and television stations are often poor training grounds for this sort of responsibility. Very seldom does anyone have the time to take a newcomer in hand and drill him or her in the niceties of sourcing and attribution. Newspaper and news agency copy desks are better forums for learning these things. In radio and television, large stations and networks expect their employees to know the rules—rules that may not have been enforced at smaller stations. Thus, broadcast journalists who begin at small stations will have to do a lot of self-teaching.)

The sentence and story restructuring just described applies also to stories from *unnamed sources,* such as the famous "high White House source" (which many journalists refer to off-mike as "a high White Horse souse"). Each news department has its own rules for the use and treatment of such questionable material, but *stylistically* all follow the same rule: *attribute at the start of the sentence:*

> A high White House source says the President is furious about the defeat of his housing bill.

or

According to a high White House source, the President is furious about. . .

-0-

Pentagon sources say the M-X missile will eventually cost triple the original estimates.

-0-

Sources in the Sanitation Department tell W-W-X-X News that the sewer system is in rapid decay.

-0-

W-W-X-X News has learned from sources in the Sanitation Department that the sewer system. . .

Apart from questions of legality and responsibility, attributing carefully has a practical aspect: it enables you to protect yourself. If *you* report something that turns out to be wrong, you are the one with the red face (or worse). However, if you attribute to someone else, you are off the hook. Some news departments insist on making corrections of false reports in later newscasts. Others don't bother with a retraction as such, preferring to treat the correct version as an update of the incorrect one. Still others say nothing, pretending it never happened, especially since the sound waves of the incorrect words are already in the neighborhood of a galaxy far, far away.

Whatever the policy, the best course is to be right and to attribute clearly in the first place.

QUOTATION

Quoting someone's words is, of course, the most direct form of attribution. However, since listeners can't see the quotation marks, broadcast writers must take special care to make clear who was talking and what was being said. Again, here's an example of the print-style model from which writers in broadcast newsrooms have to work:

> MOSCOW—Claiming that "malicious anti-Soviet hysteria" endangers the safety of its athletes, the Soviet Union Wednesday cancelled the scheduled December U.S. tour of its ice hockey team.
>
> The cancellation raises the question of whether the Kremlin might be considering a boycott of next year's Summer Olympics in Los Angeles.
>
> The action followed the cancellation of a trip to the United States by Soviet basketball players and was another indication of the deepening chill between the two nations since the Soviet downing of a South Korean airliner Sept. 1.
>
> Moscow also attacked the United States for "flagrantly violating their international commitments" in not providing normal landing rights for Soviet diplomats wishing to attend the newly opened United Nations session.

> In explaining the sports cancellations, the official Soviet news agency Tass said that when U.S. authorities "encourage anti-Soviet actions, there are serious fears that proper safety may not be ensured for Soviet players."

(Antero Pietila, Baltimore Sun)

Because the words "malicious anti-Soviet hysteria" are obviously a statement of opinion, and, in this case, propaganda, they quite properly belong in quotes. But if a newscaster were to read that first print sentence aloud, it would *sound* as if the newscaster, and thus the news department, accepted that characterization as true. The newscaster could inflect his voice in an attempt to "vocalize" the quote, and sometimes this works. But more often, relying on such performing ability leaves too much room for misunderstanding.

Broadcasters have a number of ways to make things crystal clear (at the same time as they do away with the hopscotch structure of the print story):

The Soviet Union today canceled the scheduled U.S. tour of its ice hockey team.

It said the team would be in physical danger because of **what it called** "malicious anti-Soviet hysteria."

-0-

Accusing the United States of "malicious anti-Soviet hysteria," the Soviet Union has canceled the U-S tour of its ice hockey team. . .

-0-

Ice hockey players and fans are the latest victims of the current sorry state of Soviet-U.S. relations.   The Soviet ice hockey team was supposed to tour the U-S this December.   But today the Soviets pulled out.   Moscow claimed its players would be in physical danger because of -- **in its words** -- "malicious anti-Soviet hysteria."

Note that in each case it is possible to delete the quotation marks without affecting the clarity of the spoken wording. But it is generally preferable to keep the quotation marks as a sort of visual punctuation allowing the newscaster to inflect his voice if he so wishes.

The operative phrases for direct quotation in broadcast style are

what he (she, it) called
what he (she, it) termed
in his (her, its) words
calling it
terming it
—and these are his (her) exact words—
as he (she) put it

If you want your story to contain several quotes, you should also vary the phrases you use to set them off.

Now here's an example requiring extremely careful handling because of its racial and political overtones:

> WASHINGTON—Ultraconservative Sen. Jesse Helms (R-N.C.) bitterly attacked the late Dr. Martin Luther King, Jr., in a speech Monday on the Senate floor, calling him unworthy of a holiday in his honor and denouncing him as a communist sympathizer.
>
> "Dr. King's action-oriented Marxism . . . is not compatible with the concepts of this country," Helms said as he launched a filibuster to prevent the Senate from voting on a bill to make the third Monday in January a paid federal holiday in honor of the assassinated civil rights leader's Jan. 15 birthday.
>
> "The legacy of Dr. King was really division, not love," Helms said many people in this country believe.
>
> Helms' Senate remarks seemed almost temperate compared with a report prepared by his office and released Monday that accuses King of "hostility to and hatred for America" and speculates:
>
> "King may have had an explicit but clandestine relationship with the Communist Party or its agents to promote, through his own stature, not the civil rights of blacks or social justice and progress, but the totalitarian goals and ideology of communism."
>
> Evidence "strongly suggest(s) that King harbored a strong sympathy for the Communist Party and its goals," said the report, which concluded, nonetheless, that "there is no evidence that King was a member of the Communist Party."
>
> (Ellen Warren, *Chicago Sun-Times*, Reprinted with Permission)

That's pretty strong stuff—a U.S. senator describing as a crypto-communist a man perceived as a hero by millions upon millions of Americans. This is the kind of story that, if it were a package put in the mail, would be stamped "Handle with Care."

Here's what broadcasters might do with it:

> The senator leading the fight against a national holiday for the late Dr. Martin Luther King Junior today **called** Dr. King a communist sympathizer. In a speech on the Senate floor and in a report released by his office, Senator Jesse Helms of North Carolina **denounced** Dr. King in very strong terms. Helms said, **and these are his words,** "Dr. King's action-oriented Marxism is not compatible with the concepts of this country." Helms said many Americans -- **again quoting him directly** -- believe "the legacy of Dr. King was really division, not love." The report from Helms' office said there's evidence, **quote,** "that King harbored a strong sympathy for the Communist Party and its goals," **end quote.** Helms' remarks came at the start of a filibuster against a bill to make the third Monday in January a federal holiday in Dr. King's honor.

Yes, that's a mouthful, and yes, it sounds stilted. But this is a case where the nature of the material overrides the customary informality of broadcast newswriting. The material cries out for quotation at length: You can't have a U.S. senator calling someone a communist and let it go at that.

So, in cases where you want to (or must) quote at length, it is fine to use the words "quote . . . end quote" (or "unquote"). But try not to overdo it. Rely whenever possible on the more informal phrasing.

PARAPHRASING

Most of the time, when you want to report at length on what someone has said, you'll find that it is better to paraphrase. That's because the average trained newswriter can put things shorter and sweeter than the average politician, bureaucrat, or other newsmaker. Why take 12 words for an uncontroversial direct quote when you can use half that many of your own words to say the same thing?

As we'll see when we deal in later chapters with tape recorded quotations ("actualities" in radio, "sound bites" in television), broadcasters enjoy certain advantages over their print colleagues in citing exact remarks. But things cut both ways. Let's face it: a disturbing number of people do not or cannot express themselves well, especially around nosy people with notebooks or microphones and cameras. Print writers need to judge a remark, however badly put, only for its clarity *on paper*. They can thus cite a remark which the reader might have to read twice or pause to interpret in context.

The broadcaster, however, must be understood immediately, even when using someone else's words. To this end, he can often say something *better* (more clearly, more directly) than the original speaker. Indeed, whenever he *can* do so, he *should* do so.

1. If *you* can say something more clearly and directly than the original speaker, then *paraphrase*.
2. If the original speaker's words are clear, colorful, biased, or controversial, then quote directly.

To see how paraphrasing might work in practice, here's a (fictitious) excerpt from a news conference by a tongue-tied president:

Reporter: Sir, one of the election promises you made was to seek a summit conference with the Soviet leadership as soon as possible. Is now the time? If not, when?

President: Well, you know, uh, on a summit, uh, these things have to be carefully, uh, prepared. And the, uh, atmosphere has to be right. Now, I don't think the Soviets have been helping to create the right atmosphere. Just the opposite, they've been bellicose in their attitude. So I think they'll, uh, have to bend toward peace. They have to, their words and actions, prove it. When that happens, I'll know it and know how to respond in kind. But for now and the, uh, near future, no, I don't think a summit conference would be, uh, useful.

And here's a comparison of print and broadcast versions of those rambling remarks, showing how the broadcaster needs to paraphrase while the print writer does not:

print: WASHINGTON—President Richard E. Roe, accusing the Soviet Union of displaying a "bellicose" attitude, Thursday ruled out a summit conference "for now and the near future," unless the Soviets prove they want it by "their words and actions."

broadcast: President Roe today ruled out a summit conference in the near future.   The president said Soviet words and actions show there'd be no point to a summit conference at this time.   If the Soviets want a summit, the president said, they'll have to prove it.   In the president's words, they'll have "to bend toward peace."

Yes, the *words* in the broadcast version are very different. But the *meaning* is undistorted.

SAY, SAID

I come back to these words because they are so important. "Say" is the most useful verb in the broadcast journalist's vocabulary. It is simple, direct, and unambiguous. I wish I had a penny for every time it's used in broadcast copy. I might soon become wealthier than Saudi Arabia.

You should resist the temptation to spice things up by using such verbs as "state" and "declare." Forget the spice. Stick with the meat and potatoes. *Say* is the right word.

At his news conference this afternoon, the president **said** a summit meeting with the Soviet premier is unlikely in the near future.   The president **said** the conditions aren't right.   First, the president **said,** the Soviets must, in his words, "bend toward peace."   He **said** if the Soviets want peace, then, **said** the president, "I'll know it and know how to respond in kind."

That's a lot of "saids" on paper. But *aloud* they sound fine.

4
RUBBER BUGGY BUMPERS

TONGUE-TWISTERS

Admittedly, "rubber buggy bumpers" isn't as hard to say as "Thirteen thieves of Thebes thinned three thickets of thistles." The point is, no newscaster should ever be forced to attempt either one during a broadcast.

We all like "bloopers," those instances of entertainers tripping over their tongues on the air. Such boners are rarely heard these days, since virtually all entertainment programming is recorded on film or tape and the bloopers edited out. Sports is just about the only entertainment still broadcast live.

News, on the other hand, is almost always delivered live. Even in those instances where the East Coast edition of the network news is taped for later replay in the Pacific and Mountain time zones, the content is "protected"; that is, news staffs on the West Coast update and change the newscast as necessary, right up to and during the rebroadcast. Even the 24-hour all-news radio and TV outlets are programmed live.

Live programming inevitably results in occasional mistakes and miscues, both human and electronic. The goal is to keep such miscues to a minimum. There is no need to manufacture them by using the wrong language, the language of tongue-twisters. For example, there is no good reason to write,

> Federal narcotics agents have **thwarted** a cocaine smuggling ring.

when it's just as easy to write,

> Federal narcotics agents have **broken up** a cocaine smuggling ring.

"Thwart" is hard to say. "Break up" is not. In this context they mean the same thing, but "break up" is better in broadcasting.

The same is true of "furor," which is spoken better as "stir" or "outburst," and "cause a furor" is better put as "cause a scene." Sometimes the problem pops up not in single words but in word combinations:

> Governor **Shuster** signed the legislation at seven this morning. . .

That sentence contains an overabundance of sibilants ("s"-sounds), guaranteed to leave many a newscaster hissing or spitting. We can fix the problem by choosing slightly different wording.

> Governor Shuster signed the bill this morning. . .

(By the way, the words "bill" and "law" are far preferable to more formal words such as "legislation," "ordinance," or "statute." In everyday speech, people are more likely to say "drunk driving **law**" than "drunk driving **statute.**")

Another sound to watch out for is the letter "p":

> Police **apprehended** a dozen **picketing grape-pickers**. . .

might be better rendered as

> Police arrested a dozen picketing farm workers. . .

("Apprehend" is also a no-no. "Arrest" will do just fine.)

There's no room in this book to list every hard-to-pronounce word or word combination that comes to mind. The point is to sensitize you to the problem. For a career in broadcast news, you must train yourself to recognize potential tongue-twisters and to change your wording when necessary. The best way to do this is to read your copy aloud—always.

JARGON

One of the joys of writing the news for radio and TV comes in deflating the pretentious prose and overblown language of many officials, bureaucrats, and "experts" in many fields. It kind of makes you feel like a David cutting a Goliath down to size. The following are exaggerations, but just barely:

Reporter: Well, Senator, have you decided to run for president?

Senator: I am studying the position with a view toward making a determination.

Translation: I haven't made up my mind yet.

-0-

Student: Dr. Pangloss, why did you give me a failing grade?

Professor: Your compository perambulations have no *raison d'être* in the cadre of a syntactical module.

Translation: Neither you nor I can write a simple declarative sentence.

Who knows what causes some people to talk or write this way? Is it a way of showing intelligence or erudition? Is it a form of elitism? Whatever the reason, such locutions should not be used in writing broadcast news.

This is not a matter of "writing down" to the mass audience. It is a matter of being understood. English is one of the world's richest languages. It long ago supplanted French as the language of diplomacy and German as the language of science. Good writers of English rejoice in finding the right word. But writing the news requires only a relatively small "telling" vocabulary. It is not a sign of poor education or lack of intelligence to keep language simple in telling the news. Rather, it is a sign of wanting to be clearly understood.

You should almost think of yourself as a foreign language translator who must render the *sense* of people's thoughts in completely different words. Confronted with overblown or hifalutin language, you must ask yourself, "What does this *mean*? And how can I rephrase it so that other people will understand?"

One way of measuring the understandability of the words you'd like to use is to turn your friends, neighbors, or relatives into sounding boards. Read them your copy aloud and see if they understand. If you don't have time for that—and in the news business you probably won't—you should at least ask yourself, "If I put it this way, will people I know understand what I'm saying?"

All I can offer you here are guidelines:

1. Avoid redundancy.

Politician: I want the American people to realize their **hopes and aspirations.** (Strike one or the other; they mean the same thing.)

Witness: The truck narrowly **missed hitting** the car. (Strike "hitting.")

Salesman: This model contains many **new innovations.** (Strike "new.")

2. Avoid foreign words and expressions for which there is an ample English equivalent.

Politician: The housing bill has no **raison d'être.** ("The housing bill is unneeded," or "There's no reason for this housing bill.")

Professor: The Soviet Communist **Weltanschauung** results inexorably in paranoia. ("The Soviet Communist view of things results in paranoia.")

3. Avoid unfamiliar or complicated words where simpler words will do.

Restaurant Critic: The chef's **gustatory** instincts were **awry.** ("The cook's taste buds were flat.")

| Art Dealer: | Heavens knows where the populace acquired this predilection for antediluvian tableaux! ("It's a shame people prefer paintings done in a natural style.") |

4. Avoid clichés.

| Guest Speaker: | I'm **pleased as punch** to address this assemblage of **movers and shakers.** ("I'm very happy to address this important group.") |
| Football Coach: | We're gonna **get up** for this one and really **sock it to 'em** and **come up smellin' like a rose.** ("We're going to win big next Saturday.") |

5. Avoid mixed metaphors.

| Politician: | I'm **throwing** the tax bill for **a long pass** and hoping someone **crosses home plate** with it. (mixing football and baseball) |
| Historian: | Roosevelt was a **colossus,** taking the world of economic troubles **onto his back.** (confusing the Colossus of Rhodes with the Atlas of Greek myth) |

6. Avoid trendy, overworked expressions that become clichés.

| Reporter 1: | The **bottom line** was he had to start all over again. (Make it "result" instead of "bottom line.") |
| Reporter 2: | The administration hopes to get its foreign policy back **on track** by next year. (Make it "straighten out" or "reorganize" or "adjust.") |

Entire volumes have been written on how to recognize and translate such jargon (*Less than Words Can Say* by Richard Mitchell and *Strictly Speaking* and *A Civil Tongue* by Edwin Newman, to name just three recent ones). Learning to write and express oneself clearly is a lifelong pursuit. But newswriters can't wait till age 40 to develop the knack. To earn a paycheck, they must be able to write clearly from day 1. Believe me: despite the examples of jargon and fractured syntax you may occasionally hear on your local news programs, the best and lasting preparation for a career in broadcast news is learning to write well.

SLANG

Just as jargon and pretentious language must be "translated down," so must substandard or unsuitable language be "translated up." Solecisms such as "ain't got" and "can't hardly" are taboo if they're *your* words. If they're someone else's words, someone you wish to quote, then the matter must be decided on a case-by-case basis. That's because some slangy words or expressions lend color to a story. So let me make this distinction:

Slang is permissible when it is *both* (1) widely understood and (2) spoken by a news*maker*, not a news*caster*. Put another way, you may quote people in the news who use slang, but you yourself may not use it.

yes: The senator **called** the president's remarks **"dopey"** and **"tomfoolish."** (It's clear that the senator used those words.)

or: The senator termed the president's remarks stupid. (paraphrase)

but not: The senator said the president's remarks were dopey and tomfoolish. (Sounds like the newscaster is using those words.)

-0-

yes: In farmer Smith's words, "You can't hardly get them kind of ducks no more." (Substandard English quoted for colorful effect.)

or: Farmer Smith said that breed of duck is a rare bird indeed. (Paraphrasing to retain semblance of colorful effect.)

but not: Farmer Smith said you can't hardly find them kind of ducks no more. (Substandard writer and newscaster.)

Again, space does not permit an exhaustive listing of slangy examples. Your dictionary and language guide will indicate if a word or expression is considered slang. Suffice it here to warn you to keep your ears open to the way you and your friends talk.

Each of us spends most of his or her time in a limited setting among people of the same general group, whether at home, at school, or in the office. We converse so often with these people that we no longer question certain words and expressions, without realizing that people on the next block or on the other side of town may not know what those expressions mean, or may think they mean something entirely different.

For example, a student newscaster wrote,

After his lecture, Professor Carmichael attended a beer and munchies . . .

On her university campus, the term "beer and munchies" was a well-known way to describe a get-together where food and beverages were served. The food was not necessarily snacks, and the beverage was not necesssarily beer. The expression had thus taken on a generic meaning quite apart from its component words. Although virtually everyone on campus understood it, the radio station served several communities well outside the campus. The station was known to have many, many listeners in those areas who were not or had never been students; they simply liked the programming. For them, the term "beer and munchies," especially used as a noun, was either confusing or meaningless. The student newscaster, aware she was addressing an audience not just of students, should have written,

After his lecture, Professor Carmichael joined students for refreshments.

A mistake like this isn't the end of the world, but it's the kind of thing a broadcast newswriter has to watch for.

The same watchful eye should be kept on idiomatic expressions and colloquialisms. Because such language is often colorful, it can and should be used in broadcast newswriting, but *judiciously*. It must truly lend color, be widely understood, and should be grammatically accurate as well.

no: The mayor, **looking like Uncle Ned's whiskers,** attacked the city council for what he called "laziness." (Was the mayor angry? Red-faced? Disheveled? This kind of idiomatic expression shouldn't be used; few people understand it.)

-0-

no: Seriously injured was 34-year-old Yvette Taylor of suburban Woodfield. **The Taylor woman** was taken to Saint Francis Hospital. (Colloquial in the South-Central states, but grammatically poor. Make it "Mrs. (or Miss) Taylor.")

Again, one could fill a book (or several) with examples. But you know your specific audience better than I do, and I leave it to you to judge each case on its merits.

IMPACT OF WORDS

Broadcast journalists have a special responsibility to watch their tongues. That's because spoken words drive more deeply into the psyche than do written ones. This becomes apparent even in childhood. Somehow, the words, "Fe, Fi, Fo, Fum, I smell the blood of an Englishman," just don't seem to strike as much terror on the page of a book as they do from the mouth of a parent. And at the very next words, uttered in Dad's best Ugly Giant voice—"Be he live or be he dead, I'll grind his bones to make me bread!"—some youngsters retreat under the covers.

In the broadcast news business, we don't want to send listeners retreating under their figurative covers. We recognize that, even for adults, words invested with the dimension and fullness of the human voice contain a special power to move people emotionally, to grab at their guts, and sometimes to make them act rashly or foolishly.

Above all, broadcasters must remain calm in their words and tone of voice. We've come a long way since a radio program—Orson Welles' *Mercury Theater* production of "War of the Worlds" in 1938—was able to make thousands of Americans believe that Martians had landed. But we can never come so far as to drain spoken words of their emotional impact. Here are a few cases in point.

The word "violence" is tricky and troublesome. It carries more impact spoken than written. If we say,

Violent clashes marred an antinuclear demonstration today in West Germany . . .

we lead listeners to expect some awfully bloody details. But if it turns out that the "violent clashes" amounted to half a dozen people slightly injured in a series of shoving matches, we have grossly overstated the case and robbed the words of their true meaning.

There is a way to avoid this: *be specific* as to what happened, *without* characterizing it as "violence" or "violent." Let the facts speak for themselves.

A distinction should be made, too, between "wounds" and "injuries." They are *not* synonyms. If we say,

The bomb *wounded* six people . . .

the meaning is that the bomb was *deliberately* detonated. If we say,

The bomb *injured* six people . . .

the meaning is that it went off *accidentally*. In newsroom parlance, injuries happen in accidents, wounds in deliberate violence such as war or terrorism. If you think such distinctions are small or unimportant, you had best stay out of the news business, especially broadcasting.*

Even more caution, perhaps, is required for stories involving race or religion. In the first instance, you have to decide if a story really *does* involve either of them. If we say,

A group of New England congressmen, *including two blacks,* called today for

reform of the income tax laws . . .

we are mentioning race unnecessarily. The race of the congressmen has nothing to do with the issue being addressed.

And if we say,

In a *rash of anti-Semitism* in France, vandals today painted swastikas on two Paris

synagogues . . .

we are again wildly overstating. "Paris" does not equal "France," and "two synagogues" defaced do not constitute a "rash of anti-Semitism." The facts in this

---

*There is argument over whether broadcasters should say "people" or "persons." Those who prefer "people" say it is more conversational. Those who prefer "persons" say the word "people" applies only in the cultural or anthropological sense, as in "the American *people*." I am strongly for "people" instead of "persons," and I am using it throughout this book.

story are bad enough and speak for themselves. They do not need "punching up" through the addition of inaccurate, inappropriate, or emotional language.

Well, I won't belabor the point—which is simply this: do *not* include details of race, religion or national origin *unless* such details are germane to the point of the story. In fact, it might be a good idea to mutter to yourself, "Fe, Fi, Fo, Fum!" every time you come across a story involving

> Race
> Religion
> Violence
> Bodily injury (blood and gore)
> Bodily functions
> Sexual conduct

Measure your language. You are speaking to *people,* not to clumps of earth.

OBSCENITY

Obscenity is in the eye of the beholder. One man's "art" is another man's "pornography." The U.S. Supreme Court has held that obscenity shall be determined by community standards. What may be held to be obscene in Roanoke may not necessarily be held to be obscene in Milwaukee; the people in those two communities may have different standards.

That said, broadcast standards, in actual practice, are far more strict than print standards. Reading is a deliberate act. Listening or viewing can happen by accident. A 3-year-old will not read words that he may accidentally hear. All of which is not to say that broadcasters are prudes. It's just that broadcasting, by its very nature, reaches a wider audience than print. And since broadcasters are forever trying to reach an even wider audience, it stands to reason that they do not want to risk offending people.

And make no mistake about it: people *are* easily offended. Although standards in entertainment programming have been relaxed over the years (not long ago it was forbidden to say "hell," "damn," "bastard," or "son-of-a-bitch," even in the context of dramatic dialogue), standards remain strict in news programming. Specifically, it is taboo to use the name of the Lord in a profane way or to use the popular words for excrement, genitalia, or sexual activities.

The vast majority of newsmakers understand this and consequently watch their language in public, especially when cameras and microphones are present. But sometimes they forget themselves and let slip an occasional "Shit!" or "God damn it!" On such occasions, the words are edited out—or "bleeped"—in news broadcasting. (There are exceptions. In 1984, CBS did not edit the word "shit" out of remarks by former President Richard Nixon.)

A celebrated case in point: Earl Butz, the Secretary of Agriculture under the Nixon and Ford administrations, had, much like Interior Secretary James Watt under the Reagan administration, an unfortunate proclivity for putting his foot in his mouth. On one occasion, following the Pope's proscription of birth control pills, Butz blurted, "He no play-a da game, he no make-a da rules," a remark for which he expressed regret. But in 1976 another Butz remark became known when it was leaked to the news media. Butz was quoted as saying, "Coloreds? All they want is loose shoes, tight pussy, and a warm place to take a shit."

Well, we've all heard people make such remarks. But for a U.S. *cabinet officer* to tell such a "joke," even in what he assumed to be private and trusted company, was quite another matter. Just the use of the term "coloreds" for blacks was enough to indicate an insensitive, if not completely backward, view of the state of race relations in the United States.

And 1976 was an election year as well. The heat became too much, and Butz resigned. Indeed it was widely reported, but never confirmed, that President Ford had *demanded* the resignation.

The point of this story is that the *text* of the "joke" was never reported in broadcast news programs. It could not be, for the language forbade it. Most newspapers and magazine did not quote the text either, for the same reason; instead, they substituted blanks for the potentially offensive words. Broadcasters had to find euphemisms, alternately calling the "joke" profane, obscene, or a racial slur.

Today, there may be a handful of radio stations, probably on FM, which would carry the text verbatim, almost certainly late at night. But such stations are on the fringe of news broadcasting. Overwhelmingly, commercial and noncommercial stations alike would *not* report the text, not even with a prior warning to listeners.

PRONUNCIATION

Print writers do not have to concern themselves with pronunciation. Broadcasters do. Indeed, in spoken news, pronunciation forms part of the substance. In addition, broadcasters help to set the standards of spoken English for society at large. That is a major responsibility, and it is not going too far to say that broadcasters have a *duty* to know correct pronunciation. This applies whether you are writing words that you yourself will say on the air or writing them for someone else. Pronunciation is part of the job.

Some words, such as "controversial" and "comptroller," have only one correct pronunciation, con-tro-VER-shul and con-TRO-ler, respectively. Anything else is wrong. No matter that many people say "con-tro-VER-si-al" or "COMP-tro-ler." "Many people" are not broadcast newsmen. Broadcast standards should be high. There is no pronounced fifth syllable in controversial and no pronounced "m" or "p" in comptroller, period.

However, many other words have more than one acceptable pronunciation, for example, words like "extraordinary," which may be pronounced either "ex-tra-OR-din-a-ree" or "ex-TROR-din-a-ree." Dictionaries usually list such alternative pronunciations and sometimes specify which pronunciation is "preferred." That's why, as mentioned a few chapters ago, clear pronunciations should be a major factor guiding your choice of dictionary.

But no dictionary that I know of will be of much use in finding the right pronunciations of names and places currently in the news, especially foreign names and places. Many experienced radio newscasters and TV anchors make it their business to learn foreign language pronunciation. But they are a distinct minority, and writers should not rely on them. Yet, how is a writer to know how to pronounce Giscard d'Estaing (French), Ianes (Portuguese), Walesa (Polish), or Nagy (Hungarian)?

There are some specialized pronouncing dictionaries on the market, but these are mostly inadequate or expensive. On the other hand, the *Music Lovers' Encyclopedia,* a moderately priced, one-volume work, contains a succinct, multi-language pronunciation guide for languages from Arabian to Welsh.

In addition, the broadcast wires of the two major news agencies, AP and UPI, transmit daily pronunciation guides for current names in the news. The trouble is, typically AP will give one pronunciation and UPI another, and sometimes both are wrong.

So here's a method that almost always works: pick up the phone and call the nearest embassy, legation, consulate, trade representation, news organ, or cultural organization of the country or national group of the person whose name you wish to know how to pronounce, and ask! Far from being annoyed, these representatives of foreign countries, nationalities, and cultures are pleased to be of assistance. Some of them are downright flattered that you have taken the time and trouble to get the pronunciation right.

PHONETICS

Okay, now you know how to pronounce Giscard d'Estaing, Ianes, Walesa, and Nagy. But unless you know how to put it on paper, the knowledge will remain exclusively yours. In short, you will need some sort of phonetics to render strange words pronounceable at a glance.

You can't use a dictionary system of diacritical marks because they are even harder to decipher than foreign languages. What you need is something simple that appeals to the eye. I've been using such a system in this book. Its simplicity and eye appeal stem from three sources:

1. Lack of diacritical marks (with two exceptions)
2. Upper/lower case typing
3. Syllabication by sound rather than spelling

On the copy page, the phonetic rendering may come either *in place of* the correct spelling or *immediately following* the correct spelling and *in parentheses:*

either: Polish Labor Leader Lek Vah-WEN-sah says he . . .

   or: Polish Labor Leader Lech Walesa (Lek Vah-WEN-sah) says he . . .

-0-

either: Former French President VAH-lay-ree ZHEES-kar Day-STANH has published some controversial memoirs . . .

   or: Former French President Valery Giscard d'Estaing (VAH-lay-ree ZHEES-kar Day-STANH) has published some controversial memoirs . . .

The second way is the more common.

Either way, the stressed syllable is all capitals and the unstressed syllables are all lower case, except for the first letter of proper names. The object is to keep the typed copy pages as clean and legible as possible.

Any system of phonetics, including the one that follows, will have short-comings. Even though most foreign languages have regular pronunciations (unlike English, which has enough irregularities to buffalo even the most talented linguist), many have sounds that can only be approximated by the English alphabet. The nasal sounds of certain French endings (*vin, chanson*), the guttural sounds of some German (*Ich, Buch*) and Dutch (van Gogh) consonants, the harsh sibilants of some Russian (*tovarishtch*) and other Slavic speech components—all require more than a simple rendering on a typed copy page. In these cases, the writer and newscaster should confer well before air time to make sure that the pronunciation is voiced by the former to the latter.

Another word of caution: it isn't always necessary to render *exact* pronunciations of foreign names and places. If we said "München" instead of "Munich," only the fluent German speakers in our audience would know where we were talking about. What *is* necesssary is to avoid the sort of mispronunciation which gives the impression we haven't the foggiest idea what we're saying.

ACTUAL	PHONETIC	AS IN
a	a	fat, glad
a, é	ay	late, great; *passé* (Fr.)
a, o	ah	father, car, clot, body
ão	onh	Macão, gabão (Portuguese)
b	b	boy, build
c, k, ch	k	cord, kelp, chemical
c, s	s	cede, sulk
ch; c, cc	ch	cheap, beach; *città, bacci* (Ital.)
ch (guttural), gh	kh	loch (Scottish), *Bach* (German), Gogh (Dutch)
d	d	dog, dud
e; ä	e	neck, edge; *Gärtner* (Ger.)
e, ee	ee or ey	cede, seek
eu, ö, ü	ŏŏh	*feu, peu* (Fr.), *schön, kühn* (Ger.)
f, ph, v	f	feet, phone; *Vogel* (Ger.)
g	g	get, go
g, j	j or dj	gem, ledge, join
h, j	h	how, him; *joya* (Span.)
i	i	bit, miss
i, y, ll	y	bite, sky; *llegar* (Span.)
l	l	lips, fill
m	m	man, ember
n	n	not, knot
n (terminal)	nh	*vin, bon, sang* (French)
ñ; gn	n'y	niño, *piña* (Spanish); *bagno* (Ital.)
o	o	note, goat
oi	wa	*moi, trois* (Fr.)

ACTUAL	PHONETIC	AS IN
oo	ŏo	foot, put
oo, u	oo	moon, shoot, butte, suit
oy, eu	oy	boy, soy; *Heute* (Ger.)
p	p	pot, slip
qu	qu or kw	quart, quiz
r	r	rude, car
rr, rr (rolled)	rr	*trois* (Fr.), *perro* (Sp.)
sh, sch, sz, s	sh	rush, *Schade* (Ger.), Szell (Hung.); *depois* (Port.)
t	t	ten, twit
th	th	thick, thin (hard sound) *and* this, the (soft sound)
u	u	nut, spun
v, w	v	vice; *warm, Wein* (Ger.)
w	w	wax, wait
wh	wh	what, whoosh
x	x	extra, sex
z	z	size, maze
z, j	zh	azure; *muzik* (Russ.); *je* (Fr.)

Almost insurmountable obstacles occur in attempts at phonetic rendering of languages based largely on tonal scales or click sounds. Chinese, for example, has been transliterated in so many ways over the years that, depending on date and origin of publication, you may see the Chinese capital city written as *Pekin, Peking, Beiping,* or *Beijing.* This last spelling is the closest to actual pronunciation—"Bay-ZHING"—but, lacking a bilingual source to check each case as it comes up, you'll have to do a lot of guesswork. (If you're a news junkie, you will have heard reporters based in Beijing and will have kept your ears open for the way *they* pronounce the names and places they are closest to.) As for African languages using click-sounds—well, you can't win 'em all.

5
FARAWAY PLACES, NUMBERS, TITLES, AND ABBREVIATIONS

SITUATING TIMBUKTU (THE "WHERE" ELEMENT)

For the record, Timbuktu (Tim-buk-TOO) is a town in Mali, Central Africa. In colloquial usage, it has come to mean any obscure, faraway place—a sort of Podunk or West Overshoe, only more distant. Since people don't carry detailed maps in their heads, in broadcast news we have to tell people where the Timbuktus and Podunks are located.

This is especially true in radio, where no one can see a map or a dateline. But even in television, where maps are often used as graphic elements behind the anchorman, the visual aid is quickly lost, leaving people perhaps to wonder where things are taking place. So in radio and TV *both,* you should name the location (the "where" element) near the *start* of a story and then *rename* or *reinforce* it later on if the story runs longer than 25 to 30 seconds.

The "where" element is important psychologically as well as informationally. Upon hearing the location of a story, listeners automatically reach a decision of how much attention they will pay. It will come as no surprise to you that most people are more interested in what happens down the block than in what happens halfway around the world. They are more interested in events close to home or in places they have visited, or where they have friends and relatives than in, to them, obscure points on a map.

So it is essential that broadcast writers and reporters spell out where things are happening. They must make obscure places at least a trifle less obscure in the mind of the listener. The best way to do this is to state an unfamiliar location *in terms of a more familiar location.* There are a number of ways of expressing this.

print model: TAYLORSVILLE, KY—A coal mine collapsed during the early shift Monday morning, killing at least 11 miners and sending at least 14 others to nearby hospitals, authorities said.

broadcast
rewrites: A coal mine collapse killed at least 11 miners today **in Taylorsville, Kentucky, about 30 miles southeast of Louisville.**   At least 14 miners were injured.

-0-

At least 11 miners died in a coal mine collapse this morning **in the town of Taylorsville, southeast of Louisville, Kentucky.**

-0-

A coal mine collapse **in Kentucky** today. . . At least 11 miners were killed **in Taylorsville, midway between Louisville and Frankfort.**

-0-

In Taylorsville, Kentucky -- that's about 30 miles from Louisville -- a coal mine collapsed this morning, killing 11 miners.

-0-

At least 11 miners are dead in a coal mine collapse **in north central Kentucky. It happened in Taylorsville, outside of Louisville.**

However, if you happen to be working at a station in the Louisville-Taylorsville-Frankfort region, where people *already know* the geography, you need only write,

A coal mine collapsed **in Taylorsville** this morning, killing at least 11 miners. . .

And if your station is *in* Taylorsville or a nearby community, you can come right out and name the mine and its address:

At least 11 coal miners died this morning **in the Cardwell Number Four mine on West Burnham Road.**   The mine collapsed just after nine A.M. . . .

You see, just as stating the "when" element depends on a combination of time of occurrence and time of broadcast, so stating the "where" element depends on a combination of (1) the location of the event and (2) the location of your station. Unless you work at a network, where you must write for a widely scattered audience, you must tailor your copy to suit the needs of your specific local audience. This is part of what's called "localizing" the news, and we shall deal with it in a later chapter. It is sufficient to note for now that you who read this book, almost without exception, will begin your careers at a local station; and most of you will remain at local stations throughout your careers, simply because that is where the vast majority of the jobs are. Thus you would rewrite the following story differently, depending on the location of you and your audience:

> SOUTH CHARLESTON, W.Va. (AP)—A natural gas explosion destroyed a crowded supermarket Monday, injuring at least 17 people, authorities said.
>
> All employees and customers were believed accounted for, said a state police superintendent, but searchers continued to use shovels to dig for more victims possibly trapped inside.
>
> "All those who were in the store have now been accounted for. We no longer expect to find any bodies," said Supt. John O'Rourke, but he said he could not rule out the possibility that someone may be in the debris.
>
> The explosion occurred shortly after an employee lit a cigarette in the supermarket, said State Trooper A. W. Robinson, but he said it was not immediately known if the cigarette caused the explosion.
>
> Also under suspicion was a major gas line about 40 feet from the Foodland supermarket that was accidentally ruptured about noon by construction crews working on an Appalachian Corridor G highway project, said Bill Reed, district manager for Colombia Gas of West Virginia. The line was leaking at the time of the blast, he said.

If you were writing for a network or a local station *far away* from the scene, you might make it,

> At least 17 people have been hurt in a gas explosion at a supermarket **just outside of (or near) Charleston, West Virginia. . .**

If your station is closer to the scene, say, in the same state or a bordering state, you might make it,

> **In South Charleston, just west of Charleston,** a gas explosion today injured at least 17 people at a supermarket. . .

And if your station is in the immediate area, you might make it,

> At least 17 people are hurt in a gas explosion **at the Foodland supermarket near the Appalachian Corridor G highway project.** . .

Note that in the first example, only the larger, better known place is named in the lead, and in the third example the exact location is named. As the audience grows more specific, so does the "where" element grow more specific.

Do not be disturbed that spelling out the "where" element causes you to write extra words and thus eat up precious air time. The extra words are normal and necessary in broadcasting. Again, the objectives are clarity and immediate understanding.

As for reinforcing the "where" element, the wording can be much simpler. In fact, a single word will usually suffice, that word being the name of the location used as an adjective: "The New York Governor," "The Taylorsville mine," "The reaction of the Roanoke town council," and so on. In the case of the preceding South Charleston explosion story, "where" reinforcement might go this way:

> A natural gas explosion injured 17 people today at a supermarket **near**
>
> **Charleston, West Virginia.** The explosion leveled the store, but rescuers who
>
> combed the debris say all shoppers and employees are now accounted for. The
>
> supermarket was near a gas line and highway project in the town of **South**
>
> **Charleston.** **West Virginia** state police speculate the explosion was caused when
>
> a lighted cigarette touched off leaking gas fumes. A gas company official confirms
>
> the gas line was leaking at the time of the blast.

The desirability of renaming the location in the body of a broadcast story is one major difference with print style. Another major difference is that sometimes you don't have to name the location geographically *at all*. In broadcasting, some "datelines" are superfluous:

> The White House announced today *in Washington.* . .
>
> -0-
>
> *In Paris,* the French government said today its soldiers will stay in Lebanon. . .

In these examples, naming the city was unnecessary. *Of course* the White House is in Washington and the French government is in Paris! It is only when events occur *outside* their accustomed place that it's necessary to tell where:

> President Smith announced today **at Camp David.** . .
>
> -0-
>
> Governor Thompson, **on a visit to Rockford**, called today for a massive highway
>
> repair project. . .

Normally, those two officials would be located, respectively, in Washington and Springfield. Had they made news in those locations, naming the cities would have been superfluous. But since they spoke elsewhere, the specific "where" had to be included.

While we're on the wording of the "where" element, consider the following:

> Prime Minister Margaret Thatcher of Britain warned today that **that country** will
>
> not tolerate Argentinian occupation of the Falkland Islands. . .

The wording "that country" is an example of a writer obeying the dictum, probably laid down by a high school English teacher, always to avoid repeating the same word and, conversely, always to find a different word. In broadcasting, this is not, repeat *not,* always desirable. It sounds stodgy, unclear, or both. The lead should read

> British Prime Minister Margaret Thatcher warned today that Britain will not
>
> tolerate. . .

Similarly,

> The mayor of Warsaw today told the people **of that city** that they face serious
>
> food shortages this winter. . .

should read

> The mayor of **Warsaw** today told the people of **Warsaw** they may face serious
>
> food shortages. . .

In short, if you've found the right word, it's better to repeat it than to stretch for another word.

"WHERE" AS TRANSITION

The use of transitions (or "links") between stories will be discussed in Chapter 13 on radio news. However, as noted previously, story order in radio newscasts is usually decided only a few minutes before air time, so as to lead with the freshest news. Thus, the writer cannot always know in advance which story will precede the one he or she is writing, or which story will follow, making it impossible, or at least highly risky, to write a specific transition. That's where the "where" element comes in.

If you *start* a story with the "where" element, especially if it is the kind of story that will "play" on its own (that is, it is not specifically related to another story in subject matter), that story can then be placed virtually anywhere in the newscast without rewriting:

> **In Poland,** Solidarity Leader Lech Walesa (Lek Vah-WEN-sah) led a silent vigil. . .

In Boston today, Mayor Kevin White. . .

-0-

On West 23rd Street this morning, a bus jumped a curb. . .

Using "where" as a transition making a clean break from an as yet unknown preceding story is also useful in TV news, especially in news departments with limited writing staff. In large news departments, a producer can assign a writer to handle a group of stories destined to run together in a specific segment of a newscast; the writer will thus have time to link the stories with creative transitions. But in smaller news departments where the work load is heavier, writers have less time to spend on such niceties; they will find that using the "where" element as a transition comes in very handy.

But, again, a caution: Do not overdo it. You can't start *every* story with "where." If you did, the newscast would sound staccato.

NUMBERS

Many news stories deal in some fashion with numbers, usually in the form of statistics issued by companies, government agencies, or international organizations. Journalists come upon an unending stream of statistics to measure the economy, law enforcement, defense procurement, crop production and so on. Broadcasters (who also rely on statistics to measure audiences, the ratings) treat numbers very differently from print journalists, chiefly by using *fewer* of them.

Numbers on paper can be reread. Numbers on the air are heard once. A steady barrage of them can lead to a condition jocularly known as MEGO— short for "My Eyes Glaze Over." Here's an example of the statistics-laden copy streaming into broadcast newsrooms:

> DETROIT (AP)—Domestic automakers wrapped up their best model year in two years as late September car sales surged 7.9 percent ahead of year-ago figures, U.S. carmakers said Tuesday.
>
> Imported cars sold at a near-record pace in the model year but fell 9.1 percent in September from a year ago because of low inventories, the companies said.
>
> As a whole, estimated sales of 8.81 million foreign and domestic cars in the model year that traditionally runs from Oct. 1 to Sept. 30 were up 14.7 percent from 1982 and the best since 1981's 8.95 million.
>
> The six major domestic automakers sold 6.48 million cars in the model year, up 16.8 percent from 1982. The 1982 model year was the worst since 1961, while the 1983 model year was the best since 6.59 million cars were sold in 1981.
>
> In late September, domestic automakers delivered 241,198 cars compared with 223,512 a year earlier. The daily selling rate of 26,800 was the highest since 33,756 were sold each day in the period in 1978.
>
> General Motors Corp. said it sold 144,841 cars in late September, a 7.9 percent boost. For the month, GM shipped 314,315 cars, a 4.2 percent gain. GM's model year tally was 3.88 million, a 14.4 percent gain over 1982 and the best since 4.03 million were delivered in 1981.

Ford Motor Co.'s late September sales totaled 58,657, a 13.2 percent improvement over a year earlier. In the month, Ford shipped 133,442 cars, up 21.2 percent. The model year tally was 1.48 million, up 14.8 percent from 1982 and the best since 1981's 1.49 million.

Chrysler Corp. delivered 27,279 cars between Sept. 21-30, a 2.6 percent increase over a year ago. In September, it sold 64,061 autos, up 16 percent. The model year count was 819,209, a 24.4 percent boost over 1982 and the best since 1979's 986,647.

Whew! If read on the air in anything approaching that fashion, virtually the entire listening audience would be MEGO'd. Would *you* stay tuned for it?

Broadcasters must translate this mesmerizing hodgepodge into a readily understandable story. To do it, they would

1. Report only the most important numbers
2. Round those numbers off
3. Never report a statistic without telling its significance.

And, to enable a newscaster to read numbers aloud correctly, writers would

1. Spell numbers out where necessary
2. Use hyphens in fractions and seriated numbers

Thus, the preceding wire service story might go something like this as rewritten for broadcast:

It's been a good year for the American car industry. Figures just released in Detroit show U-S carmakers sold **nearly six-and-a-half-million** cars in the model year **1983.** That's up **almost 17 per cent** from the year before. The biggest gain was at Chrysler, which boosted sales by **nearly 25 per cent.**

That's a 20-second story. You may argue that the story was worth more than 20 seconds. But chances are, the person next to you may argue 20 seconds was too much. The point is, the only way to make the story clear is to keep the statistics to a significant minimum.

Print writers can be lazy. They can routinely list all (or nearly all) the statistics and leave it to the reader to decide what's interesting or significant. A broadcast writer must shoulder a larger burden and make that decision for the listener. Making that decision intelligently assumes a high degree of training, experience and news judgment. Well, no one said the job was easy.

As for copy appearance, numbers should appear on the page according to the way they should be *spoken*.

Rule: Spell out all numbers which are subject to error in pronunciation.

For example, most people seeing the year written in figures—let's use 1986—would say "nineteen eighty-six." So it's safe to write the figures "1986" in broadcast copy. But what about the year 2017? Is it "two thousand seventeen" or "twenty seventeen"? You have to decide how you want it to be said and then you have to write it that way.

The same problem occurs in street addresses, which are expressed differently in different cities, according to colloquial usage. In one locality, the address "3049 E. Main St." might be pronounced "three-oh-four-nine east Main Street," while in another locality the pronunciation might be "thirty forty-nine east Main Street." Again, you have to decide which is right.

Some early textbooks in radio/TV news have attempted to list rules for when to use figures and when to use words. However, all such lists are virtually worthless because, in actual practice at professional newsrooms, no such formal rules exist. Hence, the only rule you can consistently put into practice anywhere and everywhere is to write numbers the way they are to be said.

With that proviso, here are five general guidelines for preventing common errors:

1. Beware of long numbers. A number scripted as "4,372,612" is destined to tie up a newscaster's tongue. Make it easier to say: "four million, 372-thousand-612" or, better, "nearly four-and-a-half million."
2. Never begin a sentence with a figure. Write it out: "Twenty-six people suffered smoke inhalation today . . ."
3. Spell out all signs, fractions and decimals: "$600" becomes "six hundred dollars" or "600 dollars"; "5½" becomes "five-and-a-half" or "5-and-a-half"; "1.8 million" becomes "one-point-eight million" or "1-point-8-million."
4. Personalize numbers for the audience:

print: CHICAGO—The City Council voted on Thursday to raise $2.4 billion through a 1 percent retail sales surtax, effective next Monday, to finance construction of a crosstown expressway.

b'cast: Starting Monday, **you'll** be paying for the new cross-town expressway whether **you** use it or not.   The city council today passed **a surtax that'll add a penny to each dollar you spend at the store.**   The retail surtax is designed to raise the nearly two-and-a-half billion dollars the expressway is expected to cost.

Explaining a money figure this way is very effective in broadcasting. It tells the effect on your audience's spending power in a direct, personal way.

5. Never use Roman numerals or mathematical symbols. Only gladiators in the Colisseum would have understood "Superbowl XVII." Make it "Superbowl Seventeen." It's also "Pope Paul the Sixth." And while Albert Einstein wrote "e = mc²," he *pronounced* it "E equals M-C squared." Always spell out "plus," "minus," "times," "divided by," and so on.

LISTS

Like long series of numbers, long lists tend to quickly bog down both newscasters and listeners. Here's a "list" story in print style:

JERUSALEM—Crowds of Israelis jammed stores and service stations throughout the country Tuesday to buy milk, bread, salt, sugar, frozen meat, canned goods, imported delicacies, gasoline and other commodities affected by drastic government economy moves that will raise prices as much as 50 percent by Thursday.

If you tried to say all that on the air, you'd lose listeners well short of the checkout counter. For radio and TV, the shopping list must be condensed:

Israelis rushed today to stock up on **gasoline and basic food items** in order to

beat huge price increases set for later this week. . .

Another type of "list" story occurs when a newsmaker touches on a large number of issues, such as at a presidential news conference. A print writer, after putting the most important issue in the lead, can go on to write, "The president also made these points:". The print writer then lists them point-by-point. If you tried that in broadcasting, you'd wind up with a sentence long enough to make the *Guinness Book of Records*.

So you must avoid the "these points" language. Instead, you include whatever you wish to report by sticking to the simple language mentioned earlier: "The president *said*," "The president *went on*," "The president *also said*," and so on.

AGES

In broadcasting, a person's age almost always *precedes* his or her name or title:

Police arrested 24-year-old Max Murkle. . .

-0-

Police arrested Max Murkle, a 24-year-old computer programmer. . .

However, broadcasters do not include people's ages in news stories as often as do newspapers. There's no hard and fast rule about when and when not to include a person's age, except, of course, when the age itself is an interesting part of the story:

The 7-mile Chesterton marathon was won today by a grandmother.   Forty-four-

year-old Elise Harvey was greeted at the finish line by her daughter, 22-year-old

Cornelia, and her grand-daughter, 18-month-old Elaine. . .

(Note that this story is a case where the passive voice works better for storytelling effect.)

SPELLING

Okay, I admit it, many broadcast newsmen are notoriously bad spellers. Accustomed to having their words heard instead of seen, their attitude has been one of "Aw, what the hell, no one will know if I write 'sez' instead of 'says'."

Well, friends, things have been changing rapidly—thanks to technological advances in television. In modern TV news, writers, reporters and producers most emphatically *do* need to spell correctly. Here's why:

CBS News

WMAQ-TV, Chicago

CBS News

These off-monitor photos show just some of the elements that have become standard in both local and network newscasts. Computers and electronic titling machines permit TV journalists to include textual material along with graphics to enhance the content as well as the form of broadcast stories. Titling machines called "character generators" enable the insertion not only of statistics but also of key portions of documents, quotations, and so on. These same machines are used to insert wording in shots known as "bumpers," visual headlines usually seen between newscast segments, just before commercial breaks.

Obviously, the spelling of this material must be accurate. Misspelled words are a bad reflection on the news department as a whole—and downright embarrassing for the writer who makes them.

More and more, TV newswriting is becoming an outlet for certain creative instincts common among writers in all media; namely, the coining of puns. The writers at CBS News seem to excel at this. Here are a couple of bumper copy creations that have appeared on CBS newscasts:

On a story about a pet bird owners convention:

COMMON CAWS

On a story about a dispute over the allocation of beer distributorships:

AT LAGERHEADS

And this one, authorship unknown, that popped up on TV stations all across the country after the creation of "life" in a test tube by DNA manipulation:

DESIGNER GENES

In a few years, it could be you inventing such word play, which is broadcasting's equivalent of headline writing. But you have to be a good speller. It's doubtful that a poor speller would have thought to use these homophones.

NAMES AND TITLES

As a people, we Americans have a worldwide reputation for informality. We don't like fancy titles, preferring to address each other as human beings rather than as officeholders. We are quick to call strangers by their first names, which is a way of lessening (in form if not in fact) the distances created by age, education, social station, and personal wealth.

Of course, there are limits. It is only with tacit permission that a student addresses a professor by first name, or a patient his doctor, or a reporter a high elected official. However, when the titleholder is not present, we usually refer to that person by last name only.

Most of the time, broadcasting seeks to reflect the informality of American manners. *On first mention*, a newsmaker is identified by *title, first name*, and *last name* (no middle initial):

> Secretary of State George Shultz
> Mayor Ed Koch
> Senator Edward (*not* "Ted" or "Teddie") Kennedy of Massachusetts

On second mention (and all subsequent mentions), the newsmaker is identified by *last name only*.

> Shultz also said . . .
> Later, Koch visited . . .
> Kennedy denied the charge, saying . . .

There are four generally recognized exceptions to these rules:

1. The president of the United States is usually referred to as "Mr." or "President" on *every* mention. Chauvinistic as it may be, the same courtesy is *not* extended to leaders of foreign countries, who get last-name-only treatment on second mention.
2. Members of the clergy are re-identified by title on each subsequent mention:

> Terrence Cardinal Cooke (1st); Cardinal Cooke (2nd)
>   -0-
> Rabbi Arnold Gold (1st); Rabbi Gold (2nd)
>   -0-
> (The) Reverend Jerry Falwell (1st); (the) Reverend Falwell (2nd)

3. Some news organizations insist that women be identified as "Miss" or "Mrs."—but never "Ms." Thus:

Prime Minister Margaret Thatcher (1st); Mrs. Thatcher (2nd)

-0-

Actress Elizabeth Taylor (1st); Miss Taylor (2nd)

Other news organizations insist that women be given the same rough treatment as men—just plain Thatcher and Taylor.

4. In obituaries, the deceased is often identified by full name on both *first* and *last* mention:

Earl Tupper, whose name became a household word because of the plastic containerware he marketed so successfully, died today in Costa Rica.   **Tupper** founded the Tupperware company in 1942, became wealthy, and retired in 1973. **Earl Tupper** was 76.

Frequently in the news, the title or role of a newsmaker is more important to immediate understanding of a story than his or her name. Thus, first mention can be of title or role only, leaving the name itself to a follow-up sentence.

print: FAIRWAY, Kan. (UPI)—"Doonesbury" creator Garry Trudeau will take a leave of absence early next year and temporarily cease production of his Pulitzer Prize–winning comic strip in more than 700 newspapers, Universal Press Syndicate officials said Wednesday.
      "I need a breather," Trudeau, 34, told Universal Press Syndicate officials in a telephone conversation from his home in New York City.

b'cast: Doonesbury is going on extended vacation -- or, more exactly, his creator is.   Garry Trudeau, whose "Doonesbury" comic strip appears in some 700 newspapers, says he needs a rest. . .

or

The creator of "Doonesbury" says he'll take a leave of absence next year -- and take his comic strip along with him. Cartoonist Garry Trudeau says. . .

Sometimes it is preferable in broadcasting to omit names altogether if they are obscure and not relevant to understanding the story:

print: SINGAPORE (UPI)—Garlic, known to scare away vampires and members of the opposite sex, may soon do the same to mosquitoes, two Indian scientists say.
      The pungent herb has been found to be an effective pesticide, New Delhi scientists A. Banerji and S. Amonkarby said in an article in the Singapore Scientist Tuesday.

b'cast: Two Indian scientists have come up with what they say is a new and effective way to chase mosquitoes: squirt them with garlic.   The scientists report. . .

or

      Bothered by mosquitoes?   Well, two Indian scientists say they've found a product that'll drive mosquitoes away.   The product is garlic. Of course, it may drive your friends away, too. . .

(This last version is an example of a "kicker," a light item used at the end of a radio or TV newscast. More on kickers in Chapter 13.)

CONTRACTIONS AND "NOT"

You've probably noticed that I've been using contractions liberally in this book. (There, I did it again.) That's because, being characteristic of informal speech, they are desirable in broadcast writing.

However, caution is advised when using *negative* contractions and the word "not." You'll find in writing the news that "not" is used predominantly to stress something important. Most news stories and newsmakers state things positively. So when you hear a negative, indicating something out of the ordinary, you might want to shun the contraction. For example,

      President Jones says he **won't** visit the Philippines next month.

Since this development was unexpected (the visit had been scheduled), it should be stressed for the sake of clarity:

      President Jones says he **will not** visit the Philippines next month.

Many broadcast newswriters like to underline the word *not* in all their copy, just to make sure that the newscaster doesn't slur it or gloss it over.

Another reason for caution with negative contractions is that the "n't" sound tends to be lost in pronunciation, possibly causing serious misunderstanding among listeners.

ABBREVIATIONS AND ACRONYMS

By now you don't have to be bludgeoned about the head regarding the need to prepare copy that will not trip up radio newscasters or TV anchors. No doubt you have already guessed that abbreviations are to be avoided. Well, a *few* abbreviations are okay—"Mr.," "Mrs.," "Dr."—ones that are common and clear-cut. But a newscaster might do a double take on "Card." or "Msgr.," so they should be spelled out entirely—"Cardinal" and "Monsignor"—on *every* mention.

Rule: Do not use abbreviations.

What about all those government agencies—FCC, FAA, FHA, SEC, and so on? They should be *hyphenated* in broadcast copy: F-C-C, F-A-A, S-E-C. However, if the agency is relatively obscure (that is, if most listeners wouldn't recognize it by its initials), then it should be *named* on first mention and its letters used only on subsequent mention:

> The **Securities and Exchange Commission** filed suit against two Wall Street
>
> firms today for alleged stock manipulation.   The **S-E-C** suit charges that the two
>
> firms. . .

Once again, the practice is to write things the way they are to be said. Thus,

> **N-double-A-C-P** leader Benjamin Hooks says. . . (*not* "NAACP" or "N-A-A-C-P")

As for acronyms (initial letters pronounced as a word), the practice is to begin with a capital letter and put all remaining letters in lower-case. Thus,

> **Nato** commanders met in Brussels today. . .
> -0-
> Senator Murphy said **Nasa's** budget should be increased drastically. . .
> -0-
> In Vienna, the **Opec** ministers ended their meeting without a decision on oil
>
> prices. . .

Some initials and acronyms are so obscure that they require virtual translation to be comprehensible. For example, CINCPAC, which is pronounced "Sink-pak" and which is the Pentagon abbreviation for "Commander-in-Chief, Pacific," should be rendered as "The U-S Pacific Command" or "U-S Naval headquarters in the Pacific." In other words, whenever you come upon an abbreviation or acronym for an agency whose function you do not know, find out what that agency does and include that information, if pertinent, in your story:

> The **Government Accounting Office -- that's the agency that oversees federal**
>
> **spending** -- says the Commerce Department is overspending its budget.   The
>
> **G-A-O** says the Commerce Department spends 40 million dollars a year just
>
> for paper. . .

VISUAL PUNCTUATION

Punctuation in broadcast copy is solely for the eye of the newscaster, as an aid to phrasing, inflection, and emphasis. Since it is not seen by the public, it does not have to follow the rules of print. In fact, a print punctuation mark such as a semicolon (;) is totally worthless in broadcast script.

On the other hand, certain types of punctuation are very helpful visually, especially commas (,), dashes (--), ellipses (. . .), and, to a lesser extent, colons (:). Even the lowly hyphen is helpful as a visual aid because it serves to break up long words that are not hyphenated in print: *life-long, hodge-podge, multi-faceted,* and so on. Such hyphens (which I've been using even in the textual portions of this book) help the newscaster's eye to break up long clusters of letters and thus aid phrasing and pronunciation.

Inevitably, each newswriter evolves a pattern of visual punctuation with which he or she feels personally comfortable. Some writers use visual punctuation to break down entire story sentences phrase by phrase:

> Mayor Tom Smith said today. . .he will not seek re-election to a third term.   The
>
> mayor. . .who was considered a shoo-in. . .said he is. . .in his words. . ."growing
>
> tired and stale."

But by far the most common type of visual punctuation is the <u>underlining</u> of key words. Although this is typically done by newscasters and writers who announce their own copy, it can also be done by writers writing for other people, provided that the people being written for don't object. With underlining, the preceding copy might look this way:

> Mayor Tom Smith said today he will <u>not</u> seek re-election to a third term.   The
>
> mayor, who was considered a <u>shoo</u>-in, said he is, in <u>his</u> words, "growing <u>tired</u> and
>
> <u>stale</u>."

To repeat, broadcast punctuation is a matter of personal choice—just as long the choice aids clarity.

The same is true of paragraph structure. Only the newscaster can see where a new paragraph begins—and he or she may not even care. Newscasters scan the copy just ahead of what they are saying. Thus, starting a new paragraph within a story may actually make it harder for them to scan ahead comfortably. But, again, this is a matter for each writer to decide.

6
TIME AND TIMING

We are almost ready to begin our detailed coverage of radio news, then of television news. But first a word from our stopwatch. . .

I said earlier that the way in which a broadcast story is written depends largely on how much air time is allotted to it. It will be useful, at this point, to examine that proposition more closely. Ultimately, you can't beat the clock. But at least you can try to keep it from beating you from the very first tick.

The time of a story read *live* as part of a newscast (as opposed to taped material) is expressed to the nearest 5 seconds. That is, if your stopwatch reads 10, 11, or 12 seconds, the time is expressed as ":10." If the stopwatch reads 13, 14, or 15 seconds, the time is expressed as ":15." And so on, always rounded off to the nearest :05.

To determine the actual air time of written copy, there is no better or safer way than to read it aloud before it leaves the typewriter. In radio, some writers and newscasters count the number of 70-space lines as a way of *estimating* story times. However, such line counts, while time-saving when you're in a hurry, are often unreliable for the simple reason that different people read aloud at different rates. And in TV news, where lines of copy are sometimes only one or two words long, estimating time by line count would be more complicated than would reading aloud for actual time. So it's best all around to rely on the stopwatch for true timing.

In the real world of broadcasting (as opposed to the ideal world), most stories in any given newscast are very short, running around :10 or :15. A few stories run slightly longer, around :20 or :25. Rarely does a *live* story run longer than :30. That's because the practice is that any story worth more than 30 seconds is also worth having a reporter file a spot or supply taped material.*

In radio, most writers and newscasters determine for themselves the desirable time for each live story. In television, that determination usually falls to a producer. Whichever, the net result is about the same when it comes to writing: a short story time leaves less room for inventiveness and originality than does a long story time.

To illustrate the work and thought processes entailed in all this, I've chosen a somewhat "typical" news story as it was received in broadcast newsrooms all across the country via wire service teleprinter, plus some examples from actual broadcasts showing how the writing and approach varied depending on the air time allotted to it. First the wire service story:

> NEWARK, N.J. (AP)—A federal judge Monday struck down a New Jersey law requiring a minute of silence each day in public schools, saying the law had a "religious purpose" and was unconstitutional.
>
> United States District Judge Dickinson Debevoise, acting on a suit brought by the American Civil Liberties Union, ruled the law requiring the pause at the beginning of each school day violates 1st Amendment guarantees of separation of church and state.
>
> The ACLU, representing a high school teacher and several students and their parents, contended the legislature enacted the law as a way of allowing prayer in the classroom.
>
> Debevoise agreed, saying "The law does not have a bona fide secular purpose. It advances the religion of some persons by mandating a period when all students and teachers must assume the traditional posture of prayer of some religious groups."
>
> He also said that through the law the state "injected itself into religious matters by designating a time and place when children and teachers may pray."
>
> The silent minute law was enacted by the Democratic-controlled legislature last Dec. 16 over the veto of Republican Gov. Thomas Kean, who said the measure posed constitutional problems.
>
> Debevoise issued a restraining order preventing the law from taking effect after the ACLU sued in January on behalf of Jeffrey May, an Edison science teacher who was disciplined for refusing to conduct a moment of silence.
>
> The state Senate and Assembly intervened as defendants in the case when New Jersey Atty. Gen. Irwin Kimmelman refused to defend the law's constitutionality.

(Some of you may want to stop right here, before reading the professional broadcast versions, to test your own ability to decide what to write and how to write it. You might want to try both a 10-second version and a 25-second version.)

No matter how much or how little time is allotted for a story, the broadcast newswriter's first task is mentally to reduce it to its bare bones. In this story,

---

*All such elements of broadcast news have specific names, but at this stage I don't want to complicate matters by introducing them. They'll occur soon enough in coming chapters.

virtually everyone would agree that the skeleton is, "Federal judge overturns state law requiring minute of silence in public schools." Right away, the writer knows that *any* broadcast version, regardless of length, *must* include this essential information.

Next, the writer asks himself about the *significance* of the event: What does it mean? What is the real issue here? Again, virtually everyone would agree that the issue here involves religious prayer, specifically, the issue of separation of church and state. (The issues in news stories are not always as clear cut as in this one.) So that is the second piece of essential information that must be included in the minimum story time.

Well. If the writer has only 10 seconds of air time, he or she can stop thinking and start writing, because, as the saying goes, "That's all she wrote." There simply will not be time to tell anything else. In fact, it won't be easy to cram in the *essential* stuff.

Here are two 10-second versions:

A federal judge has struck down a New Jersey law which requires a minute of

silence at the start of each public school day.   He says it violates the constitutional

separation of church and state.

(Chet Douglas, ABC Radio)

-0-

No moment of silence in New Jersey public schools.   A federal judge today struck

down a New Jersey law requiring a minute of silence each day, saying the law had

a religious purpose and was unconstitutional.

(Bill Diehl, ABC Radio)

Newswriter Jerilyn Cascino of WBBM-TV, Chicago, reads her copy aloud against her stopwatch to obtain an accurate timing—the only reliable method of figuring time in broadcasting.

Note that in each case, the writer barely had time to do little more than rewrite the wire service lead, changing the wording a bit and shortening the sentences. In the first version, note the use of the present perfect and present tenses. In the second version, note the use of an incomplete sentence in the lead. Beyond that, there's not much to note, except that both versions contain the essential information—the event and its significance. Bare bones news.

Now here's what happens when the writer gears up a notch—to 15 seconds:

> A federal judge in Newark today struck down as unconstitutional a state law
>
> requiring a minute of silence at the start of each class day in the public schools.
>
> The judge said the law violates the First Amendment, because "the state injected
>
> itself in religious matters by designating a time and place when children and
>
> teachers may pray."
>
> (Judy Muller, CBS Radio)

This writer has used the additional 5 seconds to include two more elements: the specific place (Newark) and the judge's very words (in a voice-inflected direct quote).

Okay, let's say that the writer decides or is told to do the story in 25 seconds. Now there's time for more than the essence, a whopping 10 extra seconds! Here's where the writer at last has some real choices. But the choices of what? More direct quotes from the judge? The background of the case? Reaction to the decision? The parties involved?

So once again the writer must do some thinking and deciding before hitting the typewriter keys. His reins, although slackened somewhat, are still pretty tight. He might not like *any* of the information supplied in the AP account; thus he may check the wires to see if there's any later or additional information, or he may pick up the newsroom phone and dig for fresh information. And here's what he may come up with:

> A New Jersey federal judge today struck down as unconstitutional a state law
>
> requiring a minute of silence at the start of each public school day.   The judge
>
> ruled the law violates the First Amendment by forcing students and teachers to
>
> assume what he called "the traditional posture of prayer."   The state assemblyman
>
> who sponsored the law criticized today's ruling.   He said the judge, and I quote,
>
> "is assuming that what somebody is THINKING is unconstitutional."
>
> ("CBS Evening News")

The newswriter who prepared that copy chose to devote a few seconds to the losing side in the case. Was it a conscious effort to provide fairness and balance? Perhaps. But perhaps it was just an effort to ensure that the version broadcast at that hour by CBS would be both newsworthy and different from every other version on competing stations and networks.

Whatever the case, think of all the information that still had to be left out because of time limitations: Who was the judge? Who brought suit? Who was the defendant? What was the background? What were the reactions to the decision? What happens next?

Are broadcast writers doomed to eternal frustration because of limited air time? Not at all. Because a story that gets only 10 seconds at 2 o'clock may get 1 minute and 10 seconds at 3 o'clock—but in a very different form from print. Here's yet another broadcast version, from CBS Radio, of the same story:

(Richard C. Hottelet)   A federal judge has struck down New Jersey's mandatory minute of silence at the start of each public school day.   Jeff Grant of station W-C-B-S reports from Newark.

(Jeff Grant)   The controversial law was passed by the state legislature last December over Governor Tom Kean's veto. But in January, the American Civil Liberties Union went to court, seeking to overturn the statute. The A-C-L-U argued the law violated the First Amendment's separation of church and state, and U-S District Judge Dickinson Debevoise (De-be-VOYS) agreed. In a 39-page opinion, Debevoise ruled the minute of silence injected the state into religious matters "by designating a time and place when children and teachers may pray, if they do so in a particular manner." A-C-L-U Attorney Ann McHugh said this decision should lay to rest any effort by other states to institute moments of silence.   Lawyers for the state legislature have not decided whether to appeal the ruling. Jeff Grant, for CBS News, Newark, New Jersey.

While not an example of sharp or inventive writing, this broadcast excerpt does serve to show the true nature and structure of "length" in broadcast news. And that is details beyond a story's essence are usually supplied from audio and/or video sources *outside the studio*. Since these sources and their treatment differ in radio and television, we must now consider these media separately.

One last word before taking the plunge: some of you may be thinking, "Well, hell, I'm not interested in radio, so I'll just skip on to television." Think again. It doesn't work that way, either in life or in the classroom. The techniques of television grew out of, and presuppose a knowledge of, the techniques of radio. You cannot learn one set of techniques without first learning the other. The basic terminology, the basic writing skills, are the same. So are the sources of news, interviewing techniques, and so on. So let's talk microphones before we talk cameras.

7

IS ANYONE LISTENING?

MURROW'S LEGACY

Chances are, you've never heard of Gabriel Heatter or H. V. Kaltenborn. But in their day, these news commentators were as well known as John Chancellor and Bill Moyers are today.

The difference is, few people recognized Heatter and Kaltenborn at the local supermarket—because they spent their commentating careers in radio. You can bet that for the sake of privacy, Chancellor and Moyers sometimes think Heatter and Kaltenborn had it pretty good.

If your parents are 45 or older, they probably have childhood memories of the family gathered near a huge radio console (with vacuum tubes, of course; there were as yet no transistors, printed circuits, or microchips) tuned to Jack Benny, Fred Allen, or "Yours Truly, Johnny Dollar." Even now, many people of that generation (myself included) can hum the themes from "The Lone Ranger" and "Let's Pretend."

At any rate, radio in the 1920s, 1930s, and 1940s was as big, culturally and socially, as TV is today—in news as well as in entertainment. If fact, the very first U.S. radio broadcast was news: the 1920 Harding-Cox presidential election returns over Westinghouse station KDKA in Pittsburgh.

In its first two decades, radio news did not have a "broadcast style." Writing and presentation were in newspaper style, which was only natural inasmuch as print was the only possible training ground. But as radio grew to rival newpapers and magazines as a deliverer of information and as an advertising medium, broadcast news staffs began to evolve some of the writing techniques discussed in the first six chapters of this book, especially brevity and informality. Although there were a number of pioneers in this, men whose early careers peaked just before and during World War II, one man above all is credited with bringing to broadcast news the stamp of genius. That man was Edward R. Murrow. For broadcasters, the name Ed Murrow occupies the same high place as, for print journalists, do the names Horace Greeley and Joseph Pulitzer.

By the outbreak of World War II, Murrow, from his base at CBS in London, had assembled a network of correspondents across Europe who, by short wave, telephone, and transatlantic cable, reported not just the events of the war, but also its *sounds*. For the first time, American listeners could hear not just the voices of the reporters and the voices of Hitler, Churchill, Stalin, and Mussolini, but the actual sounds of bombs exploding, air raid sirens shrieking, anti-aircraft batteries pounding, and fighter planes roaring overhead.

Murrow's own broadcasts from London during German air raids stand even today as models of the art of broadcast reporting. Here's part of his first such live broadcast, delivered from the roof of the BBC building:

I'm standing on a rooftop looking out over London. At the moment everything is quiet. For reasons of national as well as personal security, I'm unable to tell you the exact location from which I'm speaking. Off to my left, far away in the distance, I can see just that faint red angry snap of anti-aircraft bursts against a steel-blue sky, but the guns are so far away that it's impossible to hear them from this location. About five minutes ago the guns in the immediate vicinity were working. I can look across just at a building not far away and see something that looks like a flash of white paint down the side, and I know from daylight observation that about a quarter of that building has disappeared, hit by a bomb the other night.

I think probably in a minute we shall have the sound of guns in the immediate vicinity. The lights are swinging over in this general direction now. You'll hear two explosions. There they are! That was the explosion overhead, not the guns themselves. I should think in a few minutes there may be a bit of shrapnel around here. Coming in, moving a little closer all the while. The plane's still very high. Earlier this evening we could hear occasional--again, those were the explosions overhead. Earlier this evening we heard a number of bombs go sliding and slithering across, to fall several blocks away. Just overhead now the burst of the anti-aircraft fire. Still the nearby guns are not working. The searchlights now are feeling almost directly overhead.   Now you'll hear two bursts a little nearer in

a moment.

There they are!   That hard, stony sound.

I don't know about you, but I get a chill just seeing those words on paper. Imagine what they must have been like coming through a radio!

And if you think *that's* good, listen to how Murrow could describe an air raid with time to write copy before going on the air:

It was like a shuttle service, the way the German planes came up the Thames, the

fires acting as a flare path.   Often they were above the smoke.   The searchlights

bored into that black roof but couldn't penetrate it.   They looked like long pillars

supporting a black canopy.   Suddenly all the lights dashed off and a blackness fell

right to the ground.   It grew cold.   We covered ourselves with hay.   The

shrapnel clicked as it hit the concrete road nearby.   And still the German bombers

came.

Ed Murrow went on to pioneer in the development of television news and documentary techniques and later became head of the United States Information Agency under President John F. Kennedy. He died a premature death from cancer in 1965, having secured the premier place in the pantheon of broadcast journalism.

Although the techniques and technology of radio news have changed considerably since Murrow's heyday, his overall concept of the use of the medium is still very much alive: radio journalists seek to transmit not only the cold hard facts of events but also their sound and their feel.

There is a tendency among broadcast journalism students, never having heard the reportorial and writing artistry of Ed Murrow, Robert Trout, Edward P. Morgan, and other radio news practitioners, to give short shrift to radio in favor of television. Such students may be making a big mistake. Radio news, because of its inherent emphasis on words rather than on pictures, content rather than image, and because of its closer ratio of humans to machines, is frequently the more effective and professionally satisfying medium. And, on the practical level, radio salaries are often on a par with television's.

DRIVE TIME = PRIME TIME

Radio lost much of its audience to television in the 1950s, *except* (and this is a very big exception) at two distinct times of day: morning and early evening. People may be watching "Three's Company" and "Dallas" at night, but they are listening to the radio while traveling to and from work.

In the morning especially, when people wake up, shower, eat breakfast, and go to work, radio's audience is much much larger than television's. Morning is truly radio's Prime Time. Only, in the radio business it's called "Morning Drive Time" or just "AM Drive." This is when local stations schedule their main news efforts, frequently programming solid "news blocks" of 2, 3, or even 4 hours. Morning Drive Time is from 6 A.M. to 10 A.M.

Of secondary (but still major) importance in radio is the period from about 3 P.M. to 7 P.M., known (not surprisingly) as "Afternoon Drive Time" or (you guessed it) "PM Drive." Once again between these hours, local stations concentrate their news efforts, hoping to attract a huge share of the people heading home from factory or office, mostly by car.

The rest of the time, 16 hours out of 24, plus weekends, local stations (except for several dozen all-news stations around the country) content themselves with a modest schedule of newscasts. But considering that there are some 8,200 AM and FM radio stations in the United States, that's an awful lot of broadcasters writing and/or announcing an awful lot of newscasts, day in, day out, in an unending torrent.

Of course, some of those stations don't broadcast any news at all. And some, as noted, broadcast news and nothing but news 24 hours a day. But most, no matter what their style of entertainment programming, fall somewhere in between.

FORMATS

In broadcasting, the word "format" is used to describe both the specific form and the general content of programming. For example, a station that plays Country and Western music is said to have a "Country and Western format." If it programs, say, a 5-minute newscast at the start of each hour, it is said to have a "news-on-the-hour format."

As you might expect, given the large number of radio stations, the variety of news formats is positively bewildering and lends itself to only broad categorization:

1. News-on-the-hour—anywhere from 1 to 10 minutes of news every hour, either network or local, but usually a mix of both
2. News-on-the-half-hour—similar to news-on-the-hour, but almost always locally produced
4. Fifteen-minute newscasts scattered at fixed times from early morning through late evening
5. News blocks—30-minute or 60-minute segments scheduled during AM Drive and PM Drive
6. "Headlines" or "newsbriefs"—30-second or 60-second summaries of one-sentence versions of the latest stories

The important thing to note at this point is that, whatever the format, a news story does not exist in a broadcasting limbo; it is always part of a structure called a newscast.

Each network and local station devises a format for its newscasts. For example, the format (at this writing) for CBS Radio Network News calls for 6 minutes of news-on-the-hour, including 2 minutes of commercials, presented roughly in the following fashion:

Opening theme—known as a "signature," a "sounder," or "beeps," featuring a series of tone signals or musical notes readily identifiable as belonging to CBS.

Sign-on—an introductory identification line including the names of the programming source and the newscaster (as in, "CBS News, This is Reid Collins.").

Section One—a first body of news containing the top one or two stories of the hour.

Commercial cue—a short sentence or phrase to alert listeners that the news will continue after a commercial break (such as, "More news in a moment" or "More news after this").

First commercial—either one 60-second commercial or two 30-second commercials played back-to-back. (The content and production of commercials is not a concern of the news department except insofar as the subject matter of a commercial might cause shock among listeners. It would be unwise, for example, to follow a news story about somebody's mouth being badly burned with a commercial for a breath freshener or an air crash story with a commercial for an airline company. In such cases, the commercials are pulled off the air, *not* the news stories.)

Section 2—another body of news.

Commercial cue—making a break to the second commercial.

Second commercial—similar to the first commercial break.

Section 3—the concluding body of news, including, if time and context allow, a final light item known as a "kicker."

Sign-off—a closing line re-identifying the newscaster and the source of programming ("Reid Collins, CBS News").

Such a format is typical of radio news formats just about everywhere in that it affords great flexibility. It can be revised drastically depending on the nature and flow of the news. A truly major news development, reported live, could lead to indefinite postponement of the commercials and continuation of the broadcast until there were no further details to report. Any format—and there are literally hundreds of them—is designed to give a station or news department a distinctive "sound" on an hour-to-hour and day-to-day basis.

In addition, many stations revise their standard formats frequently as they experiment with ways both to build their audiences and to fit their news presentation within the overall framework of their programming. Any newsman who stays at the same station for a few years will probably live through several format changes. Someone who joins a station with a Talk Radio format (telephone call-in and discussion) featuring 5 minutes of news every hour and half-hour may suddenly find himself working for a Soft Rock station with 60-second newsbriefs once an hour. That's because, except for very successful stations with long-standing high shares of a very fractionalized audience, local stations are constantly scrambling to snare a significant audience share to "sell" to advertisers.

You should not be shocked at this. Broadcasting is a business, and the news is part of that business. While newsmen generally have nothing whatever to do with the preparation and selling of commercials, they must be aware that the format of a newscast is designed as part of a sales package to potential advertisers. Even National Public Radio (NPR), which serves a network of mostly non-commercial stations, occasionally changes its format to serve the needs of its affiliated stations which, do not forget, are competing for audience in local marketplaces.

I stress this because I don't want you to go into the news business blindfolded. Just as a newspaper may put a human interest or soft feature story on the front page to attract readers to build circulation and thus attract advertisers, so a radio station might decide that the audience *it* wishes to attract will sit still for only 60 seconds of news rather than 6 minutes. If that bothers you to the extent that you wish to do something about it, then you should go into station management rather than the news department.

At many stations, newscasters must announce any live commercial copy scheduled within their newscasts. The commercials are written at advertising agencies or by staffers of the sales department, never the news department. However, the newscaster, as the "on-air talent," is expected to give the ad copy his or her best reading. Sometimes it comes as part of the newscast format itself:

Good morning. I'm Joe Doaks with the latest W-W-K-K news . . . brought to you by McNulty Chevrolet . . . where Smilin' Ed McNulty always gives you the best deal on a new or used car . . .

In the "golden days" of radio, such copy would always be read by staff announcers, to safeguard an image of strict separation of news and commerce. Nowadays, while staff announcers abound in television, they are a dying breed in radio. Today a station that wants to keep its news staff "untainted" by contact with commercials will have the disk jockey or call-in host read the open, close, and live commercials while the newscaster sticks to the news. Newcomers seldom have a chance to begin their careers at such stations, and they should not be surprised to find themselves reading the plug for Smilin' Ed, however much they may oppose the practice.

MARKETS

If I have seemed to be dwelling just now on the commercial aspects of radio—the business side—it's because you need to understand how broadcasters conduct their affairs, of which the news department is just one division. Radio stations, and television stations, too, measure themselves for sales purposes (and by extention for news purposes) by a combination of their signal strength and the size of the local marketplace.

Signal Strength

To begin broadcasting, and then to remain on the air, a station owner requires a license from the Federal Communications Commission (FCC), the agency that regulates all broadcasting in the United States. The FCC assigns each local station not only its specific frequency on the AM or FM band, but also the power and direction of its transmitter. This isn't as easy a matter as it sounds because radio waves, especially on the AM band, behave erratically and fluctuate with atmospheric conditions, especially at night. Therefore, a station whose signal is precise and narrow during the day may interfere with some other station's signal at night. The FCC thus strictly limits the frequencies, directions, and power of transmitters. The dial is very crowded indeed.

If you are trying to reach a large audience, you obviously want as strong a signal as you can get, in as heavily a populated an area as you can find. The FCC, however, has set maximum AM transmitting power at 50,000 watts. If you've ever dialed your car radio at night and suddenly brought in a station from the other end of the country, you were probably hearing a 50,000-watter. There are very few of them. All other stations are considerably weaker in transmitting power, down to a low of 1,000 watts during the day and 250 watts at night.

The size of a station's news department will be largely determined by its signal strength. The higher the strength, the bigger the potential audience, the bigger the potential profits (through the sale of commercial time), and the bigger a news staff you need and can afford.

Market Size

The other determining factor is the size of the local area itself. In broadcasting, size is determined not by geographical area but rather by population density. "Market size" thus refers to the potential listening audience and the number of radio (or TV) sets in a given area, not city limits or other geographical or geopolitical demarcations.

For example, the "Los Angeles market" does not mean the city of Los Angeles. It means the Los Angeles metropolitain area within reach of local radio and TV signals. The same is true of every metropolitain area in the United States. (See the chart on page 80 to find the "designated ranking" of your metropolitan area.)

For all purposes, including news, broadcasters break market sizes into three main categories:

1. *Major markets* are the country's 10 or 20 largest. They correspond for the most part to the country's largest cities. However, because of the standard of measurement just explained, some smaller cities, geographically close and thus yielding high population density, are served by the same stations; this boosts them into the major market category: San Francisco/Oakland, Dallas/Fort Worth, Tampa/St. Petersburg, and so on.

2. *Medium markets* are the next largest population areas: Indianapolis, Sacramento, Louisville, Portland, and so on.

3. *Small markets,* the most numerous category, are the least populated areas: Laredo, Peoria, Tallahassee, and so on.

As with signal strength, it's easy to understand the link between market size and news department size: the bigger the one, the bigger (usually) the other.

But of course we are really talking about more than size. We are also talking about professional competency. Although there are many exceptions (No station of whatever size in whichever market has a corner on either excellence or, conversely, ineptitude), it is generally true that the larger the market, the greater the professional demands and the higher the pay. This accounts for the usual (but by no means required or unconditional) career track for broadcast journalists: small market to medium market to major market to network. Mistakes and lack of professionalism that can be abided at a lower level are not tolerated at a higher one.

Naturally, there are excellent news departments at all levels, just as there are poor ones. A broadcast journalist may find that he or she is perfectly content, personally and professionally, to remain at a station in a small or medium market. (You've probably heard the old saying about being a big fish in a small pond.) But the goal of the vast majority of young people entering broadcast news is to go as high, as far, and as fast as they can.

The alphabetical listing and ranking of broadcast markets in the United States as of September 1984. Rankings 1–20 are considered major markets, 21–80 medium markets, and the rest small markets. Shifting population patterns eventually result in a rise or drop in ranking, but such fluctuations are relatively minor on a year-to-year basis.

Designated Market Areas

Market	Hshld. Rank	Market	Hshld. Rank	Market	Hshld. Rank	Market	Hshld. Rank
Abilene-Sweetwater, TX	156	Des Moines-Ames, IA	70	Las Vegas, NV	106	Roanoke-Lynchburg, VA	66
Ada-Ardmore, OK	173	Detroit, MI	7	Lexington, KY	82	Rochester, NY	72
Albany-Schenectady-Troy, NY	50	Dothan, AL	160	Lima, OH	193	Rockford, IL	111
Albany, GA	155	Duluth, MN-Superior, WI	119	Lincoln & Hastings-Kearney-Grand Island, NE	88	Roswell, NM	194
Albuquerque, NM	63	El Paso, TX	109	Little Rock-Pine Bluff, AR	54	Sacramento-Stockton, CA	23
Alexandria, LA	176	Erie, PA	137	Los Angeles, Palm Springs, CA	2	Salisbury, MD	165
Alexandria, MN	162	Eugene, OR	125	Louisville, KY	44	Salt Lake City, UT	41
Alpena, MI	204	Eureka, CA	183	Lubbock, TX	140	San Angelo, TX	195
Amarillo, TX	122	Evansville, IN	89	Macon, GA	139	San Antonio, Victoria, TX	45
Anchorage, AK	163	Fairbanks, AK	202	Madison, WI	104	San Diego, CA	25
Atlanta, GA	15	Fargo-Valley City, ND	104	Mankato, MN	187	San Francisco-Oakland, CA	5
Augusta, GA	105	Flint-Saginaw-Bay City, MI	53	Marquette, MI	188	Santa Barbara-Santa Maria-San Luis Obispo, CA	117
Austin, TX	87	Florence, SC	133	Mason City, IA-Austin-Rochester, MN	141	Savannah, GA	106
Bakersfield, CA	149	Fresno (Visalia), CA	64	Medford-Klamath Falls, OR	154	Seattle-Tacoma, WA	14
Baltimore, MD	20	Ft. Myers-Naples, FL	123	Memphis, TN	38	Shreveport, LA	55
Bangor, ME	153	Ft. Smith, AR	148	Meridian, MS	170	Sioux City, IA	136
Baton Rouge, LA	91	Ft. Wayne, IN	93	Miami-Ft. Lauderdale, FL	13	Sioux Falls (Mitchell), SD	97
Beaumont-Port Arthur, TX	127	Gainesville, FL	167	Milwaukee, WI	29	South Bend-Elkhart, IN	83
Beckley-Bluefield-Oak Hill, WV	147	Glendive, MT	205	Minneapolis-St. Paul, MN	16	Spokane, WA	69
Bend, OR	201	Grand Junction-Montrose, CO	189	Minot-Bismarck-Dickinson, ND	146	Springfield-Holyoke, MA	95
Billings, MT	168	Grand Rapids-Kalamazoo-Battle Creek, MI	39	Missoula, MT	172	Springfield, MO	84
Biloxi-Gulfport, MS	184	Great Falls, MT	177	Mobile, AL-Pensacola, FL	62	St. Joseph, MO	181
Binghamton, NY	118	Green Bay, WI	68	Monroe, LA-El Dorado, AR	115	St. Louis, MO	18
Birmingham, Anniston, AL	40	Greensboro-H.Point-W.Salem, NC	52	Monterey-Salinas, CA	110	Syracuse, Elmira, NY	61
Boise, ID	138	Greenville-New Bern-Washington, NC	96	Montgomery, AL	113	Tallahassee, FL-Thomasville, GA	129
Boston, MA, Manchester, NH, Worcester, MA	6	Greenville-Spartanburg, SC-Asheville, NC	36	Nashville, TN Bowling Green, KY	28	Tampa-St. Petersburg, Sarasota, FL	17
Buffalo, NY	32	Greenwood-Greenville, MS	175	New Orleans, LA	33	Terre Haute, IN	121
Burlington, VT-Plattsburgh, NY	99	Harlingen-Weslaco-Brownsville, TX	128	New York, NY	1	Toledo, OH	60
Butte, MT	179	Harrisburg-Lancaster-Lebanon-York, PA	41	Norfolk-Portsmouth-Newport News, VA	47	Topeka, KS	144
Casper-Riverton, WY	186	Harrisonburg, VA	196	North Platte, NE	203	Traverse City-Cadillac, MI	134
Cedar Rapids-Waterloo, IA	77	Hartford & New Haven, CT	24	Odessa-Midland, TX	150	Tri-Cities, TN-VA	81
Champaign & Springfield-Decatur, IL	73	Hattiesburg-Laurel, MS	164	Oklahoma City, OK	43	Tucson (Nogales), AZ	86
Charleston-Huntington, WV	46	Honolulu, HI	79	Omaha, NE	71	Tulsa, OK	57
Charleston, SC	114	Houston, TX	11	Orlando-Daytona Beach-Melbourne, FL	31	Twin Falls, ID	197
Charlotte, NC	34	Huntsville-Decatur, Florence, AL	90	Ottumwa, IA-Kirksville, MO	191	Tyler, TX	158
Chattanooga, TN	80	Idaho Falls-Pocatello, ID	159	Paducah, KY-Cape Girardeau, MO-Harrisburg, IL	76	Utica, NY	157
Cheyenne-Scottsbluff-Sterling, CO	182	Indianapolis, IN	22	Panama City, FL	171	Waco-Temple, TX	98
Chicago, IL	3	Jackson, MS	85	Parkersburg, WV	185	Washington, DC, Hagerstown, MD	8
Chico-Redding, CA	142	Jackson, TN	190	Peoria, IL	101	Watertown, NY	180
Cincinnati, OH	27	Jacksonville, FL	65	Philadelphia, PA	4	Wausau-Rhinelander, WI	132
Clarksburg-Weston, WV	166	Johnstown-Altoona, PA	78	Phoenix, Flagstaff, AZ	24	West Palm Beach-Ft. Pierce, FL	67
Cleveland, Akron, OH	11	Jonesboro, AR	174	Pittsburgh, PA	12	Wheeling, WV-Steubenville, OH	112
Colorado Springs-Pueblo, CO	103	Joplin, MO-Pittsburg, KS	124	Portland-Poland Spring, ME	75	Wichita Falls, TX & Lawton, OK	126
Columbia-Jefferson City, MO	130	Kansas City, MO	30	Portland, OR	21	Wichita-Hutchinson, Ensign, Garden City, Great Bend, Hays, KS	58
Columbia, SC	92	Knoxville, TN	59	Presque Isle, ME	200	Wilkes Barre-Scranton, PA	49
Columbus-Tupelo, MS	145	La Crosse-Eau Claire, WI	93	Providence, RI-New Bedford, MA	35	Wilmington, NC	151
Columbus, GA	116	Lafayette, IN	192	Quincy, IL-Hannibal, MO-Keokuk, IA	152	Yakima, WA	120
Columbus, OH	37	Lafayette, LA	107	Raleigh-Durham, NC	42	Youngstown, OH	94
Corpus Christi, TX	131	Lake Charles, LA	161	Rapid City, SD	161	Yuma, AZ-El Centro, CA	178
Dallas-Ft. Worth, TX	10	Lansing, MI	100	Reno, NV	143	Zanesville, OH	198
Davenport-Rock Island-Moline, IL	75	Laredo, TX	199	Richmond, Petersburg, Charlottesville, VA	56		
Dayton, OH	51						
Denver, CO	19						

Source: Standard Rate & Data Service, Inc.

JOB TITLES AND DUTIES

The staff of a radio news department can vary in size from 1 (in the case of a daylight-only station in or near a major market or a medium-power station in a medium or small market) to more than 50 (at local all-news stations in major markets and at networks). The larger the staff, the more specialized the work of each member. Conversely, the smaller the staff, the more multifaceted the work.

As a rule, news staffers at small stations in large markets and at large stations in small and medium markets are expected to be able to "do it all": write, report, interview, operate portable and console recording equipment, edit tape, and announce newscasts. Thus, except at networks, all-news stations, and some large stations in major markets, a certain degree of on-air performing ability is required. Given the choice between an applicant who can write well and one with a "good" air voice, a local station with a limited budget will usually hire the latter—although what it really wants is someone with both talents.

Compared with TV budgets, radio news budgets are small. Staff size is customarily kept to an essential minimum. And since, in the real world, station owners and executives generally consider the "sound" of the station to be the most important commercial factor, on-air performance is given priority.

Even at networks, where it was once the norm for writers to write copy for newscasters or announcers, that is now the exception. In modern network radio, the voice you hear on the air is almost always the person who wrote the newscast. So the "Jack-of-all-trades" nature of jobs in modern radio news extends from the lowest level to the highest.

And that is why I'm putting "Jack-" or "Jill-of-all-trades" at the top of the following rundown of job titles and duties.

Staff Newsman (or Newswoman)

Writes and gathers local news, assembles full newscasts (from wire services for national and international news), and reads them on the air. Conducts telephone interviews ("foners"), records them on tape, edits excerpts for inclusion in newscasts, covers stories in the field with a portable tape recorder, and phones in reports both live and on tape. May have to read live commercial copy during own newscasts—and may have to substitute for a vacationing disk jockey as well as clean the office coffee pot, take transmitter readings, empty the waste baskets, and sweep the hallway during a night shift. (I kid you not.)

News Director

The boss. Hires, fires, and auditions all applicants. At many local stations, also writes and reads newscasts as well as sets work schedules, orders equipment, and tries desperately to cover the news on the inevitably inadequate budget set by top management. Accepts ultimate responsibility for the success or failure of the staff (of which he or she may be the only member).

Newscaster

Writes and reads scheduled newscasts. At small and medium stations, a newscaster will typically handle one newscast per hour in an eight- or nine-hour shift as well as periodic headline summaries and bulletin interruptions of entertainment programming to report major stories. At networks, the work load is somewhat lighter—one newscast every two hours—but the quality of the writing is expected to be much higher. At all-news stations, the newscaster's work load may be extremely heavy inasmuch as he or she must prepare very long chunks of programming, perhaps 1 hour of air time with 2 hours of preparation time. Whew!

Reporter

A terrific, accessible job for a newcomer. Armed with a tape recorder and phone connection cables, radio reporters cover breaking stories and/or beats such as city hall, police, sports, and so on, and call in from the field with taped or live material. Demands for performing ability are less stringent for reporters than for newscasters, the only requirements being the ability to write and speak clearly. In radio, field reporters are the only staff members who get to witness events at the scene.

Newswriter

Actually a misnomer. In modern radio, "newswriters" per se exist only at networks, all-news local stations, and a very few other stations with large news departments. And they do very little writing. In the main, they oversee the editing of taped material from field reporters and network closed-circuit feeds. They also work the phones and conduct interviews on fast-breaking stories (although their voices are generally cut out of what goes on the air), help write copy for newscasters hard-pressed by the clock, and keep an eye on the wire machines for bulletins and major developments requiring previously written copy to be updated. Accessible to newcomers, but hard to find.

News Editor

A rare beast in modern radio, existing chiefly at networks and all-news stations. Editors decide content and story order of each newscast, proofread all copy prepared by newscasters and newswriters, select the tape to be aired, and help direct coverage from field reporters.

Producer

Another rare beast, to be found only at networks and all-news stations. Producers are in charge of special broadcasts such as fast-breaking major developments requiring massive coverage, documentaries, and weekly or monthly interview or news-in-review programs that entail invitations to panelists and the selection of a moderator.

Intern

Not to be confused with "inmate." Some news-conscious stations, networks, and group broadcasters (such as Westinghouse and Metromedia) hire recently-graduated college journalism majors for three- or six-month terms as interns. Such trainees, while not permitted to write or announce news, or handle equipment, are allowed to help with research, assemblage of wire copy, delivery of tapes and scripts, and so on—in general to observe firsthand and learn how the news department works. Such jobs, while they often pay only a pittance, very often lead to full-time jobs with the station or company. In other words, go for it.

Desk Assistant

Formerly called "copy boy" and still called "gopher"—as in "go for coffee." A kind of glorified receptionist, answering phones, taking messages, emptying ashtrays, and so on. Minimum wage and minimum future.

To my knowledge, there are no accurate figures on the number of jobs of any of these categories open at any given time. Such figures are virtually impossible to assemble because openings (and closings) pop up helter-skelter as stations expand or curtail their news coverage, or employees move on to other jobs. But it's safe to say that there is *always* a need for young people who can write and/or perform well and who are willing and able to stand the long hours and low starting pay in the news business.

One's early years in any business are sometimes called one's "salad days"— because one is earning just enough money to buy salad for lunch. This is especially true in journalism, where starting salaries (see Chapter 23, "Job Hunting") are lower than in other professions such as engineering, law, and medicine. However, journalism, especially the broadcast branch, is constantly in need of youthful, ambitious newcomers who are content with salad while awaiting steak.

8
SOURCES OF NEWS

Radio stations (and TV stations, too) compile their news from three main sources:

1. News agencies (also called wire services)
2. Network news services
3. Their own reporters

The exact mix of these sources depends on the size of the station, the market, and the news department. It's risky to generalize about such a multi-faceted industry, but overall, radio stations emphasize local news because they are broadcasting to a local audience. So whenever possible, they rely on local staff newsmen to cover local stories, either in the field or by recorded telephone interview. For world and national news, they rely on both the wire services and the network news organizations with which they may be affiliated.

But even in covering just the local news, many stations can't possibly hire enough reporters to cover everything. In this they face the same problem as newspapers, but even more so: there are seldom enough reporters to go around. Thus, like newspapers, radio stations rely on local news agencies to help cover local news, which they then have to rewrite in broadcast style.

NEWS AGENCIES

In a nutshell, news agencies were created as cooperative efforts by newspapers to help fill the enormous gaps in news they could not cover by their own separate efforts. The very first news agencies were European: Havas (French) founded in 1835, Wolff (German) in 1849, and Reuters (British) in 1851. In the United States, the Associated Press (AP) was begun in the 1870s and United Press (UP) in 1882.

After an intricate series of mergers, false starts, and fresh beginnings, two American news agencies remain today: the Associated Press (AP) and United Press International (UPI). Each offers a wide variety of news wires, many of which are tailored specifically for use by radio and television stations.

Part of UPI sales brochure for DataNews. Stations purchasing the service, as with AP's AP-TV, can order the mix of news and sports that best suits their needs.

What is

Broadcast DataNews

It is UPI's high-speed, computer-oriented system for delivering news and story ideas to your newsroom. Copy is sent by UPI bureaus throughout the world to subscribing stations at 1,200 words per minute —20 times faster than conventional wires.

(UPI)

A Partial List of UPI Broadcast DataNews Subscribers

Networks
American Broadcasting Companies
Columbia Broadcasting System
Missouri Network
Mutual Broadcasting Co.
National Broadcasting Corp.
National Public Radio
Voice of America

Television

Ames WOI-TV	Milwaukee WITI-TV
Atlanta WAGA-TV	Philadelphia KYW-TV
Baltimore WMAR-TV	St. Louis KMOX-TV
Boston WNAC-TV	St. Louis KSD-TV
Charlotte WRET-TV	St. Louis KTVI-TV
Chicago WBBM-TV	Salt Lake City KSL-TV
Cincinnati WCPO-TV	San Diego KCST-TV
Cleveland WJKW-TV	Seattle KIRO-TV
Columbus WCMH-TV	Sioux Falls KELO-TV
Dallas KDFW-TV	Springfield WICS-TV
Dallas WFAA-TV	Tulsa KTEW-TV
Los Angeles KNXT	West Palm Beach WPTV
Memphis WMC-TV	

Radio

Ames WOI	New York WHN
Boston WHDH	New York WNEW
Bucyrus WBCO	New York WOR
Chicago WBBM	Pittsburgh KQV
Cleveland WERE	St. Louis KSD
Dallas WFAA	Salt Lake City KSL
Houston KTRH	San Francisco KCBS
Los Angeles KNX	Seattle KIRO
Miami WINZ	

Source: UPI.

Like so much in our day and age, AP and UPI have undergone, and are still undergoing, major technological changes. With the advent of satellite transmission and high-speed printers, each agency has designed a space-age service bringing the news to subscribers faster and in greater volume than ever before possible. AP calls its new service AP-TV, and UPI calls its new service DataNews.

But these services, which began in the 1980s, are relatively expensive and beyond the financial reach of all but the biggest and richest broadcast news organizations. Since they produce 20 times the output (yes, 20 times!) of older services, they use up 20 times as much paper, with the result that paper costs alone can ruin a small station's budget. So most stations continue to buy the older, slower wires. Today, a newcomer entering broadcast news must understand the operation of both the older and the newer wires.

The "A" Wire

The so-called "A" wire is a news agency's main transmission service for the most important, breaking world and national news. It is written, edited, and slugged in newspaper style, transmitted in AM and PM cycles geared to newspaper deadlines. However, it is also the most comprehensive wire on which to base any rewritten broadcast version of a story. The "A" wire, either AP's or UPI's, or both, is bought by virtually every big-city radio station whose news department has a policy of rewriting every word it broadcasts. (Much "A" wire material is included in both AP-TV and DataNews.)

Here's how AP's "A" wire looks as it comes over the printer (teletype machine):

```
A233
     U 1 BYLZYVZYV A0588
AM - TURKEY - QUAKE, 1ST LD, A222, 230
EDS: DEATH TOLL CLIMBS TO 509. SURVIV
ORS ENDANGERED BY COLD.
BY ISMAIL KOVACI
ASSOCIATED PRESS WRITER
     ISTANBUL, TURKEY (AP) - A MAJOR EARTHQUAKE STRUCK EASTERN TURKEY
EARLY SUNDAY AND OFFICIALS SAID AT LEAST 509 PEOPLE WERE KILLED.
NEWSPAPERS SAID 50 VILLAGES WERE LEVELED, AND THE DEATH TOLL WAS
EXPECTED TO CLIMB.
     ABOUT THREE HOURS EARLIER A QUAKE ROLLED THROUGH THE HINDU KUSH
MOUNTAIN RANGE, 1,400 MILES TO THE EAST ON THE BORDER BETWEEN
AFGHANISTAN AND PAKISTAN, SHAKING ISLAMABAD AND REACHING AS FAR AS
```

INDIA'S KASHMIR STATE. THERE WERE NO IMMEDIATE REPORTS OF CASUALTIES OR DAMAGE. MORE THAN 12 HOURS LATER, A STRONG QUAKE SHOOK SOUTHWESTERN JAPAN, BUT NO CASUALTIES WERE REPORTED.

THE DEVASTATING QUAKE STRUCK TURKEY AT 7:12 A.M. (11:12 P.M. EST SATURDAY) AND WAS FELT IN MOUNTAINOUS PROVINCES BORDERING IRAN, SYRIA AND IRAQ.

NIGHTFALL AND INTERMITTENT SNOWFALL IN SEVERAL AREAS HAMPERED RESCUE EFFORTS. A LOCAL ARMY CORPS MOBILIZED ALL ITS SOLDIERS TO HELP THE SURVIVORS AND CLEAR DEBRIS IN COMMUNITIES REACHED EARLIER IN THE DAY.

DROPPING TEMPERATURES THREATENED THOUSANDS OF HOMELESS SURVIVORS IN REMOTE TOWNS, LOCAL OFFICIALS SAID. TEMPERATURES OF 35 DEGREES FAHRENHEIT WERE EXPECTED.

AUTHORITIES SAID THE QUAKE WAS BELIEVED TO BE CENTERED IN ERZURUM AND KARS PROVINCES, WHERE MOST OF THE DAMAGE WAS DONE, BUT IT ALSO SHOOK THE PROVINCES OF BITLIS, MUS, DYARBAKIR, BINGOL, VAN AND MALATYA, ACCORDING TO THE MARTIAL LAW COMMAND OF THE EASTERN REGION.

JOURNALISTS IN: 6TH GRAF

AP-NY-10-30 1738EST

A235

U 1 BYLZYVWYF A0568

AM - GRENADA - PRESS, BJT, 560

AMERICAN COMMANDER BATTLING SNIPERS,

REPORTERS

BY **KERNAN TURNER**

ASSOCIATED PRESS WRITER

BRIDGETOWN, BARBADOS (AP) - THE U.S. MILITARY COMMANDER OF THE GRENADA TASK FORCE IS F

BUST IT

AP-NY-10-30 1757EST

A236

B A BYLZYVVYX A0615

AM - OBIT - LILLIAN CARTER, 30

BULLETIN

AMERICUS, GA. (AP) - LILLIAN CARTER, THE MOTHER OF FORMER PRESIDENT JIMMY CARTER, DIED SUNDAY IN AMERICUS-SUMTER COUNTY HOSPITAL AT AGE 85, OFFICIALS SAID.

MORE

AP-NY-10-30 1758EST

A237

U 1 BYLZYVEEV A0572

AM - MISSING SHIP, 340

NO SIGN OF MISSING OIL DRILLING SHIP

PEKING (AP) - SEARCHERS TURNED UP NO FURTHER SIGNS SUNDAY OF AN AMERICAN OIL DRILLING SHIP OR ITS 81 CREWMEN, MISSING SINCE A TYPHOON FIVE DAYS AGO IN THE SOUTH CHINA SEA.

"UNFORTUNATELY, THESE SEARCHES ARE SOMETIMES A LONG AND HARD JOB," SAID U.S. AIR FORCE SENIOR MASTER SGT. BILL BARCLAY AT THE WEST PACIFIC RESCUE COORDINATION CENTER ON OKINAWA.

EARLY SUNDAY, FOUR SHIPS SEARCHED AN AREA WHERE A PLANE HAD SPOTTED WHAT MIGHT HAVE BEEN SURVIVORS, BUT FOUND NOTHING, SAID AIR FORCE LT. COL. JACK GREGORY OF THE RESCUE CENTER.

"IT DOESN'T MEAN THEY AREN'T THERE, BUT WE HAVEN'T FOUND THEM," HE SAID.

BARCLAY SAID TWO U.S. NAVY P-3 PLANES CONTINUED TO TAKE TURNS SEARCHING FOR THE 5,926-TON GLOMAR JAVA SEA, WHICH HAD BEEN DRILLING FOR OIL SOUTH OF CHINA'S HAINAN ISLAND BEFORE TYPHOON LEX HIT IT WITH 75 MPH WINDS.

THE SHIP, CARRYING 42 AMERICANS, 35 CHINESE, TWO SINGAPOREANS, AN AUSTRALIAN AND A FILIPINO, WAS DOING THE EXPLORATION FOR ARCO CHINA INC., A U.S. COMPANY WORKING UNDER A CONTRACT WITH CHINA.

THE SHIP'S HOUSTON-BASED OWNER, GLOBAL MARINE INC., SAID IN HONG KONG THAT THE SIGHTING OF WHAT MIGHT HAVE BEEN TWO OR THREE SURVIVORS WAS MADE ABOUT 60 MILES NORTHWEST OF THE DRILLING LOCATION.

GREGORY SAID THREE CHINESE SHIPS AND A VESSEL BELONGING TO GLOBAL MARINE, THE SALVANQUISH, WENT TO THE AREA.

EARLIER, CHINA'S OFFICIAL XINHUA NEWS AGENCY SAID CHINA HAD SENT FOUR SHIPS TO FIND A LIFE RAFT FLASHING DISTRESS SIGNALS IN THE AREA.

THERE WAS NO WORD FROM CHINESE OFFICIALS SUNDAY ON ANY FINDINGS. THERE ALSO WAS NO REPORT ON A CHINESE SHIP THAT WENT TO INVESTIGATE A LARGE UNDERSEA OBJECT WITH SONAR EQUIPMENT AND UNDERWATER TELEVISION APPARATUS.

THE OBJECT, DISCOVERED NEAR THE DRILLING SITE WITH SONAR EQUIPMENT, WAS REPORTEDLY ABOUT 328 FEET LONG, 164 FEET WIDE AND 66 FEET HIGH, ABOUT THE SIZE OF THE MISSING SHIP.

SO FAR, SEARCHERS HAVE REPORTED FINDING TWO FENDERS FROM THE MISSING SHIP, MORE THAN 10 LIFE JACKETS AND AN EMPTY LIFE RAFT.

AP-NY-10-30 1805EST

A238

U 1 BYLZYVRYR A0235

AM - GRENADA - PRESS, BJT, 560

AMERICAN COMMANDER BATTLING SNIPERS, REPORTERS

BY KERNAN TURNER

ASSOCIATED PRESS WRITER

BRIDGETOWN, BARBADOS (AP) - THE U.S. MILITARY COMMANDER OF THE GRENADA TASK FORCE IS FIGHTING TWO BATTLES - ONE WITH THE RESISTANCE ON THE ISLAND AND ANOTHER WITH THE FRUSTRATED INTERNATIONAL PRESS TRYING TO COVER THE INVASION.

VICE ADM. JOSEPH METCALF III SAYS HE HAS ORDERED NAVAL PATROL BOATS TO SHOOT AT UNAUTHORIZED SMALL CRAFT ATTEMPTING TO LAND REPORTERS AND PHOTOGRAPHERS ON GRENADA. JOURNAL

BUST IT

AP-NY-10-30 1807EST

A239

U A BYLZYVQYV A0617

AM - OBIT - LILLIAN CARTER, 1ST ADD, A236

,110

URGENT

AMERICUS, GA.: OFFICIALS SAID.

MRS. CARTER HAD BEEN AT THE HOSPITAL FOR ABOUT A WEEK. THE FORMER PRESIDENT AND HIS WIFE, ROSALYNN, HAD BEEN AT THE HOSPITAL FOR THE DAY.

"MISS LILLIAN," AS HER NEIGHBORS IN PLAINS, GA., CALLED HER, LIVED ON THE FRINGES OF POLITICS FOR MOST OF HER LIFE.

HER FATHER, JIM JACK GORDY, A POSTMASTER, NEVER RAN FOR OFFICE. BUT SHE RECALLED DURING AN INTERVIEW IN 1976 THAT HE "WAS THE BEST, BIGGEST POLITICIAN IN THIS PART OF THE WORLD. HE KEPT UP WITH POLITICS SO CLOSELY THAT HE COULD TELL YOU - ALMOST WITHIN FIVE VOTES - WHAT THE PEOPLE WHO WERE RUNNING WOULD GET IN THE NEXT ELECTION."

MORE

AP-NY-10-30 1810EST

A240

R 1 BYLUIVCZC A0614

AM - GRENADA - PRESS, 560

AMERICAN COMMANDER BATTLING SNIPERS, REPORTERS

BY KERNAN TURNER

ASSOCIATED PRESS WRITER

BRIDGETOWN, BARBADOS (AP) - THE U.S. MILITARY COMMANDER OF THE GRENADA TASK FORCE IS FIGHTING TWO BATTLES - ONE WITH THE RESISTANCE ON THE ISLAND AND ANOTHER WITH THE FRUSTRATED INTERNATIONAL PRESS TRYING TO COVER THE INVASION.

VICE ADM. JOSEPH METCALF III SAYS HE HAS ORDERED NAVAL PATROL BOATS TO SHOOT AT UNAUTHORIZED SMALL CRAFT ATTEMPTING TO LAND REPORTERS AND PHOTOGRAPHERS ON GRENADA. JOURNALISTS PRESUME HE IS JOKING.

METCALF, COMMANDER OF THE 15,000-MEMBER INVASION FORCE, ALSO HAS REJECTED COMPLAINTS FROM THE PRESS ABOUT RESTRICTIONS, SAYING HE IS PROTECTING REPORTERS' LIVES BY NOT GRANTING THEM FREE ACCESS TO THE ISLAND.

DRESSED IN A BERIBBONED WHITE UNIFORM , METCALF TOLD REPORTERS AT A NEWS CONFERENCE SATURDAY TO STOP TRYING TO TAKE THEIR COMPLAINTS TO A HIGHER AUTHORITY.

"THE BUCK STOPS WITH ME. IF YOU WANT TO ARGUE WITH SOMEBODY ABOUT IT, YOU'VE GOT TO ARGUE WITH ME, NOT THE D.O.D. (DEPARTMENT OF DEFENSE), NOT ANYBODY ELSE BUT ME," HE SAID.

EARLIER IN THE DAY, WHEN HE WAS WEARING A JUMPSUIT AND VISORED CAP, METCALF GREETED A POOL OF REPORTERS IN GRENADA ON A CLOSELY GUARDED VISIT TO THE EMBATTLED ISLAND.

"ANY OF YOU GUYS COMING IN ON PRESS BOATS?" METCALF ASKED. "WELL, I KNOW HOW TO STOP THOSE PRESS BOATS. WE'VE BEEN SHOOTING AT THEM. WE HAVEN'T SUNK ANY YET, BUT HOW ARE WE TO KNOW WHO'S ON THEM?"

A NUMBER OF TIRED CORRESPONDENTS HAVE RETURNED TO BRIDGETOWN AFTER HIRING BOATS THAT WERE TURNED AWAY OFF THE COAST OF GRENADA BY NAVY WARSHIPS, BUT THERE HAVE BEEN NO REPORTS OF JOURNALISTS DUCKING U.S. BULLETS.

METCALF, A NATIVE OF HOLYOKE, MASS., IS A 1951 GRADUATE OF THE U.S. NAVAL ACADEMY. HE IS COMMANDER OF THE 2ND FLEET.

THE COMMANDER'S ENCOUNTERS WITH JOURNALISTS HAVE REVEALED A TOUGH YET GOOD-NATURED PERSONALITY. HE GREETS THOSE ON THE POOL TOURS AT PLANESIDE, SHAKING HANDS AND ASKING THEIR NAMES.

BUT WHEN PRESSED FOR SPECIFIC INFORMATION, HE OFTEN SAYS, "I HAVEN'T THE FOGGIEST IDEA." HE TOLD ONE PACK OF PERPLEXED REPORTERS, "I LOVE THAT QUOTE."

ON SOME OCCASIONS, HE HAS MISLED REPORTERS. WHEN ASKED ABOUT THE CAPTURE SATURDAY OF BERNARD COARD, THE POLITICIAN BELIEVED TO HAVE PROVOKED THE EVENTS LEADING TO THE SLAYING OF PRIME MINISTER MAURICE BISHOP, METCALF AT FIRST TOLD A NEWS CONFERENCE THAT GRENADIANS HAD DETAINED COARD.

TOLD THAT A MARINE OFFICER HAD DESCRIBED TO THE PRESS POOL HOW COARD HAD BEEN SURROUNDED BY MARINES IN A HIDEOUT AND ORDERED TO COME OUT OF THE HOUSE OR GET BLOWN UP, METCALF SAID, "OK, LET'S BE TECHNICAL, OK?"

PRESSED FURTHER BY THE REPORTERS, METCALF ACKNOWLEDGED HE WAS AT A

MARINE COMMAND POST WHEN COARD WAS BROUGHT IN AND WAS AWARE THAT THE MARINES HAD CAPTURED HIM.

DESPITE HIS RESTRICTIONS, METCALF INSISTS HE WANTS "THE NEWS MEDIA TO GET ON WITH THE LEGITIMATE BUSINESS OF PUBLIC INFORMATION."

METCALF ACCEPTED FULL RESPONSIBILITY FOR KEEPING REPORTERS OUT OF GRENADA DESPITE "ENORMOUS PRESSURE IN WASHINGTON TO GET REPORTERS IN THERE" AND CALLED HIMSELF THE JOURNALISTS' "BEST FRIEND."

"I WANT TO GET YOU THERE, BUT BY GOLLY I'M GOING TO INSIST THAT YOU CAN BE SUPPORTED WHEN YOU GET THERE," METCALF SAID.

"I'M NOT A DOG IN THE MANGER," HE SAID. "YOU MAY THINK I AM . . . BUT I'M REALLY NOT."

AP-NY-10-30 1820EST

A241

  U A BYLUIVZVT A0619

AM - OBIT - LILLIAN CARTER, 2ND ADD, A239

, A236,170

URGENT

AMERICUS, GA.: NEXT ELECTION.

MRS. CARTER WAS OFFERED HER HUSBAND'S SEAT IN THE GEORGIA LEGISLATURE WHEN HE DIED DURING HIS FIRST TERM IN 1953, BUT SHE DECLINED.

"I WAS TOO SHOCKED BY HIS DEATH," SHE SAID LATER. "BUT I THINK IF LATER THEY OFFERED THE LEGISLATURE SEAT TO ME AGAIN, I WOULD HAVE TAKEN IT."

A GRAVESIDE SERVICE FOR MRS. CARTER WILL BE AT 3 P.M. TUESDAY AT THE LEBANON CEMETERY IN PLAINS.

MRS. CARTER HAD 15 GRANDCHILDREN AND EIGHT GREAT-GRANDCHILDREN.

SHE CAMPAIGNED ACTIVELY FOR HER SON WHEN HE RAN FOR GOVERNOR OF GEORGIA IN 1970, BUT HER ROLE IN HIS 1976 PRESIDENTIAL CAMPAIGN, WHEN HE LOST TO RONALD REAGAN, WAS MORE SEDATE. HER JOB WAS TO CARE FOR GRANDDAUGHTER AMY, THEN 8, THE ONLY CARTER CHILD LEFT AT HOME.

IT WAS THE SECOND DEATH IN THE FAMILY IN JUST OVER A MONTH.

EVANGELIST RUTH CARTER STAPLETON, CARTER'S SISTER, DIED SEPT. 26 AT

AGE 54 AFTER A MONTHS-LONG STRUGGLE WITH PANCREATIC CANCER.

    MORE

AP-NY-10-30 1824EST

A242

    U A BYLUIVBYL A0622

AM - OBIT - LILLIAN CARTER, 3RD ADD, A241, A

239, A236, 200

URGENT

AMERICUS, GA.: PANCREATIC CANCER.

    IN 1964, MRS. CARTER WAS A DELEGATE TO THE DEMOCRATIC NATIONAL

CONVENTION AND WAS ASKED TO SERVE AS CO-CHAIRMAN OF LYNDON B.

JOHNSON'S LOCAL CAMPAIGN HEADQUARTERS.

    "AT THAT TIME, PEOPLE AROUND HERE DIDN'T LIKE JOHNSON BECAUSE HE

WAS FOR THE BLACKS," SHE ONCE SAID. "ANYWAY, I WAS DELIGHTED TO DO

IT, TOOK THE JOB AND THE BLACKS HAD ACCESS TO THE OFFICE OVER AT THE

HOTEL JUST LIKE THE WHITES."

    MRS. CARTER WAS KNOWN FOR BEING LIBERAL ABOUT RACE IN AN ERA WHEN

MOST OF HER NEIGHBORS WERE EXACTLY THE OPPOSITE.

    A REGISTERED NURSE, SHE USED HER KNOWLEDGE OF MEDICINE TO HELP MANY

POOR BLACKS IN PLAINS.

    CARTER RECALLED THAT HIS MOTHER "TAUGHT US BY HER DAILY EXAMPLE TO

HELP THE WEAK AND HANDICAPPED EVEN WHEN IT WASN'T THE COMFORTABLE OR

SOCIALLY ACCEPTABLE THING TO DO."

    BORN AUG. 15, 1898, IN RICHLAND, GA., ABOUT 20 MILES FROM PLAINS,

MRS. CARTER ATTENDED PUBLIC SCHOOLS THERE AND STUDIED NURSING AT THE

NOW-DEFUNCT WISE CLINIC IN PLAINS. SHE EARNED HER NURSING DEGREE AT

GRADY MEMORIAL HOSPITAL IN ATLANTA.

    SHE MARRIED JAMES EARL CARTER SR., A PEANUT FARMER AND BUSINESSMAN,

IN 1923.

AP-NY-10-30 1828EST

Allowing for one lengthy story that has been omitted here, that's approximately 40 minutes' worth of "A" wire. The copy has been reproduced at length to give you a feel for this kind of basic raw material and to demonstrate in this and later chapters some of the things that broadcast newswriters have to watch out for.

First, let's make sure you understand what you are seeing, going back to the start of the series, numbered "A233." Each story, you will have noticed, begins with a number. That is how this particular version of the wire story will be referred to in any upcoming additions, revisions, or corrections.

Just underneath is "U 1 BYLZYVZYV A0588." Forget it. It's an internal AP code.

Next, "AM—Turkey—Quake, 1st Ld." "AM" means the wire is sending its stories for next morning's newspapers. "Turkey—Quake" is the slug, and "1st Ld" (short for "First Lead") means the story contains the latest information that the agency could find. This may be updated by later stories for the AM cycle; if so, they will be denoted "2nd Ld," "3rd Ld," and so on.

Next, on the same line, see "A222, 230." The first number, A222, is the number of the previous story on the Turkey Quake which A233 updates. The second number, 230, is the number of words in story A233, rounded off to the nearest 10.

The next line, beginning "Eds: Death toll climbs . . .," calls writers' and editors' attention to the specific information making this story newsworthy.

Underneath this is the AP writer's byline. Then follows the story proper.

Skip now to the end of the story, where you find the words "Journalists in: 6th graf." This tells you that you will find the rest of the story by going back to the sixth paragraph of A222, which begins "Journalists in," and picking up the copy from there.

Now the final line: "AP-NY-10-30 1738EST." "AP" is obvious. "NY" is the identification of the AP bureau from which the story was edited and transmitted, in this case New York. "10-30" is the date, October 30. And "1738EST" is the exact time, based on a 24-hour clock, that the story was "timed off," the time transmission of that story ended, including the time zone: 5:38 P.M. Eastern Standard Time.

With minor variations, the organization of UPI's "A" wire resembles AP's. Each gives specific directions, in highly abbreviated form, to guide editors and rewriters to find things quickly.

Now while this may be "old hat" to those of you who may have worked or interned at newspapers, for most of you it is new and perhaps a bit complicated. So take a few moments and go back over the material provided. If you ever hope to reach the higher echelons of the broadcast news business (networks and major markets) where such wire service material is common, you will have to learn how to read it quickly. A professional radio or TV newsman would be expected to be able to scan all of the foregoing material, and know what to save for broadcast rewrite, *in less than 1 minute.*

Broadcast Wires

I must be honest with you: chances are, unless you've got a real head start and knack for this, you will *not* begin your career at a station that buys an

"A" wire. *Most* radio stations don't buy it. If they did, they'd also have to hire people to rewrite it for broadcast. And they haven't got the money for that—or if they have, they don't want to spend it.

So what do they do? They buy a wire that is already rewritten in broadcast style. AP and UPI both offer not one but several. Some contain local and regional rewrites, in addition to world and national. Some contain sports. Some contain the weather. AP-TV and DataNews contain it all.

Such services, commonly known as "radio wires," have distinct advantages and disadvantages. Before we go into those, first take a look at some AP broadcast wire copy. The AP packages this material in 60-second chunks called "Newsminute" and in 2:30 chunks called "Newswatch." Here's a "Newswatch" that incorporates material from the "A" wire copy in the previous pages:

V2307

R D

AP-19TH NEWSWATCH

HERE IS THE LATEST NEWS FROM THE ASSOCIATED PRESS:

OFFICIALS IN AMERICUS, GEORGIA SAY THAT LILLIAN CARTER -- MOTHER OF FORMER PRESIDENT JIMMY CARTER -- HAS DIED AT THE AGE OF 85. MRS. CARTER HAD BEEN IN THE HOSPITAL FOR ABOUT A WEEK -- ALTHOUGH THERE'S NO IMMEDIATE WORD ON THE CAUSE OF HER DEATH. IT'S THE SECOND DEATH IN THE CARTER FAMILY IN JUST OVER A MONTH. THE FORMER PRESIDENT'S SISTER -- EVANGELIST RUTH CARTER STAPLETON -- DIED OF CANCER ON SEPTEMBER 26TH.

IT LOOKS LIKE ONE OF THE ADMINISTRATION'S MAIN STATED REASONS FOR INVADING GRENADA (GRUH-NAY-DUH) WASN'T MUCH OF A REASON AT ALL. ALL ALONG, OFFICIALS HAVE BEEN SAYING THEY WERE AFRAID THE U-S CITIZENS ON THE ISLAND WERE IN DANGER OF BEING TAKEN HOSTAGE. BUT U-S INTELLIGENCE SOURCES ARE NOW SAYING THERE WAS NO CLEAR EVIDENCE THAT SUCH A TURN OF EVENTS WAS LIKELY.

ACCORDING TO A TOP U-S OFFICIAL, THE U-S FORCES IN GRENADA HAVE UNCOVERED SOME SECRET DOCUMENTS ABOUT GRENADA'S RELATIONS WITH OTHER COMMUNIST NATIONS. DEPUTY SECRETARY OF STATE KENNETH DAM SAYS THE

PAPERS SHOW GRENADA ENTERED INTO MILITARY SUPPLY AGREEMENTS WITH CUBA, NORTH KOREA AND THE SOVIET UNION. HE MADE THE COMMENT ON THE C-B-S PROGRAM "FACE THE NATION."

AUTHORITIES IN TURKEY REPORT MORE THAN 500 DEATHS AS A RESULT OF A MAJOR EARTHQUAKE THAT STRUCK EARLY TODAY. NEWSPAPERS SAY 50 OF TURKEY'S VILLAGES WERE LEVELED. ACCORDING TO OFFICIALS, COLD AND SNOW IN MANY AREAS ARE HAMPERING RESCUE EFFORTS AND ARE LIKELY TO CAUSE MORE DEATHS.

A SCIENTIST WITH THE GOVERNMENT'S HAWAIIAN VOLCANO OBSERVATORY SAYS HAWAII'S KILAUEA (KIH-LUH-WAY-UH) VOLCANO IS READY TO ERUPT AGAIN. KILAUEA'S LAST ERUPTION ENDED ON OCTOBER SEVENTH. THE GEOLOGIST SAYS MOLTEN ROCK CONTINUES TO COLLECT AT THE VOLCANO'S SUMMIT -- AND THE NEXT WAVE OF VOLCANIC ACTIVITY COULD COME AT ANY TIME.

V2309

R D

AP-19TH NEWSWATCH-TAKE 2

LAST WEEK, THE CITIZEN-LABOR ENERGY COALITION WAS TELLING NATURAL GAS CUSTOMERS THAT THEY CAN LOOK FOR THEIR BILLS TO RISE AN AVERAGE OF 21 PERCENT THIS WINTER. TODAY, THE CONSUMER AND LABOR ORGANIZATION SAYS THE STUDY THAT PRODUCED THE FIGURE WAS WRONG. THE COALITION SAYS THERE WERE ERRORS INVOLVING 20 OF THE 80 CITIES STUDIED.

HOSPITAL OFFICIALS IN FORT LEE, NEW JERSEY REPORT THE DEATH OF PIONEER ANIMATOR OTTO MESSMER. HE WAS 91. MESSMER WAS THE CREATOR OF "FELIX THE CAT" -- ALTHOUGH IT WAS THE STUDIO HE WORKED FOR AND NOT MESSMER WHO GOT THE CREDIT.

THE TINY VILLAGE OF LIJAR IN SOUTHERN SPAIN HAS APPARENTLY DECIDED TO LET BYGONES BE BYGONES. THE VILLAGERS HAVE SIGNED A PEACE TREATY WITH FRANCE -- ENDING WHAT WAS OFFICIALLY 100 YEARS OF WAR BETWEEN THE SMALL TOWN AND

THE NEIGHBORING COUNTRY. THE WHOLE THING STARTED IN 1883 WHEN THE KING OF

SPAIN WAS INSULTED AND HIT WITH STONES IN PARIS. THE WAR WAS DECLARED TO

DEFEND THE KING'S HONOR -- AND ENDED TODAY WITH A FESTIVE CEREMONY.

APTV-10-30-83 1841EST

Again, UPI offers similar summaries in broadcast style, every hour, 24 hours a day.

The advantages of such pre-rewritten copy:

1. It saves time and money.
2. It's easy to read at a glance — no complicated directions to follow.
3. It allows local newsmen to devote their entire attention to local newsgathering and preparation.

The disadvantages are:

1. Every station buying and airing the product unedited sounds identical. You could turn the dial and still hear the exact same words.
2. The radio wires are *slower* to move major stories. Don't believe me? Check back to that "A" wire bulletin about the death of Lillian Carter. It was timed off at 5:58pm Eastern Standard Time. Now here's how it moved on the broadcast wire:

V2295

U A

AP-U R G E N T

LILLIAN CARTER

(AMERICUS, GEORGIA) -- OFFICIALS SAY LILLIAN CARTER, THE

MOTHER OF FORMER PRESIDENT JIMMY CARTER, DIED TODAY IN

AMERICUS-SUMTER COUNTY HOSPITAL IN GEORGIA AT AGE 85.

APTV-10-30-83 1802EST

That version was timed off at 6:02 P.M.—4 minutes *later* than the "A" wire version. And it happens that those 4 minutes are the difference between getting the story on the 6 P.M. newscast and having to wait till the next newscast, maybe an hour later.

In radio news, minutes count BIG.

3. The radio wires make it next to impossible to be creative or original, because they do not give you enough detail. No further details of the Lillian Carter story moved on the radio wire until 6:41 P.M. However, if you had had "A" wire A239 (Carter, 1st add) from which to rewrite, you had enough details to say something like,

Miss Lillian Carter died a short time ago in Americus, Georgia. Her son, former

President Jimmy Carter, was at her bedside.

The "A" wire story buried this last fact. But since it adds dimension and detail, I, a writer, choose to give it high prominence in *my* version of the story, a version that, I hope, will sound original and *beat the competition.*

As you can see, I am a fervent advocate of the "A" wire. And, indeed, much "A" wire material is included in the high-speed AP-TV and DataNews services. At this writing, not many stations could afford them. Perhaps with time, or eventual computerization eliminating hard-copy paper costs, more stations will buy them or at least buy the "A" wire. In the meantime, newswriters and newscasters restricted to using the radio wires alone will find it difficult to come up with the colorful detail or different angle to make their stories sound distinctive.

Many radio journalists scorn stations with such limited source material, calling them "rip-and-read" operations, after the practice of ripping the copy off the printer and reading it on the air unedited. Of course, in a limited job market, not everyone has the choice of where he or she will work. In the meantime, there are all those bills to pay.

City Wires

Some large metropolitain areas have home-grown news agencies usually called City News or City News Bureau. These began as cooperatives among local newspapers and are now supported as well by radio and TV stations. Again, their purpose is to provide reliable coverage of local and regional events beyond the personnel abilities of any single news organization.

As a rule, extreme care must be taken in handling copy from such local agencies. Most of them operate on a shoestring. Typically, they serve as training grounds for print journalists who are just out of school and still wet (if not drenched) behind the ears. The copy tends to be poorly written, unclear, inexact, and convoluted in the extreme.

That said, such city wires are also extremely valuable. They provide coverage of the nitty-gritty news stories that many big newspapers and broadcasters tend to neglect, sometimes to their dismay and regret: the "routine" homicide that turns out to be a VIP, the "routine" political campaign speech that turns out to be a bombshell, the "routine" court trial that reveals the appearance of a surprise witness, and so on.

In addition, city wires serve as conduits for the scheduling of events, from news conferences to rallies and marches. A single call to a city wire from a newsmaker or would-be newsmaker ensures that word of the upcoming event will get to just about every newsroom in town, enabling coverage to be planned ahead of time.

NETWORK NEWS SERVICES

Let's say that you are the owner of a 1,000-watt AM radio station in a small market or in a fringe (suburban) area of a medium or major market. The low power of your transmitter and your limited potential for building a large audience (measured in total listenership), and thus charging high rates for commercials, preclude hiring a large staff for your news department. You just can't afford it. Yet you are a reponsible broadcaster in that you consider the news an important element in community life. So how, given your limited budget, do you go about providing a balanced diet of local, national, and world news?

First, you hire two staffers for your news department—a news director and a staff newsman of the news director's choosing. They will concentrate on gathering, writing, and announcing local news. They will work six-day weeks (standard at the small-station level) to cover weekends, and their shifts will overlap on weekdays to begin local coverage during AM Drive and maintain it through PM Drive, and yet allow them to share the labor at midday when the bulk of the news breaks. You are buying a regional radio wire from either AP or UPI to provide your two-person team with news from the state capital. But you don't want them ripping and reading the world and national news, because that's what's being done at competing stations, and you don't want to sound like them.

So, to provide your listeners with well-written, well-delivered world and national news, you decide to affiliate your station with a network news service. But of what time, length, and format? Here, as of 1984, were some of your choices:

News-on-the-hour
News-on-the-half-hour
News-on-the-quarter-hour
News-at-fifty-five (5 minutes before the hour)
One-minute "capsules"
Two-minute newscasts
Three-and-a-half-minute newscasts
Four-minute newscasts
Four-and-a-half-minute newscasts
Five-minute newscasts
Five-and-a-half-minute newscasts
Six-minute newscasts

Fifteen-minute newscasts
Five-minute sportscasts
Business and financial newscasts (varying length)
Commentaries
News analysis
Feature newscasts
Religion newscasts
Closed-circuit feeds of news reports and actualities

And you'd have no shortage of suppliers, all eager to get their services (and thus their commercials) into your market. You could choose from among

ABC News (six different services aimed at different types of local audiences: "Information Radio," "Contemporary Radio," "Entertainment Radio," "Direction Radio," "FM Radio," and "Rock Radio," each service offering a newscast at a fixed time every hour)
CBS News
NBC News
Mutual News (also offering several different services)
UPI Radio News
AP Radio News
National Black Network
Various state and regional networks, depending on your area

And that's just in English. You could also get network news in Spanish if that was the predominant language of your target audience.

You see, what we're dealing with here is free enterprise—"Competition" with a capital "C." The only restraint on you as a station owner is that with few exceptions based on transmitting power, direction of signal, and market saturation, only one network service per station is allowed in each market. So if a station in your listening area were already affiliated with CBS News, you would have to shop around for another service.

For example, you as a station owner would negotiate an affiliation contract with the network you choose (if you both want each other). The contract entitles you to air the newscasts and feature material from that network, at your discretion but under certain conditions. For example, you don't have to carry the network's 10 A.M. news, but if you do, it must be at the time the network broadcasts it; you can't record it and play it later.

The network pays you a small percentage (and I do mean small) of the revenue it receives for its network commercials, and it formats (structures) its newscasts in such a way that there are 30-second or 60-second "holes" in which you may insert your own local commercials. (You can recognize such holes by the strictly worded cues that precede them: "You're listening to NBC News, . ." "This is Information Radio News, . ." etc.)

You also receive, at certain fixed times each day, a closed-circuit feed (heard by the station but not the public) of reports, actualities, and features which you may record and air at your discretion, perhaps in your own local newscasts sold to local sponsors.

So everybody's happy: you because you've got your professional national and world news, and a package into which to insert your own commercials, and the network because it has now extended its voice into your market, thereby increasing its total audience for its news identity and the commercials it carries. Capitalism at work.

Of course, apart from station management and seasoned radio journalists, only news junkies and shut-ins are truly familiar with the breathtaking variety of network news offerings available for local broadcast. That's because very few stations broadcast the full gamut of services from the networks with which they are affiliated. You have to spin the dial all day just to get an idea.

In fact, I suggest you do just that: spend a day or two spinning the AM and FM dials in your area, and notice the high quality of the network writing. Only listeners to CBS affiliates can hear such gems as Charles Osgood's "Newsbreak" and "The Osgood File." Only listeners to ABC affiliates can hear the stylistic virtuosity of Paul Harvey's "News and Comment."

Closed-Circuit Feeds

It's likely that many stations in your area purchase not only a radio wire from AP or UPI, but also an attendant audio service which is fed closed circuit via a line from the telephone company. Such feeds are scheduled at fixed times, usually once an hour, but they may be augmented in the case of major, breaking news. The content of such feeds is sent over the wire printer. UPI's looks like this:

```
NU--R

Z2271NU--R

           R R NETWORK-HOURLY NEWSFEED 0377

10-29 810P⟨

FOLLOWING CUTS FED AT 8:10 and 10:10PM EDT=

⟨

⟨

83 :45 V-A WA -(ARMS)- (VICKI BARKER W-PRES⟨

REAGAN) PRES RESTATES COMMITMENT TO NUCLEAR⟨

ARMS REDUCTION IN WKLY RADIO ADDRESS⟨

⟨

84 :41 V-A WA -(DEMS)- (VICKI BARKER W-REP⟨

LEE HAMILTON, D-IND) DEMOCRATIC RESPONDENT⟨

URGES GOVT TO KEEP MARINES IN LEBANON⟨

⟨

85 :46 V NEW YORK -(SPRINT)-⟨
```

```
(MICHAEL LYSAK W-MARK HOCHMAN,⟨

OF SUMERVILLE, N J) PHONE SERVICE⟨

CUSTOMER ALLEGES RIPOFF⟨

86 :46 V NEW YORK -(REAGAN)-⟨

(JACK VAIL) SURVEY SHOWS PRES⟨

REAGAN GETTING FAVORABLE REACTIONS⟨

TO BEIRUT AND GRENADA POLICIES⟨

⟨

87 :25 A TULSA, OKL -(GRENADA)-⟨

(U-S AMBASSADOR TO UNITED NATIONS⟨

JEANE KIRKPATRICK) VOTING MEMBERS⟨

IN THE GENERAL ASSEMBLY SHOULD KEEP⟨

THEIR STORIES STRAIGHT (TIRED OF THAT) ⟨

88 :16 A TULSA, OKL -(GRENADA)-⟨

(U-S AMBASSADOR TO UNITED NATIONS⟨

JEANE KIRKPATRICK) THEIR DEAL OF⟨

SUPPORT FOR U-S MILITARY ACTION IN⟨

GRENADA (WORLD TODAY)⟨

(EDS: CUTS 87-88 REFER TO A RECENT VOTE⟨

TAKEN IN THE U N GENERAL ASSEMBLY CONDEMNING⟨

U-S INVASION OF GRENADA, WHICH THE U-S VETOED)⟨
```

To explain the foregoing requires using a few terms with which you may not be familiar. Later chapters will consider these things in depth; they are the basics with which radio journalists must deal as a matter of course. But for now we'll keep the jargon to a minimum.

Each item to be fed at the times specified (in this case 8:10 and 10:10 P.M. Eastern Standard Time) is called a "cut." Each is numbered consecutively throughout the day. This particular UPI Newsfeed contains cuts 83 through 88.

Following each cut number is its *exact* running time (to the second, *not* rounded off. This is on *tape,* and in both radio and TV, everything on tape is timed *exactly.*). That's followed by a letter or two. "V" stands for "voicer," a voice report *without* an actuality. "V-A" stands for "voicer-actuality," meaning that the report contains the voice of a newsmaker as well as that of the reporter. In the business, this is known as a "wraparound," or just "wrap," because of the reporter's voice "wrapping around" someone else's.

Next comes an abbreviation for the location of the report. In cuts 83 and 84, "WA" stands for Washington, D.C.

Then, in parentheses, comes the name of the reporter and, where applicable, the name of the voice in the actuality, followed by a brief description of the report's content. The information in parenthesis also serves as the slug.

Cuts 87 and 88 are denoted "A," which stands for "actuality," in other words the voice of a newsmaker. In this case, it's U.N. Ambassador Jeane Kirkpatrick, speaking in Tulsa. The words in parentheses at the end of cuts 87 and 88—"tired of that" and "world today," respectively—are called "outcues" or "endcues." An outcue is the final few words of an actuality or report.

Okay, this sounds a bit complicated. Patience. By the end of the next few chapters, you'll be bandying about those terms like a pro.

LOCAL REPORTING SOURCES

To state the obvious: the most important source of local news is the talent of the reporter—his or her intelligence, curiosity, drive, capacity for hard work, and "nose for news." Without the reporter all the microphones, recording gear, telephones, wire services, police and fire radios—*all* of it is worthless. As I said in the Preface to this book, broadcast journalism depends on brain power, not electronic wizardry.

In the real world, local broadcast newsmen are at a disadvantage compared with their print colleagues. The latter usually outnumber the former, often by a wide margin. That example of the two-person radio news department I mentioned a little while ago was very close to the norm, at least in small markets.

Nevertheless, I put it to you that even a news department of that size can, on a regular basis, beat the print competition despite its numerical handicap. Here are some of the tools it uses in the process:

> *Fire radio*—a receiver tuned to the frequency of the local fire department, to intercept dispatching announcements.
>
> *Police radio*—one or several receivers (depending on the size of the city and the number of police frequencies in use) tuned to intercept calls of "distress" and "crimes in progress."
>
> *Direct telephone lines*—lines that bypass the station switchboard and go directly into the newsroom and the recording studio, enabling newsmen and their contacts to maintain confidentiality as well as the uninterrupted taping of phone interviews.
>
> *Newspapers*—yes, newspapers—a good source of story leads and background material.
>
> *Files*—where scripts and newspaper clippings should be stored for ready access. Keeping and updating files on local events and trends is a habit best formed early in one's career.
>
> *Street indexes*—also called "Criss-Cross" directories, published by the telephone company and listing names and phone numbers by street address instead of alphabetically, enabling newsmen to locate and identify witnesses to events occurring in local neighborhoods.

Number file—a Rolodex or index card file of private telephone numbers frequently used by the news department to reach officials, politicians, bureaucrats and so on.

Little black books—your own private property, and perhaps your most valuable piece of property, containing the names, addresses, and phone numbers of *your* news sources, many of them inevitably confidential. This is customarily the single item that a newsman or woman does *not* share with his or her colleagues, except under special circumstances on a case-by-case basis—and even then only with the permission of the confidential source.

The way a two-person radio news staff can beat a ten-person newspaper staff is to be aggressive, by picking up the telephone and calling officials and unofficial sources *on a regular, recurring basis*. It is *not* sufficient to sit back and let the news come to you. You must go out after it.

Police do not always use their radios when something's happening. The mayor does not normally call the news media when he's about to do something. Teachers don't call the media before deciding to strike. The way things generally become known (unless they are scheduled long in advance) is that *one reporter*, either through routine or luck, learns of something, reports it, and it is then quickly picked up by his or her competitors. You will not be that one reporter by sitting on your duff and waiting for the news to come to you. You must go out after it, chase it, hound it, all day, every day.

Welcome to the news business!

9
TAPE I: ACTUALITIES

In 1961, a portable tape recorder featuring excellent sound reproduction weighed more than 20 pounds and cost more than $1,000. Two decades later, a portable recorder with equivalent sound weighed less than 1 pound and cost less than $100.

Tape recorders have become so ubiquitous and affordable that it's difficult to imagine radio journalism without them. Even print journalists, who used to scoff at reporters carrying tape recorders, now themselves carry cassette or microcassette recorders—driven to it, in part, by having misquoted people whose exact words were there on radio for everyone to hear.

The proper use of a tape recorder and the ability to integrate tape recordings into newscasts are skills *demanded* of today's radio journalists. On average, about one-third of every newscast is on tape, either in the form of actualities (the voice of a newsmaker or the natural sound of an event) or reports from the field. Just tune in any newscast, anytime, anywhere; the newscaster's voice isn't on very long before a different sound source is heard. And with very rare exceptions, those other sound sources are on tape.

In fact, "tape" is how professional broadcasters refer to such material, regardless of its content. "What tape do I have for the next show?" is a question you'll hear in any radio newsroom anywhere in the country.

This chapter and the next are devoted to the different kinds of "tape" and how they are edited and prepared for broadcast. We will take it slowly, because this is where broadcast news is radically different from print journalism. Nothing of what follows has its equivalent anywhere in newspapers or magazines.

TYPES OF ACTUALITIES

Voices of Newsmakers

These are the standard, most frequently heard kinds of actualities. Nothing, repeat, nothing, conveys the "feel" of an event as well as the voice of someone who took part in it or witnessed it. Yes, there is a writer's skill, and, yes, there is the writer's ability to paraphrase. But what writer can convey the emotional power of Rev. Martin Luther King, Jr.'s "I have a dream!" The forlornness of Richard Nixon's "I shall resign the presidency effective at noon tomorrow." The faraway yet breathtaking essence of Neil Armstrong's "A small step for a man, a giant leap for mankind"?

These words, uttered in living memory, are lodged deep within our collective and individual psyches not so much for their substance as for the way and the context in which they were said. And, in particles of magnetic tape, they are preserved for generations to come.

At first glance, actualities appear to be the equivalent of print's direct quotes. But they are not, and it is misleading to consider them as such. For one thing, words in print have no "voice." They are disembodied, appearing only as ink on paper. As such, a direct quote, preceded or followed by the identification of who said it, seems to flow in context. But on the air, the quote and the identification of the speaker are accomplished by *two voices,* two different sounds from two different sources. Unless handled in a special way, they would not seem to flow; instead, they would seem jarring and incongruous.

More on the "special handling" coming up. But, first, the actualities themselves. How do you choose them? What standards guide their selection? Answering these questions is tricky, because, in the last analysis, each case must be decided on its own merits. But by and large, there are five standards on which to judge actualities:

1. **Informational Content.** This is by far the most frequent basis for selection. Almost every speech, news conference, or interview contains one or more portions, brief excerpts, which reflect the crux of the remarks as a whole. Journalistically speaking, the crux is overwhelmingly the "what" or the "why," perhaps both. In short, the *main point* (or points) of a spoken context is what most often makes the best actuality (or series of actualities).

2. **Colorful Details.** Sometimes, the main point of a spoken context can be stated more quickly and clearly by the newswriter than by the speaker. In such cases, the colorful or quirky remark might make the better actuality. Suppose that the president of the United States, in a speech somewhere, proposes a long series of controls on the food industry to guarantee the purity and safety of food products on supermarket shelves. And suppose his recitation is so long-winded and boring that a newswriter could summarize the proposal in two sentences.

Good-bye, actuality. But suppose that the president had ad libbed, "You know, the only reason I'm making these proposals is because I found a staple in my Corn Flakes this morning," followed by audience laughter. Suddenly, you've got your actuality: that remark, *including* the audience reaction.

3. **Emotional Impact.** Very often the flavor or weight of a set of remarks is carried not so much by the words as by the speaker's tone of voice, his attitude. Rev. Martin Luther King, Jr.'s "I have a dream" speech at the Washington Monument in 1963 is an example. So is the reaction of somebody to a piece of good news or a piece of tragic news. If you ask the winner of a million-dollar state lottery for his reaction, you are obviously going to hear words to the effect, "I'm very happy." But his tone of voice will tell you just *how* happy. The words themselves are nothing without their emotional weight.

4. **Sound Quality.** Except in rare cases (when a piece of tape is of historic value or was exceptionally hard to obtain), actualities must sound clear technically. Every word must be understandable. The voice can't sound mushy or too distant from the microphone. Obviously, you can't control the quality of receiving equipment used by listeners. But at the point of transmission (i.e., the newsroom or studio), there must be no straining of ears or shaking of heads over the text of an actuality (or any piece of tape). (A common standard for judging sound quality is to answer the question, "Will this be understood by a commuter over his car radio while driving 55 miles-an-hour in moderate traffic?")

   If the sound quality is poor, the tape is labeled "UFB" (Unfit For Broadcast) and is junked.

5. **Length.** There is no "optimum" length for an actuality. Each news organization sets its own standards for length. In the end, you can't control the way people talk; thus, some actualities will be very short, others very long. I have found over the years that, roughly speaking, no actuality should run less than 10 seconds or longer than 30 seconds in radio. But so much depends on what "sounds right" that each case is different.

Natural Sound ("Wild-Track" Audio)

Sometimes the best actualities are not words in the form of prepared or ad lib remarks. Sometimes they are the natural sounds of events, such as chanting, singing, sirens, police bullhorns, railroad cars clacking on rails, machinery in operation, computers beeping, and so on. For example (to follow up on a model story used earlier in this book), when President Ronald Reagan signed the bill making the third Monday in January a National Holiday in honor of Rev. Martin Luther King, Jr., the crowd of onlookers in the White House Rose Garden spontaneously began singing "We Shall Overcome." The natural sound of the crowd in song was a terrific actuality, more telling than anyone's prepared remarks.

Radio reporters are always on the lookout for such natural sounds (sometimes called "wild-track" audio), which they record "in the clear," that is, without spoken commentary. The tape is then incorporated into stories and newscasts.

Q-and-A

Q-and-A, short for "question and answer" and sometimes written "Q/A," is the kind of actuality that includes the *reporter's* voice as well as the newsmaker's.

An actuality may begin with a newsmaker's remark, continue with a reporter's follow-up question, and conclude with the newsmaker's answer. Because such a structure often results in lengthy actualities, Q-and-A's are seldom heard on network radio, where newscasts tend to be short. However, they are used very liberally in local radio news where more time is allotted for local stories.

A second kind of Q-and-A is composed solely of the reporter's voice. It results from a form of taped "debriefing" in which someone in the studio (a newscaster or newswriter) questions a reporter in the field, usually by telephone, about the story the reporter has just covered. The conversation is taped, and the reporter's ad lib answers are excerpted and edited in the same way as a newsmaker's. Such taped Q-and-A's (although they are really just A's) are incorporated into stories and newscasts in the same way as newsmakers' voices and natural sounds, and thus qualify as actualities.

INTERNAL EDITING

Content

The content of taped actualities is an editorial decision in the same way that print journalists decide which of their notes to include in a story and which to reject. Journalists, *not* the newsmakers, control the structure and content of their stories in all media.

For radio journalists, this means freedom to edit out extraneous remarks, as long as such editing *does not distort the speaker's meaning or intent.* Clearly, internal editing demands a high degree of journalistic integrity. Former President Richard Nixon once declared, "I am not a crook." Any journalist who edited out the word "not" would deservedly have been fired on the spot.

More than likely, the case will be something like this: Mayor Smith says,

> The tax bill is a sham from stem to stern. *Now wait a minute, folks, let me answer this question.* It takes money from the poor and puts it into the pockets of the rich.

Clearly, the second sentence (in italics) is an interruption of some kind and not a part of the mayor's train of thought. You as a radio journalist would edit that sentence out, butting together the first and third sentences into a single actuality.

Of course, internal editing can get much trickier. Suppose that the mayor had said,

> The tax bill is a sham from stem to stern. *Its proposal at this time is a blight on the citizens of our fair city, a stain on our civic pride, a caving in to greedy instincts.* It takes money from the poor and puts it into the pockets of the rich.

This time the radio journalist has a choice: to use the remark unedited *or,* for the sake of brevity, to edit out the second sentence. Again, the meaning is not distorted.

However, suppose Mayor Smith had said,

> The tax bill is a sham from stem to stern. *And the property assessment indicator is no bargain, either.* It takes money from the poor and puts it into the pockets of the rich.

Much as you might like to edit out the second sentence, you can't do it honestly. That's because the "it" at the start of the third sentence could refer to the tax bill, the assessment indicator, or both. You just don't know for sure. So your choices are to use the actuality in its entirety, or not to use it at all.

Internal edits need not be confined to single sentences. A remark from one part of the text may be butted to a remark that came minutes later (but not hours or days), as long as the resulting actuality is faithful to the sense of the remarks as a whole. I can't stress this too strongly. Responsibility in editing is at the heart of broadcast journalism.

Inflections

Sometimes you won't be able to edit an actuality for the most desirable content. That's because human speech patterns won't always let you.

All human languages rely, to varying degrees, on rhythms and inflections to help convey meaning. Some Oriental languages rely on inflections so heavily that, in Chinese, for example, one "word" can have four or five different meanings, depending on its tonal inflection.

English, on the other hand, uses inflections sparingly, usually at the end of a phrase or sentence. The sentence, "You are going," ends in a *down* inflection. But if we add a question mark, "You are going?" the inflection is now *up*, indicating doubt or that something is to follow.

Many speakers tend to ramble, unsure of where the thought or sentence will end. Such speakers end their sentences with unnatural *up* inflections. The result, in tape editing, is that it's hard to find a place to end the actuality without letting it go on to an undesirable length. For the sake of flow and normal speech patterns, actualities should end with *down* inflections. In other words, natural speech rhythms should be retained in editing and ending actualities. Otherwise, they sound unnatural, in fact, sound "edited."

Most beginners discover the inflection problem through trial and error. But they soon develop an ear for inflections and can predict in advance whether a certain edit will work.

WRITING TO ACTUALITIES

You may have wondered why so few examples appeared in the foregoing discussion of actualities. The reason has to do with the "special handling" I mentioned. You see, actualities do not exist in a void. No one edits a piece of tape, picks it up, and plays it on the air by itself. Stories with actualities (or *any* kind of tape) have a special structure, which I will now define and illustrate.

Briefly put, a radio news story containing an actuality begins with scripted copy called a *lead-in*, continues with the actuality, and concludes with more scripted copy called a *tag*. These terms are universally accepted in both radio and TV news. However, there are variations. A lead-in may be referred to as the copy "going into" an actuality and a tag as the copy "coming out" of it. Tags are also sometimes known as "write-outs," but this terminology is rare.

Before considering these elements separately, a few words about the approach: In print journalism, a writer conceives a story at the outset as a lead followed by various supporting elements, including direct quotes. He chooses the quotes he needs only when the time comes to put them on paper.

But in broadcast journalism, the writer *begins* with the taped quote. That is a *given*. His task thus becomes to write copy both before and after the actuality that will ensure that the entire structure flows from beginning to end *without being redundant*. Bear this work approach in mind.

Lead-ins

A lead-in accomplishes two things: it begins a story, and it sets the stage for the actuality. Thus, it serves as a lead (in the broadcast, not print, sense), and it identifies the voice we will hear next. Otherwise, the sudden appearance of a different voice would disorient the listener. And if the lead-in did not establish the context for the taped remarks, that, too, would disorient the listener.

Tags

Tags also serve a double function: to reidentify the voice we have just heard and to carry the story a step farther. However, tags are more flexible than lead-ins. In fact, they can often be dispensed with altogether, *provided* that the text of the actuality constitutes a natural end to the story, and *provided* that the speaker is a familiar voice.

Okay, now for some examples:

(lead-in)   President Reagan is in New Jersey today, campaigning for the G-O-P candidate for the U-S Senate, Congresswoman Millicent Fenwick. The president used the occasion to call for a crackdown on crime:

(actuality)   (Reagan) Many of you have written to me how afraid you are to walk the streets at night. Many older citizens are frightened to go out even during the daytime. It's time to get the hardened criminal off the street and into jail. (applause)

(tag)   The president also denied charges by Democrats that his administration has been hard-hearted when it comes to America's poor. The president said his battle against inflation has delivered more purchasing power to poverty-level families.

(Stephani Shelton, CBS Radio)

That manner of handling the story is special to broadcast journalism. In print journalism, the writer would have to have led with something on the order of, "President Ronald Reagan, declaring 'it's time to get the hardened criminal off the street and into jail,' called Monday for stricter anticrime legislation."

But if this broadcast newswriter had begun that way, she would have obviated the need to use that particular actuality. It would have been redundant and would have wasted precious air time. Since she was given an actuality with that text, she had to find a way to tell the story without upstaging the news contained in it.

Note that the actuality was edited to include the applause in reaction to the president's remarks. If he had been booed, that, too, would have been included. A crowd's reaction is part of the scene, part of the "feel." Including the applause also enabled the newscaster to begin the tag *over* (hence the term "voice/over") the last second or two of the actuality. This resulted in a continuous flow of sound.

All right, here's another:

(lead-in)   A special honor today for Steven Spielberg, who directed the summer box-office smash "E-T."   Spielberg was in New York, where he received the United Nations Peace Medal.   In accepting the medal, Spielberg compared the U-N with E-T:

(actuality)   (Spielberg) They both have the desire and the need to communicate, often to "phone home," (laughter) to understand the care and the love, regardless of nationality.   This film is dedicated to all such children, of all ages, in all the world.   Thank you very much.   (applause)

(tag)   Movie Director Steven Spielberg.

(Bill Diehl, ABC Radio)

Note that the actuality cannot stand on its own. It begins with the pronoun "they." Thus, the lead-in had not only to identify the speaker and establish the context, it had also to spell out who "they" are. Otherwise, the actuality would make no sense.

Note also that the tag is a simple reidentification of the speaker. The writer could have gone on to report more of Spielberg's remarks, but this would have been anticlimactic.

Once more into the breach:

(lead-in)   President Reagan and his special envoy Phillip Habib met at the White House today to discuss the Lebanese situation.   And afterwards, the president announced that American G-Is in Beirut would soon be leaving:

(actuality)   (Reagan) With the evacuation complete, and the authorities asserting their control throughout Beirut, I am pleased to announce that the multi-national force will commence its withdrawal from Beirut Friday, September Tenth, day after tomorrow, and the United States Marine contingent should be among the first to leave.

(tag)   The Americans will depart despite strong requests from the Lebanese government that they stay on indefinitely.

(Steve Porter, NBC Radio)

To take this in reverse order, note that the tag does not reidentify the speaker. That's because the president's voice is heard so often that, while it must be identified going in, it need not be reidentified coming out—everyone recognizes it.

You'll agree, I think, that the most important part of this story, its essence, is the president's announcement of a specific date for a U.S. pullout from Beirut. Yet the writer did not say this in his lead, knowing the president would say it in the actuality. Does this mean that broadcasters *always* have to hedge in the lead when they are using tape? No. Remember, this was just one newscast. Here's how the same writer led the story in the next newscast, one hour later:

> The American G-Is in Lebanon will pull out on Friday.   President Reagan,
>
> following a meeting with his special Middle East envoy Phillip Habib, announced
>
> the pullout at the White House this afternoon. . .
>
> (Steve Porter, NBC Radio)

Now let's move on to something more difficult—a story with *two* actualities, requiring a "bridge" of copy tying the two together:

(lead-in)   The government's new off-shore oil and gas leasing plan came under fire today at a hearing on Capitol Hill.   Leading the attack was Democratic Senator Walter Metzenbaum of Ohio:

(actuality 1)   (Metzenbaum) It would seem to me that the program to lease 200 million acres a year for five years is absurd.   And its only conceivable result will be the most monumental giveaway in the nation's history: vast and immensely valuable public resources leased out at bargain basement prices, and in all probability leased out to the largest corporations in America.

(bridge)   But Interior Secretary James Watt said Metzenbaum and others were off-base in their criticism of the leasing plan:

(actuality 2)   (Watt) There's a basic lack of understanding that what we're talking about is the far-out lands under the oceans -- not the coastal beach areas.   And too many people have, without understanding or intentionally without understanding, have made comments and conclusions that are not accurate or fair.

(tag)   Watt, who was testifying before the Senate Energy Subcommittee, said the plan would create jobs, strengthen national security, protect the environment, and reduce the nation's dependence on foreign oil.

(George Engle, ABC Radio)

In a one-sentence bridge, the writer has reidentified Metzenbaum while at the same time setting up the context of Watt. This kind of writing is not easy for most newcomers; it requires a lot of practice, a lot of experience working with tape. But the key to it, I think, is the acceptance of the non-inverted-pyramid structure of broadcast news. The first thing out of the newscaster's mouth does not have to be the essence of the story (although it may very well be), just as long as the essence is contained somewhere by the end of the story.

How about a story incorporating natural sound?

(actuality 1)	(chanting) "Win, Jesse, win. . .win, Jesse, win. . .
(bridge)	(voice/over) To the chant of "Win, Jesse, win," civil rights leader Jesse Jackson announced today he's a candidate for the Democratic presidential nomination. (tape out) Jackson says that he is running for office to affirm his belief that leadership has no color or gender:
(actuality 2)	(Jackson) I seek the presidency because there is a need to inspire the young to hold fast to the American dream, and assume their rightful place in the political process.
(tag)	With Jackson now in the race, there are 8 announced candidates for the Democratic presidential nomination.

(Ann Taylor, NBC Radio)

It was a bit risky to have begun that story with natural sound because the writer couldn't be sure what kind of story would precede it. In any case, it worked here. The bridge (which, you'll recall, is a kind of tag/lead-in between two pieces of tape) repeated the words "Win, Jesse, win" because it was possible some listeners wouldn't understand the tape. This way, the writer left no doubt.

Please notice how absolutely impossible it would be for print journalism to attempt this sort of structure. It just wouldn't work. (If you think I'm biased in favor of broadcast news in this instance, you're right.)

Now for some Q-and-A:

(lead-in)	The Marine contingent in Beirut may be augmented. In Saint Paul, Minnesota, today, Defense Secretary Weinberger said 800 U-S Marines will go ashore this weekend. Their numbers may be increased to 12-hundred if conditions warrant. Weinberger also said two or three other countries have expressed an interest in sending troops to join the peace-keeping force, in addition to the U-S, Italy, and France. ABC's Carole Simpson asked Secretary Weinberger about that when he landed at Edwards Air Force Base near Washington a short time ago:
(actuality, Q/A)	(Weinberger) Somebody asked me if there were any other countries wanting to come into the multi-national force. I said some "might."

I didn't have any countries in mind, but some might.

(Simpson) Will that be to augment U-S troops?

(Weinberger) No, it'll just be to add to participation in the whole force. But we haven't had, I haven't any idea whether they will or not. There are no negotiations pending. It was just a casual answer to a casual question.

(Simpson) Does that mean it might be more protracted than we originally thought?

(Weinberger) No, no, no. The time of the mission won't change. It'll be a limited time.

(tag) Weinberger would not say when that "limited time" might expire.

(ABC Information Radio)

Some editors might not have used that tape at all, on the basis that it doesn't do much to bolster or add detail to the story. But in broadcasting, both radio and TV, news departments will go a long way to put the voice of a newsmaker on the air, especially when their own reporters go out of the way to provide the tape. And, remember, no one newscast chronicles history. Next hour, this story might have been given 10 seconds total, or dropped altogether in favor of fresher news.

Here's an example of the other kind of Q-and-A, where the reporter himself is treated as an actuality:

(lead-in) A few moments of high drama today. . .amid the hours of tedium at the occupied Polish embassy in Bern, Switzerland. A diplomat the terrorists did not know was hiding in the building all this time. . .got away. . .with some help from Swiss police. ABC's Bob Dyke, who's been covering the story in Bern, says it began to unfold when police units showed up at the embassy building in force:

(actuality, Q/A) (Dyke) A van with blankets over the window drove away. Later, we learned that police had rescued from inside the embassy someone, uh, who was not a hostage, but had managed to hide away in the building when the compound was seized last Monday.

(tag) Correspondent Dyke says photographers had spotted the man several hours earlier when the man held a piece of paper up to the top floor window. But police asked reporters not to mention it so the terrorists wouldn't find him. They didn't. He's now been identified as Polish diplomat YO-seff SO-zee-ak. . . his post at the embassy unknown.

(ABC Entertainment Radio)

Again it might be argued that this piece of tape does not add substance to the story. However, it undeniably adds presence. Between the lines, it tells listeners, "Hey, look at us, we're Johnnie-on-the-spot with all developments in this story." However you may feel about such boosterism and self-promotion, there still remains the fact that journalism is fiercely competitive, nowhere more so than in broadcasting. Part of the nature of the business is to make sure listeners *know* when you're Johnnie-on-the-spot. It goes with the territory.

SCRIPTING ACTUALITIES

In a radio news script, stories with tape inserts do not appear as I have presented them thus far. From time to time, for the sake of clarity and to illustrate points about story structure and development, I will continue to write out verbatim transcripts. However, in broadcast copy, a verbatim of the tape itself, whether an actuality or a report, does not appear. Instead, the story on page 110 would appear this way:

Shelton
10/28, 2p

reagan-crime

(:35)

President Reagan is in New Jersey today...campaigning for the G-O-P candidate

for the U-S Senate...Congresswoman Millicent Fenwick. The President used the

occasion to call for a crackdown on crime:

> TAPE: Reagan #2
>
> RUNS: :16
>
> ENDS: "...into jail (applause)."

The President also denied charges by Democrats...that his administration has

been hard-hearted...when it comes to America's poor. The President said his

battle against inflation has delivered more purchasing power to poverty-level

families.

Although the specific form for such tape-integrated copy varies slightly at each news department, the basics are pretty much standard throughout the industry.

In the *extreme* upper left of the page are the writer's name, the date, and the hour of the newscast. In the *extreme* upper right are a one- or two-word slug and the *total* story time, rounded off to the nearest :05 and circled. The total story time obviously can't be included until the writer has completed the story, read it aloud against a stopwatch, and figured in the tape time; the story time is usually handwritten because by the time it's calculated, the page is already out of the typewriter.

The tape cues, which are radically indented and bracketed (or circled), are for the benefit of *both* the newscaster and the engineer who plays the tape; each must know *exactly* how the tape ends. These are called "cue lines."

The first cue line ("TAPE: Reagan #2") identifies the actuality by name and number. The number is necessary because several cuts will have been made from a given set of remarks.

The second cue line ("RUNS: :16") gives the *exact to-the-second* running time of the tape.

The third cue line (ENDS: ". . .into jail (applause).") tells the *exact* words and/or *sounds* that conclude the tape. This is called an "outcue" or an "endcue." (The *opening* words or sounds are called the "incue.") I stress that the outcue must be an *exact* version of the final *sounds*. The engineer must know when to kill the sound on the tape playback machine, and the newscaster must know when to resume reading copy.

These three cue lines are included for *each and every* piece of tape within a story. At networks and some major market stations, copy pages containing tape are typed with at least one carbon, the carbon copy going to the broadcast engineer. Elsewhere, the newscaster in the studio and the engineer in the control room are in direct line of sight of one another in order for the newscaster to throw a hand cue to the engineer to start the tape. And at small stations, the newscaster operates the machinery himself.

On the next two pages are two more scripted examples of stories cited earlier.

The script on page 118 seems a bit complicated, until you realize that all words circled or in brackets are internal instructions *not* to be read on the air, the rest being copy *for* air. Every step of the way, both the engineer and the newscaster have been told what to do and where and when to do it.

Note also that in calculating the story time, the only portion of the first actuality that was added was the "ESTABLISH & FADE" portion, about :05. The other :10 of the chanting actuality was played under the newscaster's first sentence, then faded out entirely. (If you think *this* is complicated, just wait till we get to television!!!)

The government's new off-shore oil and gas leasing plan came under fire today at

a hearing on Capitol Hill.   Leading the attack was Democratic Senator Walter

Metzenbaum of Ohio:

> TAPE: Metzenbaum #1
>
> RUNS: :23
>
> ENDS: ". . .corporations in America."

But Interior Secretary James Watt said Metzenbaum and others were off-base in

their criticism of the leasing plan:

> TAPE: Watt #4
>
> RUNS: :20
>
> ENDS: ". . .accurate or fair."

Watt, who was testifying before the Senate Energy Subcommittee, said the plan

would create jobs, strengthen national security, protect the environment. . .and

reduce the nation's dependence on foreign oil.

(OPENS W/TAPE)

> TAPE: (Chanting) (EST. & FADE)
>
> RUNS: :15
>
> ENDS: ". . .win, Jesse, win!"

(VOICE/OVER) To the chant of "Win, Jesse, win," civil rights leader Jesse Jackson announced today he's a candidate for the Democratic presidential nomination. (TAPE OUT) Jackson says that he is running for office to affirm his belief that leadership has no color or gender:

> TAPE: Jackson #3
>
> RUNS: :14
>
> ENDS: ". . .the political process."

With Jackson in the race, there are now 8 announced candidates for the Democratic presidential nomination.

TRICKY LEAD-INS AND OUTCUES

Suppose that we have an actuality of the president of the United States with the following text:

> The world cannot tolerate this kind of behavior. It amounts to international piracy. We will ask the United Nations for a resolution demanding a Soviet withdrawal—an IMMEDIATE Soviet withdrawal.

As previously noted, the lead-in should *not* use the same words or tell the same information as the actuality. If it did, there would be no point in using the actuality at all. For example, the lead-in should *not* say,

> President Jones reacted angrily today to the Soviet seizure of a disputed island in
>
> the Sea of Japan.   **The president said the world cannot tolerate such behavior:**

Those are the wrong words because they are redundant. For the same reason, the lead-in should not use the words "international piracy," again because they're already in the actuality. The trick is to find the kind of language that tells part of the news, without telling the *same* news. For example,

> An angry reaction from President Jones today to the Soviet seizure of that disputed
>
> island in the Sea of Japan.   The president called for international action:

Now the actuality fits right into the flow of the narrative.

As for the matter of inflections, lead-ins, too, must pay heed to normal speech patterns. Suppose that I lead in this way to the preceding actuality:

> President Jones reacted angrily today to the Soviet seizure of a disputed island in
>
> the Sea of Japan.   **The president said:**

Try reading that out loud. Notice where your voice is on the word "said"? The inflection is "up." It would end "up" even higher if it had been phrased, "Said the president:"

What's wrong with that? Well, nothing, provided that the engineer plays the tape *immediately*. If he's not paying attention, or there's a long pause between your voice and the start of the tape, the result is dead air. And dead air is disorienting. So in all things *live*, do *not* end lead-ins with "up" inflections. Save such razzle-dazzle for *recorded* reports, where there is no chance for a miscue. Besides, "down" inflections sound more natural. And in the event of dead air, the effect is not as disorienting.

As for the outcue to that actuality, read it carefully. The president *repeats* the final words—"Soviet withdrawal." If we typed the outcue this way,

The Making of a Tape Cartridge

a) WMAQ (Chicago) radio newswriter/assignment editor Tom Clark does a rundown as he monitors a telephone feed from a field reporter.

b) Broadcast engineer Gregg Schatz manually edits the quarter-inch reel-to-reel tape according to Clark's directions . . .

c). . . then dubs the edited tape onto a cartridge, making sure the cart is carefully labeled.

d) The cart is placed among others at the disposal of newscaster/news director Walt Hamilton as he writes an upcoming newscast.

e) Control room engineer Don Witt logs the cart before loading it into a playback machine . . .

f) . . . and it is then aired on cue during Hamilton's newscast.

> ENDS: "...Soviet withdrawal."

the newscaster might come in *too soon* with the tag copy. This must be prevented. Here's how:

> ENDS: "...Soviet withdrawal." (DOUBLE OUTCUE)

The additional words "DOUBLE OUTCUE" in parentheses and capital letters ensure that the newscaster and the engineer both know that the words of the outcue will be heard twice.

EDITING EQUIPMENT AND DUBBING

To understand the radio news system of cue lines, slugs, and ID numbers, you have to understand something about tape recording and playback machines.

Tape recordings made in the field by reporters are on standard-sized audiocassettes—*good-quality* cassettes, not the three-for-a-dollar kind from the corner drugstore. However, even the best quality cassette tape has two drawbacks: it is too narrow and it moves too slowly to be edited properly. Besides, you'd have to break the cassette to get at the tape.

Instead, the slow-moving cassette tape is dubbed in the studio onto console machines using reel-to-reel quarter-inch tape moving at much greater speeds. Original material recorded in the studio, such as telephone interviews and network closed-circuit feeds, is recorded directly onto the reel-to-reel machines.

Actualities, reports, and so on, are edited on these consoles. Once edited, the tapes are dubbed again, this time onto cartridges called "carts" for short. You've all seen cartridges like these; in stereo stores they're called "8-track cartridges." In radio news, the carts are the same size but work slightly differently. The tape inside each cart is on a continuous loop, the length of tape differing with each cart. Some carts thus run as short as :10, others as long as 10:00. If an actuality runs, say, :18, it will be transferred to a 20-second cart.

Each cart is labeled. *Carefully* labeled. On the label are

1. The name of the person speaking
2. The place at which he or she was speaking
3. The number of the cut
4. The exact running time
5. The outcue

That is all vital information for any newswriter, newscaster, or engineer who handles the cart. And the bigger the news department, the more vital the label information—because the cart will pass through just that many more hands. No one should ever arrive at the start of a shift, pick up a cart presumably for a newscast, and have to wonder, "Now what the hell is this?" So, in the preparation of carts as in the preparation of news copy itself, neatness and precision count. That, too, goes with the territory.

10
TAPE II: REPORTS

Reports, known as "spots" in radio news, are the second major category of tape that must be integrated into newscasts. In addition, writing and voicing reports in local radio is likely to be the main task of newcomers to large news departments. So we're now going to consider them in detail.

TYPES OF SPOTS

Voicers

A voicer is a spot composed entirely of the reporter's voice. No actuality or other sound source is included.

Here are two competing voicers, reporting the mysterious absence of the Soviet Communist party boss from one of the USSR's major public events:

#1   Soviet leader Yuri Andropov was a no-show at Moscow's Red Square for today's

anniversary celebration of the Bolshevik Revolution.   Soviet Defense Chief Marshal

Dimitri Ustinov officially opened the ceremonies and delivered a nationally broadcast

speech from atop Lenin's tomb.   Nothing was said publicly about Andropov's absence from the country's most important celebration.   A Soviet official told Western journalists that Andropov had a cold.   Steve Mallory, NBC News, Moscow.

(runs :29)

#2   Yuri Andropov's failure to appear at the military parade in Red Square, celebrating the anniversary of the Russian Revolution, has caused a storm of speculation about his health.   It was unprecedented for the leader of the Soviet Union not to show up on such an important occasion.   And with unseasonably warm weather, diplomats and observers were extremely skeptical about the official Soviet reason -- that Andropov has a common cold.   Instead tonight there is serious and informed speculation that he may have had a major operation for either heart or kidney problems, and is recuperating.   Talk about a possible successor has commenced among the foreign community.   But Soviet sources downplay the talk, stressing that there is none of the nervousness and gossip in the bureaucracy that usually occurs when a Soviet leader is seriously ill.   Andropov posters, and his name, were in the front line of all the ceremonies and media coverage today, leaving little doubt that he is still the leader of the Soviet Union.   But he has not been seen in public since August 18th. . .and many diplomats tonight are asking, How much longer can his lack of visibility go on?   Don MacNeil, CBS News, Moscow.

(runs 1:05)

It's difficult not to be judgmental in assessing these spots—but clearly the longer one allowed the reporter to break away from the strict, bare bones facts to present a fuller picture of the events and their ramifications. However, bear in mind that reporters, newswriters, and editors do not decide formats for spot length. That decision comes from top management, based on assessments of the target audience or of the expressed desires of the local stations affiliated with a network.

Wraparounds

A wraparound—or "wrap"—is a spot that contains one or more actualities. A wrap is, in effect, a self-contained story structured as lead-in/actuality/tag/sign-off.

Here are two competing wraparounds on a White House ceremony for the American medical students "rescued" in the recent U.S. Marine invasion of the island of Grenada:

#1   (opens w/military band music)

(voice/over) The band played, and there were handshakes and smiles, as 450 students gathered on the South Lawn with representatives of the military who brought them off

Grenada. (tape out) President Reagan served as master of ceremonies, as it were, but the spotlight was on the students, who had asked for a forum to express their thanks. Jeff Geller of Woodridge, New York, was once a skeptic about the military. Not any more:

(geller) It is one thing to view an American military operation from afar and quite another to be rescued by one.

And Jeanne Joal of Albany, New York:

(joal) I never had so much faith or pride in my country than during the 24 hours I spent under war conditions in Grenada.

The students will complete the semester in the States, returning to Grenada when conditions are better. David Rush, NBC News, at the White House.

(runs :45)

#2 The students thanked the president and the U-S military, to whom they said they owed a debt they could not repay. They talked of pride in their country and a reassessment of what they called their "liberal political views." This was clearly music to the ears of the president, who, in keeping with the tone of today's meticulously staged event, criticized those who opposed the invasion of Grenada:

(reagan) It's very easy for some smug know-it-alls in a plush, protected quarter to say that you were in no danger. (sustained applause) I have wondered how many of them would have changed places with you. (laughter)

Mr. Reagan also brushed off comparison of the Grenada operation and the Soviet invasion of Afghanistan. He emphasized that U-S troops will soon leave the Caribbean island. But he said, "don't hold your breath for the Soviets to leave Afghanistan." John Ferrugia, CBS News, the White House.

(runs 1:01)

(The second report was broadcast 1 hour later than the first, which may explain the emphasis on the president's remarks, which followed those of the students.)

ROSRs

ROSR (pronounced RO-zer) is an acronym for "Radio On-Scene Report," a term coined at ABC Radio News in the 1960s. ROSRs have since become a standard form throughout the industry and can be heard on all networks and major local stations.

A ROSR is simply this: A reporter in the field talks into his tape recorder, either extemporaneously or from prepared notes, describing a scene or event as it occurs before his very eyes. In other words, the reporter *pretends* to be broadcasting live, trying to capture the color and feel of an event.

This ad lib narrative may go on for several minutes—as long as the event continues or the reporter does not run out of things to say. From time to time, or at the very end, the reporter "wild-tracks" a sign-off stating his or her name and location.

Once back in the studio, this lengthy running account is edited down into short chunks, each about the length of a spot, with a sign-off edited to the end of each chunk. The result is often a vivid piece of radio reportage, bringing the listener into the scene on the old Ed Murrow model.

ROSRs must really be heard to be appreciated. They are usually punctuated by background sounds lending presence to the reportage—which, of course, is the intended effect. Here's one by a CBS reporter who accompanied Israeli troops on a drive into Beirut, Lebanon:

> I'm with a forward Israeli tank unit . . . rolling forward in the center of West Beirut
> . . . (gunshots) . . . tanks are coming up . . . (tanks firing) . . . heavy machine guns
> on the tanks (machine gun firing) trying to pick out sniper positions in the buildings
> above us.   Israeli troops back against the walls of this street, amid the rubble . . .
> thick black smoke rising just in front of the tanks (tank shell explosions).   The
> tank's now charging forward, turret swinging . . . (machine guns and sniper fire) . . .
> firing toward sniper positions, the machine guns opening up.   It's twin firing its
> heavy cannons into the buildings . . . thick smoke clouding everything in front of
> us. Israeli troops here with us against the walls of the buildings . . . (more tank
> fire). Larry Pintak, CBS News, with the Israelis in West Beirut.
>
> (runs 1:03)

I don't know how that ROSR sounded before it was edited, but the finished product sounded like the reporter was where no human being should be without a titanium suit.

Here is a calmer sort of ROSR, from NBC Radio, recorded while the Israelis were heading in the opposite direction, *out* of Beirut. A steady rumble of motorized army vehicles is heard in the background:

> I'm standing beside a column of Israeli soldiers who're beginning their individual
> pullout of West Beirut.   This has been going on now for several days . . . but
> tomorrow, all of the Israelis are supposed to be out of this section of the city, which
> was once a stronghold of the Palestine Liberation Army . . . (sirens).   Their pullout
> has been controversial. The multinational force . . . has refused . . . to come in
> until the Israelis get out of West Beirut.   But another French unit arrived today,

after another 350 French paratroopers came in yesterday.   Ike Seamans, NBC

News, West Beirut.

(runs :39)

As you may have surmised, ROSRs are often the product of a radio journalist's efforts to cover disruptive or violent events. The reporter is acting as the listener's eyewitness at places and events that are, shall we say, unsafe for tourism. ROSRs are not always informative, but that is not their chief purpose. Their purpose is to capture the *texture* of a time and place.

LENGTH OF SPOTS

The trend in recent years has been toward brevity in radio spots. Where 60 seconds (expressed as "1:00") or 1:15 was the norm, it is now the exception. In commercial radio in the mid-1980s, the 60-second spot, as a normal and desirable running time, existed only at CBS Radio and a few local stations. Elsewhere, spots ran anywhere from :30 to :45, depending on subject matter. On non-commercial National Public Radio, spots occasionally ran several minutes, but NPR represented only a very small part of a very large industry. (Remember, "length" in broadcasting is a relative term. In case of major news developments, "desirable" running times go out the window, and reportage continues as long as necessary.)

As we shall see shortly, the perceived need for brevity imposes a certain type of structure on many spots.

SIGN-OFFS

Every spot, whether voicer, wrap, or ROSR, concludes with a sign-off. Sign-offs in broadcasting are roughly the equivalent of a combination of a newspaper byline and dateline—roughly but not exactly. For one thing, sign-offs do not contain the date. They do contain at least two elements:

1. The reporter's name
2. The reporter's location

. . .Pye Chamberlayne, Washington.
(UPI Audio)

. . .Jack Vail, New York.
(UPI Audio)

And most sign-offs contain a third element:

3. The reporter's news organization

. . .David Rush, NBC News, Washington.

. . .Richard C. Hottelet, CBS News, at the United Nations.

Whenever possible, sign-offs emphasize the *closeness* of the reporter to the story:

. . .Bill Plante, CBS News, *with the president* in New Orleans.

. . .Larry Pintak, CBS News, *with Israeli forces* in Lebanon.

There are strict rules for expressing proximity to the story in a sign-off. Obviously, the president of the United States was not looking over Bill Plante's shoulder as Plante filed his report. They weren't in the same room. Maybe not in the same building. But Plante (and the rest of the White House press corps) had followed the presidential party around all day. Their assignment was to cover the president, to be with him whenever possible (or allowed by the White House). So the sign-off "with the president" is correct. If Plante had merely rewritten his copy from wire services—in fact had not been "with the president"— he could *not* use those words in his sign-off.

Rule: No Reporter May Ever Sign Off from Where He Has Not Been in Connection with a Story.

He need not be at that location at the moment of filing his story. But he must have been there to cover it, at least in part.

And in fact many spots written in radio are merely rewrites from wire service copy or are based on telephone interviews. In those cases the sign-off contains the reporter's name, news organization, and *city*. No further specification is legitimate. No reporter must ever give the impression of having been somewhere he has in fact not been.

There are a few other twists to sign-offs. The general public is largely unaware of them, but they are strictly understood inside the industry.

One is a matter of professional standing. Only a full-time staff member of a news organization may use the name of that organization unqualifiedly in a sign-off. Nonstaff reporters, such as part-time "stringers" or local staffers of independent or network-affiliated stations, must include the word "for" in the sign-off:

> . . .Jeff Grant, *for* CBS News, Newark, New Jersey.

> . . .JoAnne Nader, *for* NBC News, Boston Heights, Ohio.

These two sign-offs are examples of local reporters who, either by volunteering or by request, got their voices onto network newscasts. For this they were paid a fee by the network.

Still another signoff variation is one that *omits* the reporter's location altogether:

> . . .Garrick Utley, NBC News.

> . . .Lynn Scherr, ABC News.

Such sign-offs might indicate that the reporter voicing the report did not actually cover the story in person. Typically, the story that is the subject matter of the spot might have taken place in a location different from the reporter's. Or such a sign-off might indicate that the reporter is merely narrating material written by someone else.

Some news organizations—CBS, for one—strictly forbid such ambiguous sign-offs. And if the correspondent did not personally write the report, then the lead-in uses tip-off wording such as, "Our report is narrated by . . ."

Note that sign-offs to *newscasts* are not subject to the rule of stating location. In local radio, it's assumed that the newscaster is in town and in the studio, not announcing from a vacation cottage in Acapulco. And in network radio, although most newscasts originate from New York or Washington, the practice is to omit the location in the sign-off as a kind of gimmick to make the news organization seem omnipresent—sort of like saying, "If we don't tell 'em where we are, maybe they'll think we're everywhere." (On such matters are careers sometimes made or broken. No kidding.)

To sum up: sign-offs to reports must be accurate. It is unethical to "invent" a sign-off.

CHARACTERISTICS OF SPOTS

To attempt to tell you exactly how to write a radio news spot would be just as impossible as telling you how to construct a snowflake. Each is different. Writing (hence, journalism) is an art, not a science.

However, I can offer guidelines regarding the content and structure of spots in general. And this much I can state unequivocally: it is impossible to tell the history of the world in 45 seconds. So don't even try.

Beginners have a tendency to think that their spots must be comprehensive, must trace the history of an event from its early beginnings, through its current developments, and on into an analysis of its possible ramifications. That is far, far too much territory for a radio spot. Instead, the focus must be kept narrow, on the current developments. History (background) should be kept to a minimum—only enough, in fact, to make the current developments clear. And the analysis should be kept out altogether or confined to the telling of what will (or might) happen next. (And I do mean *next*—not down the road a decade or two.)

Specifically (which means "specifically, in general"—there are always exceptions),

1. Spots should be limited in subject matter. A spot should deal only with the story immediately at hand: its facts, limited background, and significance. Spots should *not* deal with related stories; related stories will be treated in separate stories scripted by the newswriter/newscaster and/or by other reporters in their own spots. Limit the content to what *you* have seen or learned.
2. Spots should be limited geographically. A spot should treat events that occur at the location stated in the sign-off or close to it—*not* events occurring elsewhere. Again, events elsewhere, however related, will be treated in spots from those locations, not yours.
3. Because of the brevity of spots formatted by most commercial radio outlets, it is frequently best to begin a spot on the assumption that the latest, most important details will be stated *in the lead-in* and, therefore, need *not* be repeated in the spot itself, which would eat up precious time. (I'll try to make that last sentence clear in the pages that follow.)

LEAD-INS TO SPOTS

Spots, like actualities, do not exist in a void. Structurally, they require lead-ins to

1. Set the stage of the story
2. Identify the reporter and most often his or her location

The lead-ins and copy pages to the voicers and wraps at the start of this chapter went like this:

Maus   andropov   (:35)
11/7, 7p

There was a big show in Moscow today. . .but the Soviet Union's "Mr. Big" wasn't

there. NBC News Correspondent Steve Mallory has a report:

> TAPE: Mallory #1
>
> RUNS: :29
>
> ENDS: ". . .NBC News, Moscow."

(Mike Maus, NBC Radio)

WT
11/7, 7p

andropov

A man set himself afire in front of the Lenin mausoleum in Moscow's Red Square

today -- but no one knows what he was protesting. . .and probably no one ever will

find out.   It happened a couple of hours after the Revolution Day parade, and the

big news out of that was that the number one man was not there.   Don MacNeil

reports:

> TAPE: MacNeil #2
>
> RUNS: 1:05
>
> ENDS: ". . .CBS News, Moscow."

(The World Tonight, CBS Radio)

Walden   grenada students   :55
11/7, 11a

There was a big celebration at the White House today. . .as students from Saint

George's University Medical School on Grenada met with the president and with

some of their rescuers.   NBC News Correspondent David Rush was there:

> TAPE: Rush #1
>
> RUNS: :45
>
> ENDS: ". . .at the White House."

(Alan Walden, NBC Radio)

Hottelet   grenada students
11/7, 12p

President Reagan talked about the Grenada operation this morning with some of

the evacuated American students who had found themselves part of the problem.

John Ferrugia at the White House:

> TAPE: Ferrugia #2
>
> RUNS: 1:01
>
> ENDS: ". . .the White House."

(Richard C. Hottelet, CBS Radio)

THROW LINES

In the lead-ins to spots, the copy immediately preceding the spot is sometimes referred to as the "throw line," after the old-time radio terminology of remote broadcast announcers who would conclude by saying, "And now we throw it back to you in the studio." The wording of throw lines varies considerably, but they all include the name of the reporter and, most often, his or her location. (Just to avoid confusion, the throw lines in the two lead-ins we just quoted are "NBC News Correspondent David Rush was there" and "John Ferrugia at the White House.")

It is possible, and often desirable, to merge the throw line with the lead-in copy as a whole. For example,

President Jones won a major victory today for his tax reform plan.   But, *as Jill*

Doaks reports from the White House, that victory came at a high price:

Burying the throw line that way still makes clear to listeners that they are about to hear a different voice.

Some local news departments instruct newswriters and newscasters to omit the throw line entirely and to write the lead-in in such a way that the opening wording of the spot flows from the lead-in without it. In most cases, however, the result is a jarring, disorienting break in the flow because all of a sudden, unexpectedly, the listener hears a different voice for which he was not prepared. Therefore, if I were a news director, I would insist that throw lines be included. (But again, such format decisions are not up to writers and newscasters.)

"HARD" VERSUS "SOFT" SPOTS

The exact wording of a lead-in depends on the *opening* wording of a spot. This is true of all spots and all lead-ins. They are inseparable, part of the same structure.

Here is the working-level process:

1. A reporter covers a story.
2. A reporter writes one or two spots on the story.
3. The spots are fed to the newsroom, where they are put on cart.
4. One of the spots is given to a newswriter/newscaster for inclusion in the upcoming newscast.
5. The newswriter/newscaster tailors the lead-in to fit the content and opening wording of the spot.

It is important to understand this process because spots can open two basic ways:

1. By stating the latest, most important news in the opening sentence. Such an approach is called "hard leading."

2. By deferring the latest, most important news until later in the spot, or by omitting it altogether. Such an approach is calling "soft leading."

If the spot opens the first way, with a hard lead, its lead-in should be soft—because if it, too, were hard, the top of the structure would be redundant and sound careless as well as repetitive. Conversely, if the spot begins soft, the lead-in must be hard—because if it, too, were soft, the listener would have to wait too long before learning the real news.

To make clear the difference, here are two spots on the same story, the first hard, the second soft. Both are by Richard C. Hottelet of CBS News:

#1: (HARD LEAD)

The Arab states, which have been talking about expelling Israel from the current session of the General Assembly, have now decided to pull back. Instead of challenging Israel's credentials in a routine vote next Monday, the Arabs and others will express reservations about Israel's presence in drastic terms. They will denounce Israel as a member which violates international law and specifically refuses to obey numerous Assembly resolutions on Palestinian rights and withdrawal from occupied territory. Many Arab and Islamic states, as well as African and Western countries, were appalled by the idea of trying to expel Israel. They saw it derailing a Middle East process which may just be starting to move again. And some of the Arabs argued privately that it could only heal the breach between the Reagan administration and the Begin government. Most did not have the confidence to make these points publicly, but they seemed to have sunk in. Unless the radical Arabs go back to the original idea, or Iran picks it up next Monday, the issue appears to have been shelved for this year. Richard C. Hottelet, CBS News, United Nations.

(runs 1:03)

#2: (SOFT LEAD)

Two weeks ago, radical Arab states proposed that Israel be thrown out of the current session of the U-N General Assembly. The idea was to call for rejection of Israel's credentials when the report of the Credentials Committee comes up for approval next Monday. The proposal stirred up a storm. Most Western countries saw it as unwarranted and illegal distortion of the spirit and letter of the United Nations charter. Washington served official notice that if Israel were excluded in this fashion, the United States would walk out with it and, more than that, would withhold American payments to the United Nations' regular budget. Since the United States pays 25 per cent or more of the U-N's expenses, this would have been a disastrous political as well as financial blow to the organization. Many of the Arab states, and of the larger Conference of Islamic Countries, opposed the action of expelling Israel, especially at a time when Arab leaders are consulting with the United States about plans for peace in the Middle East. This afternoon, the Arab group of nations at the U-N decided NOT to try to reject Israel's credentials, but simply to express their reservations about Israel's presence. Richard C. Hottelet, CBS News, United Nations.

(runs 1:09)

These spots are slightly atypical in that the latest news—the Arab back-down—while a major development, needs considerable backgrounding and explanation to make clear its significance. Notwithstanding, the two spots are written in diametrically opposed ways. Spot 1 contains the hard news in the opening sentence. Spot 2 defers the hard news until the very last sentence. Spot 1 thus required a soft lead-in:

Here in New York, the United Nations has apparently been spared a crisis that,

Richard C. Hottelet says, could have put it out of business:

> TAPE: Hottelet #1
>
> RUNS: 1:03
>
> ENDS: " . . . CBS News, United Nations."

(Dallas Townsend, CBS Radio)

And spot 2, which would only tell the hard news almost a minute in, required a hard lead-in:

At the United Nations, Arab nations have backed away from their campaign to

oust Israel from the General Assembly. More from Richard C. Hottelet:

```
TAPE: Hottelet #2

RUNS: 1:09

ENDS: " . . . CBS News, United Nations."
```

(Stephani Shelton, CBS Radio)

The ability to tailor a lead-in to suit a spot is, like writing stories with actualities, a basic craft in both radio and television newsrooms. It can almost be reduced to a formula (but don't push the formula too far):

> Soft-led spot requires hard lead-in.
> Hard-led spot requires soft lead-in.

TAGS TO SPOTS

Normally, there is not (repeat *not*) a tag after a spot. That is because the sound source (the reporter) includes his or her own reidentification in the form of a sign-off, which makes a natural break from one story to the next. Structurally, the spot amounts (or should amount, if it's been written correctly) to the last word in the newscast on the specific story it concerns.

Occasionally, however, there may be a late-breaking development that updates a spot in a significant way. A news agency, for example, may report new information between the time a spot was filed and the time it is to go on the air. In such a case, the newsroom must choose between two editorial options:

1. Junk the spot and substitute a fresh spot or writer-written version containing the new information.
2. Play the spot and update it with a tag.

The choice depends on the individual case. If, logistically, it is a relatively easy matter to get an updated spot by air time from the reporter, so much the better; the new spot will simply be substituted for the old. If, however, the reporter is unavailable (for example, he or she may be covering another story by then), or if time is very short (which is often the case), and the original spot is well written and otherwise rich in content, then a tag is in order.

Suppose, for example, that a reporter covering a union meeting on whether to strike says, in concluding his spot, "Results of the strike vote are expected shortly." And just before air time, AP sends a bulletin announcing the result of the vote in favor of a strike. This is quite clearly a major update. To include the information in the lead-in to the spot would negate any reason for using it, because it ends with dated information. So instead a tag would be written to this effect:

And, we've just received late word that the union HAS voted to strike.

To repeat, the use of such tags is rare. Newsrooms would rather not use them at all, preferring to have the latest word from the reporter. Unfortunately, for logistical and technical reasons, it isn't always possible.

PROTECTING CONTENT OF SPOTS

And speaking of logistical and technical problems: I said at the start of this book that one reason for the artificiality of much newspaper writing is the delay between the time a story is written and the time it is seen by readers; the facts may have changed in the meantime. Well, the same thing can happen in broadcasting if the reporter is not careful about which facts to include and which to leave out.

You see, radio and TV reporters are not always near a telephone, much less a satellite transmitting station. They are often out "in the boonies" (boondocks), covering floods, earthquakes, wars, pestilence, famine—and all manner of things that wreak havoc on humanity but on which reporters thrive. Can you imagine trying to find a phone booth in a war zone? Or tape editing equipment in Bangla Desh?

You get the point. Reporters are literally out of touch for long periods of time. So when they finally do find the means to feed (or fly) their spots back to their newsrooms, they do not want their material junked because it was dated by air time. Thus they "protect" their copy. Here's what I mean:

Go back to pages 86–87 for the AP "A" wire story (A233) slugged "Turkey—Quake." Take a minute to reread it.

Okay. Natural disasters such as this one, as well as accidents and acts of war or terrorism, inevitably cause casualties. This AP First Lead reports "at least 509 people were killed" in the quake and "the death toll was expected to climb" as rescuers discovered more victims.

If a radio spot from a staff or free-lance reporter in Istanbul (the closest and most likely telephone and satellite link) included the figure "509 killed," the spot would likely be dated by air time, because by then more victims would have been found and added to the count. In fact, the death toll in this quake rose steadily, hour by hour, until it had reached 1,350 three days later. So what to do?

The solution is for the reporter to omit the casualty figures entirely. Yes, *omit entirely.* The reporter confines the spot (or spots) to those facts that are *not* likely to change, such as the quake's location, intensity, time of occurrence, conditions in the area, the scope of rescue efforts, and leaves for the *lead-in,* written thousands of miles away, the inclusion of the latest casualty figures. Such a spot might *begin* this way:

The quake struck early this morning. . .rolling through mountainous areas along

Turkey's borders with Iran, Syria, and Iraq.   Reports reaching here in Istanbul say it leveled some 50 villages, many of them in hard-to-reach areas. The Turkish

Army has mobilized rescue teams. . .but their efforts are being hampered by

darkness, cold, and intermittent snow. . .

A spot written this way will "stand up" for quite a while, at least until daybreak in Turkey. It is "protected" against predictable changes in the story. Any such changes will be reported in the lead-in, which (remember the process) is the last step before air. The reporter in Istanbul (let's call him "Joe Doaks") knows that his spot will be preceded by lead-in words such as

A major earthquake struck Eastern Turkey today, killing at least _____

people. Joe Doaks has more on the story from Istanbul:

You may be asking, "Why this way?" Isn't Joe Doaks in Istanbul thousands of miles closer to the scene than any newswriter/newscaster in a U.S. newsroom? Isn't he in a better position to report the latest casualty figures?

No, probably not. Joe Doaks may be *your* man in Istanbul, but he's not the *only* one there. He's still some 1,400 miles from the scene of the quake. Even if he were at the scene, it wouldn't do you any good, the "scene" being a vast area (without telephones or shuttle flights) beyond the coverage abilities of any one reporter. There'd be no way for him to get a voicer back to you until he reached Istanbul, and who knows when that might be?

Joe is in fact in the right place, along with a lot of other reporters for other news organizations. All the news of the quake is, sooner or later, filtering through Istanbul, probably relayed through military communications. Some of those other reporters work for news agencies, agencies whose wires your newsroom buys. The *wires* will carry the latest casualty figures, and that information will go to whoever writes the lead-in to Joe's spot. In fact, the newsroom in the United States will probably learn the latest casualty figures *before* Joe does.

That's how the multifaceted news business works. So in radio we want the voice of Joe Doaks supplying color and detail which he is in a position to provide, and we want the latest information which he cannot provide without dating himself by air time, but which we will get from other sources.

This technique of protecting reportorial copy, which you should henceforth listen for as you continue on your way to news junkie-hood, is *standard* in both radio and television. You must master it if you wish to progress in a career as a broadcast reporter, for it applies to the bus accident just down the block as well as to an earthquake halfway around the world.

Again, each case must be weighed on its own merits. But, in general, protected spots should *omit*

Death and injury figures
The condition of people in hospitals
The specific time of an event

In general, they should *include*

> The circumstances of the event
> What led up to the event (limited background)
> What is likely to happen next (but *not* immediately)

Unfortunately, many fledgling reporters learn how to protect their spots the hard way, by busting their tails to get a story, only to see their material not used on the air because it was dated and made irrelevant by breaking events by air time.

OVERNIGHTS

Let's say you are working the PM shift in radio—3 P.M. to 11 P.M. or 4 P.M. to midnight. Unless you're at a network or exceptionally well-staffed local station, you will turn out the lights as you leave the newsroom, because the AM shift won't be in for four or five hours yet. The wire machines will be left running, but for all intents and purposes, the news department will be closed overnight.

All right, in walks the AM shift. They check the wires. But what do they do for fresh tape? There's been no one to prepare it, right?

Wrong. *You* prepared it before you left last night. How? By writing and recording a spot or two on events that occurred late in your shift. You tailored them specifically for use during AM Drive by rewriting the "when" element to suit the circumstances.

Suppose, for example, that you covered a fire that was brought under control at around 10 P.M. In your spots that evening, you spoke of "tonight's fire" and concluded by saying that "Officials suspect arson and have begun an investigation." Fine. But in your overnight versions, which are simply called "overnights" or "o'nites," you must change the wording to correspond to the projected time of broadcast. You might say

> Arson investigators *this morning* are looking into *last night's* fire on the West Side. . .

> or

> Arson *is* one possible explanation fire officials *are giving* for the fire that destroyed
>
> a warehouse on the West Side. . .

Yes, the AM shift could simply have rewritten fresh copy from the overnight wire service material. But that's not what your news director wants. What he or she wants is fresh *tape* to enliven and enrich newscasts, tape which only *you* as the reporter of the story can provide. And since you can't work a 24-hour day (at least not *every* day), the tailoring and protection of spots for later use is another standard task of the radio journalist, from small markets to networks. (Of the two Richard C. Hottelet/United Nations spots on pp. 133–34, spot 2 was aired at 3 o'clock in the afternoon, and spot 1 was aired at 8 o'clock *the following morning.* Spot 1 was written as a protected overnight.)

SPOT VARIATION

A reporter is expected to write not one but several spots on each story that he or she covers. The object is to provide newswriter/newscasters with fresh material for newscasts, of which there may be 24 or more each and every day. Normally, a spot is aired just once or at least not again for six or eight hours. It is not a matter of changing a word here and there to make a "new" spot. It means a complete rewrite.

Here once again we are dealing with a facet of news broadcasting for which there can be no hard or fast rules. But there is a "typical" cycle of spot variation, based on the way most news stories break. It is this:

1. The first time a story hits the air, it is entirely new. No one's heard it before—not even the person who writes the lead-in—because the reporter has called it in well before the wire services can move it. Therefore, this first spot should be *hard-led*. It should contain the full story, starting with the latest, most important details.

2. The second time around, it is likely both that the wire services have moved the story and that some listeners already have heard it. The second spot should thus be the reporter's main effort, the one in which he tries for stylistic effect, for which he will need every precious second of his allotted time. Therefore, spot 2 should be *soft-led*, leaving to the newsroom the task of writing a hard lead-in.

3. Spot 3, if it is aired at all, will only be heard many hours later. Spot 3 should thus be either fully protected, or be an overnight altogether.

Three spots, three different approaches, per story:

1. Hard lead
2. Soft lead
3. Protected and/or overnight

FREE-LANCERS

One main way that local reporters progress in their careers to major markets and networks is through "exposure" in those markets and networks. "Exposure" is a BIG word in broadcasting. For a broadcast reporter, "exposure," or time on the air, means the same thing, career-wise, as getting on the front page in newspapers. The more exposure you get, the more you are "known," both by the public and by prospective employers.

Sooner or later, no matter where your location and local station, something will happen of importance to your region or to the country as a whole. At that time, you will probably have the opportunity to write and voice a spot or two for the regional or national network with which your station is affiliated. There's no telling when or where such an event will occur. But it *will* occur, mark my words. And at that time you had best be prepared to write a spot of network quality.

In truth, that standard of quality is not as high these days as it once was.

That's because of the relative decline of network radio in favor of television as the nation's primary broadcast news source. Here are two competing network spots filed by local staff reporters:

(John Bohannon, NBC Radio) They've been talking now for 28 hours. . .and it appears that the United Auto Workers and Chrysler are just one issue away from an agreement. We get the latest from JoAnne Nader of W-K-Y-C, Cleveland:

(JoAnne Nader spot) Marathon talks between Chrysler and the Twinsburg auto workers are entering their 28th straight hour. Union leaders say that one important issue stands in the way of a tentative agreement. Local President Bob Weissman says bargaining has suddenly taken a "crazy turn," and it will take Chrysler two hours, quote, "to come to their senses." No comment from Chrysler yet, but it seems both sides are at a stubborn, yet critical point in negotiations. I'm JoAnne Nader, for NBC News, Boston Heights, Ohio.
(runs :30)

-0-

(Frank Setapani, CBS Radio) Officials of Chrysler and the United Auto Workers are continuing their efforts to settle the Twinsburg, Ohio, parts plant strike that has forced the closing of Chrysler assemblies in the United States and Canada. . .and idled some 20-thousand auto workers. We get the latest from Mary Lou Johanek of CBS affiliate W-J-K-W, Cleveland:

(Mary Lou Johanek spot) Union officials say negotiations have reached an impasse over two issues. Both are safety-related. One involves job qualifications for crane operators at the Twinsburg plant. The union wants licensed, trained employees on the equipment. The other issue involves oil spills in the plant and the union's demand for more janitors. Local union officials are now waiting for reaction on those proposals from company officials. The union's goal is to settle today and schedule a ratification vote tomorrow for the 32-hundred strikers. If the new contract is approved, the plant could reopen with the midnight shift tomorrow night. Mary Lou Johanek, for CBS News, Twinsburg, Ohio.
(runs :37)

Both of those local reporters got paid a very nice free-lance fee for their spots. But perhaps more important, their names became known at their stations' networks.

Well, you never know what'll happen.

11
TAPE III: INTERVIEWING AND EDITING

Radio news has a great advantage over television in that newsmakers can be interviewed and tape recorded by telephone. Radio is thus much speedier in assembling and airing breaking news, despite recent advances in live TV transmission capabilities.

Every radio journalist has a favorite story about getting the ideal phone interview: the gunman holding hostages inside a bank, the public figure gone into hiding following reports of a major scandal, and so on. Such stories may be apocryphal, but they do illustrate the goals of radio journalists: to reach the right person, to reach him *first*, and to reach him *exclusively*.

In real life, it seldom works out that way. But it's worth a try every time.

FONERS

Tape recorded telephone interviews are called "foners" (sometimes spelled "phoners"). This bit of broadcast jargon takes the verb *to do*, as in "do a foner" or "I did a foner with Alderman Spock."

Federal law permits the tape recording of telephone interviews *only with the subject's permission*, either tacit or expressed. Upon reaching an interview subject, you *must* inform him that you are taping the conversation, thus giving him a chance to decline. Some news departments require the subject's verbal permission, expressed clearly on the tape, before allowing the interview to proceed.

Naturally, there are some exceptions. If perchance you *do* reach the gunman holding hostages (which at some news departments would violate a policy of non-interference in criminal matters where lives are threatened), you are obviously not going to begin the chat by asking, "Please, sir, may I pretty please have your permission to tape this interview?" Someone who is clearly breaking the law at the time you reach him is not going to sue you for invasion of privacy.

EQUIPMENT

There are certain technical problems in doing foners. The first involves the sound quality of the phone lines themselves, which is very often poor—poor, that is, when compared with live or studio-quality sound. And lately, despite sweeping technological advances in communications, telephone sound quality has actually been growing *poorer* because of the proliferation of cheap, gimmicky telephones and the overcrowding of satellite channels. Local and regional telephone companies say that quality will improve once they install fiber optics lines, but at this writing, such changes are well down the road.

Thus, radio news departments use specialized equipment to record optimum-quality telephone sound. The recording phone itself is a separate line bypassing both the switchboard and the newsroom and is located instead in a studio or quiet nook near a console recorder. The handset is equipped with a "push-to-talk" button or switch, which, unless pushed, kills the handset microphone, thus shutting off extraneous noise from the reporter's end. Reporters must push the button or flick the "talk" switch whenever they want their questions to be heard and recorded.

The recording line number (large news departments have several recording lines) is unlisted and is engraved in the memory of newsroom personnel; it's the same number reporters use to phone in their reports and actualities.

(In a pinch, a portable cassette recorder with a phone recording attachment can be used to do foners. But the resulting sound quality is usually very poor, making much of the tape UFB.)

REACHING THE SUBJECT

Since foners are often done in connection with breaking stories, speed is of the essence. If you linger in trying to reach a newsmaker, chances are you'll get a busy signal because the competition has reached the newsmaker first. So you've got to move fast.

Over time, you will have compiled your own list of names and private telephone numbers, your own "little black book." The newsroom, too, probably maintains a Rolodex file of important and frequently called names and numbers, which each staffer is expected to correct and update as changes warrant.

On breaking stories, however, such sources may be of no help. You'll have to find new numbers—and find them *quickly*. Elementary as it may sound, you should lunge for the telephone book instead of dialing Directory Assistance. The telephone book is quicker than "Information," which is really of help only in learning new listings or numbers outside your metropolitan area. (It's amazing how many people refuse to consult the phone book first, just because it's all the way across the room. You'd think they needed cross-country skis to reach it.)

If the telephone book is of no help, *then* dial "Information." If that's no help, or if there's no answer at the subject's home or office numbers, then call known relatives or associates of the subject for possible leads to his or her whereabouts.

There's also the street (Criss-Cross) index, published by the phone company in many cities, listing residential, building, and business numbers by street address rather than alphabetically. All you need to know is the approximate address of a person or place; you can then use the street index to find the specific address and phone number.

Here's an example of how radio newsmen can use the street index to do effective foners. Let's say that a fire breaks out on the far side of town. You are the only newsman on duty at your station; there is no reporter to go to the scene. Your fire radio has announced the address or approximate location of the fire. You check the street index for telephone numbers of businesses or residences *across the street* or *nearby* the fire. And you call those numbers to tape "eyewitness" accounts of the fire from people within sight of it.

INTERVIEWING TECHNIQUES

The first thing to do upon reaching an interview subject is to identify yourself by name and station call letters. There must be no misrepresentation; this is a matter of ethics, if not law. Then you explain briefly why you are calling (most times it'll be obvious) and ask permission to tape record the conversation.

That's the easy part. The next part—the interview itself—is truly the highest art of journalism. Well, not always. Many times, two questions—"What happened?" and "What do you think about it?"—will suffice. But other times, when you are talking to people who may have something to hide or who you suspect are being less than truthful or forthcoming, the ability to conduct a fruitful (from your point of view) interview can spell the difference between getting a story and missing it.

Although I am about to suggest some guidelines for interviewing, I must say ahead of time that interviewing is a talent developed over time and with much practice. Fortunately, there is no shortage of role models available for you to watch and emulate, even as you develop your own abilities. I'm speaking particularly of Mike Wallace ("60 Minutes," CBS), Ted Koppel ("Nightline," ABC), Robert MacNeil ("The MacNeil-Lehrer News Hour," PBS), and Phil Donahue ("The Phil Donahue Show," syndicated). On network radio, there is Larry King (weeknights, 11 P.M. or midnight, depending on time zone, over the Mutual Broadcasting System). And in local radio, almost evey market has one or two talk or telephone call-in hosts who consistently bring out (or wring out) the best and most newsworthy in their interview subjects. (I would have included Barbara Walters of ABC, but at this writing she was limiting her considerable talents to "celebrity" interviews of strictly entertainment value.)

What unites these and other effective interviewers, first and foremost, is their *knowledge of the subject matter*. They come prepared. Nothing turns off an interviewee more quickly and thoroughly than an interviewer who does not know what to ask.

Broadcast journalists, while inherently generalists because of the hop-scotch nature of the news business, must nevertheless prepare themselves for interviews. On the workaday level, this may mean no more than reading every available bit of wire copy before placing a call. But it must be done. You must have a pretty firm idea of what questions to ask.

Avoid "Yes-No" Questions

Remember that what you are after in doing a foner is not just information, but information that can be excerpted as actualities. Therefore, questions that can be answered by a simple "yes" or "no" should be avoided.

If you ask Senator Piltdown, "Do you think the tax bill will pass?" you will likely get a one-word answer (well, maybe not in the case of Senator Piltdown). So instead you should phrase the question, "What will happen to the tax bill?" or "How do you assess the tax bill's chances?" Such phrasing forces the interviewee to be more forthcoming.

Similarly, in interviewing witnesses to events, do not ask, "Did you see the bridge collapse?" Instead, ask, "What did you see?" and "What did it look like?" You must oblige people to use *their* words, not parrot yours. (Sometimes, no matter how hard you try, all you'll get are one-word answers. In such cases, actualities may be excerpted as Q-and-A.)

Sticking to the Point

It goes without saying that your questions should stick to the subject matter; that's why you called. More difficult, though, is getting the *interviewee* to stick to the point. Some people express themselves poorly. Some are nervous being interviewed by reporters. Still others are reluctant to answer your questions, refusing to be pinned down or preferring to utter self-serving comments on matters closer to their hearts than to yours. There's the story of the Texas senator who, when asked his stand on the Equal Rights Amendment, replied, "Some of my friends are for it, some of my friends are against it, and I never disappoint my friends."

You must not let people get away with such evasion. Politely but firmly, you should repeat the question, remarking if necessary that the interviewee's previous answer was unresponsive.

Many people in the public eye, especially politicians, have considerable experience in dealing with reporters and the media. Many of them know your technical requirements as well as you do, as well as the questions you are likely to ask. Such people are very skilled at using the media for their own ends. They have certain points to make—and will make them no matter what you ask or how many times you ask the question. In such cases, it's well to remember that *you* are conducting the interview; if the interviewee, who *agreed* to be interviewed, doesn't want to answer your question, make him *say* he doesn't want to answer it—on tape.

Listening

It seems silly to have to mention this, and yet, failing to *listen* to a person's answers to your questions is a common cause of flubbing interviews. If you are not listening carefully to a response, if instead you are going over in your mind the wording of your next question, you may miss the most newsworthy part of the interview, and thus miss the ideal chance to ask a follow-up question.

Almost every broadcast newsman has a personal horror story of "letting the big one get away," and almost always the reason was failure to listen carefully (or failure to prepare for the interview by reading background material). Such disasters can usually be avoided. Here's how:

Jot down a few questions in advance. But do *not* look at your written questions during the interview *unless* your mind suddenly goes blank or the interview is not proceeding smoothly. Those written questions are nothing but a kind of crutch to be used only in an emeregency. But having them around frees you to concentrate on what the interviewee is saying instead of mentally thrashing about for what to ask next.

Handling Difficult Interviewees

Now about those nervous or inexpressive interviewees: Herein lies much of the art of broadcast interviewing, for it is often necessary to put people at ease or flatter their egos before they will open up. There is, I suppose, a certain amount of shamelessness involved in getting people to give you the information you want in the form you want it. But it goes with the territory.

Sensing trouble ahead, you might, for example, begin a foner with small talk and gradually work the conversation into the subject matter you really want. Or you could phrase your questions as an appeal for help, reminding the interviewee that he or she is the expert, while you, a mere reporter, need educating.

You can appeal to the interviewee's ego, his sense of self-worth, by reminding him how much you enjoy talking to him because he usually makes things clearer than other interviewees.

Shameless flattery? Trickery? Yes, in a way. But perfectly legitimate. He *did* agree to be interviewed, and he is free to stop at any time.

What you must never (repeat *never*) do is misrepresent your credentials.

"Good Tape"

After some practice doing foners and interviews in the field, you will develop an ear for a good actuality even as the words are spoken. You will begin to recognize "good tape" even before it's on tape.

A broadcast interviewer must learn to listen closely for both information *and* good actualities. The corollary is that he or she must also be able to recognize "bad tape" in order to shift gears in the course of an interview.

Some people ramble on and on. Others use specialized jargon or technical language your audience won't understand. Still others mumble indistinctly even while they're telling you what you want to know. In all such cases, where you fear the remark will not make a good actuality, you should *ask the question again,* perhaps phrasing it a bit differently. You may have to "play dumb," saying you don't quite understand. Or, on rare occasions, you may simply explain that you've got a technical problem with the answer, that listeners won't understand unless the answer is phrased better and more concisely. This is not telling a person what to say or "staging the news" in any way. It is merely a technical requirement of the medium, in the same way that a print reporter asks someone to speak slowly to be quoted accurately.

Whatever method you use, you'll find that, nine times out of ten, the second time a person says something makes "better tape," because, in effect, it has been rehearsed.

Remember, the real objective in doing foners and taped interviews in the field is not only to get information in a form *you* can understand, but also in a form your *audience* will understand.

"Off the Record"

Each news organization has its own specific rules regarding off-the-record interviews, that is, remarks that, by agreement with the interviewee, you will not attribute to him or her. Whatever the rules of your news department, it is expected in radio that you will *turn off your recorder* for anything stipulated "off the record." Obviously, a tape recording would be a "record," solid proof of the remarks of which you promised there would be no proof.

There's no *law* that says you have to turn your recorder off. But if you don't, that's the last you'll ever hear from that particular source and, once the word gets out, the last you'll hear from many such helpful sources. Like so much of the news business, especially (as we'll see) in television, this is a matter of ethics.

You are probably aware that, in some states, courts have ordered reporters to divulge their sources and that some reporters have been held in contempt of court and sent to jail for refusing to do so. Other courts have ordered broadcasters to turn over their unused (unaired) portions of tape—their "outtakes"—for use in trials. These are matters of vital interest to journalists in all media. This book, which is designed as a practical guide for fledgling broadcast journalists, does not have space to chronicle such matters, except insofar as they may affect writers and reporters on the everyday working level. Suffice it to say at this point that journalistic ethics, while often established by individual news departments, are ultimately a matter of personal choice, except where specified by law.

EDITING PROCEDURES

Someone can show you how to cut and splice reel-to-reel quarter-inch audiotape in a matter of moments. If you have average manual dexterity, you'll become fast and smooth at it within half an hour. So that's not what this section is about.

Instead, it's about the process of monitoring tape-recorded material for possible actualities and then finding those actualities quickly to get them on the air ahead of the competition.

The degree of a radio journalist's hands-on participation in technical matters depends on the size of the market. At small and medium market stations, radio journalists are called upon to do everything: to operate the console tape gear, cut and splice tape, prepare carts, and so on. At major markets and networks, they are forbidden to touch the equipment; labor contracts stipulate that only members of the engineering and technical unions may do that. In *all* markets, however, it is the journalists, not the engineers, who decide the form and content of what goes on the air.

Tape Counters

To the type of tape recording, editing and playback gear described at the end of Chapter 9 must be added one item: a tape counter, calibrated either in feet or in time code. Such a counter is a tape editor's best friend, because it enables him or her to locate a particular remark on Rewind or Fast Forward without having to listen to the entire tape all over again. The counter must be "zeroed"—reset to zero—at the start of each reel of tape and then *not touched* until editing of that reel is completed; otherwise, the editor's rundown notes (discussed next) would be worthless. A zeroed footage counter looks like this: 0000. And a zeroed time code counter like this: 00:00. The footage counter advances in consecutive numbers from 0001 to 9999. The time-code counter advances the same way a digital clock or stopwatch does, in minutes and seconds, from 00:01 to 59:59. (Trust me, you'll know it when you see it.)

Rundowns

Whenever tape is involved, taking notes in broadcasting is considerably more taxing than when there is no tape. Without tape, a newsman's notes reflect only the informational content of a set of remarks. With tape, the notes must also reflect the wording of desirable actualities and where to find them on the tape reel. Such notes involving tape, in both radio and TV, are called "rundowns."

Taking a good (i.e., practical) rundown comes with concentration and practice. Each broadcaster evolves a system best suited to him or her. Some write by hand, others use a typewriter. As a practical matter, it's best to learn how to take a rundown by hand, because you can't always count on there being a typewriter around.

Over the years, through my own trial and error and by observing others, I've found that the best way to go about it is to divide the notepaper (legal pads are the best) into right and left sides. On the right go my notes on informational content and on the left go my notes on the tape. In my tape notes, I include counter readings, so I know where to find the cut, and the incue (the first three words) of the cut, to remind me of how it starts. Since I don't know what cuts I want until I've listened to the entire tape, my left column looks like a series of numbers and incues, some of which I will have underlined or starred to show that, yes, this or that cut was indeed a good actuality. I can now rewind the tape machine to the counter number of the cut I want to edit and put on cart and use my right-column notes to write the lead-in and tag.

that, yes, this or that cut was indeed a good actuality. I can now rewind the tape machine to the counter number of the cut I want to edit and put on cart and use my right-column notes to write the lead-in and tag.

I know this sounds complicated. And it *is* complicated until you get used to it. You have to think and write fast. You have to make quick decisions. The objective is to get the story, including an actuality, on the air before your competitors do.

12
FIELD REPORTING

Like the doctor with a paging device and the beat cop with a sidearm, the radio reporter is never without a tape recorder. The recorder virtually becomes an extension of the reporter, a tool ready for use at a moment's notice, and without which he cannot perform his job.

This book is not going to recommend specific models or brands of portable cassette recorders; new models are arriving on the market all the time, adding to the bewildering array already available at all price ranges. However, cassette recorders, no matter how sophisticated or what their control configuration, will not automatically record the crisp, clear sound required for broadcast quality. Their successful use depends on the ability of the user to handle them properly.

BASIC FEATURES OF RECORDERS AND CASSETTES

Regardless of brand name or cost, any cassette recorder for professional broadcast use should have the following *minimum* features:

1. A directional or semi-directional hand microphone (with or without a remote control switch)

149

2. A tape counter (for fast location of actualities)
3. An output jack (usually labeled "Earphone" or "Monitor")
4. An input jack (usually labeled "Auxilliary Input"; on some models, the "Microphone" input will serve for this purpose)
5. A shoulder strap (to free the hands for holding the mike and taking notes)
6. An earphone (for private listening in the field)

The following additional features are helpful:

1. A battery-level indicator (to show when the batteries are losing power)
2. A "Cue/Review" function (to permit speedy relocation of incues and outcues)
3. A "Pause" control (to permit precise stopping and restarting).

Cassettes

Audiocassettes for professional use must be of high quality. Cheaply made, inexpensive cassettes break easily or fail to function, causing you to lose or miss a potentially important recording.

Cassettes should be a *maximum* of 60 minutes in length (30 minutes per side). Longer cassettes (lasting 90 or 120 minutes) have transport systems that cause jamming or stopping in small, battery-powered machines.

It is *not* necessary to use top-of-the-line, high bias tape cassettes, which are designed for the home stereo buff. Normal bias ("low noise") cassettes are sufficient for radio news usage.

Batteries

Always use long-lasting alkaline or rechargeable batteries, *not* standard or so-called "heavy duty" batteries. Only premium batteries have enough strength and staying power to serve reliably in the field.

TESTING FIRST

Before leaving the station on an assignment, the reporter should test the recorder thoroughly to avoid a mishap in the field. Here's a checklist:

1. Make sure that the batteries are fresh. Do *not* rely on a battery-level indicator.
2. See that the recording and playback heads are clean. If they are dusty or dirty from tape particle buildup, clean them with a cotton swab (a "Q-tip" will do) dipped in head cleaner solution or denatured alcohol.
3. Record something and play it back. *Speak* (do *not* blow) into the microphone, and watch that the tape transport system is moving smoothly. If the playback sounds mushy or distorted, change the batteries and cassette, and try again. If you still don't get crisp, clear sound, get a different recorder; the one you've been testing needs professional maintenance.

BACKUP AND ACCESSORY EQUIPMENT

In addition to the gear just listed, full-time radio reporters carry an array of backup and accessory equipment enabling them to record under a variety of conditions and to feed the material back to the station over its recording line. This gear is small and light and fits easily into a small shoulder bag, where the recorder itself may be stored when not in use. This accessory gear includes

1. A spare set of fresh batteries
2. Several spare cassettes
3. A patch cord for recording from a mult-box or other tape recorder (discussed shortly)
4. An acoustic coupler for telephone transmission (discussed shortly)
5. A roll of adhesive tape (discussed shortly)
6. A small clamp (discussed shortly)

Each item of standard and accessory equipment has an important use which may not be apparent to the novice reporter or student reading this book, so I am going to explain why each is necessary and how it is used.

MICROPHONES

Many portable cassette recorders are manufactured with a built-in microphone, usually along one edge of the recorder. Most professional radio reporters do *not* rely on this built-in mike. For one thing, it would require them to hold and move the recorder itself during recording; this is unwieldy, no matter how compact the recorder. But more important, the built-in mike is omni-directional: it records sound indiscriminately from all directions. Thus, it is likely to capture and enhance unwanted background noise, instead of just the sound you want.

That's why professionals prefer a small hand mike that, when plugged into the recorder, overrides (in fact, disconnects) the built-in mike. The hand mike is directional or semi-directional. That means it must be pointed directly at the desired sound source. But it provides sharper, clearer sound.

If the hand mike has a remote control switch, the switch should always be left in the "on" position, and the recorder's own controls used for on/off operation. That's because the remote control function doesn't control the recorder's full circuitry. In the "off" position, it doesn't really turn the recorder off; left unattended, this will drain the batteries. Thus, to avoid accidental drainage, it is better to rely on the recorder's master controls only.

Automatic Volume

Most modern recorders are also equipped with an automatic volume feature (usually abbreviated as AGC, for Automatic Gain Control), freeing the user from having to adjust the recording level to suit the sound source. At best, this feature is a mixed blessing because it does *not* operate like the human ear. It cannot distinguish between wanted and unwanted sounds. The circuitry automatically boosts the machine's sensitivity to weak sounds and lowers it to loud sounds. But suppose you *want* the weaker (i.e., less loud) sound?

That's where the hand mike proves useful once again. Its directionality permits you to point it close to the specific sound source you wish to record and thus eliminate much of the unwanted sound. The recorder itself, being dumb, can't make editorial decisions. Without a human hand and ear to guide it, the machine records everything indiscriminately.

Mike Placement

For some mysterious reason, beginners sometimes think that a cassette recorder mike will record a speech or news conference from across the room. Thus placed, what it will record is mush. Because of the features already described, it'll give equal weight to the speaker's voice, the person coughing next to you, your own breath and heartbeat, and the power lawn mower chugging along outside.

In short, microphones must be held or placed *close* to the desired sound, which is usually someone's mouth. Depending on the quality of the microphone and the recorder, and the amount of ambient noise, the optimum distance is from *6 to 18 inches.* Any closer will overemphasize the speaker's popping of P's and spitting of S's, and any farther will put the voice "off-mike" ("echo-y" and indistinct).

Clamps and Adhesive Tape

In case you were wondering, the clamp and adhesive tape are not for the purpose of stemming the flow of a reporter's blood spilled chasing a story. They are for the purpose of affixing a microphone in the right position.

The "typical" reporting assignment often involves covering a speech or news conference at which the speaker is either sitting at a table or standing at a rostrum. Although some hand mikes come with a collapsible stand allowing them to be placed at the correct angle on a flat surface, the stand won't work on a rostrum, which is slanted. Thus, the mike must be clamped or taped in a suitable position (aimed toward the speaker's mouth).

In practice, there are usually other broadcast reporters at such assignments, all with the same mike placement problem. So as a matter of course they agree among themselves to help each other with taping or clamping their mikes. If there is a "house" mike (one set up by whoever manages the premises), the radio reporter has only to tape his or her own mike to it.

Recording From Loudspeakers

This is to be avoided whenever possible. A loudspeaker is only as good as the sound system connected to it. Frequently, house sound systems and loudspeakers, being designed to amplify sounds over large areas, are bassy and full of static. Such sounds captured by your own microphone will be terrible and only marginally of broadcast quality. That's why broadcast reporters make every effort to arrive at events *early,* in plenty of time to set up their own microphones.

(In certain cases, whether because of crowded, chaotic conditions, lack of permission to set up sound gear, or your own late arrival, you will have no choice but to record from a loudspeaker. If so, you should hold the mike close enough to the loudspeaker to capture that sound only, eliminating as much as possible the sounds from other sources, such as applause or the comments of people nearby.)

The best sound quality for broadcast news is in the *treble* register, the opposite of the bassiness of most large loudspeakers. So if your recorder has a tone control (which is inoperative in the Record mode), it should be turned to *full treble* during playback.

PATCH CORDS

There is still another way of recording certain events, one that bypasses your own microphone altogether. But for this you'll need what's called a "patch cord," enabling you to plug your recorder directly into someone else's equipment.

Thanks to the Japanese, patch cords have been pretty well standardized with eighth-inch plugs (also called "Sony plugs") at each end. However, some news organizations use equipment requiring pin-plugs (also called "RCA plugs"), and a few others use European-made gear requiring DIN plugs. So a patch cord has to be suited to specific equipment.

Mult-Boxes

At locations used frequently for news conferences and announcements—such as city hall and the governor's office—house sound systems have been built specifically for the use of radio and TV news teams. These include a podium-mounted microphone connected to a small amplifier and a so-called "mult-box," short for "multiple plug box." With such devices, radio reporters (or TV sound technicians) need not set up their own microphones. Instead, they use patch cords to link their recorders and the mult-boxes, resulting in clean, crisp recordings. (They haven't invented a machine to ask questions yet, but they're probably working on it.)

The patch cord may also be used to connect two tape recorders for the purpose of dubbing from one to the other.

ACOUSTIC COUPLERS (FEED CORDS)

An acoustic coupler—or "feed cord"—enables a reporter to transmit his or her tape-recorded material back to the station via telephone. One end attaches to the Output or "Monitor" jack of the cassette recorder, the other to the telephone. This device is the only means of sending broadcast-quality taped sound back to the studio. (You can't hold up the recorder's speaker to the phone mouthpiece; the sound quality is UFB.)

In 20 years, I have seen or used half a dozen different types of acoustic couplers, each successively designed to overcome technological advances or de-

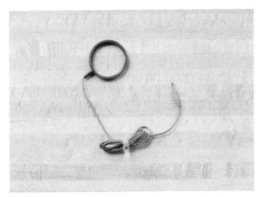 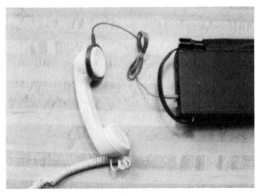

One type of acoustic coupler for use with standard office, residential, and pay telephones. The plug end fits into a tape recorder's "Monitor" or "Earphone" jack.

The coil end fits around the *ear* of the telephone. Since this kind of coupler does not cut off the phone's built-in microphone, one hand must be firmly clamped over the mouthpiece to eliminate outside noise.

sign and manufacturing changes in telephones. And you know what? By the time this book is published, probably none of them will be in use. That's because of the destandardization of consumer telephone equipment. Telephones today don't always *look* like telephones. They can look like Mickey Mouse or a plastic blob.

Well, never fear—broadcast technology is coming to the rescue. Even as I write, several firms are designing new types of acoustic couplers for use by radio reporters. They will be "on line" (as they say) by the time you are. What will *not* change are the various procedures for calling in and feeding live and/or taped material.

STICK TO BUSINESS

Whenever you call in from the field with spots or actualities, you will be using your station's recording number. On the answering end will be either a fellow newsman or a broadcast engineer. Whoever it is, do *not* engage in small talk. There may be other reporters trying to phone in or staffers trying to do foners. You mustn't tie up the recording line. So state your business and get on with it.

FEEDING "LIVE" VOICERS

"Live" in this sense means that you will announce your voicer live over the phone for recording inside the studio. This is the simplest and most straightforward of all feeding procedures and requires only that you be calling from a quiet place and have your copy cleanly written. Here, step by step, is how to go about it:

1. Identify yourself.
2. State that you are doing a voicer, and briefly tell its subject matter.

3. Tell its approximate running time. This is important because the person on the other end will attempt to record the spot *directly onto cart,* thereby skipping the step of dubbing from reel-to-reel. (The console machine will be running anyway, as a backup.)

4. Await the instruction to "give a level." This refers to the sound level of your transmission, which must be set properly on the studio recording gear.

5. Go ahead with the level by delivering the first two sentences of your spot *at the volume and tone of voice you will use in actual delivery.* (The purpose is to set the actual level, not the rehearsal level; so they must be the same.)

6. Await instructions, if any, to speak louder or softer. Once the level is set, you will be told to "Count down and go."

7. Precede your spot with a *countdown.* That means you start by saying, loudly, clearly, and in tempo, "Five-four-three-two-one." Then you pause a beat (about half a second) and go directly on with your voicer. The countdown, which is used for spots in TV as well as radio, enables the recording engineer to know when to start the cartridge machine. Without a countdown, such coordination would not be possible. The engineer will hit the Record button during your half-second beat. Thus, it's essential that the countdown be done in cadence.

8. If you "bobble" (make an error in delivery or pronunciation) in a *short* spot, pause a few seconds, then do it over from the top, *including* a new countdown. (The cart is blown, so now the operator is working with the console reel-to-reel recorder.) If you bobble in the *first half* of a *long* spot, again do it over from the top with a new countdown. But if you bobble in the *second half* of a long spot, pause a few seconds, then resume *from the start of the sentence in which you bobbled.* (The tape operator will splice the spot together before transferring it to cart.)

9. After your sign-off, *remain silent.* Give the engineer a chance to kill the Record circuitry before you talk.

10. Do not hang up until the engineer confirms that everything has been received "loud and clear."

At first glance, this process may seem complicated and time consuming. In fact, it is precisely the opposite. The procedure is designed to ensure technical quality and speed.

FEEDING TAPED VOICERS

Sometimes you won't be able to find a quiet phone. You may have to call from an outside pay phone or from an inside phone where your voice might disturb other people. In such cases, it's best to record your voicer on your own tape recorder, then feed the tape back to the studio. That procedure is slightly different.

BEFORE CALLING IN,

1. Record your spot in a quiet place, *with* a countdown. You may do it as often as you like (until you're satisfied), but the countdown must be on the tape just before your spot.

2. Attach your feed cord to the phone. Cue the cassette to your spot. Now you're ready to call in.

1–4. Same as for live voicers.

5. Play the first 10 seconds of your recorded spot. Adjust the level if and as instructed by the technician.

6. Await the instruction to "recue and go."

7. Rewind your recorder to the start of the taped countdown, pause, then play the countdown and spot in their entirety.

8. After the sign-off, do *not* stop your tape machine immediately because this would cause a loud click back in the studio. Again, give the engineer a chance to stop his or her own recorder.

9. And, again, await the "all OK" before hanging up.

FEEDING ACTUALITIES AND WRAPS

Feeding actualities proceeds exactly like feeding taped voicers, except, of course, that there is no countdown; the level is given by playing the first few seconds of the desired cut. Feeding wraparounds, however, can be complicated for newcomers because it requires both manual dexterity and the ability to deliver copy without bobbling. What you attempt to do is read your lead-in live, play your taped actuality, and resume live with your tag as you simultaneously shut off your recorder. Few radio reporters can do this without considerable practice.

(Time permitting, it isn't even necessary. The lead-in, actuality, and tag can be fed separately, then spliced together by the tape operator before timing and transferal to cart. Unfortunately, "time" doesn't always "permit.")

Here's the procedure:

1. Hook up before calling in.

2. Go through the identification and description procedures listed earlier.

3. Give levels *both* on yourself and the tape. The engineer will have you adjust the tape level until it corresponds as closely as possible with your live announcing voice.

4. Carefully recue the taped actuality to the starting point and press the Pause button. (The Pause control, when released, makes the tape transport system start up quicker and cleaner than the on-off circuitry.)

5. Array your copy comfortably in front of your eyes.

6. Poise a finger above (but not touching) the Pause button.

7. Count down and go, releasing the Pause button at the end of your lead-in, and hitting it again at the end of the actuality at the same time as you continue with your tag and sign-off copy.

8. Cheer for yourself if you get it on the first try. (But only after remaining silent for a few seconds.)

GOING LIVE

Occasionally, you will be covering a major, late-breaking story that calls for you to report live during a newscast or in a bulletin interruption of non-news programming. Learning how to do this in radio is perhaps the best preparation for doing it in television.

Live reports from the field (often called "live-shots") are usually via two-way radio or cordless telephone, but they may also be done over a regular telephone. The sound quality of two-way radio is generally awful, so many news departments prefer the telephone. The line used is the station's recording number, which can be patched directly onto the air.

Obviously, the important thing in covering a major, breaking story is to find a phone in the first place. On a hot story, everyone—print, radio, and television—wants the phone. Networks have been known to hire flunkeys just to monopolize a telephone so that it will be available for the network's reporter whenever he or she wants it, or they install their own phones. But for the sake of argument, and sanity, let's assume here that you've got the phone.

The line will not be patched onto the air until the very second you are to go on. In the meantime, an engineer or fellow newsman will be on the other end, telling you, in terms of minutes and seconds, how long you've got before you're on the air. ("You go in four" means you're on in 4 minutes; "In thirty" means you're on in 30 seconds; and so forth.) The last word you'll hear is "Go!" which means you "take a beat" (pause half a second), then deliver your report. Obviously, you do *not* deliver a countdown in this case. You're already on the air!

Things need not be so nerve-wracking. Some stations can patch their programming into the telephone, so that you can hear what's on the air. This is called Program Audio. If you can hear it, you no longer need time cues and commands from the studio engineer. You can hear yourself announced (a throw line with your name on it), and you just take it from there. Furthermore, you can converse with the studio newscaster, answering any questions (Q-and-A) he or she might have.

MOBILE UNITS

Many stations maintain at least one mobile unit—a car, van, or station wagon equipped with a powerful two-way radio, as well as recording and transmission gear, enabling a reporter (who also drives the darned thing) to reach isolated locations speedily and call in reports without having to rely on the telephone. Because of the transmitting power of such units, sound quality is usually excellent. It's the hand-held "squawky-talkies" that are often unreliable. (More on this in Chapter 22 on coming technology.)

BACK IN THE STUDIO

When there are no further reporting assignments, the field reporter usually returns to the station instead of going straight home, because there's still work to be done. There are those overnight and protected spots to write and record for use that night and early the next morning.

It is important that these spots be recorded in the studio instead of in the field. That's because the audio quality is better. The material phoned in from the field has a tinny sound at best, especially the actualities. Many stations like their reporters to drop off their cassettes at the station on a routine basis, so that the better quality audio from the cassettes may be substituted for the phone-quality sound thus far on carts. Naturally, the reporter, too, sounds better in a studio-quality recording.

However, since the reporter will no longer be writing and recording at the scene of a story, it may be necessary for him or her to change the sign-off. Some stations are firm in ruling that to use an on-scene sign-off, the reporter must be at the scene at the time. Others allow the use of an on-scene sign-off as long as the reporter was there at some time to cover the story, even though he or she is now back in the studio.

As we shall see, this latter procedure is more typical of television than of radio.

AND NOW A WORD FROM . . .

. . . the brain. So far, this is the first chapter in this book to have dealt more with technical matters than with news content. In a way, this reflects the reality of a newcomer's first experiences in a broadcast news department. Inevitably, he or she becomes swept up into "*our* way of doing things."

And, in truth, no one is born doing countdowns and hooking gadgets into telephones. There is undeniably a modicum of technical proficiency required of broadcast journalists that is not required of their print counterparts.

But this technical proficiency comes in a few short weeks or months. I have seen students who didn't know a microphone from a wall socket return within six months on the job to show me a few new technical twists with a tape recorder rigged out with more buttons than a sailor's suit.

The point is (excuse me for beating you about the head with it) that technical proficiency is the *easy* part of the broadcast news business. More difficult by far, and what you should be concentrating on, is the *editorial* sense required of a good journalist: the ability to transform complicated reality into clear, concise English sentences. *That* is what you should be working on—now and during your entire journalism career.

13
NEWSCASTS

Along with the writing of spots, the writing and assembling ("producing") of newscasts is the most creative and challenging job in radio news. So far, this book has dealt with the components of newscasts:

1. Scripted stories without tape (called "readers")
2. Actualities
3. Reports

Now it's time to bring these components together, to examine how they interact within the framework of a newscast.

It is well to bear in mind the *nature* of most radio news in the United States (and overseas, too), which is overwhelmingly the reporting of late-breaking developments, told briefly. Although most newscasts are short, they come hard and fast—every hour or half-hour, depending on the station—a fresh "edition" as many as 24 or 48 times a day. Each newscast is different, consisting of a different mix of stories of different lengths, rewritten, updated, and handled differently from hour to hour.

Thus, it is necessary to approach the writing and assembling of radio newscasts with an attitude different from newspapers and television, whose "editions" are longer but fewer and farther between. One cannot expect from a single short radio newscast the same sort of "definitive" treatment of the day's news as from a single edition of a newspaper or a single telecast. Instead, a day's radio newscasts must be regarded as a whole for any true assessment of quality of coverage.

This is important psychologically as well as journalistically. A newswriter/newscaster need not feel that he or she has failed if an important story gets only 10 seconds on one newscast, as long as it receives adequate time on a different newscast. Radio newscasts are trade-offs whose value can only be assessed in the aggregate.

All of which is not to say that a single newscast, however ephemeral its nature, cannot be a creative, skillful, tasteful, sensitive, and perceptive account of the day's news. Quite the contrary. Those are precisely the qualities to strive for. And professional newswriter/newscasters *do* strive for them, and very often achieve them.

There are a number of "highs" in the broadcast news business. One of them is beating the competition on a major story. Another is writing a newscast that "sings"—the copy so sharply written, the stories flowing so smoothly into each other, that the writer and listener both are sorry when it is over.

NEWSCAST LENGTH AND STRUCTURE

From the earlier remarks regarding formats (Chapter 7), you have no doubt gathered—correctly—that newscasts come in an infinite variety of lengths and structures. However, you have only to listen to local radio virtually anywhere in the country for a day or two to realize that the most "typical" format is 5 minutes, usually on the hour, but sometimes on the half-hour. "Typically" (I insist on using the quotation marks), it is a mix of local, world, and national news, with the emphasis on the local. "Typically," it contains 1 commercial minute (one 60-second commercial or two 30-second ones), reducing the actual news hole to 4 minutes.

Such a newscast—which is so "typical" that we will use it as a model—would be structured in two basic parts called *sections* (in some places called *segments*), divided by the commercial:

SECTION 1

Sign-on at 00:00:00 (if on the hour)
Lead local or non-local story
Related stories (if any)
Secondary stories (local or non-local)
(COMMERCIAL)

SECTION 2

More secondary stories (local or non-local)
Local sports (if any that day)
Local weather
Sign-off at 00:05:00

The only hard-bound rules in this format are

1. The newscast must start precisely on the hour.
2. The commercial must be included *somewhere* in the newscast.
3. The newscast must conclude with the local weather forecast.
4. The newscast must be off the air *no later than* 5 minutes past the hour. (Ending a few seconds early is okay, but *not* a few seconds late.)

Everything else—the number of stories, their lengths, their placement, the mix of local and non-local, which ones will include tape, exactly where to break for the commercial—is up to the newswriter/newscaster. He or she thus has *complete editorial control*. Whatever the editorial choices, they are guided by three basic considerations:

1. To tell the *latest* news
2. To tell the *most important* news
3. To maintain listener interest and attention

Consideration 1 is a matter of keeping up with the news wires and the reporters in the field. Consideration 2 is a matter of news judgment and experience. And consideration 3 is a matter of ability to write and communicate. It is consideration 3 that eventually determines the success or failure of a career in broadcast news.

STORY COUNT

Only in extremely rare cases—maybe once or twice a year—will an entire newscast be devoted to just one or two stories of transcendent importance. At all other times, the "typical" 4 minutes available for news must be parceled out, stingily, to a host of stories, all crying in varying degrees for attention.

Thus, our model newscast, at any given hour, would contain anywhere from 6 to 10 different or related stories, each of different length.

Since newswriter/newscasters cannot know precisely what will be the latest or most important news by air time, their first task is to prepare for all eventualities. They do this by

1. Reading and "tearing down" (separating and reassembling) all available wire service copy from the preceding several hours and arraying it story by story in a convenient place (usually a desktop)
2. Familiarizing themselves with all available tape, both actualities and reports
3. Reading the station's newscasts from the preceding 4 to 8 hours
4. Ascertaining the whereabouts of all reporters, with an eye toward the tape they are likely to be feeding within the next few hours

This preparatory process—known as "reading in"—is essential as a first step. The material being read and sifted will almost always be fresh news—that is, news that has not yet appeared in the newspapers or on television. Only radio, with its build-in speed and immediacy, can for technical reasons afford to concern itself chiefly with "the top of the news."

Each newswriter/newscaster evolves his or her own system of reassembling wire copy. Since wire copy continues to pour in without stop, it can quickly clutter one's work space. Most newswriter/newscasters thus form a habit of throwing away immediately all wire copy which they know they will not need—stale news, long features, esoteric sidebars, and so on. Some divide the copy into neat piles of "local," "foreign," and "domestic." Others divide into piles of "set" (stories not likely to change by air time) and "breaking" (stories that are likely to change by air time).

Whatever the system, the essential thing is to read *everything* before deciding which stories to include in a newscast. (Once writing begins, it is best to leave the breaking stories for last, since they are the most likely to change and, tackled too early, could entail unnecessary or time-consuming rewrites.)

STORY LENGTH

Deciding how much air time each story is "worth" is a matter on which reasonable men and women will differ. There is no such thing as an "optimum" length, all length being relative to the structure as a whole. One person's "short" is another person's "long."

In radio, where the range is from :10 minimum to about 1:30 maximum (for an important story involving tape), one need not become preoccupied with the "worth" of most stories within a single newscast, for a story that gets only :15 in one newscast may get 1:15 in the next. (Or it may be left out altogether in favor of a different story.)

What can be said definitively about story lengths is that they should vary widely within each newscast. The AP "Newswatch" summary in Chapter 8 is *not* a good newscast. It contains eight stories, all but one of which are the same length. On the air this sounds dull. It lacks pacing and variety. For better or worse, a newscast is a kind of "show" or "performance." Sameness of length results in a dull show. And a dull show fails to fulfill condition 3, maintaining listener interest.

So a newswriter/newscaster must make a deliberate effort to vary the running times of the stories chosen for the newscast. This goes along with a writing approach that has been stressed throughout this book: decide the time of a story *before* writing it. It may come out a few seconds long or a few seconds short, but you will have a target to shoot for as well as an almost certain knowledge of what details you can include.

LEAD STORIES

Deciding the lead story of a newscast—a decision made only moments before air time—usually provokes the most heated discussion in the newsroom. Again, reasonable men and women will differ, and differ strongly.

Much of the time, of course, the lead story will jump out and grab you by the throat. Stories with great immediacy, importance, or impact virtually "tell themselves."

But at other times, on slow news days (which all journalists detest), you could literally begin digging into the waste basket to find a lead story, hoping against hope that it was buried in a piece of wire copy you overlooked or rejected.

There is an unfortunate tendency in some news organizations, on slow news days, to "hype" stories out of proportion to their true importance, to use overly dramatic language such as "war of words" or "dropped a bombshell" when there was neither hostility nor air raid. This technique, almost always employed for strictly commercial reasons to attract an audience, debases the English language and, in the long run, debases listeners' trust in the offending station's news team.

So what to do if there's no clear or obvious lead story? Well, some newswriter/newscasters flip a coin. However, certain other solutions are much better. One is to lead with a human interest story instead of with a hard news story, especially if the former involves health, medicine, or everyday science (a new household invention, for example). Another is to lead, in a general way, with the weather, returning to the specific forecast at the end of the newscast.

Whatever the merits of one possible lead versus another, it is well not to waste too much time in deciding. Remember, if you lead with story "A" at 10 A.M., you can lead with story "B" at 11 A.M. One newscast is just one *installment* of the news, not the day's definitive record.

Still another way to resolve the problem of stale or slow news is to rewrite stories to stress what is *about* to happen or what is *expected* to happen. This technique works best during early-morning newscasts, especially when there have been no major news developments since the previous evening. Sometimes, what is *going* to happen is more immediate and newsworthy than what has already happened.

STORY PLACEMENT

Following selection of the lead story, the rest of the stories are not just thrown together helter-skelter. Instead they are grouped in some sensible or logical way so that, as much as possible, they flow one to another until they come to a natural break. Modest transitions (discussed shortly) may be required either between groups of stories or between stories in a group. But if stories are clearly written at the outset, only a slight pause between them by the newscaster will be sufficient.

The intention to group related stories should be in the newswriter/newscaster's mind even as he or she writes the newscast. This makes it possible to write smooth transitions and to order the newscast by grouped rather than individual stories, without getting caught short for time just before air.

There are several bases on which to group stories:

1. *By subject matter,* such as labor relations, politics, economic news, medicine, science, and weather among others
2. *By geography,* such as U.S. region, Western Europe, Eastern Europe, the Far East, the Middle East, and so on
3. *By newsmaker,* such as Congress, the Supreme Court, the president, governor, or mayor taking different actions on different matters

Remember that grouped stories, however related, should still be typed one story per page. This is to permit the sudden deletion, if necessary, of just one story and the subtraction of just that story's running time from the total.

TAPE PLACEMENT

There is a sort of Eleventh Commandment in radio newscasting: "Thou shalt use tape." Based on studies of listening habits and patterns, commercial station managements are convinced that audiences quickly become bored with "static" newscasts, that is, where the only thing heard is the voice of the newscaster. So they instruct newswriter/newscasters to include tape in every newscast, the object being to enliven the "sound" of the news as well as its content. The risk in such a policy is that, depending on circumstances, the tape available may not be newsworthy—in which case its use amounts to cosmetics only. Management's answer to such criticism is, "If you don't like the tape you've got, do foners until you *are* satisfied." So one way or another, there *will* be tape in just about every commercial newscast.

In structuring a newscast, the rule is not to use all the tape in the same place. Rather, it should be divided among newscast sections. Our model newscast, with its two sections, would ideally have one piece of tape in each section, not two in one and none in the other. It doesn't matter if the total tape is two actualities, two reports, or one actuality and one report. The point is to vary the newscast's pacing, both in story length and in tape placement.

As with all things in this book, I don't want you to accept my word alone on this. I want you to listen to the stations in your area. Take notes if you have to—or a rundown of several newscasts, noting story count, length, placement, and tape. Or better yet, arrange to visit one or two of your local stations. Talk to the staff newsmen and women. Ask them about their news departments' formats and policies regarding the use of tape and so on. Unless it's a very heavy news day, professional broadcast journalists are, as a rule, pleased to welcome students and "show them the ropes."

So far, this chapter has dealt with the approach to newscasts as a whole. Now let's move on to specific problems of writing individual and grouped stories.

TRANSITIONS

In broadcasting, a transition—sometimes called a "tie-in" or "link"—refers to the word or words connecting two different stories, whether they are related or unrelated. Print's way of linking related stories is to write them as a "roundup" in one overall story, a structure that, as we've seen, does not work well in broadcasting. And print doesn't link different stories at all; it merely publishes them in a different column or page. That, too, doesn't work in broadcasting, since there are no "columns" or "pages"; a newscast goes from beginning to end, leaving the listener with no option but to stay tuned or to tune out altogether. Thus, *occasional* transitions are necessary to help the newscast flow smoothly.

I stress the word "occasional" because, as with so much of broadcast style, effective use of a technique depends on using it sparingly. On average, there should be no more than one or two transitions per newscast. Otherwise, they call attention to themselves and detract from the stories themselves.

A few transitions are so standard that they long ago reached the status of cliché: *meanwhile, meantime, in the meantime,* and *elsewhere.* Sometimes, because of the pressure of the clock, newswriter/newscasters will grab one of those cliché transitions, however reluctantly, because there's no time to come up with something more inventive.

However, as noted in Chapter 5, the location of a story—the "where" element—often makes a simple, handy transition, one which the writer can use to open a story even though he doesn't yet know its ultimate position in a newscast:

In New York, Mayor Ed Koch said today. . .

-0-

In Washington today, the Labor Department reported. . .

Stories begun that way will fit almost anywhere in a newscast. If the first of these two examples winds up following another story set in New York, then the copy would be changed at the last minute to read *"Also in New York,"* or *"New York's Mayor Ed Koch,"* or something similar.

In the second example, the writer knows that a Labor Department story always comes out of Washington and therefore normally would not even mention the city; but here he does so to make a smooth transition from the preceding story, which he knows will be on a different subject.

Often the best transitions are those which specifically tie one story to another:

Federal spending wasn't the only thing on the president's mind today. . .

-0-

While the Israelis remained adamant, the P-L-O was showing some flexibility. . .

-0-

Arizona's loss was Nevada's gain. . .

Such specific tie-ins work only if they are strictly accurate. If the writer has to stretch too far for them, they fall flat and call undue attention to themselves. So unless a good transition springs to mind quickly, suggesting itself, as it were, it is best to keep it simple:

At the same time. . .

-0-

In other economic (medical, political, etc.) *news.* . .

-0-

Also downstate (upstate, etc.). . .

Remember that transitions should be used sparingly. A well-written newscast may require no transitions at all, as long as the writer has varied his or her approach to stories that are *inherently* related. For example, here are three grouped stories that took a total of 40 seconds of air time:

(HONDURAS)

Terrorists in Honduras holding 105 hostages say they will start killing their captives one at a time, starting two hours from now, if their demands are not met. The terrorists are demanding freedom for some 80 political prisoners in Honduras, and softening of the country's three-month-old anti-terrorism law.

(BRUSSELS)

Four people were wounded today in Brussels when a man with a machine gun opened fire on a synagogue during Rosh Hashanah services. The gunman escaped.

(PARIS)

French police have arrested 14 people and uncovered a cache of weapons and explosives in Paris. Officials say they believe the 14 are part of the terrorist group "Direct Action." That group has claimed responsibility for recent anti-Jewish violence in France.

(Robb Armstrong, CBS Radio)

Note that those three stories, whose common thread is terrorism, could have been read *in any order*. If the writer had used a transition, the flexibility of story order would have been destroyed. Instead, each was written on a separate page to stand on its own and eventually linked with the others by placement (story order) rather than transitional words.

UPDATING

Newswriter/newscasters write many more versions of the same story than do writers in print or in television. A staff newsman in local radio may write up to eight 5-minute newscasts per shift. In all-news radio, the work load is heavier still. In the case of a major story, the demand is for a fresh version every hour or so, sometimes every 20 minutes. By and large, staff newsmen are *not* permitted to air the same version twice, no matter how much time has elapsed between the two.

This can and does become challenging. Once you have written two long versions, two medium versions and two short versions, all of the same story, where do you go from there?

Fortunately, the solution comes in most cases through the natural development of the story itself, the twists and turns it takes as new information becomes known. Each twist and turn can be used to revise the story and perhaps give it a new lead. This process is called "updating." Here's how one network, CBS Radio, updated one major story throughout much of the broadcast day:

Time	Order	Content
12p	lead	The battle over the Equal Rights Amendment is back in Congress. One year after the first unsuccessful effort to pass it, backers are hoping they will have better luck this time around. Neil Strawser reports:

(wrap) Backers of the E-R-A are pleased with the strategy they have chosen. It takes a two-thirds vote to bring the Amendment up under suspension of the rules, but it also takes a two-thirds vote to pass it. They believe they have the votes. The procedure prohibits amendments and limits debate. The backers say E-R-A has already been debated for years. But Republicans are outraged. . .including their leader, Bob Michel (MY-kel):

(act.) I think that just does violence to the whole legislative process. I'm sure they're going to be many many members on our side who would support E-R-A and would hope to do so next year, when we have an opportunity to consider it under an open rule, offer amendments, and all the rest.

Senate Leader Howard Baker said he won't tie up the Senate with E-R-A in the closing days of this session, but some knowledgeable sources say E-R-A may not reach the Senate floor until after the 1984 elections. Neil Strawser, CBS News, Capitol Hill.

-0-

| 1p | 2 | The House has begun debate on a revived Equal Rights Amendment. Under rules set by Speaker Thomas O'Neill, total discussion is limited to 40 minutes, and amendments are prohibited. This has caused an uproar among Republicans: |

(act.) I don't really believe that anybody expects that E-R-A is gonna pass this way, on a suspension of the rules. And I tell ya, it's not gonna pass in the last three days of the Senate. I'm for E-R-A. I supported it in the past. But I'm not gonna support it in the Senate

in the last three or four days. So I think it does injury to the cause
of the E-R-A to bring it up in this way.

Senate Majority Leader Howard Baker. Womens' rights groups and Right-
to-Life advocates were reminding members of the House today that they'll
be held accountable for the way they vote on the E-R-A bill.

-0-

2p   lead   Debate is under way in the House on a new Equal Rights Amendment.
Tempers flared over a Democratic maneuver limiting the debate and
prohibiting opponents from tacking on amendments to the bill.

-0-

3p   lead   The House is now taking a roll-call vote on a revived version of the Equal
Rights Amendment. The surprise development has angered Republicans,
who charge "steam roller" tactics by the Democrats in an effort to
embarrass the Republicans. They say the Democrats were not allowing
debate or amendments, a breach of normal House procedure. Republican
Hamilton Fish of New York said the effort does not do justice to the E-R-A:

> (act.) I suggest it is less a commitment to equal rights, that it is more
> of what we have witnessed repeatedly this fall: partisan politics in
> search of a campaign issue. We should refuse to cooperate with this
> approach. A no vote, my colleagues, is not a vote against E-R-A,
> but a vote for respect for the United States Constitution.

Several Democrats said they wanted members of Congress to be on the
record on this issue. . .as Election Year approaches.

-0-

4p   lead   An attempt to revive the Equal Rights Amendment failed today in the
House of Representatives. Neil Strawser reports:

(wrap) A switch of six votes would have meant victory for E-R-A. It took
two-thirds. E-R-A lost by a vote of 278 yeas to 147 nays. Republicans
and some Democrats had argued that the Democratic leadership was trying
to ramrod the bill through without allowing amendments, to make sure
E-R-A did not mandate abortion or require women to go into combat.
And Republican Hamilton Fish, an E-R-A supporter, charged Democrats
with trying to put Republicans on the spot:

(act.) A no vote, my colleagues, is not a vote against E-R-A, but a
vote for respect for the United States Constitution (applause).

Speaker O'Neill, winding up debate, scoffed at opponents for trying to hide
behind such arguments:

(act.) If you think this is the escape, then vote no. If you truly
believe in a constitutional amendment for women's rights, now is the
time, and vote yes (applause).

But O'Neill lost, and Fish announced he will attempt to bring E-R-A back
to the floor under a rule allowing amendments. But apparently it can't
happen yet this session. Neil Strawser, CBS News, Capitol Hill.

(anchor tag) Senate Republican Leader Howard Baker said he didn't think
the Senate would take up E-R-A until next year. . .and perhaps not until
after the 1984 elections.   Baker also said. . .

(tag used as transition to another Senate story)

-0-

5p   lead   (opens w/actuality)

(act.) By this vote, the ayes are 278, the nays 147, one member
voting "present." Therefore, the two-thirds not having voted yes,
the rules are not suspended.

That's the Clerk of the House, with parliamentary talk meaning the Equal
Rights Amendment was defeated today, six votes short. This despite the
wagging finger of House Speaker Thomas O'Neill.   House Republicans
were infuriated because O'Neill and the rest of the Democratic leadership
barred them from modifying the E-R-A proposal in any way.   O'Neill
issued a warning to those members who declared their opposition because
of insufficient debate and no amendments.   Said the Speaker, wagging the
finger, "You're not fooling anybody. In your hearts you were never with
us."   To which, Republican Representative Larry Craig of Idaho replied,
challenging the leadership's tactics and saying, "Shame on you, Mr.
Speaker, shame on you."

-0-

6p   2   Another attempt to put an Equal Rights Amendment into the U-S
Constitution died today in the House of Representatives.   The final vote,

278 to 147, was six votes shy of the two-thirds necessary for passage.
Republicans were angered by a parliamentary move that prohibited
amendments and limited debate to 40 minutes.   Some Republicans said
they wanted to discuss such issues as abortion and women in combat.
Democratic Representative Mary Rose Ocher of Ohio says those issues
just provided a handy excuse for voting no:

> (act.) There can be no other more pro-life issue than to be for the
> Equal Rights Amendment.   And I suspect, without impugning the
> reputations of any of my colleagues, that a lot of people use that as
> an excuse to oppose us.   And they can dream up all kinds of
> reasons, emotional issues, that are divisive among those of us who
> believe strongly, simply to see the defeat of this amendment.

-0-

7p   3   The battered Equal Rights Amendment came to a vote in the House of
Representatives again today. . .and went down to defeat.   The vote, 278
to 147.   Jacquilyne Adams covered the story:
(wrap) With only six more votes, supporters of the Equal Rights
Amendment could have won passage in the House.   But a number of
members, like Republican Hamilton Fish, argued and voted against the
E-R-A, because the amendment was brought to the floor under a
procedure normally used for non-controversial amendments, and because it
prohibited debate on abortion and women in combat:

> (act.) I suggest it is less a commitment to equal rights, that it is more
> of what we have witnessed repeatedly this fall: partisan politics in
> search of a campaign issue.

But Speaker Thomas O'Neill discounted the opponents' arguments:

> (act.) You want to hide behind something that we have done, the
> strategy which we have brought out?   You're not fooling anybody.
> In your heart you were never with us.   You were looking for the
> escape.

After the vote, E-R-A supporters said they were sorely disappointed, but
glad that now they have the names of their opponents. Women's groups
say they'll target each one for defeat -- 15 per cent of House Democrats,
two-thirds of House Republicans.   The E-R-A is expected to return to the

House floor next year. . .before the 1984 election.   Jacquilyne Adams,
CBS News, on Capitol Hill.

-0-

8p   lead   It's called the Equal Rights Amendment.   It says equality of rights under
the law shall not be denied or abridged by the United States, or by any
state, on account of sex.   Today a revived effort to make the E-R-A a part
of the Constitution went down to defeat in the House of Representatives.
The proposal fell six votes short of the two-thirds majority needed.
Republicans were angered by the restrictions set by the Democratic
leadership to limit debate and bar amendments to the measure.   As might
be expected, women's groups such as the National Organization for
Women denounced the House action. Judy Goldsmith, the president of
NOW:

(act.) Votes such as today's virtually assure that the gender gap will
continue to grow, as women become more determined to remove
from office those who do not support our rights.

-0-

9p   3   The House of Representatives today killed a new version of the Equal
Rights Amendment. The House vote was six votes short of the two-thirds
majority needed to send the measure along to the next step in the
ratification process. Republicans in the House said they were angry over a
parliamentary move that limited debate to 40 minutes. But Cathy Wilson of
the National Political Women's Caucus says that's a weak excuse:

(act.) I think that they are influenced by the right-wing tone that has
been set by the president of our country, Ronald Reagan.

-0-

10p   3   An effort to revive the Equal Rights Amendment failed today in the House
of Representatives, coming up six votes shy of the two-thirds majority
required for approval. The Democratic leadership ruffled the feathers of
many Republicans, and some within Democratic ranks, by limiting debate
and barring any amendments to the proposal. House Speaker O'Neill
accused E-R-A opponents of using the restrictions as an out for voting no.

By now, you should understand enough of broadcast style and structure
to be aware on many levels of the way CBS Radio handled that story. You noticed
how the content kept pace with the breaking elements of the story, stressing
their immediacy, and yet always retaining the main point, the essence.

You noticed how the story length varied, running as short as around :15 to as long as around 1:30.

You noticed how the story placement varied, sometimes as the lead, but moving up and down in order until, finally, when there were no further developments, dropping well back in the newscast. (By midnight, the story was not even included in the hourly newscast.)

You noticed how the approach and treatment varied, from a straightforward reader, to a lead-in and a spot, to a lead-in with an actuality, sometimes with a tag, sometimes without.

Of course, CBS News is a large organization of many experienced, talented people. This may not be the case in the places you first find work. But your job in updating the news will be the same no matter where you are, even if you have to do it all by yourself.

LOCALIZING

If you received the following wire service story in your newsroom, how would you lead *your* radio version of it?

A246

R W BYLUIVVYX A0575

AM-CONGRESSIONAL DISTRICTS, 550

CENSUS BUREAU DETAILS MAKEUP OF CONGR

ESSIONAL DISTRICTS

BY RANDOLPH E. SCHMID

ASSOCIATED PRESS WRITER

WASHINGTON (AP)—THE NATION'S RICHEST AND MOST WELL-EDUCATED CONGRESSIONAL DISTRICT IS MARYLAND'S 8TH IN SUBURBAN WASHINGTON.

THE POOREST, BASED ON PER FAMILY INCOME, IS NEW YORK'S 18TH, THE SOUTH BRONX.

THE DISTRICTS WITH THE MOST FAMILIES WITH CHILDREN? ALSO THE SOUTH BRONX, FOLLOWED CLOSELY BY UTAH'S 3RD DISTRICT.

THOSE WITH THE MOST UNEMPLOYMENT ARE IN MICHIGAN; THOSE WITH THE LEAST UNEMPLOYMENT ARE IN TEXAS. DISTRICTS WITH THE OLDEST POPULATION ARE IN FLORIDA; THOSE WITH THE YOUNGEST ARE IN UTAH.

THOSE FACTS AND MORE ARE PACKED INTO A NEW CENSUS BUREAU STUDY, WHICH ALSO REVEALS THAT DESPITE REDISTRICTING AFTER THE 1980 CENSUS, THE POPULATIONS OF THE NATION'S 435 CONGRESSIONAL DISTRICTS STILL VARY WIDELY.

THE GOVERNMENT REPORT SAYS THE LEAST POPULOUS CONGRESSIONAL DISTRICT HAS ONLY 55 PERCENT AS MANY PEOPLE AS THE MOST HEAVILY POPULATED ONE.

SOUTH DAKOTA, WHICH LOST ONE OF ITS SEATS IN THE HOUSE OF REPRESENTATIVES AFTER THE NATIONAL HEAD COUNT, BECAME THE NATION'S LARGEST SINGLE DISTRICT WITH 690,768 PEOPLE, THE STUDY SAID.

THE LEAST CROWDED DISTRICT IS THE 2ND DISTRICT OF MONTANA WITH 376,619 PEOPLE, THE REPORT ADDED.

THIS DISPARITY NOTWITHSTANDING, THE BUREAU'S REPORT NOTED THAT WITHIN STATES, DISTRICT POPULATIONS ARE NEARLY EQUAL.

THE STUDY WAS BASED ON A SERIES OF STATE-BY-STATE REPORTS OF CONGRESSIONAL DISTRICTS ISSUED OVER THE PAST SEVERAL MONTHS.

OUT OF 435 SEATS IN THE HOUSE OF REPRESENTATIVES, 411 WERE WITHIN 1 PERCENT OF THE AVERAGE DISTRICT POPULATION FOR THEIR STATE AND 15 VARIED BY LESS THAN 5 PERCENT, THE STUDY SAID. THE REMAINING SIX WERE STATES WITH ONLY ONE SEAT.

THE SHARP VARIATION BETWEEN STATES IS CAUSED BY THE REQUIREMENT THAT CONGRESSIONAL DISTRICTS BE ENTIRELY WITHIN ONE STATE, AND THE LIMIT OF 435 SEATS. THUS, WHEN THE LIMITED NUMBER OF SEATS ARE DIVIDED AMONG THE STATES, SOUTH DAKOTA QUALIFIES FOR ONLY ONE, WITH 690,768 PEOPLE.

MONTANA'S POPULATION OF 786,690 GIVES IT TWO SEATS, BUT BOTH THOSE DISTRICTS BECOME RELATIVELY SMALL AT 410,071 AND 376,619 PEOPLE.

NATIONWIDE, THE AVERAGE POPULATION OF A HOUSE SEAT IS 519,328 PEOPLE, THE STUDY SAID.

THE SUN BELT'S RAPID GROWTH WAS REFLECTED IN ITS HOUSE SEATS, WITH THE FASTEST GROWING DISTRICTS BETWEEN 1970 AND 1980 BEING THOSE IN PALM BEACH, FLA., HOUSTON, TEXAS AND CARLSBAD, CALIF.

FLORIDA'S 18TH DISTRICT IN MIAMI AND MIAMI BEACH IS THE ONLY ONE IN THE NATION WHERE THE MAJORITY OF RESIDENTS ARE FOREIGN-BORN, BUT CALIFORNIA'S 24TH AND 25TH DISTRICTS ARE CLOSE BEHIND AT OVER 40 PERCENT. THE TWO CALIFORNIA DISTRICTS ARE IN HOLLYWOOD, THE SAN FERNANDO VALLEY AND CENTRAL AND EAST LOS ANGELES.

BLACKS MAKE UP THE MAJORITY IN 15 DISTRICTS AND HISPANICS WERE A MAJORITY IN NINE, THE REPORT SAID.

FLORIDA'S 13TH (SARASOTA-FORT MYERS), 8TH (WEST ST. PETERSBURG) AND

18TH (MIAMI AND MIAMI BEACH) HAD THE HIGHEST MEDIAN AGE, WHILE THE YOUNGEST WERE IN UTAH'S 1ST (OGDEN) AND 3RD (PROVO) DISTRICTS.

MARYLAND'S 8TH DISTRICT IN AFFLUENT MONTGOMERY COUNTY, A SUBURB OF THE NATION'S CAPITAL, HAS THE NATIONS'S HIGHEST SHARE OF COLLEGE GRADUATES AMONG CONGRESSIONAL DISTRICTS. THAT IS 43 PERCENT OF PEOPLE AGED 25 AND OLDER.

THAT SAME DISTRICT HAD THE HIGHEST MEDIAN INCOME IN THE NATION AT $33,404 PER FAMILY. THE LOWEST WAS NEW YORK'S 18TH DISTRICT WITH $8,448 PER FAMILY.

NEW YORK'S 18TH DISTRICT IN THE SOUTH BRONX ALSO HAD THE HIGHEST SHARE OF FAMILIES WITH CHILDREN AT 67 PERCENT, JUST AHEAD OF UTAH'S 3RD DISTRICT WHICH HAD 66.4 PERCENT.

UNEMPLOYMENT RATES WERE LISTED AS HIGHEST IN MICHIGAN'S 1ST AND 13TH DISTRICTS, BOTH IN DETROIT, AND LOWEST IN TEXAS'S 3RD (NORTH DALLAS), 7TH (WESTERN HOUSTON) AND 26TH (SUBURBAN FORT WORTH) DISTRICTS.

AP-NY-10-30 1851EST

The answer, as you no doubt have guessed, is that your handling of the story depends on where your local station is located, which means that the lead will be different in each locality. There are more than a dozen locations (in this case, congressional districts) named in the AP story, which was written for national (i.e., network) consumption. But local audiences are more interested in local events, and it is the job of local newsmen to pull local elements out of national stories and give them more prominence.

This is called "localizing" the news, and it should be done with *every story*, not necessarily in the lead, but definitely somewhere in the local rewrite.

For example, a plane crash in a distant city might be rewritten this way:

A _____(your city)_____ man was among 17 people who died today in a plane crash in New Jersey. . .

You would then go on to tell the "local man's" name, age, and address. Furthermore, you would attempt to contact the victim's relatives or business associates via recording phone for biographical material and so on. (If you are squeamish about making such calls—and many people are—you should be aware that contacting bereaved friends and relatives is a routine part of the news business. Naturally, one must be tactful and sensitive in the process.)

Not every story can be localized; local newsmen should not invent local angles where none exists. However, it's a rare story out of Washington or a state capital that doesn't have ramifications, or at least reaction, on the local level. Local newsmen should constantly be asking, "What is the effect of this story on people in my listening area?"

If the defense budget is cut, do any of the cuts affect local defense contractors and their employees? If the president or the governor proposes a highway reconstruction bill, would local roads and traffic patterns be affected? How do local elected officials feel about it? What are their reactions and counterproposals? If the Supreme Court rules on abortion, what are the reactions of local pro- and antiabortion groups? And what are their next moves?

The examples are endless. And so must be your efforts to find local angles. You are broadcasting to neighbors and fellow residents who have an immediate interest in such things. You are also competing with newspapers and other local stations. You can bet that the competition won't be sitting back waiting for local angles to drop into their laps. They'll be out there digging for them.

TEASERS

A "teaser" is a sentence or phrase designed to whet a listener's appetite for a story and make him or her stay tuned a while to hear it, usually through a commercial. For example, our model newscast might use a teaser just before the commercial, then tell the story itself as the first item following the commercial: "The latest on the Middle East . . . right after this . . ."

There are two types of teasers. The first amounts to a one-sentence "headline" containing the crux of the story:

The president says "no" to a tax increase. Details in a moment. . .

The second type "hooks" the listener *without* telling the crux of the story:

The president wrestles with taxes. The winner after this time out. . .

The choice of which type of teaser to use is, I believe, a matter of journalistic ethics. The first type, by telling the main point of a story and trusting interested listeners to stay tuned, backs up a news department's claim to be accurate and to be first in telling the news. The second type, while undoubtedly more inventive, says, in effect, "Hey, we've got the news, but we're not going to share it with you just yet." The second type promotes an image of the news as entertainment.

Although some local news departments have firm policies on which type of teaser to use, most do not, leaving the choice up to the individual newswriter/newscaster. So in the end it's a matter of which type of image a newsman wants to project of *himself*.

KICKERS

By its very nature, any newscast is overwhelmingly devoted to stories involving serious issues. Seldom is there any time for lighter human interest stories, except at the very end of a newscast or just before the local sports and weather. Such a lighter item is known in broadcasting as a "kicker."

Kickers are important psychologically—a way of saying to the listener that the world is not coming to an immediate end despite the bleak picture painted by the news stories he's heard so far. And for the newswriter/newscaster, writing kickers is a sort of release from the tension of writing sober, issue-oriented copy all day.

There are no firm rules on which stories make good kickers. However, there are a few rules on what *not* to use:

1. Kickers should never treat serious issues lightly.
2. Kickers should never make fun of people or beliefs.
3. Kickers should never be cruel to people, animals, or religious institutions.

In short, kickers should be in good taste. While most are funny, they need only provide a pleasant contrast to the serious news that precedes them. They're the newscaster's way of saying, "Things aren't quite as desperate as I've just made out."

Here are a couple of nice ones, by George Engle of ABC Radio, which illustrate the proper tone and approach:

Eight million dollars is a lot of overtime -- but that's how much doctors at three university clinics in West Germany collected last year. Officials decided they'd look into the matter, and they found an easy explanation: The doctors were cheating. It wasn't hard to figure it out. They put in for extra pay for working on special days -- February Thirtieth. . .June Thirty-first -- days the calendar doesn't even acknowledge are there.

-0-

A new weapon in the age-old battle between man and mosquito: Two scientists in New Delhi say garlic does the trick. They've discovered garlic not only helps stimulate the human system and fight bacteria -- a little spray of garlic oil also kills the mosquito. However, at the dosage they're recommending, it could kill your social life as well.

As in writing transitions, it is best not to reach too far in writing kickers. Nothing falls flatter than an unfunny joke. Kickers should be attempted only when they strike the writer's fancy by suggesting themselves on first reading. A potential kicker that has to be studied closely probably isn't going to work.

STOCK REPORTS

Also written as "stox"—referring to the stock market.

Financial, or Wall Street, news is a standard part of many afternoon newscasts. The information moves hourly on the radio wires. Unless the news department specifies otherwise, stock reports in regular newscasts should be kept very short. The story should be limited to the latest Dow Jones *industrial average* (not other averages), whether trading has been "light," "moderate," or "heavy," and, time permitting, the price of gold in New York. Here's an example:

> On Wall Street at this hour, the Dow-Jones industrial average is UP
>
> one-point-eight-two, in moderate trading.

(Mitchell Krauss, CBS Radio)

Short and sweet. Further details should be left for longer newscasts scheduled in PM Drive.

SPORTS

For reasons which I've never been able to learn precisely, broadcast sportswriting is the most overblown, cliché-ridden prose to be found anywhere. I lost track long ago of how many times I've heard such clunkers as "He really came to play" or "He's some kind of player." Apparently, many sports broadcasters do not realize that such clichés tell us *nothing* and that they are a vacuous substitute for real description.

The same goes for sports interviewing, which frequently doesn't rise above the level of "Hey, Coach, are ya gonna win next Saturday?" Just once I'd like to hear the coach answer "Naw, we haven't got a prayer."

There is some good sportswriting to be heard on network broadcasting—notably by Ray Gandolf and Dick Schaap at ABC and Brent Musburger at CBS—but by and large the territory is a vast wasteland of substandard prose.

Nevertheless, sports occupies a large niche in the American psyche, and sports reportage does have a place in local radio newscasts. But that place is strictly limited to *major* developments, such as the signing of a new coach or star player, and to the scores of games involving local teams. In this, a certain amount of home-team boosterism is permissible:

> Bad news last night for the Redbirds -- They lost to Atlanta, 6 to 4.

When giving the scores, newswriters/newscasters should *avoid* cliché verbs such as "trounced," "walloped," "slammed," "nipped," and so on. In most cases, the scores speak for themselves. The simple verbs *won, lost, beat* and so on, are sufficient. Unusual or dramatic circumstances in the game should be incorporated into a clear sentence:

In sports, Atlanta beat the Redbirds six-four last night on a ninth-inning homer by Dale Murphy.

Keep it simple to avoid being trite.

WEATHER

Like sports and the stock market, the local weather forecast moves over the radio wires. And like sports and the stock market, the weather should be kept *short:* just the forecast and the hourly readings.

With weather, as with sports, there is an unfortunate tendency in broadcasting to grab the nearest cliché:

Better get out those umbrellas -- the weatherman says it'll rain tonight. . .

Please resist this temptation. Most of your listeners are wise enough to realize that if rain is forecast, they should probably bring along an umbrella. They don't need you to offer childish advice. And *who* is "the weatherman"? Is he related to the Sandman? Leave the silliness to the disk jockey. As for you, just keep it short and to the point:

The weather forecast: Possible rain tonight, with a low around 50. Clearing by morning, with a high tomorrow around 70.

Because the weather is "typically" the closing item in a newscast, it is well to write it in such a way that it can be shortened or lengthened at a glance from the newscaster. That's because, while it's easy to begin a newscast on time, it's tricky to end it on time. A certain amount of flexibility is needed to enable the newscaster to "stretch" or "get off."

Therefore, the weather should be written (on a separate page, of course) something like this:

The weather forecast calls for possible rain tonight, with a low around 50.

Clearing by morning, with a high tomorrow around 70. (Turning colder by

Thursday, and more rain expected by the weekend.)

At _____ o'clock, the airport temperature was _____.

The humidity was _____ per cent.

And the wind was _____ at _____ miles per hour.

The blanks are filled in with the latest readings just before air time, and the material in parenthesis, as well as the hourly readings, may be read or deleted as time warrants. Many news departments have standardized format sheets for the weather; the blanks need only be penciled in on the way to the announce booth.

PAD AND PROTECTION

Situation: You are on the air, delivering the hourly newscast. You read the lead-in to a 45-second spot and cue the engineer (or hit the Start button yourself). Nothing happens. Silence. The cart is broken and doesn't play. What do you do? (multiple choice)

a. Scream for help
b. Start whistling "You Are My Sunshine"
c. Tip-toe out of the studio and lock yourself in the washroom
d. Fill your remaining time on the air with a detailed technical explanation to the audience of how carts are made and supposed to work
e. None of the above

Yes, fans, choice "e" was the correct one. Since you were a professional radio newswriter/newscaster, you went into the announce booth *prepared* for something to go wrong. What you did was to bring along *at least 60 seconds too much copy.* These were stories you wrote at the beginning of your shift—good stories that you weren't quite sure would get on the air. You also brought a scripted version of the story that would have played on that defective cartridge. You were prepared with all that backup material because, from bitter experience, you have come to believe in "Murphy's law," which states: "Anything that *can* go wrong *will* go wrong."

Good old Murphy. He must have worked in broadcasting. Your station has spent untold tens of thousands of dollars on equipment, yet can't get you on and off smoothly because of a 14-cent wire spring in a cartridge. So it goes.

In broadcasting, the scripted version you brought along for the taped story is called "protection." The 60 seconds of extra stories you brought along are called "pad," because you needed the copy to pad the newscast, to make up the air time you lost when the cart malfunctioned.

Believe me, you only need to get caught once without pad and/or protection, and you will make it your business never to let it happen again.

SPECIAL WRITING PROBLEMS

Unclear Stories

You'll recall that I advised never to write or go on the air with a story you don't understand. That was advice for the ideal world. In the real world, however, you might have to do it once in a blue moon. So here's what to do: attribute the story to the news agency that sent it to you, and read it *word for word* in the news agency's language. It may sound stilted, and it may be wrong, but at least you and your news department are temporarily off the hook.

Teamwork

Often there will be a conflict in factual accounts of a story. One source, a wire service, will say one thing, and another source, your reporter, will say something else. In such cases, it is common practice to trust your own reporter and go with his or her version. It may prove to be wrong, but a news department works as a team, and you should let your own team members run with the ball.

Giving Credit

No journalist likes to be beaten on a story. But it happens. Sometimes the competition, whether newspapers, television or other radio stations, will out-hustle you on a story. When this occurs, it is best to remember the Golden Rule: Do unto others. . . . You should credit your competitor by name:

The New York Times reports this morning that. . .

-0-

Newsweek magazine quotes administration sources as saying. . .

-0-

Channel Nine reports the mayor will. . .

-0-

The mayor told W-W-K-K Radio in an interview that. . .

At the same time, however, you and your news department should be hustling to get your own angle on the story. And once you do, you no longer need to credit anyone else. The story is now yours and may be reported as such.

SPECIAL TECHNICAL MATTERS

Scripts

Broadcast scripts are never stapled or clipped together until *after* they've been aired. The pages must be kept loose. That's to permit the newscaster to slide the pages noiselessly as they are read on the air. It also permits him or her to drop or rearrange pages at will either before or during a newscast.

Slug and Time Placement

There is a practical reason for insisting that slugs and times be written in the *extreme* upper edge of a page. A newscast script is customarily held in one hand, slightly fanned vertically. This permits the newscaster to see at a glance, without fumbling pages, which stories remain and how long each runs, in order to get off the air on time.

Backtiming

Okay, you've written a terrific kicker. It runs :20. You want to end the newscast with it, just before sign-off. How do you *ensure* you will begin reading it on time, in order to get off the air on time?

By "backtiming" it. You *subtract* the time of your kicker from the time you must be off the air (00:05:00):

$$:05:00$$

$$-\quad\ :20$$

$$=\ :04:40$$

You write and circle the notation

BY :04:40

in the upper right corner of the copy page. This reminds you at a glance of the latest time you may begin reading the story and still get off the air on time.

The technique of backtiming may be used for the weather or any other item with which you want to end a newscast. It may seem a bit complicated to you now, but after a few months on the job, you'll be doing double and triple backtiming, just to give yourself a challenge.

"EQUAL TIME" AND THE "FAIRNESS DOCTRINE"

As we've seen, broadcasting in the United States is subject to federal regulation; the "justification" is that, while private industry owns the means of putting programs on the air, the public owns the air waves through which programs are sent.

There are two federal regulations which broadcast news personnel should understand, even though neither one applies to regularly scheduled newscasts. The first is the so-called "equal time" rule established in section 315 of the Federal Communications Act. The rule requires any station that gives or sells air time to one candidate for political office to give or sell equal time, on a like basis, to all other candidates for the same office. Although the regulation is clearly intended to provide equal access to all candidates, broadcasters have fought it up and down the line because in practice it has meant that stations must set aside precious air time for fringe candidates—of, say, the Dipsy Doodle Party—as well as for Republicans and Democrats. In any event, the rule does *not* apply to newscasts and other regularly scheduled news programs, so you do *not* have to keep track of how many minutes and seconds you devote to each candidate.

The second regulation is the so-called "Fairness Doctrine," which requires stations airing controversial viewpoints (say, in editorials or special news broadcasts) to present opposing viewpoints as well. Again, this does *not* apply to regular newscasts. But it does apply to a station's news programming as a whole, insofar as that programming must be fair and balanced. Again, the intent is to prevent abuse by a perhaps biased station owner. The important thing to remember is that if you are doing your job as you should, doing your best to report the news accurately and impartially, you need not concern yourself with the federal regulations. You are a journalist, not a federal watchdog.

(As this book was being published, the FCC, under Reagan-appointed chairman Mark Fowler, was considering whether to rescind or modify the Fairness Doctrine. You should make it your business to keep informed of the results.)

PERFORMING ABILITY

In newscasting, as opposed to field reporting, a high degree of performing ability is required. Since the goal is to communicate the content of the news, the newscaster's voice and speech patterns must not detract from what he or she is saying. That is perhaps a negative way of describing minimum performance skills, but it is more accurate than trying to describe a "good" voice, which is a subjective characterization.

Diction

I have noted elsewhere the necessity to know correct pronunciation. To this I must now add correct *enunciation,* the ability to speak clearly and distinctly—what at one time was called "diction." A newscaster simply cannot afford sloppy diction.

Unfortunately, by the time you are old enough to read this book, you are already at an age when your speech habits have become firmly set. It is only with considerable effort and constant practice that you will henceforth be able to correct any flaws. There is no time to waste. And you will need qualified supervision. That old orator's ploy of rehearsing with a mouthful of gravel doesn't work if you're alone; besides, you might swallow the gravel.

Voice Quality

This is the element of performance that you can do the least about. The human voice goes through a series of changes as one grows to adulthood. The change is more noticeable in men's voices than women's, going from a boyish tenor to an alto, baritone, or bass. In women, the voice remains at a higher pitch altogether, finally settling into a lyric soprano, mezzo soprano, or contralto. By the time you are of an age to read this book, your larynx and resonating chambers will have stopped growing, and your voice quality will remain basically unchanged for the rest of your life. For newscasting, the most "desirable" voice qualities are in the lower two registers, both in men and women. Sorry, you lyrics and altos, but that's the way it is.

Fortunately, the days are long gone when "golden tonsils" or a booming basso profundo were required of anyone who wished to get on the air. Broadcasters, especially news departments, have of late relaxed some of the old strictures, including some of the silly ones. It was long thought, for example, that people would not accept women as newscasters or reporters, since they didn't sound "authoritative" or "in charge." This has, of course, proved to be utter nonsense, with the result that performance standards have altered for men as well as women. Now the overriding prerequisite is the ability to communicate clearly.

Accents

Due in large part to network broadcasting, U.S. regional accents and speech rhythms are not as diverse as they once were. The voices that one hears on radio and TV, in any part of the country, tend to be speaking "standard American."

Nevertheless, many natives of New England, New York, New Jersey, Boston, Chicago, the Mid-South, and the Deep South are immediately recognizable by their accents. There is nothing wrong with accents in news broadcasting—as long as they are moderate and do not call such attention to themselves that they detract from the communication of news content. Thus, accents that are thick and that permeate a person's speech are not acceptable, except at the smallest local station level, where most listeners share the same accent.

The most "desirable" accent is no accent at all, which is clearly impossible, but by which is meant the "standard American" mentioned earlier, a voice whose region cannot be determined. (The comedian George Carlin, in a monologue parodying radio announcers, begins by saying, "Hi, I'm from Nowhere.") Natives of the Upper Middle West and the Pacific Northwest come closest, by birthright, to speaking the "standard American" sought by broadcast executives.

Practice

Most people don't really know what they themselves sound like. They hear their own words in a sort of "re-resonated" fashion, the sounds reaching their auditory senses both from the interior and the exterior. Listeners hear only the exterior sounds—your "real" voice.

So the first step in developing and improving your voice and diction is to discover how you really sound. And for this, you need a good tape recorder, hooked up to a good loudspeaker. Everybody sounds tinny over the minispeaker in a portable cassette recorder.

It is natural to be apprehensive or shy about recording yourself at the start. Fine. The point is to get started. Lock yourself in a room and record yourself reading some broadcast-style news copy (*not* newspaper articles). Listen to the tape. Go over it sentence by sentence. Are you communicating? Are you stressing the right words? Are your inflections natural? Or do you sound forced, unnatural, stagy? Re-record the copy as often as you must until *you yourself* are satisfied.

Then, and only then, should you seek a second opinion. And, because these matters tend to be subjective, a third opinion. And not just *any* opinions. Opinions must come from qualified persons—people who understand vocal structures, habits, and diction, ideally people who also understand news broadcasting.

And, then, having lost your reticence, practice some more. Join the staff of your campus or corporate closed-circuit radio station so that you can begin delivering regular newscasts.

The important thing, if you hope to become a professional (i.e., paid) radio or television newscaster, is to starting working toward it *now*.

14

IS A PICTURE WORTH A THOUSAND WORDS?

PROCEED WITH CAUTION

Because the technical requirements of television news are often baffling to newcomers, I have made every effort to keep things simple and straightforward wherever possible. However, much of the material *cannot* be understood without a thorough familiarity with the material in the first two sections of this book (or other texts on writing and radio news).

Television news is written in virtually the same style as radio news. There are differences here and there, and these will be pointed out. But the same informal language and the same linguistic elements are used in both media.

The structures, too, are basically the same: lead-in/actuality, lead-in/report, and so on. Sometimes different terms are used to describe these structures, but again, in essence, their handling is similar if not identical.

The overall approach to TV news is, of course, quite different from radio. But students who do not understand the components of broadcast style and the handling of broadcast news sources, interviewing techniques, story structure, and so on, will be at a loss in trying to fathom television. There are no shortcuts—either to learning or to a career.

Anchorman/commentator Jim Ruddle prepares to deliver the news headlines from the WMAQ-TV, Chicago, newsroom. Such "mini-newscasts" go by various names—"Newsbreak," "Digest," "Capsule," etc.

If you work in TV news, the answer to the question posed in this chapter's title is almost always a resounding *Yes!*

TV journalists will concede that some words—*mother, country, love*—may, on occasion, be worth a thousand pictures. But they will emphasize that TV news gathering is overwhelmingly the pursuit of the right picture and that TV news presentation is influenced fundamentally by the availability of that picture.

THE RIGHT PICTURES

On a recent Tuesday in early summer, of all the stories of national interest, two stood above the rest: At 1:30 A.M., Eastern Daylight Time, a 100-foot section of the Connecticut Turnpike Bridge, near Greenwich, collapsed. Several cars and trucks plunged into the Mianus River 70 feet below, killing three people.

Some 14 hours later, in midafternoon, the U.S. Senate, by a vote of 50 to 49, defeated Congress's first attempt ever to change the Constitution to allow the 50 states to make their own laws on abortion.

On almost every journalistic basis, print or broadcast, the second story was the more important. No issue had so excited the public interest, was as fiercely debated, as abortion. Only a few days before the Senate vote, the U.S. Supreme Court had affirmed that the Constitution forbade the federal and state governments from banning abortions. The powerful "Right-to-Life" lobby, representing the views of many millions of Americans, had proclaimed that the only remaining alternative was to change the Constitution. The vote in the Senate, which fell 17 votes short of the required two-thirds majority needed for constitutional amendments, was a huge defeat for the antiabortion forces.

The bridge collapse in Connecticut, while especially tragic for the victims, and while indicative perhaps of the unsafe state of many other bridges across the United States, was simply not in the same class. And, by broadcast standards, it was, by early evening, already stale news; it had been on the air since early morning in newscast after newscast and was front-paged in afternoon newspapers. The abortion vote, on the other hand, was fresh and immediate news—a major story with which to lead the evening TV newscasts.

And yet, at 6:30 P.M. Eastern Daylight Time, the first feed of the "CBS Evening News" opened this way:

Good evening . . .

For the want of some pins, the bridge was lost.   That was the speculation today, as authorities investigated the fatal, pre-dawn collapse of a major highway bridge section in Connecticut, outside New York City.   And, officials said, the accident points up a threat that spans the continent.   We have two reports, beginning with Richard Wagner:

Wagner's taped report, narrated over aerial and ground views of the collapse aftermath, explained that several steel "pins" (actually rods 7 inches in diameter and 10 inches long) had apparently come loose, unlinking a center section of the bridge and allowing it to break away. The second report promised in the lead-in was on the wider problem of the precarious condition of bridges all across the United States, some in need of urgent repair at enormous cost, at a time when public funding was virtually nonexistent. In other words, the reporter was implying, there might be another bridge collapse at any time, perhaps far more deadly than the present one.

There followed a 60-second commercial break. *Then* came the abortion story, 6 minutes into the newscast. It was a 40-second reader—no tape.

The issue here is not about the merits of the bridge story. It was clearly important and deserved major coverage. And CBS did a first-rate job, detailing the story clearly and graphically. Even the lead-in shows a love for language (it was probably written by a newswriter; at major markets and networks, anchors seldom write their own copy). The lead sentence is a literary reference to the poet George Herbert ("For want of a nail, . . ."), and the metaphor "threat that *spans* the continent" is a nice touch.

The abortion vote story was also told clearly by CBS. But why did it not lead the newscast? Because *pictures* of a collapsed bridge, especially as taken from a helicopter, are far more spectacular and dramatic than are sketches from the Senate floor, where cameras were not permitted.

It is important to understand that the question here is *not* a matter of a "right" lead or a "wrong" lead. No doubt many "CBS Evening News" staffers would have preferred to lead with the abortion vote; such things are always dicussed, and one side eventually prevails.

No, the question here is the *nature of the medium.* TV news thrives on pictures. It always attempts to tell a story visually. This makes it relatively hard to *show* a story about a senate vote and relatively easy to *show* a story about a bridge collapse. The drama of the visual elements is inherently different.

It is absolutely essential to understand the primacy of the picture in television news—because it pervades not just what viewers see, but also what they don't see: how the news is covered.

THE RIGHT COVERAGE

Situation: An early spring thaw, coupled with heavy rainfall, causes severe flooding in a Midwestern state. Whole communities are cut off by road and rail. Telephone and electric lines are down. You are a TV reporter, and you and a cameraman are assigned to cover the flood. The only way into the area is by helicopter. The only helicopter available is a two-seater, one seat for the pilot. If you're a print or radio reporter, in you climb. But in TV, that single passenger seat is for your cameraman. You yourself, temporarily grounded, may have to rely on secondary sources in writing your narration.

That situation is not hypothetical. It happens repeatedly in TV news gathering, where the rule is *the camera comes first.* Not only is the camera first in, *it is also first out.* What good are the pictures if they don't arrive at a place where they can be edited and transmitted?

Television correspondents are thus required to be far more than mere reporters. They must also be on-the-scene producers, directors, and logisticians. They must know how to get *to* the story, how to shoot it, how to write it, and how to get it back to a transmission point.

Television newswriters, too, face a bigger challenge than their print or radio counterparts. For them, too, the picture is paramount. Their copy must tell the correct news, but it must be worded in such a way as to make use of whatever pictures are available. As in radio with the use of actualities, the available pictures in television are not always the ones the writers would ideally have chosen. They must make do with what *is* available and tailor their copy accordingly.

Television news is thus the medium where a journalist is most apt to forget why he or she is there in the first place, which, as stated repeatedly in this book, is to tell the news as clearly and accurately as possible. In TV, matters can get so complicated in the effort to *show* the news, as well as tell it, that TV journalists can find themselves playing with machines instead of language—to the detriment of the latter. So TV journalists must pause from time to time to remind themselves that they are in charge, not the machines.

This self-appraisal becomes ever more necessary because of the inexorable march of technology. Modern TV news is a so-called "high-tech" industry, and, as in other such industries, there is a tendency to use technology just because it exists. This was the case, for example, when live minicam transmission was introduced. To remain competitive, local stations acquired the necessary gear at great expense. Suddenly, reporters and camera crews found themselves going live at the slightest excuse, whether or not such coverage was justified journalistically, because stations had to prove to viewers that they were keeping up with the latest technology. The networks, too, although generally more concerned with journalistic content than local stations, are constantly experimenting with technical advances in electronic graphics to enhance the "look" of their newscasts.

Much as TV journalists may rail against such electronic razzmatazz, they must accept it as normal in a commercial, profit-oriented enterprise where the ultimate goal of ownership and management is to increase viewership and thus increase advertising revenues. As a purely practical matter, TV journalists must understand the capabilities of the hardware to make it work *for* them instead of against them.

THE RIGHT STUFF

The "right stuff," the term used by author Tom Wolfe to describe the attributes of American astronauts and test pilots, can be applied to the men and women who make TV news a career. In print and in radio, the journalist essentially works alone, whether writing or reporting; other people are present at various stages, but the final product, a story, is essentially the work of a single person. Not so in television. TV news is a group, or "team," endeavor. Each member of the team contributes to what is finally seen on the air. A reportorial effort is actually the combined work of an assignment editor, a reporter, a cameraman, a producer, and a tape editor, with, at the larger news departments, the efforts as well of a field producer, a writer, a sound technician, and an assistant producer—not to mention the studio crew of camera operators, floor director, teleprompter operator, and the control room crew of director, switcher, audio technician, assistant director—*and* station staffers such as graphic artists and electronic titling operators. Believe me, that is a *crowd*. The staff required to put together a newscast in television outnumbers a radio staff by about ten to one. The capital investment in equipment is higher by an even greater proportion. In many respects, a TV newscast resembles the classic definition of a camel: "a horse designed by a committee."

So having the "right stuff" in television involves being able to work smoothly with other people. This is not just some inspirational slogan from Boy Scout or Girl Scout camp. It is real. *Nobody* in television works alone. The iconoclast, the curmudgeon, the churl, can function quite safely, if insecurely, in print and in radio. But, in television, his professional life may be short, unhappy, or both. An even disposition and a high boiling point are important qualities in TV news personnel.

So is stamina. The working hours in most forms of journalism are long, sometimes grueling. But nowhere are they longer than in television.

Reporters in print and radio can gather stories by telephone. TV reporters must go to the scene. Thus, to the time spent in purely journalistic functions such as researching, covering, and writing a story must be added the traveling time to and fro, the editing time, and the time to protect any breaking angles for late-night or next-morning telecasts. It is routine for TV reporters and cameramen to work 12, 14, or even 16 hours a day, frequently without enough time off in-between to sit down and eat a proper meal.

Anchors and producers, too, often work long hours, especially during coverage of major breaking stories. In TV, there always seems to be a "crisis" of one kind or another. Indeed, it was said of Walter Cronkite, because of his ability to remain alert and calm for long stretches, that he had "iron pants."

In mentioning all these matters, it is not my intention to discourage you from choosing a career in TV news. On the contrary, by painting a realistic portrait of what occurs behind the calm façade of what the public sees, I'm trying to give you a balanced foundation on which to make your own decision.

You see, the wonder of TV news, with so many cards stacked against it, is that most of the time it works so well.

JOB TITLES AND DUTIES

Recent years have seen a virtual explosion in TV news programming in the United States. In 1960, the typical network or local newscast, including sports and weather, ran 15 minutes, once or twice a day. Nowadays, a network may broadcast 4 or 5 hours of news daily. Some local stations in major cities broadcast 3 or 4 hours daily of local news and news-features. And on cable, Cable News Network programs not one but *two* 24-hour all news services. In many markets, news is the *only* programming produced at the local level.

There are some 850 commercial VHF and UHF television stations in the United States. When you add in cable, non-commercial, and CATV (community) television broadcasting, you wind up with an almost indescribable array of news and news-feature formats. News departments come in all shapes and sizes—from a dozen overworked, underpaid staffers to an army several hundred strong. Job titles and duties vary widely, not only from market to market but also within each market. Small markets, as well as many medium markets, demand many abilities in news department personnel—the abilities to report, write, shoot and edit tape, and to produce and anchor newscasts. In larger markets, the work grows more specialized. For example, the category of "newswriter," someone who does nothing but write copy and oversee the editing of tape and the preparation of graphics and titles, generally does not exist until the level of major markets or networks. Thus, the following breakdown of job titles and duties describes specialized roles that in actual practice may be interwoven or combined according to the practice of individual stations.

News Director

As in radio, the news director is the boss, running the news department and accepting responsibility for the work of its members. However, given the higher financial stakes in television, the news director usually does not have the final say on whom the station hires as principal news, weather, and sports anchors; the last word on that usually goes to the station's general manager. The news director does hire—and fire—everyone else, as well as draw up the budget.

Assistant News Director

Generally speaking, this position does not exist at the small market level. It may not exist even in larger markets. Wherever it does exist, however, it usually entails the assumption of duties such as setting work schedules, sorting through job applications, inventorying supplies and equipment—in short, many of the bureaucratic duties that can take a news director's mind off daily news coverage.

Executive Producer

Again, found only at larger stations in larger markets and at networks. Where he or she exists, the executive producer assumes many of the day-to-day responsibilities of the news director, especially regarding daily news coverage and "news specials," which are programs on events such as election returns, important news developments, interviews of VIPs, and so on.

Producer

The boss of any given newscast. The producer decides which stories will be included, in what order, how long they will run, how they will be handled, and by whom. The producer directs specific coverage by reporters and cameramen, decides what graphics will be used, proofreads writers' and reporters' copy, and is present in the control room during the telecast to handle any last-minute changes.

Assistant Producer

Found only at large news departments. As the name implies, assistant (or associate) producers help producers in all the functions just listed, except for being present in the control room, where too many cooks can spoil the broth.

Assignment Editor

Also known as "assignment manager," the logistical linchpin of the news department. The assignment editor keeps track of all scheduled and breaking news events, dispatching reporters and cameramen to cover as many of them as possible. Since there is almost always more happening than it is possible to cover, the assignment editor plays a precarious guessing game, warily budgeting out the available staff at this location or that, hoping that the big news won't occur at precisely those locations that he or she has neglected.

To be able to estimate travel time to and from story locations by reporters and crews at far-flung locations in the field, assignment editors must know intimately the geography of the station's coverage area as well as its traffic patterns; the flight schedules at local airports; the locations of all hospitals, fire stations, and police stations, the city morgue, and federal, state, and city buildings; and so on.

The assignment desk is truly the hub of the news department—the scene of all action, both outgoing and incoming.

The assignment desk at WMAQ-TV, Chicago, is equipped with fire and police radios tuned to scan different frequencies, WATS telephone lines, an internal paging system, an electronic paging system to contact employees in the field, a two-way radio transmitter, local maps and street guides, and complete airline and ground transportation schedules. The lower bank of monitors are tuned to competing stations, and the upper bank of monitors to the station's minicam units.

Reporter

The foot soldier of the news department. At large news departments, some reporters have specific beats, such as city hall or consumer affairs. But most TV reporters are general assignment (G-A) reporters who are relied on to cover the day's breaking events.

Reporters receive their assignments through the assignment desk, then, unless it's a major breaking story, research the story by telephone, set up interviews, and assess possible shooting locations. They then proceed with cameramen to those various locations to piece the elements of a story together, both informationally (content) and visually (form). (At small stations, reporters serve as their own cameramen, shooting the tape themselves.)

After the story is shot, the reporter writes a narration either in the field (called "the street"; hence, the term "street reporter") or back at the station, records it, perhaps writes a lead-in to his or her own report, then prepares for the next assignment. All producers and news directors prize reporters who are "self-starters," who come up with their own story ideas.

A reporter's workday is open ended.

Cameraman

In some places known as photographer. Another foot soldier, but armed with heavier firepower—the camera (and usually the recorder, too; only at major markets and networks are there two-person camera crews).

The cameraman is responsible for getting the right story in the technical sense, that is, that the videotape is properly framed and exposed to *show* the story. In the field, the reporter tells the cameraman what he or she wants, and the cameraman decides if it's technically possible. In other words, although the two work together, the reporter controls content, the cameraman form.

In terms of sheer physical exertion, the cameraman is the hardest-worked member of the news department. Because of the cost of equipment, there are almost always fewer cameras and cameramen than reporters. Thus, reporters share cameramen and must plan story coverage (along with the assignment editor) with this in mind.

Anchor

The key job in a TV news department, and about which there is much controversy. Since the viewing public recognizes a station's anchormen and women as that station's "news spokesmen," an enormous (and perhaps unfair) share of the news department's burden rests on their shoulders. Journalistically speaking, an anchor's duties are to read (and perhaps write much of) the newscast and to host special events coverage. Therefore, an anchorman or woman is often one of the most experienced and talented broadcasters in the news department, having come up through the ranks of writing and reporting. At the three major networks, this is usually true.

At local stations, alas, this is less often the case. The commercial system of broadcasting in the United States dictates that stations compete for audiences to sell to advertisers in order to ensure or increase profits. And that means, as a practical matter, that many, many stations will choose anchors who may lack credentials in journalism but who through looks, style, and/or cosmetics can attract and hold audiences.

That said, I am pleased to report that according to people whose business it is to deal with local news departments all around the country, there appears to be a trend toward choosing local anchors who have solid journalistic know-how. Note, however, that considerable performing ability is required, regardless of credentials. Anchors must possess a rare ability to communicate clearly with a mass audience through a camera lens—which is no small feat. Thus, anchors are paid accordingly. They are almost invariably the highest-paid members of the news department, with salaries in some of the top markets exceeding half a million dollars a year.

Weekend Anchor

A position whose importance varies with the size of the market. At many small markets, the position doesn't even exist because anchors there often work six-day weeks. But at major markets, the weekend anchor slot is customarily reserved for people who are being "groomed" to become full-time anchors or for reporters on a rotating basis. In major markets, the weekend anchor job usually pays more than the prime anchor job in medium markets.

Weekend anchors also work as street reporters at least three days a week.

Writer

Writers, where they exist as a distinct category, are the backbone of the newsroom. Under the producer's guidance, writers script all stories not self-contained in reporters' pieces (known as "packages"), choosing the specific graphic elements to illustrate their copy. They also view and do rundowns on all video-tape, choosing actualities (known as "sound bites" in TV) and scenes over which to write narration for the anchors. They also write the lead-ins to reporters' packages.

Writers keep track of exact timings as well as identifications of all people and places appearing in the soon-to-be-aired tape, to assure that the correct electronic titles are inserted into the finished product at the right time.

As do reporters and producers, writers must know the technical capabilities of the station's equipment in order to tailor their copy for maximum use of available visual elements.

Producers and other news department executives are often promoted from the ranks of writers.

Tape Editor

The videotape editor is responsible for the finished form of taped material. A cameraman may try the same shot several times (each shot known as a "take"). The tape editor chooses what he or she deems to be the best take.

A VTR editor must not only know how to operate sophisticated equipment, he or she should also understand cinematic techniques which make one image (or "scene") flow into another. There can be great art in this, and in Hollywood they give Oscars for it.

The following positions exist only at networks and major market stations:

Field Producer

A sort of advance man for a reporter and camera crew. Many stories require much preparation over a period of days or weeks. Reporters assigned to such stories may be tied up elsewhere and thus temporarily unavailable. In steps the field producer to scout locations, set up interviews (and perhaps tape them as well), and do preliminary research and writing. In some cases, a field producer may do an entire package, including writing the narration, which will then be voiced by a reporter.

Unit Producer

Just as a reporter may be assigned to a specific beat, so may a producer. Together they investigate and prepare stories in their area of competence. Typical beats utilizing unit producers are Health and Medicine, Consumer Affairs, Entertainment, and the Investigative Unit.

Researcher

An entry-level job for newcomers who don't wish to try to work their way up from smaller markets. Most of the researcher's work is drudgery: the inevitable securing or checking of statistics, legal documents, historical records, telephone canvassing, and so on. The work can be interesting if a major investigation is in progress, but mostly it involves trips to the municipal archives, the public library, the station's tape library, and a host of other sunless places. On occasion, it may lead to a job as a writer—but not as a reporter.

Sound Technician

A holdover term from the days when TV news was shot on film instead of videotape. In most major markets and at networks, the VTR camera crew is composed of two members: one who runs the camera and one who carries the recorder and monitors the sound. In small and medium markets, all the gear is carried and operated by a single person—perhaps by the reporter.

Desk Assistant

Same as in radio, with the added "responsibility" of tearing down newscast scripts and delivering them to the right people. A nowhere job with nowhere to go; for observation purposes only.

In addition to all these positions, TV newspeople also deal on a daily basis with a host of studio and station personnel—including directors, studio camera operators, audio engineers, floor directors (TDs), teleprompter operators, graphic artists, electronic titling operators, stagehands—all of whom contribute to getting the news on and off the air in the way the producer desires.

CRAFT UNIONS

Bear in mind that at many news departments, especially in small and medium markets, many of the job functions described above blend or overlap. In a small news department, for example, one person may serve as assignment editor in the morning, then produce the early evening newscast. The news director may also be the principal anchor. A reporter may double as cameraman, triple as tape editor, and quadruple as writer.

At networks and major markets, on the other hand, job duties are strictly delimited, usually by union contracts. For example, editorial personnel such as writers, reporters, and producers are not allowed to operate (or even touch) any of the equipment. Conversely, technical personnel are not allowed to exercise editorial functions. And only members of the performers' union are allowed to appear on camera. Frankly, it can all get unnecessarily complicated (if not downright silly), but that's the way it is.

Here is a list of major craft unions representing workers in broadcast news:

American Federation of Television and Radio Artists (AFTRA)—represents all performers in both news and entertainment. Membership is compulsory, except in states (chiefly in the South and Southeast) that forbid the closed shop.
Writers Guild of America (WGA)—represents news-, continuity- and screenwriters.

National Association of Broadcast Engineers and Technicians (NABET)—represents some writers, but mostly technical personnel such as cameramen, tape editors, and studio equipment operators.

International Brotherhood of Electrical Workers (IBEW)—represents same as above, depending on station and market.

News directors and executive producers are considered part of management.

If your interest is to learn TV news from the ground up, to experiment by "doing it all," you must begin at a nonunion shop. Union regulations make occupational experimentation impossible in most big cities.

15
PICTURE AND SCRIPT COMPONENTS

NEWSCAST STRUCTURE

The planning and "layout" of a TV newscast have more in common with newspaper practice than with radio. Radio is predominantly packaged in short takes, with time only for the hard news. TV, while putting the hard news at the top, has more time not only for news, but also for features, sports, weather, and editorial comment. A TV newscast is thus roughly similar in overall presentation to an edition of a newspaper, and although the hard news portions may undergo frequent revision before air time, the so-called "back-of-the-book" material is set well in advance.

Almost everywhere in the United States, TV news is programmed in 30-minute or 60-minute newscasts. This is true at all levels—local, network, and all news cable—no matter the size of the market or the total amount of news programming on a single station.

For example, a local station in Los Angeles may program 3 hours of early local news from 4 P.M. to 7 P.M. But each hour is planned and prepared as a separate newscast with different anchors, producers, writers, and feature content. Stories from reporters and other sources are repackaged and rewritten for each 60-minute newscast.

The network morning shows—"Today," "Good Morning America," and "The CBS Morning News"—although running 2 or 3 hours depending on time zone, are also packaged as 30-minute blocks. And Cable News Network programs its primary service, CNN-1, in 60-minute blocks, while its "headline" service, CNN-2, is prepared and presented in 30-minute blocks.

No matter the news organization or level, the staff of a TV newscast sits down well ahead of time, as much as 8 hours before air, to plan the show. (Yes, "show" is the right word.) The news director, executive producer, producer, associate producer, assignment editor, and perhaps a technical supervisor discuss the day's coverage: what fresh stories are scheduled, what stories to follow up from the day and night before, which reporters will be assigned, special technical matters involved in coverage (such as a need for extra personnel or equipment), and so on.

Many of these same people will meet again later to assess revisions in the show necessitated by breaking news events. At this time, a "lineup" of the show is prepared, listing specific stories and the order in which they will be presented. The "lineup," which henceforth is in the hands of the show's producer, will undergo a number of changes, right up to and during air time, as the results of reporters' and camera crews' efforts are received, viewed, and assessed. Decisions at this point come thick and fast, frequently without time for rational, considered discussion. If you visit a TV newsroom (and I emphatically advise such a visit), the hour or two before air time is not a time to ask questions or to interfere, but rather to stand aside and watch the action. Conditions appear to be chaotic—and sometimes they are. The amazing thing is how, out of the chaos, is created an orderly account of the day's news.

As in radio, TV news formats come in a bewildering variety. But, again, one day's viewing in any part of the country suffices to typify the weekday output of a local commercial station as 30 or 60 minutes of early news (at the dinner hour), followed by 30 minutes of late evening news (at 10 P.M. or at 11 P.M., depending on time zone).

"Typically," that late-evening newscast would be formatted as follows:

    11:00:30–11:06:00—hard news
    11:08:00–11:16:00—hard news and features
    11:18:00–11:23:00—news and weather
    11:24:00–11:29:30—sports and closing feature

You will note that once the "adjacency" and internal commercial times are subtracted, the hole is actually 24 minutes. And if you further subtract time for sports and weather, the actual news hole is around 17 minutes.

Of course, this is all highly flexible. On a heavy news day, the news hole would be enlarged at the expense of weather and sports. On a truly heavy day of major news, the newscast itself would be expanded altogether. However, 350 nights a year, 17 minutes of actual news time would be about right on the late show.

That is more than four times longer than a standard radio newscast—which means two things:

1. More stories are included.
2. Stories, especially reporters' packages, run longer.

To understand how everything fits into place, it is necessary, because of the complexity of television as compared with radio, to examine the components of TV news one by one, starting with the most obvious difference: the TV screen itself.

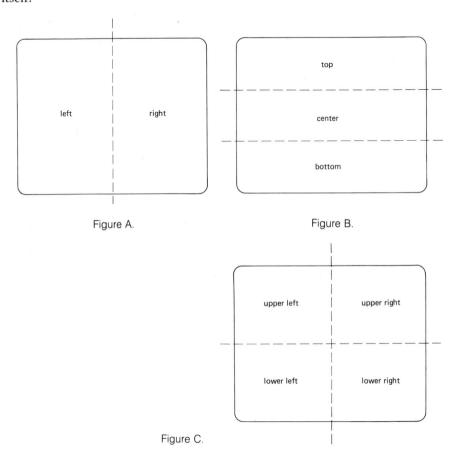

Figure A.

Figure B.

Figure C.

Picture Area

The sketches show the various ways of describing the geography of the TV picture (called the "frame"). Figure A divides the frame into right and left halves. Note that the terms apply from the *viewer's* point of view, *not* the performer's point of view; they are thus the opposite of "stage right" and "stage left." Figure B divides the frame into horizontal *thirds*. Thus, the word "top" refers to the top *third* of the frame and so on. And, finally, Figure C divides the frame into *quadrants*. The description "upper right" means the upper right *quadrant* of the frame. The significance of all this side-side, up-down will become apparent shortly.

PICTURE COMPONENTS

So far this has been pretty easy. Maybe that's because the frames are still empty. So let's fill them with something, starting with

Thanks, Dan.

That is what's known as a standard head-and-shoulders shot. It's so standard there's not even a special name for it. (After a while, you'll thank God for small favors like that.) The center of interest picturewise is in the center of the frame. There are no other visual elements to add or detract from what the center of interest is saying.

Now let's add something. Move over please, Dan.

Electronic Graphics

You've seen the preceding shot a thousand times, maybe even wondered how it's done. By electronic magic, that's how. That "thing" over Dan's shoulder (upper right, right?) is called a *graphic*. Actually, it goes by many names—*ck, rp, slide, adda, vis,* among others—but we are going to stick with the term *graphic* because that's a generic term understood in TV newsrooms everywhere.

How the graphic gets there is by one of several processes you'd need a degree in mechanical or electronic engineering to understand fully. The important thing (I never tire of stressing this) is that a writer or producer *willed it there.* A writer or producer decided what kind of graphic he wanted to illustrate the story the anchor would be reading. He then told a graphic artist what he had in mind, and the graphic artist drew it or pasted it together.

The Making of an Electronic Graphic

WBBM-TV (Chicago) graphic artist Barbara Gordon puts the finishing touches on a graphic design requested by a newswriter.

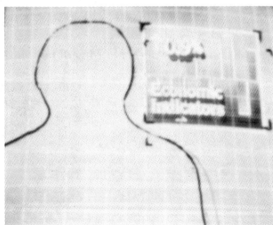

The graphic is then aligned into the position in which it will later appear onscreen and stored in a computer memory.

During the newscast, the graphic appears at the press of a button to coincide with a direction in the script. An electronic graphic may take an hour to prepare—and be on the air only a few seconds.

When the artist was done, the graphic was brought to another department where it was electronically prepared for insertion into the TV picture. Nowadays, this electronic insertion is done by either of two main processes, depending on the individual TV station:

1. *Chromakey.* In a system using chromakey, two cameras are required. One camera shoots the anchor (or reporter) off center, left or right. The second camera shoots the graphic image in the upper right or upper left. The two shots overlap and appear as one because a common color, typically blue or green, has been filtered out of the primary (anchor) shot, allowing that image to appear over the other one. (Got that? I told you you'd need an engineering degree.)
2. *DVE.* That's short for "Digital Video Electronics." You thought chromakey was magic? Wait. In DVE, the graphic is broken down by computer into digital information (you know, bits, bytes, and so on), stored in the computer's memory, and then reconstituted and inserted into the picture at the push of a button. Naturally, the primary camera (on the anchor) has moved him or her off center to create the appropriate "hole" for the insertion.

All clear? No, I thought not. Well—hear me, now—*it doesn't matter.* What matters is the thought that goes into *choosing* the graphic in the first place. That's the only *journalistic* knowledge involved. And of course it's the most important thing.

The graphic can be virtually anything the TV journalist wants. At small stations in small markets, there may not be a staff graphic artist. In that case, the station probably subscribes to a slide service that supplies photographs and generic graphics to its TV clients. Small stations tend to have the same graphic elements in their TV pictures from one end of the country to the other because they subscribe to the same slide services. But at networks, major markets, and large news departments in medium markets, the writer is limited only by his or her own imagination in choosing graphics.

It may be a map—to make clear the location of a story. It may be a photograph—to show the person or people the story is about. It may be a flag or a logo or a symbol or a statistic or a "still frame" from a piece of videotape or *anything* to help clarify, enhance, or pinpoint a key element of a story. The only thing it should *not* be is so complicated, so "busy," that it calls attention to *itself* and hence away from the content of the story.

One further thing about graphics in modern television: they can be inserted *anywhere* in the frame. The writer indicates in the script where he or she wants them (using the geographical terms that began this section), and *voilà!* Magic.

Electronic Titles

CBS News

CBS News

The writing in those frames is not the handiwork of some guy with a piece of chalk. Again, it's the work of a TV journalist who ordered a piece of electronic gadgetry to insert it there. It's called a *title*. Again, that's a generic term. Different newsrooms use different terms (*super, lower-third, cg, chyron, font,* to name but a few), depending on the type of machinery they use. But people in TV newsrooms everywhere understand what is meant by the term *title*—so that, like *graphic,* is what we'll stick with.

Electronic titles are produced by computer-assisted machines called character generators. Their capabilities vary widely. At small markets, staffs use relatively inexpensive models that produce titles of a single size and a single color. But the "big boys" use bigger machines—generators that can produce titles of any size, anywhere on the screen, in half a dozen different colors.

The preceding off-monitor photo on the left shows a title used to identify a *person;* such identification is customarily at the bottom (lower third) of the frame. A title to identify *location* (the photo on the right) is customarily at the top (upper third) of the frame. But titles can be used *anywhere*—full-screen, half-screen left or right, crawling vertically or horizontally—of the writer's choosing to add detail or clarify elements of a story, especially statistics and direct quotes.

CBS Evening News

WBBM-TV, Chicago

NBC News

As with graphics, care must be taken with titles so as not to overload the viewer's ability to read along or comprehend. This means that whatever text appears in titles should *closely match* the text the anchor or reporter is saying. Otherwise, viewers become confused instead of enlightened.

Another important point: textual material in titles, especially numbers, reverts to print style—"$1 million" instead of "one million dollars," and so on.

Broadcast engineer Karen Kors of WBBM-TV, Chicago, operates an electronic titling machine called a "Vidifont," manufactured by the French firm of Thomson CSF. Like other computer-assisted machines, it can generate characters of varying size anywhere on the TV screen.

SCRIPTING

Confusion must be avoided in TV news scripts. Not only must the copy—the news—be typed neatly and clearly, but the directions for sound and picture elements must be clear and succinct, too. So before we go any further, let's take a look at a blank script page:

In case you've never seen this kind of script paper before, here's the explanation: the *left* side of the page, up to the midline, is for *video* information and cues—everything needed to describe the TV picture; the *right* side of the page, from the midline to the endline, is for the *audio*—chiefly the text of the news story itself, but also the outcues of taped portions; the space between the midline and the endline is the only area of the page that will appear on a teleprompter. The narrow space to the right of the endline is for page numbers only.

It is unlikely that you will have this sort of script paper at your disposal. Don't worry. It's easy to simulate with standard $8\frac{1}{2}'' \times 11''$ copy paper. Merely divide the paper into roughly equal vertical halves, and type your news copy on the right half only.

Here's how to set up a TV script on standard copy paper:

1. Begin all video cues 5 spaces (Pica typeface) from the left edge.
2. Begin the news copy at the center of the page, and use a 35-space line.
3. Triple space between lines.
4. Follow the style set out in radio news to
   Type upper/lower-case.
   Not divide words between lines.
   Not divide sentences between pages.
   Draw a bold arrow in the lower right to indicate "more."

One of the first odd things you'll find about typing TV pages is that the 35-space line is so short that on occasion you'll only be able to get in two or three words. So be it. In TV, the cost of script paper is infinitesimal compared with all other costs. Don't worry about it.

A few other things, pretty much standard in newsrooms everywhere:

5. The writer's last name (or initials), the date, and the time of the newscast go in the extreme upper *left* corner, just as in radio.
6. The slug goes in the upper part of the *video* column.
7. The timing of the story, rounded off to the nearest :05, goes just beneath the slug, circled.
8. Leave *at least 1 inch* of space between the foregoing information and the first video instruction and the first line of news copy.
8. Coordinate video cues with news copy by starting them *on the same line.*

Here's what a sample page should look like:

Smith
2/27, 11pm

LAZY DOG

graphic -- fox & dog

A quick brown fox jumped today over a
lazy dog's back. The dog was caught
napping near a woodpile. The fox
escaped into the woods, and the dog was
too embarrassed to comment.

If scripting can be confusing for newcomers, it can also be confusing for professionals. That's because virtually every TV news department has its own system and its own terms to describe picture and sound elements. The terms usually refer to the specific brand or type of equipment the station uses; the equipment is manufactured by many different companies, employing many different names. So it would be pointless and confusing if I were to pick one set of terms for this book, only for you to discover a different set in your first professional newsroom.

Instead, we shall stick to generic names that are understood by just about everyone everywhere in TV news. Once you understand the elements and process of TV scripting, it will be a simple matter for you to learn your eventual employer's set of terms.

Naturally, the off-monitor photographs used in this book do not appear in real TV scripts. They are included to show the TV picture that results from a specific script instruction (or lack of instruction). Since the sample scripts were reconstructed from actual broadcasts, they show what in each case was in the mind of an individual writer or producer. A different individual probably would have done something a little bit (or a whole lot) different. So as you glance at the sample scripts, you should try to visualize how *you yourself* would have done it.

One other thing before we proceed: you are about to learn new forms—repeat, *forms*. The *substance*, however, remains in the words you use to tell a news story. Virtually all rules you have read in this book regarding broadcast style, sources of news, immediacy, localizing, and so on apply to TV newswriting. So even as you tackle and assimilate the elements of TV, remember that, in the end, the words you put in the audio column are the most important element of all.

Scripting Without Graphics

As we've seen, the simplest TV picture of all shows only the anchor as he or she delivers the news on-camera. This shot is so standard that it requires *nothing at all* to be written in the video column; a video column left blank will *automatically* result in the desired picture:

Israel says one of its warplanes was

shot down today while attacking

guerrilla bases in Lebanon. The plane

was one of four Israeli jets making an

air raid on Syrian-controlled positions

in the mountains around Beirut.

("Sunday Morning," CBS News)

Many stations and networks nowadays use two or more anchors to read alternate stories or alternate groups of stories, typically one man and one woman. Typically, writers know for whom they are writing each story. They need only include the anchor's first name in the video column, adjacent to the start of the audio column:

```
            Charles:        Israel says one of its. . .
```

Such standard shots without graphics used to dominate TV newscasts. Nowadays, with advances in electronics, they are comparatively rare and are used mainly to provide a visual change of pace. The producer of a newscast, or sometimes the director, is the one who decides which stories will be presented without graphics, as well as where they will be placed within the show.

Scripting with Graphics

As mentioned earlier, the inventiveness and originality of graphics depends both on the writer's imagination and the resources of his or her news department. At small stations and at larger stations with small news departments, the choice is limited to the graphics already on file, usually procured through companies that mail them out on a weekly basis. In large news departments and at networks, original graphics are made to order by staff graphic artists. A lead time of an hour or more is required for an original graphic. In addition to writing the story, the writer fills out an order form similar to the one shown on the following page.

As you can see, a lot of care and preparation goes into a graphic element that may appear on the screen for only a few seconds. Indeed, it may take the writer longer to arrange for the graphic than to write the story it's to be used with. That is a normal condition in TV newswriting. At small stations, the writer simply combs through the file of prepared graphics and chooses the one that comes closest to his or her needs.

Whatever a station's resources, there will often be a number of choices available for each story. Let's say the story is that the U.S. House of Representatives cuts the defense budget. Among the choices for graphics might be

A photograph of Capitol Hill
A photograph of an aircraft carrier
A photograph showing some other type of military force or personnel
Lettering saying "Defense Budget Slashed" or something similar
A generic drawing showing an element of military might, such as a rocket or bomber in flight

And so on. You can probably think of several more possibilities. The main thing is that the graphic must somehow highlight the subject of the story.

5 6 10

ORDERED BY _____   EXTENSION _____

DATE _____   DATE/TIME NEEDED _____

DESCRIPTION: CAPTION:

⊙2 NEWS GRAPHICS

Courtesy: WBBM-TV, Chicago.

In so doing, it should neither contain too little information (such as wording like "Congressional Action") nor too much information (such as the exact dollar amount by which the budget was cut). The point is to enhance the anchor's words, not to detract from them by providing more detail than can be absorbed at a glance.

As for scripting, this, too, is usually straightforward and simple. Unless specified otherwise, the graphic will appear automatically in the upper left or upper right (depending on the news department's practice), over the anchor's shoulder. All that need be included in the video column is the word "graphic," followed by a word or two describing it:

graphic -- Nobel prize

An American won the Nobel Prize for

chemistry today, giving the United States

a clean sweep of this year's Nobel

science prizes.   The winner in

chemistry: Henry Taubé (TOW-bay) of

Stanford University.

("NBC Nightly News")

It is also the writer's and producer's choice whether to include more than one graphic for a story. However, changes of graphics should not come so thick and fast as to be visually disorienting. The changes should follow both the story structure and logical thought processes, which move from the general to the specific. To change from one graphic to another, it is sufficient to script the new graphic on precisely the line of copy where it is to appear:

graphic -- the economy

The Commerce Department today

reported its main economic forecasting

gauge rose nine-tenths of one per cent

last month.   That's the thirteenth

straight monthly increase for the index

graphic -- indicators

of leading indicators, and it pointed to

continuing moderated recovery. The

report said five of the available ten

indicators rose in September.

("CBS Evening News")

The graphics we have considered so far should be kept simple for another reason: they occupy less than one quarter of the TV screen and are thus unsuitable for close scrutiny. But suppose we want to include more information or show more detail? In that case, we may decide to fill the entire screen with the graphic. Because this amounts to a visual deviation from a standard shot, we must give the right instruction for it in the video column. We do so by adding the word "full" (short for full-screen), right after the word "graphic":

graphic -- map

A major earthquake has struck the

northwestern United States, killing two

children, injuring an unknown number

of people, and causing widespread

damage in parts of Idaho. The quake

graphic FULL -- map

was centered near the small town of

Challis, Idaho, and was felt in seven

surrounding states and Canada. It

measured 7 points on the Richter

scale -- a reading that usually means

very severe damage. Several small

towns in Idaho are reportedly

devastated, and two people are missing.

The child victims were crushed when a

drugstore wall collapsed right on top of

them. Rescue teams are being sent

tonight to remote areas of the state.

(WBBM-TV, Chicago)

Full-screen graphics are often accompanied by electronic titles, the former serving as a background for the latter.

Scripting with Titles

Most of the time, electronic titles are used simply to identify people and places. The astute among you will already have realized that the ability, through titling, to identify by *visual* means can relieve the writer of the need to identify by audio means—that is, in the news copy proper. As we shall see, this can be a boon to a writer's or reporter's flexibility in writing stories involving tape. But for the moment, let's stick to stories without tape.

As with graphics, titles must be prepared well before air. There is not enough time while a newscast is in progress for the character generator operator to type out the lettering that is to appear on the screen and then punch it up. Instead, the operator types the text of each title before air time, then stores it in the computer's memory for recall at the flick of a switch at the precise time it is called for in the script. (More magic.)

Apart from simple identifications, electronic titles can be used to

Spell out statistics
List key points
Show exact quotes
Give sports results
Give weather details
Tease upcoming stories
Identify file tape
Identify sources of tape, film, or other visuals

Because the wording in these titles must be exact and spelled correctly, and because sometimes each title contains a lot of words, the exact text is ordered by the writer handling the story, using a form similar to this one:

WBBM-TV CHARACTER GENERATOR ORDER—●2 NEWS

STORY _____ PAGE _____

AIR DATE _____ SHOW _____

WRITER _____ EXT. _____

SPECIAL INSTRUCTIONS _____

_____

PLEASE INDICATE SCREEN POSITION AND COLOR IF OTHER THAN WHITE

As with graphics, there isn't enough room to type in the script the entire description or wording of electronic titles. But it isn't necessary. All that's needed is the instruction "title" at the specific copy line where the title is to appear, its position on the screen ("full," "at bottom," "at top," etc.), plus a one- or two-word description of its contents.

In practice, such titles for use in non-tape stories also appear over a background graphic, full-screen. Otherwise, the titling would appear over the anchor. The scripting would go like this:

graphic -- court battle

A compromise that would have at least temporarily saved the jobs of 734 city workers slated for layoff. . . fell through in court today.   Judge Thomas Murray proposed that the workers be retained

title FULL -- compromise

until the end of the year.   Then, if a reevaluation of the budget shows additional money is needed to keep them on the payroll, a city council majority would approve a property tax increase to make up the difference.   But a spokeswoman for the mayor said the proposed compromise is not "feasible" under the current budget deficit.

(WMAQ-TV, Chicago)

In all the examples of graphics and titles so far, the stories began with the anchor on-camera in one way or another. But it need not, and should not, be that way with *every* story. Some stories may *open* with full-screen graphics and titles and then return to showing the anchor. Or, if the item is short, it may be told *entirely* without seeing the anchor:

graphic FULL -- stox bg & title FULL -- closing stox 	On Wall Street today, stock prices were lower. By closing time, the Dow-Jones Industrials were down more than 18 points. The average share lost 30 cents, in trading that was active.

There is an especially pesky aspect of writing and proofreading TV scripts: if anything, they must be even cleaner than radio scripts. In radio, newscasters can hunch over and squint at their copy. In TV, the anchors have to look sharp as well as sound sharp. They must be able to read the script easily just by glancing at it or by reading it at a distance over a teleprompter. Either way, clean copy is a must!

16
VIDEOTAPE I: COMPONENTS AND EDITING

We now come to what TV news is mainly about: pictures that *move*.

In a way, just a standard shot of an anchor delivering the news is a moving picture. And the appearance in different parts of the screen of graphics and titles also represents "movement" in the sense of varying the visual aspect. But what is really meant by "moving pictures" is videotape shot at the scenes of events, showing us the "action."

VIDEOTAPE TECHNOLOGY

You are fortunate to be studying broadcast news at this time. That's because, although specific technology continues to change rapidly, the overall technology has reached something of a plateau. Videotape is now the standard medium for capturing and editing moving pictures in TV news and will remain so for the foreseeable future.

In the beginning, TV news relied (in addition to the still black-and-white wirephotos available through UPI and AP to all media) on bulky sound film cameras and hand-held silent cameras, both shooting black-and-white film. With the advent of color TV came a switch to costlier chromatic film requiring lots of light as well as costlier processing equipment.

With the perfection of portable tape equipment came the switchover from film to videotape. Videotape is comparatively cheap, light-sensitive, reusable, and requires no processing. It is now the standard TV news tool in news departments everywhere. (At this writing, film is still being used at a handful of network documentary units, including "60 Minutes," "ABC News Closeup," "CBS Reports," "NBC White Paper," and "Nova" (on PBS), among others. Film is a technology you may not have to learn until such time—and I'm rooting for you— as you are firmly established in the upper echelons of TV news and documentaries.)

The public and popular perception of TV news has been lagging behind the new technical reality. People were still talking about "the film" they saw on the news, even though it was tape, which has a radically different visual quality. Even people who should know better—newspaper TV columnists, Johnny Carson, and others—were still talking about "film at Eleven." As we shall see, even professionals use a few terms held over from the film days that are no longer technically accurate but that serve to clarify meaning.

The "terminology lag" affects many news departments themselves. For example, when videotape cameras and editing equipment were first introduced into newsrooms, such systems were dubbed "ENG" (Electronic News Gathering) or "EJ" (Electronic Journalism) to distinguish them from film, which at that time was still the standard system. However, now that videotape is the *only* standard system, "ENG" and "EJ" are outmoded terms—but you will still find them in current use at many stations.

Almost everywhere nowadays, broadcast standard videotape is three-quarters of an inch (3/4″) wide and packaged in cassettes of varying length, from 10 minutes to 1 hour. TV news crews generally use a compact 20-minute cassette because of its size, weight, and stability. Three-quarter-inch tape is technically known as a "U-Matic" format. A few local stations use a professional version of the Beta home video format (half-inch tape), but such gear is not compatible with either U-Matic gear or with home consumer gear.

Videotape cassettes are factory sealed. The tape is never touched by human hands, nor should it be. A smudge of dirt or even the skin's natural oils can damage not only the tape but also the recording and playback circuitry through which it passes. All editing is done electronically. (Film is edited manually.)

The way tape works is this: sound and picture are encoded in magnetic particles on the tape's surface by the Record circuitry. Editing and Playback circuitry read this code to reconstitute the images and sounds. The sound and picture are on separate tracks, enabling tape editors to rearrange them independently of one another.

Tape gear is constantly being improved, being made lighter, more light-sensitive, more shockproof, more weather resistant, more flexible. However, the basic components remain the same, and TV journalists must be familiar with them in order to exploit their capabilities. A TV writer or reporter may never have to operate the equipment, but he or she must understand its use to integrate taped material into field reports and newscasts.

A 20-minute, compact U-Matic videocassette (top) and a standard Beta videocassette (bottom). Videocassettes are factory sealed, and the tape itself is never touched. Editing is done electronically.

CAMERAS

A portable videotape camera, popularly called a minicam, has two major components: an electronic tube to enregister the picture and a zoom lens to frame that picture. All its other components—filter, switches, viewfinder, cables—are ancillary to the lens and the tube.

Since lighting conditions vary everywhere, the lens and tube must be able to read both the amount of light and the variation of colors, whose wavelengths differ under different lighting conditions. The easiest color to "read" is white. Thus, at each new location, a "White Balance" must be taken, against which the tube accommodates to all other colors. Without a White Balance, green might look like blue or red like purple.

The picture from the camera tube is carried by electron stream to the recorder.

RECORDERS

The recorder, loaded with a tape cassette, channels the stream to the machine's recording head, which encodes the image onto the tape. The sound, a separate electron stream carried via cable from a microphone to a different input jack, is recorded on a track near the edge of the tape alongside the picture as the tape passes the recording head.

Some portable recorders also have a Playback head, as well as standard functions such as Fast Forward, Rewind, and Pause. Some camera-recorder combinations thus allow the operator to rewind the tape and play it back through the camera tube and viewfinder. This is a valuable function because it allows a reporter and cameraman in the field to check a tape before leaving a location to make sure that they've got the right action. This was impossible to do with film technology, and many a story has thus been "saved" from failure to frame or expose the desired picture properly. Not all professional tape gear has this capability.

ANCILLARY FIELD GEAR

In addition to the camera, recorder, and cassettes, field crews carry other standard equipment:

Two or more microphones to allow mixing of sound sources during recording

A tripod to ensure that the camera will not move and the picture will remain steady during long takes

A camera-mounted light (battery powered) to work along with the camera in low-light conditions

A second, stand-mounted light (AC powered) for formal, long setups in low-light conditions

A backup battery pack to replace a rechargeable battery that runs down during shooting

A roll of adhesive tape for affixing microphones and for attaching small items (photographs, documents, etc.) to vertical surfaces to permit closeup (macro) photography.

It's not hard to see why TV field crews often refer to themselves as pack animals.

EDITING CONSOLES

A videotape editing system is composed of two record/playback machines, two TV monitors, and a control deck between them. The recorded cassettes are placed in one machine, and the finished (edited) tape is built on the other machine scene by scene.

These machines do not stop and start "on a dime." They require from 2 to 5 seconds to build up to the proper speed once any of their functions is set in motion. This buildup speed is what makes the precise coordination of the editing process difficult. The control deck accomplishes this by linking and synchronizing the speeds and signals of the two machines.

The final edited version of a taped story represents only a small fraction of the total tape that has been shot. It contains only the best scenes, both journalistically and aesthetically speaking, and is thus the combined work of a cameraman, reporter, writer, and tape editor. Truly a group effort. (Except in some small markets where a single person might be expected to do everything.)

OTHER TECHNICAL CONSIDERATIONS

The TV Cutoff

Before proceeding, it is necessary to understand two more major technical points in working with tape and cameras. The first is the "TV cutoff."

The next time you watch an old movie on television, pay particular attention to the credits. You may notice that the titles seem to be off-center, either left or right. Or entire lines of titles may not be wholly visible on your set, "lost" at the top or bottom of the frame.

This is because the feature movie you are watching was made for showing in a movie theater. The movie's makers knew that every bit of the frame would be projected onto the screen. Modern moviemakers, however, realize that their movies may eventually be shown on television, so they design the credits to occupy the central position of the frame. That's because they know all about the TV cutoff.

In television, the signal passes through many different steps before reaching the home screen. And at each step of the way, a little of the image is lost along the outside perimeters. And as a TV set itself gets older, its picture tube deteriorates, resulting in more picture loss along the outside edges.

This picture loss is estimated to amount to about 10 percent of the total frame. Thus, it must be compensated for both when shooting tape and later in the selection of scenes. The TV cameraman must frame the picture about 10 percent *smaller* than the movie cameraman. And the tape editor must not choose scenes containing important action or visual elements too near the edges of the frame, where they may not be seen by viewers at home.

Dubbing

The second overall technical consideration is the sharpness of the picture. It goes without saying that the picture should be as sharp and clear as possible, since, again, some quality is lost in the various stages of transmission. But in editing tape, picture quality deteriorates with each successive dubbing. The original tape, the tape on which the pictures were shot, is called the "first generation." The tape onto which the edited version is built from the first generation is called the second generation. With modern professional equipment, there is very little loss in quality from the first generation to the second. However, if a second generation tape is used as the raw material for a re-edited version, the resulting third generation will show considerable loss in quality; the pictures will begin to look fuzzy and the colors less vivid.

This happens especially with network material recorded by local stations for inclusion in local newscasts. The final edited local tape may be a fourth or fifth generation, possibly resulting in a picture of truly marginal quality or the equivalent of radio's UFB, Unfit For Broadcast.

At most stations, the standards of picture quality are very high. So whenever possible, air tapes should be edited from first-generation cassettes.

PICTURE COMPOSITION

In the first instance, it is the people in the field—reporters and cameramen—who must understand picture composition, for it is they who provide the raw material for writers, producers, and tape editors. However, these last, too, must understand picture composition and terminology to make the best use of the raw material. Moreover, a TV journalist must at least know what his or her colleagues are talking about, whether or not he or she is ever involved in editing or shot selection.

In TV news, as in movies, there are five basic shots describing the *distance* between the lens and the subject being photographed:

ELS—Extreme Long Shot
LS—Long Shot (also called Wide Shot)
MS—Medium Shot
CU—Closeup
ECU—Extreme Closeup

Basic Shots

Extreme Long Shot (ELS)

Long Shot (LS)

Medium Shot (MS)

Closeup (CU)

Extreme Closeup (ECU)

ELS. An ELS is the widest, most comprehensive view possible of a location or event. An ELS is what a movie director might use to show two armies marching toward another on a field of battle or to show a lone horseman crossing a vast plain. Such views depend on a large screen to be effective and, therefore, are almost never used in TV news with its small screen, where the soldiers would look like ants and the lone horseman like a misshapen blade of grass.

LS. Long Shots, however, are used briefly but frequently. A shot of a building, or a stadium, or a street serves to establish the location of an event. In fact, LS's are often called "establishing shots." As you watch videotaped TV reports, you will notice that an LS is customarily used at the beginning and then again to establish a radical change of location. These shots are short because, as with the ELS, it is hard to make out details from such distance on the small home screen.

MS. This is the most frequent shot used in TV news, the one that best captures the action. A Medium Shot is close enough to the subject to show detail, yet far enough away to show what the subject is doing. It shows both the person or persons performing an action and the person or persons being acted upon.

CU. Closeups are the second most frequently used shots in TV news. CU's are used for interviews. We see just the head and shoulders of the person being interviewed or just the head and shoulders of the reporter conducting the interview.

ECU. As the name implies, this shot moves the camera in even closer. During interviews, for example, the ECU is the somewhat "artsy" shot that shows just the person's head, usually while the person is in a state of deep emotion. Some stations and cameramen overdo this shot, to the detriment of what the person is saying; the viewer becomes preoccupied with the texture of the interviewee's eyebrows rather than with his or her words. ECU's also serve to show small objects or documents closely enough to read any printed matter. Such shots are also called *Inserts,* because the shot is "inserted" at a specific point in which the script refers to the object or the text of the material being shown.

Zooms

A zoom lens gets its name from its ability to move closer or farther from the subject being photographed. To "zoom in" means to come in closer, or "tighten," on the subject. To "zoom out" means the opposite—to move farther away, or "widen," from the subject.

Zooms are used only rarely in TV news, just often enough to reframe the action during unpredictable events. They are used rarely both because they are hard to shoot without losing the focus and because they are difficult if not impossible to edit. Most zooms can be eliminated by stopping the camera, reframing the shot, and then restarting the camera.

Pans

A pan occurs when the camera itself moves, instead of just the lens. In a pan, the camera swivels sideways either to the left or to the right—as in "pan left" or "pan right." As with zooms, pans are used rarely in TV news because of the editing problems they can cause. TV newstape is shot to be edited swiftly, not to ponder over. A movie editor can take a week or a month to edit a single sequence. A newstape editor has to do it in minutes. This is news, not art.

JUMP CUTS

A "jump cut" has nothing to do with a lawn mower going haywire or with the latest craze at your local "punk" hair salon. Rather, it has to do with what happens when you edit together two *moving* pictures of the same person or object.

For example, you have a videotape of the president saying

> Senator Piltdown is single-handedly responsible for the defeat of the housing bill. (sudden coughing fit) Uh, excuse me. (clears throat) But I promise him I've only just begun to fight. I'm sending Congress a new housing bill next week.

Naturally, you'd want to cut out the coughing fit. And in radio, using audiotape, you'd have no problem. You'd simply cut after sentence 1 (". . . housing bill.") and pick up with sentence 3 ("But I promise . . . "). You've got a nice, newsy actuality, which the coughing fit would have destroyed.

But editing the videotape picture is quite a different matter. Remember, we are looking at the president in closeup. Suppose at the end of sentence 1 his head is turned to the right. Now suppose that at the start of sentence 3 his head is turned to the left, the president having turned his head somewhere in the videotape we cut out.

Edited together, the sound bite will *sound* fine. But *visually* it will appear that the president has broken his neck, suddenly, instantaneously jerking his head from right to left. In short, it will be quite obvious that something has been cut out. And it will disorient viewers to the extent that many will no longer be listening to the content, but instead will be wondering who screwed up and how. In short, a major distraction, called a *jump cut,* which must be done away with.

How? Glad you asked.

CUTAWAYS

A jump cut is literally covered up by a short scene called a "cutaway." The term comes from the expression "to cut away from the main action to something else." To *what* else? Well, in the our example here, it could be a shot of reporters listening to the president, or a shot of a TV camera trained on the president, or a shot from *behind* the president as he turns his head from left to right (*not* right to left; remember, we're watching from behind him, so the sides are reversed), or a closeup of a reporter's hands as he or she takes notes—any number of things.

But wait a minute. Where did those shots come from? I mean, we had only one camera. How could it simultaneously be shooting the president and the reporters and cameras watching him? The answer is, it couldn't. (Have you figured this out yet?) The shots were taken *at different times*. The cutaways were taken either before or after the president's remarks *with the express purpose of providing editing tools*. While the President was speaking, the camera remained on him in order not to miss any potential newsmaking remarks.

So engrave this on your memory: *next to the action itself, cutaways are the most important shots in TV news*. Camermen have been fired for failing to shoot cutaways. And reporters who forget to ask cameramen to shoot cutaways are next in line for pink slips.

The editing process goes like this: the tape editor, usually under a writer's supervision, decides which sound bites to take (the news content); then the editor uses cutaways to cover any jump cuts. Naturally, the sound from the cutaway is not used, only the picture.

I know you've seen this repeatedly on the news. But you probably didn't know what was going on or how it was done. Now you know.

Some of you may be thinking, "Hey, wait a minute! Isn't a cutaway *posed*? Isn't it *staged*? Isn't that 'staging the news'?" Posing, yes. Staging, no. Cutaways are indispensible tools in TV news production. If occasionally shots are posed for cutaways, they must be the kinds of things that actually occur during the main action itself. Reporters *did* listen. They *did* take notes. There *were* TV cameras.

In other words, as long as a cutaway is a faithful re-creation of an actual scene, no staging is involved. However, re-creation of the main action itself *is* staging, and it is absolutely forbidden. The penalty for staging is dismissal.

There are, of course, degrees in this—gray areas, if you will. Suppose that you and your camera arrive late to a mayoral news conference. May you ask the mayor to repeat his key remarks for the benefit of the camera? And if the mayor agrees to do so, is it staging?

I don't know. The answer depends on the policies of your news department and the perceived importance of the mayor's remarks, as well as the perceived importance of your audience seeing and hearing them from the mayor's own mouth.

I do know this: it is absolutely, positively, unethical staging for you to request somebody to do something on camera that he would not do privately. That would be like writing a movie script, handing it to a potential newsmaker, and saying, "Here—act this out." Strictly forbidden.

Okay, back to cases: There are two broad types of cutaways:

Reaction Shots

These are shots of the reporter listening to a speaker's or interviewee's remarks. Of necessity (the camera cannot be in two places at once), they are posed shots. Reaction shots are also known as "Reverse Angles" because, in order to tape them, the camera has had to move to the interviewee's point of view (POV), usually a 180-degree switch showing the reverse of the main shot.

More on this, including procedures and camera angles, in Chapter 19 on "Reporting."

Action Accelerators

The other broad type of cutaway is used to compress time. As we've seen over and over, time is a very precious commodity in broadcasting, so anytime that we can eliminate or compress repetitive action, we do so.

Let's say you're writing a story about a swimming competition among preteenagers at a local YMCA or elementary school pool. The videotape shows the participants jumping in, swimming to the far side, kicking off, and then returning to the near side where the camera captures them at the finish. Total elapsed time: 2 minutes.

Two minutes is an eternity for a story like this. The problem is how to show the highlights while reducing the air time and maintaining the visual flow. What you might do is begin with the swimmers jumping in and swimming a few strokes, edit in a cutaway of spectators urging them on, return to the race as the swimmers kick off on the far side, edit in another cutaway, perhaps of a coach with a whistle in his mouth, then return to the race at the finish line. Total running time: 20 seconds.

Where did those spectator and coach cutaways come from? The cameraman shot them during another heat. Were they posed? No. Did the editing give the impression that all the scenes were occurring during the same heat? Yes. But were virtually the same cutaway scenes occurring during *every* heat? Yes. Therefore, the edited tape is an accurate representation of what did occur.

That is the way TV news stories are shot. It is the way they must be shot to allow writers and tape editors to represent reality and present news content within the constraints of a limited, yet reasonable, amount of air time.

As you can see, this is no easy task, especially for the reporter and cameraman, both of whom must be thinking not only of capturing the main action, but also of how that action can be accelerated, edited down to its highlights. What is finally shown on the news is not reality. It is video journalists' *version* of reality. It is no wonder, then, that working in TV news requires the highest standards of integrity and responsibility.

RUNDOWNS

All this knowledge of shots, angles, cutaways, and so forth is essential to any writer who supervises the editing of tape for his or her story. That's because, in addition to taking notes on content and audio incues as would be done in radio, the writer in television also keeps notes in his or her rundown on the available cutaways, establishing shots, and so on, as well as their counter or time-code readings, to be able to relocate them quickly or to tell the tape editor where to find them.

WMAQ-TV videotape editor Kathy Lattazi and newswriter Linda Connolly do a rundown of a just-arrived cassette. Together they will decide which scenes to use in the edited version.

Thus, at a major market station, a writer may spend his or her entire workday on just one or two stories involving tape. Writing the actual news copy, while it is the most important part of the job, may take up the least amount of time. The rest is spent doing rundowns, supervising editing, ordering graphics and titles, and making sure that everything comes together by air time.

At smaller stations, of course, the individual work load is heavier, but there is also a higher tolerance of carelessness and error. Needless to say, it is those who can do the work *without* carelessness or error who advance in their careers.

17

VIDEOTAPE II: SOURCES AND SCRIPTING

SOURCES OF TAPED VISUALS

TV stations get the news through the same three main channels as radio stations: (1) the efforts of their own reporters, (2) the wire services, and (3) network news services. But the need for pictures, especially moving pictures, requires a host of sources just for visuals. They are, in descending order of importance,

1. Local staff and free-lance camera crews
2. Network newscasts
3. Network closed circuit feeds
4. Group or regional pools
5. Government or company handouts
6. News agency wirephotos

Local Camera Crews

Since local news takes up a major portion of a local newscast, it only stands to reason that most videotape will be from local sources. As noted, professional videotape recording and editing gear is expensive. Further, it requires constant maintenance. So it's not surprising that small-market stations have comparatively little portable tape gear. The nature of work at small-market stations is that everyone does a little (or a lot) of everything. The station's chief engineer is likely to be in charge of maintaining the minicams, as well as the rest of the station's equipment. A small-market news department has access, on average, to from two to five portable cameras, usually operated by the reporters themselves.

It is not unusual, for example, for a small-station reporter to conduct an interview by mounting the camera on a tripod, framing the shot, turning the tripod-mounted camera on, then running around in front of it to do the interview. A "one-man band."

Normally, the bigger the market, the bigger the staff and the more plentiful the equipment (except at some major market independent or nonnetwork-affiliated stations that have resigned themselves to not being competitive in news coverage). Medium market stations may have as few as 5 staff cameras and cameramen and as many as 15. Some major market stations have as many as 20, and networks have double, triple, or quadruple that number. Some networks and major market stations also have occasional recourse to free-lancers who own their own U-Matic tape gear and hire themselves out on a per diem or per story basis.

Whatever the size of the market and station, TV journalists occupy themselves with locally shot tape more than any other kind.

Network Newscasts

Of the 850 or so commercial VHF and UHF television stations in the United States, more than 600 are affiliated with one or another of the three major networks—ABC, NBC, or CBS. The remaining stations—known as "independents" even though they may be under group ownership—have far less access to tape of world and national events than do the network affiliates. Some independents have formed "mini-networks" to share visual resources; chief among them, at this writing, was INN—Independent Network News.

The three major networks and Turner Broadcasting's Cable News Network (based in Atlanta) are truly the "Big Boys" of TV news. Nowadays, the annual news budget of each major network (excluding CNN) is around $300 million. Yes, that's $300 *million. Each.* Still, hefty as that figure may sound, it represents only a small (some say shockingly small) percentage of a network's total outlay for programming of all types.

The news broadcasts of ABC, NBC, CBS, and CNN are, in effect, the United States' "national newspapers," far more so than *USA Today* or the *Wall Street Journal.* Their influence is enormous. On any given weekday evening, a single network's newscast reaches an estimated audience of some 20 million viewers. There is no competition anywhere in journalism that rivals that among the networks (except, perhaps, between the wire services). That competition, in force every minute of every day, mainly involves getting the "best" pictures of a news story or getting an inclusive interview.

Local network affiliates, who are involved in fierce competition of their own in local marketplaces, rely on their respective network news departments for the quality and abundance of the world and national videotape which they can incorporate into their own newscasts. Local stations routinely record the network news to excerpt taped visuals for local use on the late news. Small stations tend to lift the network reporters' packages "as is," that is, without re-editing. Larger stations, with more equipment and personnel, prefer to re-edit and rewrite world and national stories, tailoring them for local use.

Network Closed Circuit

Given the competition, networks tend to reserve the presentation of their "best tape" for the evening broadcast. However, since this broadcast usually comes *after* local affiliates' early news shows in the Eastern and Central time zones, local stations would be left high and dry for world and national visuals if it were not for daily closed-circuit feeds in mid-afternoon. Each network sends a daily budget of sound bites and reporters' packages on world and national stories that is recorded by local affiliates. Local stations are apprised by telex of what's coming long in advance. The telex rundown is very similar to the audio-tape advisory reprinted in the radio news section of this book, except with more details. It enables a local newswriter to script a story or a lead-in even before the closed-circuit broadcast is received.

In addition to the mid-afternoon feed, networks protect their local affiliates on late-breaking world and national stories by occasionally offering so-called "Eleventh Hour" closed-circuit feeds. These are taped packages sent over the network line at the conclusion of prime-time programming (10 P.M. or 11 P.M., depending on time zone), preceded by telex descriptions of content and cues.

These are tricky for local stations to handle since at the time they are sent, the local late news is already on the air. Thus, local stations must either air them blindly, patching in the network line precisely on cue or recording them for replay later in the local news.

Group and Regional Pools

In broadcasting, a "pool" is an agreement among stations or networks to share coverage of an event. In addition to tape of world and national news, many stations want coverage of stories of regional interest. A station may thus reach a pool arrangement with a station in a different part of the state or region for coverage of a particular story. The tape may be fed from station to station via satellite, microwave, or a line leased from the telephone company, but these methods can be very expensive, and very often the tape is flown to a local airport for pickup. A typical story shared in this manner would be a sudden unexpected action by a state legislature, the pooling stations not having had sufficient advance warning to dispatch their own reporters and crews to the state capital.

Handouts

More and more, we live in a video-oriented society. Tape recording equipment has proliferated both at government agencies and at private businesses. Sometimes, the only tape (or film) of what you want to show in a news story belongs to one of the parties involved in the story. And more often than not, the company or agency is willing to lend you the tape or provide you with a dub of it. If no such "handout" visuals were available, the public could not see much, for example, of a manned space mission, since the on-board camera facilities are owned and operated by NASA.

Local stations and networks often use such proprietary material, but under two important conditions: (1) they retain the right to edit the handout material any way they see fit, and (2) they always *show or tell the source* of it. This is usually accomplished by means of an electronic title: "U.S. Air Force film," "NASA tape," "Chrysler Corp. tape," and so on.

(The verbal or visual crediting of the source of tape not shot by a station's or network's own staffers is standard practice. Often, it is required as a condition for using the tape at all.)

This sort of "visual sourcing" tells the viewer, in effect, that "We cannot vouch for the accuracy of this tape. We got it from the source you see on your screen. We show it because it is the best illustration we could find of the story we're telling."

Wirephotos

The non-local black-and-white photographs you see in your daily newspaper come mostly from AP or UPI. They are still called "wirephotos," even though nowadays they are transmitted by satellite instead of wires (thus, even the term "wire service" is outmoded). In the days before color film (hence, long before videotape), TV news departments relied heavily on such wirephotos because they were often the only source of visuals. Today they are used very rarely—only, in fact, when they are of immediate value, as in the case of the sudden death of a well-known person of whom there is no photograph in the station's graphics file, or when they are absolutely the only visual record of an event.

In addition, many stations prefer not to use such wirephotos for technical reasons; they are, obviously, not in color, and sometimes their quality is poor due to the transmission process. Still, many stations subscribe to the AP or UPI service just to be on the safe side.

To be presented on the air, a wirephoto must be prepared either by being mounted on a card for shooting by a studio camera or be reduced electronically in the same way as other graphics.

TERMINOLOGY

Before proceeding with the methods of writing and scripting stories with tape, let's run through some of the terms we'll be using:

Sound bite—the TV term for radio's actuality. Also called *bite, talking head,* or *head.*

Lead-in—same as in radio; the copy preceding a sound bite or reporter's package. A major difference: it is no longer always necessary to identify the speaker in the news copy (audio). This can now be done visually by means of an electronic title.

Tag—same as in radio, but used much less often in TV because the change in picture provides a cleaner break than radio's change in sound.

Incue—same as in radio.

Outcue—same as in radio.

Roll cue—the 5 seconds' worth of copy immediately preceding the start of a tape. Because it takes some tape playback machines about 5 seconds to build up to speed, the director orders the machine to roll 5 seconds before the tape actually hits the air. Because this is a judgment call, it's often off by a second or two either way, which is why you sometimes see an anchor staring glassy-eyed into the camera or, conversely, why you occasionally miss the first few words of a sound bite.

Page time—the equivalent of radio's "total story time." Unlike radio, a TV news script is given sequential page numbers, usually as the producer is writing the lineup. Each *story* is assigned a page number. If a story assigned to page 3 goes longer than a single script page, succeeding script pages are numbered as page 3-A, page 3-B, and so on. The *page time*, however, is the total time of the story, no matter how many script pages, and is entered on the first story page only. Before and during a newscast, technical personnel refer to a story by its page number only, so stories are deleted, added, substituted, or updated using page numbers as identification.

Tape time—the running time from beginning to end of an unbroken length of tape.

Time cue—the specific time, measured cumulatively from the start of a tape, at which a title, graphic, or sound bite appears during the playing of that tape.

Pad—a kind of breathing space at the end of a tape. The tape editor deliberately lets the tape run about 5 seconds longer than the desired outcue (killing the unwanted sound if the tape ends with a sound bite). This additional 5 seconds, which is not meant to be seen or heard on the air, is called *pad*. *Pad* is also used (about 2 seconds' worth) at the start of a reporter's package to bridge any error in the roll cue.

Track—short for *sound track,* referring specifically to a reporter's narration.

Slippage—because of the length of a newscast and the multitude of cues, times, and machines involved, it is only natural that a few seconds will be gained or lost here and there. Usually, time is lost. In other words, the newscast is running longer than planned. The cumulative lost time is called *slippage,* and it can amount to as much as 30 seconds in a half-hour newscast, meaning that the show might run over its allotted time. Therefore, slippage is allowed for by ending a newscast with *short* items that can be dropped if necessary.

Footage—a holdover term from film, which was measured in feet. In newsroom parlance, *footage* means nothing more than "tape," as in, "We've got footage of the rally" (or whatever).

B-roll—another holdover from film. Without going into a complicated explanation, I'll just say that B-roll means approximately the same thing as footage, except that it refers specifically to tape of the exact thing mentioned in the sound track (as in, "Open the bite with the coach, then lay in B-roll of the scrimmage").

File footage—tape from the news department's tape library, in other words, tape which originally aired days, weeks, months, or years earlier, but which is being rebroadcast as part of a new story. File footage, which is often necessary to illustrate news copy dealing with background information, must be clearly labeled as such, again usually by means of electronic title. Each news department uses its own term for file footage; typical terms include "file tape," "newsfile," and "file pictures." A file footage title may simply tell the date: "June 12, 1984," "May 1981," "Last Summer," "Last Thursday," and so on.

CBS News

WMAQ-TV News

Two common ways to identify file footage by electronic title: a lower left "File Tape" (left photo) and an upper left "Newsfile" (right photo).

WRITING TO TAPE

Writing to videotape is similar to writing for radio in that it employs the same informal language of broadcast style and roughly the same structure of lead-in/bite or lead-in/report. There, however, the similarity ends.

The cardinal rule of writing to pictures is that copy and picture must be correlated. Not identical, *correlated*.

Copy delivered on-camera by an anchorman or reporter is "free." That is, it need not be tied to specific pictures because we are seeing no pictures (except, perhaps, for the over-the-shoulder graphics discussed in the preceding chapter). But once the screen is fully occupied by a graphic, title, or videotape, the "freedom" is lost. Copy must refer to what we are seeing, at the time we are seeing it.

This is absolutely fundamental. And it explains why so much money, time, and effort are spent on getting the right pictures in the first place. If the pictures show the elements of a news story specifically, the writer can combine editing and writing to tell the news "freely," to present it in whichever order and structure he or she thinks does the job best.

But things don't always work out that way. The "right" pictures aren't always on hand. Thus the writer must find some way, some language, to tell the right news while incorporating the taped visuals that are available.

One option of course, is, not to use the tape at all if it doesn't show exactly what the writer wants to tell. However, in the real world (which is so, so different from the academic world), this option is rarely exercised. The name of the game is to exploit the medium's visual aspect whenever possible. In practice, this means going with whatever tape happens to be available (as long as it's related to the subject at hand). And for the writer, this means tailoring language to fit the situation.*

*It is absolutely forbidden to *misrepresent* a piece of tape (or still photograph, for that matter). For example, you may never show tape of a demonstration that took place the day before yesterday and say in your copy that this was "today's" demonstration, even though today's demonstration may have been very similar to the earlier one. This would be completely unethical and, in fact, could be grounds for a station's ownership to lose its FCC license.

The dictum never to mispresent extends to even the smallest things. If your copy talks of "wheat fields" and if you only have tape of alfalfa fields, you may not use the tape, even though the chance of any viewers catching such a discrepancy is remote. "Truth in packaging" may not apply strictly to advertising, but it applies absolutely to TV news. No exceptions.

For example, let's say that Senator Piltdown, during a hot race for re-election, visits your town briefly as part of a whirlwind campaign swing. His visit amounts to little more than a quick stop at the airport for a speech at the terminal (the kind of "event" politicians love to stage for the exposure it gets them in the local media). You have picturesque tape of the good senator waving as he exuberantly emerges from the plane and walks down the ramp. You also have excruciatingly dull tape of the senator's remarks (Piltdown is no Demosthenes). Your best picture is the ramp footage, so you are going to use it as a visual introduction, followed by a bite of Piltdown.

Your problem is this: it takes Piltdown 12 seconds to get down that ramp. That's how long the tape runs. There's no way to shorten it without a jump cut making it look like Piltdown *tripped* down the stairs. So 12 seconds is what you've got—use it or lose it. That means you have to write 12 seconds of copy to cover the playing time, whether you like it or not.

And that copy should *not* say, "Senator Orotund Piltdown smiled and waved exuberantly as he arrived in Ourtown today" because everybody can *see* him smiling and waving. Why be redundant? And it should *not* say, "Senator Orotund Piltdown said today" because we see him *smiling, waving,* and *walking down stairs,* not *saying*—a glaring mismatch of sound and picture.

You must somehow relate what we *are seeing,* the arrival, with what we *are about to see,* part of the speech, as you tell the news. Here's one way to do it:

Senator Orotund Piltdown, *arriving in Ourtown today on part of a campaign swing,*

pressed the issues that show him gaining in the opinion polls: higher defense

spending and a crackdown on welfare fraud.

The italicized words explain the context of the picture we are seeing, and the rest of the words set up the sound bite that follows (which is on defense, welfare, or both). All the words together take 12 seconds to say. Bingo.

Now no one claims this is easy. It takes much trial and error. But after much practice, TV newswriters and reporters develop a kind of sixth sense for "writing to time." They are able, after looking at a cassette of tape just once, to tell a tape editor, "Give me eight seconds of this, four seconds of that, six seconds of this, then a bite on the incue 'Mary had a little lamb,' to the outcue 'lamb was sure to go' "—and then go back to their desks and write the proper amount of copy without ever again looking at the tape.

In other words, as was stated at the very beginning of this book, this sort of newswriting cannot be haphazard. It requires discipline. It requires the writer to assess all the available elements—story points, picture, sound, plus the allotted air time—*before* sitting down to write.

Once at the typewriter, there are two general methods of correlating sound (copy) with picture (tape): scene by scene and as a flow.

Scene-by-Scene

This technique, which is easier to learn and is frequently used by field reporters to help guide tape editors in the choice and order of scenes, employs a key word or phrase that corresponds *precisely* with the appearance of a given picture:

VIDEO	AUDIO
(victim's house)	The victim lived in *this house* on Crescent
	Drive. . .

-0-

| (suspect's photo) | Police identified *this man*—31-year-old |
| | Orotund Piltdown Junior—as the prime suspect. . . |

The copy need not contain the demonstrative adjective "this" or "these"; the mere mention of a specific name or place will suffice. The technique requires a specific picture to appear at a specific time. For this reason, it is disliked by many "creative" tape editors who resent writers and reporters, in effect, editing their pieces for them. So be it.

As a Flow

By far the more difficult, more creative, and ultimately more satisfying technique is writing that lets thoughts and subject matters flow seemingly effortlessly one to another. In this technique, the references to specific pictures are more oblique, more off-handed, more like conventional storytelling:

VIDEO	AUDIO
(victim's house)	From the outside, there was no hint of what had
	taken place in the victim's basement rec-room. . .

-0-

(suspect's photo)	And the man in custody tonight, 31-year-old
	Orotund Piltdown Junior, is said by neighbors
	to have been one of the victim's frequent visitors. . .

Do you see the difference in styles? Scene-by-scene writing makes the audio-video linkage the main business of the sentence. Flow writing makes the linkage seem incidental.

No newcomer should become flustered, upset, or impatient while learning these techniques. Unfortunately, given the pressure of deadlines and the heavy work loads in TV journalism, there is seldom time for seasoned professionals to take newcomers in hand and help them go over their copy with an eye to improving it. In practice, the atmosphere in most broadcast newsrooms is sink or swim. That's why I reiterate that the surest way to learn and to improve not just these but all techniques in broadcast news is to continue to be a news junkie. One *does* learn by watching and listening to others.

"Writing Away"

Now that I've stated the case strongly for tying news copy directly to the taped visuals, let me devote a few words to the inevitable exceptions. (Ever noticed how it's the exceptions that seem to make life difficult?) Sometimes, the most effective way to tell a story on TV is to let the picture speak for itself, or at least to let it show things not specifically described in the narration. Here, as an example, is some narration for a closing item (kicker) to a newscast:

(anchor on-cam)	And finally, there was an honored guest at today's commencement ceremonies at State
(tape)	University. Patty Cake, who followed a special curriculum on full scholarship, was graduated "magna-cum-banana." Patty had an outstanding academic record. Never once did she bite a professor. It's not known if Patty will attend graduate school. It's not even known what she'll do with the rest of
(anchor on-cam)	her diploma. Patty Cake was part of a language-learning experiment underwritten by the American Zoological Society.

Well, it's pretty clear from that copy that Patty Cake isn't human. But it *deliberately* doesn't tell you that she is a young chimpanzee or what is happening in the videotape. Here's what viewers *see:* the anchor introducing the story, then tape of Patty, wearing a cap and gown, being led by her trainer as she is handed a diploma and a banana, hugging her trainer, and then taking a bite out of the diploma instead of the banana, followed by the anchor back on camera (no doubt chuckling or smiling).

This kind of writing is called "writing away" (i.e., "away" from the precise pictures). It deliberately uses language as a counterpoint to the pictures. Neither element, neither audio nor video, can stand on its own—the video because it doesn't tell us the context, the audio because it doesn't describe the pictures. But *together* they make effective storytelling on TV.

Of all television writing techniques, "writing away" is the most fun. But, as with many things that are fun, it's easy to overdo it. Thus, you should use the technique very rarely, and *only* when there is a strong picture to go with it.

"Visual Logic" (Sequential Writing and Editing)

Way back in chapters 1 and 2, we saw how and why the structure of a broadcast news story must follow a straight line instead of jumping back and forth as may a print story. Nowhere in broadcast journalism is this more true than in editing videotape and writing narration for it. That's because the tape, which is a progression of moving images, contains its own "visual logic" reflecting the natural order of the real world.

To show you what I mean, let's say we are doing a story on the space shuttle for the Late News. We have videotape of the following events, listed in the chronological order of their occurrence:

The shuttle astronauts eating breakfast
The astronauts boarding the shuttle
The lift-off from Cape Canaveral
The shuttle separating from the booster rocket
The shuttle in orbit
The astronauts getting a phone call from the president
The astronauts conducting on-board experiments
The astronauts eating dinner

After getting his or her lead paragraph out of the way, a print writer would be free to recount these events in any order, jumping back and forth, interweaving at will. He or she could, for example, describe the astronauts' dinner and then immediately contrast this with what they had for breakfast. Or the print writer could tell how calm a certain astronaut appeared, then tell how nervous that same astronaut had been before the launch.

But the TV newswriter who wishes to show any or all of these events on tape has no such freedom of movement. That's because to reverse the natural order of things, to show people eating breakfast right *after* dinner or someone preparing for space flight on the ground *after* we've already seen him or her in space, causes viewers to shake their heads in dismay. It *looks* odd to see things out of sequence, and *seeing* is what TV news is mainly about.

So here's a guideline for writing and editing: *unless there's a compelling reason to do otherwise, always edit videotape in a natural sequence, and write your narration accordingly.*

Sequential writing and editing takes two forms: temporal and spatial. The foregoing space shuttle story, for example, can be told flowingly either by respecting a strict *chronological order,* showing things in the same order in which they occurred in real life, or by *location,* starting with what happened on the ground and then with what happened in space. Either way, however, there is *no going back.* Once we eat dinner, it's too late to eat breakfast. Once we're in space, it's too late to prepare ourselves for the launch.

Note that in either case, it is not necessary to show everything. You can pick and choose from the available tape, just as you can from the available facts. But once you do choose, you should follow the sequential order just described.

A typical handling of this story for TV would have the anchor open on-camera or with a graphic by "freely" telling the latest or most important development, then go into tape for mission highlights seen and told chronologically, and then finally back to the anchor for a tag or the next story.

SCRIPTING WITH SOUND BITES ONLY

A TV story in which the only taped part is a sound bite comes the closest to what you've already learned in radio. The basic structure is lead-in/sound bite, with or without a tag. And, like radio scripts with actualities, the TV script page does not contain the verbatim text of the sound bite, but merely the audio and video cues necessary to get it on and off the air smoothly. So, before reproducing a sample script, here is the text of the bite it incorporates:

(Charles Lichtenstein, a U.S.
Delegate at the United Nations)

"If in the judicious determination of the members of the United Nations, they feel that they are not welcome, and they are not being treated with the hostly consideration that is their due, then the United States strongly encourages such member states seriously to consider removing themselves and this organization from the soil of the United States. We will put no impediment in your way. The members of the U.S. Mission to the United Nations will be down at dockside, waving you a fond farewell as you sail into the sunset."

(runs :57)

The only other thing you need to know about the following story is that it occurred a few days after the Soviet Union shot down an unarmed Korean jetliner over Soviet territory, killing all 269 passengers and crew:

U.N. Threat

graphic -- U.N. logo

There was a diplomatic war of words at

the United Nations today between the

United States and the Soviet Union. The

Soviet delegate charged that the United

States had, quote, "grossly flouted" a host

country agreement. At issue was the

refusal of the governors of New York

and New Jersey to allow Soviet Foreign

Minister Gromyko's Aeroflot airliner to

land at regional airports this week. The

refusal was in response to the Soviets'

attack on the Korean jetliner. In

response, Charles Lichtenstein, the

American delegate, issued a startling

invitation:

tape (:57) -- FULL

title -- Lichtenstein

anchor tag

ENDS: "...into the sunset"

The U-S mission to the United Nations

issued an official statement later, saying

Lichtenstein was responding to a Soviet

provocation.   But nothing he said was

retracted.

("CBS Evening News")

The time at the top of the page just under the slug—1:35—is the total page (story) time, derived by adding the tape time to the non-tape time: :37 (lead-in plus tag) + :57 = 1:34 (rounded off = 1:35).

The direction "tape FULL" means that the sound track will be played at normal volume (rather than under the anchor's voice). The time in parentheses—:57—is, obviously, the running time of the tape. As we shall see, this is the correct position for the tape time at the start of *any* piece of tape.

The direction "title" was necessary to cue the character generator operator to punch in the correct title. As we shall see, it is sometimes necessary to type in a specific cue time during the playing of a tape.

The direction "anchor tag" was necessary following the playing of the tape to show a return to the standard shot of the anchorman.

In the audio column, the audio outcue is clearly set off from the body of the script both to prevent the anchor from reading it aloud accidentally and to enable him or her to know when to be looking back into the camera at the end of the bite. At many stations, the practice is to circle the outcue instead of (or in addition to) setting it off by typed lines.

Of course, many stories *end* with the sound bite—without a tag. So, as in radio, it is essential that the outcue be precise and indicate applause, laughter, and so on, where applicable, as well as any double outcues.

In television, as opposed to radio, it is common to edit together (to butt) sound bites from different speakers. Often one bite is a natural reaction or corollary to the bite that precedes it. This works in TV (and not in radio) because we can *see* that it's a different person. In such cases of multiple sound bites, the tape time in parenthesis is *one notation*—the *aggregate* time of all the bites together. And the outcue is the outcue of the *last bite only*. (The cue times for titles will, of course, be different.)

The only thing unusual about the handling of this story and sound bite is its length. Fifty-seven seconds is an unusually long bite, and 1:35 an almost impossibly long time for a world or national story of this nature on a local newscast. A local producer would instruct the writer to come up with a shortened version along the lines of the following one, which uses only the last two sentences of the Lichtenstein bite:

Note: The local writer did not have to insert a title for the sound bite; the title was already on the tape recorded off the network.

U.N. Threat

:40

graphic -- U.N. building

The Soviets are charging that American actions against Aeroflot, the Soviet airline, are keeping the Soviet foreign minister away from the U-N session that is about to begin. Those charges led to an American suggestion: if they don't like it here, they should consider removing themselves from American soil. That is diplomatic language for "Get lost":

tape (:17) -- FULL

```
----------------------------------------

ENDS:  "...into the sunset"

----------------------------------------
```

anchor tag

The United States contributes more to

U-N operations than any other

country—879-million dollars in the past

year.

SCRIPTING WITH ANCHOR VOICE OVER

Much more typical than stories with sound bites only are stories with tape narrated by the anchorman. The tape is edited and timed under the writer's direction and supervision, and a description of the individual scenes is *not* included in the script. The anchor does not normally look at a monitor to coordinate the copy with the pictures. That coordination is accomplished by the writer as he tailors and times his copy.

The following two scripts are competing versions of the same story as it was handled by local stations in Chicago. The only previously undiscussed direction is AVO, which stands for "Anchor Voice Over," meaning we see the tape while we hear the anchor's voice.

summer snow

graphic -- map

Four days of summer are left on the

calendar, but some western states are

already battling a major snowstorm.

tape (:15) -- AVO

As much as 17 inches of snow fell on parts of Montana last night, and by early today, half a foot was on the ground in parts of North Dakota, Wyoming, Colorado, and Oregon. Heavy snow warnings are in effect for much of the Northern Rockies, and more snow is expected tonight.

(WBBM-TV, Chicago)

early snow

tape (:20) -- AVO

title -- Billings (at top)

It's still officially summer for four more days, but you might not be able to convince the residents of southwestern Montana of that.

It snowed there today -- and it snowed a lot. At last report, as many as 17 inches were on the ground in south-central Montana -- 14 inches in the suburbs of Helena.

The snow was part of a fast-moving

storm out of Canada that hit Montana,

Wyoming, Colorado, and Washington --

where the temperature only yesterday

was 60 degrees.

(WMAQ-TV, Chicago)

It's not surprising that these two versions are similar in content and structure. The writers were working with the same basic tools: wire service copy from AP and UPI and videotape supplied by their respective networks. Furthermore, each station ran the story immediately preceding its local weather forecast. In fact, *all three* network affiliates in Chicago handled the story the same way.

So what made the difference? The writing, as always.

SCRIPTS COMBINING ANCHOR VOICE OVER AND SOUND BITES

As mentioned, video column directions must be short and precise. The one new element in the script you are about to see is the addition of time cues. Because time cues can appear difficult for newcomers, I shall first explain how tapes are played during newscasts.

As we've seen, each story involving tape is edited from bulk tape onto a single cassette; that is, there's one edited cassette for each story. Thus, by the time the show goes on the air, a stack of cassettes has been assembled near the playback machines, ready to be loaded and aired one by one at the director's order.

Once a tape starts, *it continues to run* to the end of the edited material—no stopping, pausing, or restarting. Therefore, the only accurate way for everyone (technical and editorial staffs alike) to know the precise time for a title, for full sound, or for AVO sound is to keep a cumulative (or "running") time of all necessary cues. The reference point is, of course, the start of the tape, which is clocked as zero (0:00). Every time cue after that is kept cumulatively. This is done with each and every cassette, the stopwatch always recommencing from zero.

Okay, let's look at a local script, a story about a fire in a housing complex. First, here's the text of the sound bite so that you can follow the content of the story from start to finish:

FIRE OFFICIAL

When the crews arrived on the scene, we had a fire in the basement. Uh, the building was full of smoke. We spent the first half an hour probably just evacuating the building. We got maybe 75 to 80 people out of the building.

(runs :16)

Now the script:

---

suburb fire

(1:00)

graphic -- map

tape (:55) -- AVO

title -- address

title (at :10) -- this morning

Suburban fire officials are trying to

determine the cause of this morning's

multi-alarm blaze in Northwest

suburban Des Plaines --

--a fire that destroyed a 36-unit

apartment building. Five Des Plaines

policemen, a volunteer fireman, and one

resident of the building were treated for

smoke inhalation.

No one was seriously injured. The

pre-dawn blaze started in the basement

of the building. . .and spread rapidly
through stairwells and heating ducts, up
through the roof. Some residents were
trapped for a while by the smoke and
flames. They had to be rescued by
firemen using ladders going up to the
stories and balconies:

tape (:22 to :38) -- FULL

title (at :25) -- Clark

ENDS: " . . .out of the building."

AVO (:38 to :55)

Those residents left homeless by the fire
were housed in a temporary shelter put
up by the Red Cross at a grade school.
By early afternoon, most of the burned-
out families had been relocated at
nearby motels or put up with friends
and relatives. Officials are looking into

(WMAQ-TV, Chicago)

To run this down briefly: the handwritten time circled under the slug is, of course, the page time of the story, derived by adding the total AVO time and bite time (:55) to the non-tape time (:05).

The first tape direction, "tape (:55)--AVO," sets the tape in motion; the director knows, as he zeroes his stopwatch, that the tape begins here and runs a total of :55.

The first title direction, "address," needs no time cue; stated this way it will be inserted 2 or 3 seconds in. The second title cue, however, does contain a time cue—"at :10." The writer specifically wanted it inserted at that point.

The next tape cue, "(:22 to :38)--FULL," tells the specific starting and ending times of the sound bite. It is stated in cumulative time because its actual length (16 seconds) does not tell the director anything; the time ":16" has no meaning on a stopwatch that started ticking 22 seconds earlier. What the director must know is the time *on his watch* that the sound track is to be taken full.

Similarly, the title identifying the speaker needs to come at a specific

Phil Murray, a director for WBBM-TV, Chicago, goes over the lineup for the Five O'Clock News, deciding camera placement and familiarizing himself with the order of the show's videotape, graphics, and titles.

time. Why? Suppose that the sound bite had been an edited version—two statements connected visually by a cutaway to cover a jump cut. In that case, without a specific time cue, the director might have inserted the title at a point where it would appear over the cutaway instead of over the speaker. The director cannot know how each piece has been edited; he or she can't be simultaneously in half a dozen editing rooms, keeping long lists of visual elements. The director is busy enough just making the show flow smoothly technically and depends on the writer to indicate the precise times to order picture and sound elements.

So the writer was very busy in accounting for that 1 minute of air time,

Gathering the information for the story

Viewing and running down the tape from the field crew

Learning from the producer how much air time the story would get

Supervising the editing of the tape

Ordering the opening graphic

Ordering the titles

Noting the specific times in the edited tape that the sound bite and titles were to appear

Scripting the story, incorporating all the preceding elements

Reading it aloud (or giving it to the anchor to read aloud) to make sure that the AVO timing was right

Rewriting and rescripting as necessary

And, finally, handing the script pages to the producer

Whew!

In TV news, it is standard practice to name all people seen and heard in sound bites, either by electronic title or by mention in the news copy itself, *except* when people are being used "generically." I know that sounds odd, so I'll explain: Let's say an event occurs—a march, a rally, an accident—in which a lot of people are involved somehow. Naturally, it would be impossible to interview everybody. Thus, interviews are done just long enough to find a "representative sample" of comments, opinions, and/or eyewitness accounts. These are then edited in rapid-fire fashion, just a few seconds of each person, enough to recreate the representative sample. There's a special name for this in broadcasting—MOS (short for "man-on-the-street). The term derives from the old-as-the-hills technique of bringing a microphone into the street to ask passersby their opinions on an issue of the day. This sort of MOS is still done occasionally, especially on a slow news day. But MOS has really come to mean anywhere from two to half a dozen rapid-fire sound bites or actualities of people who do not need to be identified individually.

Here's a typical example of an AVO/MOS story. Two people are used. The first says,

"I could see it. I was sitting at the window. We flew right through a huge flock of sea gulls. We hit one in front, and one went right into the engine."

And the second says

"Well, I think we're pretty lucky. We're on the ground—both feet."

The scripted story:

near miss

Tape (:37)--AVO

title--Midway

tape (:12 to :30) -- FULL

Some air travellers heading out of Chicago got to their destination a little late today -- but it could have been a whole lot worse. An Air Florida jet had to make an emergency landing at Midway Airport, just minutes after taking off for Miami. A flock of birds...also heading south...somehow got sucked into one of the plane's engines:

ENDS: "...both feet."

AVO (:30 to :37)

No one aboard the plane was injured.

The pasengers were bused to O'Hare

Airport for a later flight to Miami.

In modern television, sound bites can be extremely short, lasting as little as 3 or 4 seconds apiece. Naturally, the content must lend itself to this rather abrupt treatment. It may seem foolish to spend hours (counting traveling time) to tape an interview and then to use only 4 seconds (or none) of it, but that's the way it works out sometimes. Many news managements like bites to be kept short because this gives "movement" to a piece that might otherwise appear static." Keep it moving" is the advice they give writers and reporters, by which they mean "Keep the viewer's attention."

SCRIPTING LEAD-INS TO REPORTS

If a reporter is unavailable to oversee the editing of his or her own package or to write his or her own lead-in (reporters are often out on another assignment), that duty falls to a writer. The writer also orders any necessary titles and graphics, notes the time cues, and then scripts the lead-in to the report. In such a case, the actual writing represents only a tiny fraction of the writer's work. For in addition to the lead-in, the writer may have to prepare a cue sheet to go along with the script.

The content of a lead-in to a report in television serves exactly the same purpose and follows exactly the same style as a lead-in in radio: it introduces both the subject of the story and the reporter, as it prepares the audience for what it is about to see and hear. It is either hard or soft, depending on the reporter's opening copy. (If you didn't understand that last sentence, you better go back and reread Chapter 10.) It typically ends with a throw line such as "Joe Doaks reports:" or "We get details from Jill Jones:". But good writers try to weave the reporter's name and/or location into the rest of the lead-in copy. Here, for example, are competing network lead-ins to reports on a story about cocaine usage by Major League baseball players:

Another big-league baseball player is in the news tonight--not because of what he did ON the field, but because of what he did OFF the field.   Former Kansas City Royals pitcher Vida Blue, once one of baseball's best, pleaded guilty today to possession of cocaine. He joins three other Royals in the cocaine lineup.   And, as Jim Cummins tells us tonight, there may be others:

("NBC Nightly News")

-0-

It's a world apart from the World Series -- an underworld of whispers and pointed fingers and illicit drugs.   But it's in the courts now, and, as Frank Currier reports, the scandal of "diamond dust" continues to spread:

("CBS Evening News")

To understand how a TV newswriter goes about scripting a lead-in and attendant cue sheet, it is necessary to go back a few steps. Even before the writer comes into the process, the producer and reporter will have discussed both the content and structure of the reporter's story, as well as how much air time it will receive; the producer has the last word on these matters. The reporter then writes and records his or her narration, either in the field or back at the station. The reporter does *not* include specific times for sound bites or titles, for the simple reason that he or she cannot know such information until the report is edited.

Now the writer steps in. The producer assigns to the writer all the reporter's and cameraman's output: narration, videotape, handout material, and so on as well as any wire copy or printed background information. The producer also tells the writer how much air time is allotted to the story, including the lead-in.

The writer and a tape editor then edit the package (at small stations, the writer and tape editor are likely to be the same person), choosing the exact sound bites and noting the various cue times for requisite titles. Then the writer scripts the lead-in and cues.

Since the complete text of a reporter's package does not exist in scripted form, it is necessary to reproduce a transcript of one so that you can clearly understand what follows. Here is a report done for a local Chicago station (WMAQ-TV) about a potential environmental hazard. Although the text is self-explanatory, included in the video column are brief descriptions of the visuals:

(waste in ship canal)	v/o:	Waste -- the product of more than 75 years of unregulated dumping. . .From the mills that have fed the economic life of the nation has come a hazardous legacy.
(reporter on-camera)	o/c:	The Indiana Harbor ship canal is considered one of the most polluted waterways in the nation. The waste it holds includes the cancer-causing agent P-C-B. But now the canal must be dredged, and the problem is, where should the tons of waste be dumped?
(ship canal shots)	v/o:	One plan would have it dumped in a giant holding container in Lake Michigan, just off Jorris Park in East Chicago. That's the plan Lake County commissioners approved. It's supposed to be safe. But some people here say such a holding container would become an environmental time bomb.
(East Chicago Councilman Frank Kollintzas)		(sound bite, Kollintzas) "It's impossible to give us the security that the toxics and many of the PCBs and the mercury that they're gonna be pulling out of the canal are gonna be able to be contained in one massive land fill."

(waste, dredging, & loading gear)	v/o:	The canal must be dredged because it is filling in. Giant ships that haul the products and supplies of this area need a deeper channel. But, say some people here, there must be a safer way.
(East Chicago Councilman John Todd)		(sound bite, Todd) "My preference would be to put it on the land some place rather than in the water. It seems to me just reasonable that any problems occur, they would be far less of a catastrophe if it were on land -- such as if the container were to break."
(beaches, Chicago skyline)	v/o:	And, they say, the beaches of Chicago are not that far away.
(Todd again)		(sound bite, Todd) "We're playing with something here that is irreplaceable, the lake, and just the impact it could have on the health and welfare of the people throughout the southern lake area, possibly even the whole lake, and putting these things in a potential dangerous situation."
(canal again)	v/o:	Indiana Harbor's ship canal <u>will</u> be dredged. It will take years and will cost millions. But there will be a fight if the dredging dumping ends up
(picturesque view of Lake Michigan)		out <u>there</u> -- in the lake people here are trying to protect. Stephen Ray, Channel Five News.

That report, as broadcast with this text, ran 2:12. The cassette was labeled with the story slug, the reporter, the running time, and the show time: "Lake Fill—Ray—2:12—4:30pm" The writer's scripted lead-in and cue times went like this (the off-monitor photos are included for your benefit):

LAKE FILL

(2:25)

graphic -- map

Some East Chicago, Indiana, officials are

claiming a plan to clean up the Indiana

Harbor ship canal threatens the future

of Lake Michigan. The plan, approved

by Lake County commissioners this

week, would have P-C-Bs and other

waste placed in containers and dropped

in the lake. Stephen Ray reports:

tape (2:12) -- FULL

  (Stephen Ray)

ENDS: "...Channel Five News."

LAKE FILL
(cue sheet)

title (at :05) -- Ship Canal

title (at :13) -- Ray

title (at :50) -- Kollintzas

title (at 1:17) -- Todd

That script was comparatively easy to set up. But many reporters' packages in modern TV news are considerably more complicated. Often they contain such visual elements as full-screen graphics, electronic titles with statistics or quotations, and so forth. Each element requires a specific cumulative cue time in the script, possibly requiring the script to continue onto a separate second page called a cue sheet.

Many small market stations do not have adequate staff or equipment for such electronic razzle-dazzle. This is probably a good thing for newcomers, who are thus less distracted from writing good copy at a time in their careers when they are on somewhat shaky ground.

The same shakiness is to be expected of neophyte reporters. The next few chapters are designed to help calm the shakes.

18
REPORTING I:
THE ASSIGNMENT

Television news reporters are on call 24 hours a day. They are expected to be reachable anytime, anywhere. Even when they are away on vacation, they had better be *far* away, because when a major story breaks, vacation schedules are as worthless as three-dollar bills.

Nowadays, the beeping page device you hear go off in a public place is just as likely to be worn by a TV reporter as by a doctor. The 3 A.M. wakeup call is as likely to be a summons to cover a fire as to deliver a baby.

News events, like babies, are not born according to nice, convenient schedules. And TV reporters are more likely than print or radio reporters to have their personal lives interrupted because of TV's need for relevant pictures. The aftermath of an event, while sometimes useful on tape, simply is not good enough in the competitive world of broadcasting. The pictures are wanted *now*. The interviews are wanted *now*. The reporter's phone is ringing *now*.

Unfortunately, many young people try to get into TV news reporting because, deep down, they have the same emotional desires as many actors and models: to be loved, to become "famous," to receive adulation, to get preferential service at restaurants—and the other "perks" of work performed in the public eye. Such people quickly learn, however, that TV news reporting is nine parts preparation and hard work and one part performance. Either they learn and accept to prepare and work hard, or they drop out.

That preparation begins long before reporters receive assignments. Their news directors expect them to be the sort of new junkies mentioned 17 chapters ago, people who are on top of the news and who cannot wait to tackle fresh angles. Their news directors expect them to be self-starters and come up with their own story ideas instead of waiting for something to happen.

Then, once these reporters are on the job, the working atmosphere is one of endless competition, not just against reporters at competing stations, but also among reporters at the *same* station. Landing the major, lead story of a television newscast is like landing on page 1: you don't always get there by accident; you have to outreport your colleagues. And the competition is tough. If Reporter Smith can't handle an assignment, it'll be given to Reporter Jones, and soon Smith may be looking for a job in another line of work.

Okay, now that I've presented the tough-as-nails side of the job, I really must be fair and present the pleasant side. Sure, the pay is good (in major markets), and it's nice to get preferential service at restaurants. But when you get right down to it, the pleasant side is this: there are few professional rewards, few feelings, like having covered and presented an important story well—the feeling, difficult to summarize, of exhilaration at having been *the link* between momentous events and the public's perception of them.

Usually, such accomplishments are recognized by one's peers rather than by the public. Only one's peers know the long odds, the tension, the preparation, the hard work, that go into the final product. A simple "Well done!" from the news director is worth any amount of preferential treatment by waiters.

PREPARING THE STORY

Preparing and gathering coverage for television is a vastly different procedure from what transpires in either print or radio. A print reporter can "work the phones" (gather information via telephone interviews) and immediately thereafter begin to write the story. A radio reporter can also work the phones, recording foners for actualities where appropriate, and be ready to air the story in short order. But when a TV reporter works the phones, his or her job is just beginning.

Sometimes, before handing an assignment to the reporter, the assignment editor or an assistant will have done some preliminary work, arranging for permission for the camera to attend an otherwise private event, jotting down phone numbers of important people involved in the story, and noting their various locations and travel plans. But likely as not, the reporter himself will have to track down this information.

In working the phones, the TV reporter is seeking two types of information: details of the story itself *and* details of the visual possibilities of each story element. He may quickly learn what the story is all about, but that is just the beginning of his job. Now he must arrange for pictures and interviews to illustrate the story. He has been deciding not only whom to interview but *where* to interview him.

Interviews of people sitting in offices make for dull viewing. A factory owner's or manager's office may be plush, but it is still just an office. The person should thus be interviewed *inside* the factory, where the setting *shows* the production process. The reporter needs to know ahead of time what the picture is likely to show, whether there's enough light, and whether it's likely to be too noisy to record clear sound.

Sometimes, of course, office interviews are unavoidable. Many people are simply too busy to allow a major disruption of their schedules just to accommodate a TV camera. Just the same, the reporter always makes an effort to arrange interviews at suitable, picturesque locations. A doctor taped at a clinic is better than a doctor taped in an office. An attorney taped outside a courtoom or court building is better than an attorney taped in an office. A politician calling for increased Medicare benefits is better taped at a nursing home or "senior citizen" gathering than at a news conference.

It is a truism that news is people. No one knows this better than TV reporters, who consistently try to show those people in the visual framework of the issues. This is nothing less than the main goal of television news coverage. Newspapers can quote people at length. Radio can bring us their voices. Only television can show them to us in the "proper" setting, which serves as a visual reminder of the story's context. Which is a better, more "journalistic" picture— an auto mechanic peering out from under a jacked-up car or an auto mechanic on a coffee break?

In short, even before he leaves the station, the TV reporter must have a pretty good idea not only of what the story is, but also how he will tell it and what it will look like. He must clearly have thought out the pictures he will need, element by element and location by location.

Although I've made this sound terribly organized, almost as if taping the story elements were a mere formality, it is often far from it. Often, the picture you want is inaccessible. Often, interview subjects refuse to go on camera. Often, nobody's home or you get a busy signal. Often, when someone does answer, the reply is "No comment." Often, there's too little notice to plan ahead because the story is breaking and the reporter and cameraman must fly out the door. Often, it's a hit-or-miss proposition. Chaos, I regret to report, is a way of life in many TV newsrooms—cowboys trying to round up stampeding cattle with too few horses.

All of which does not mean no attempt is made. The attempt is *always* made to get a story. If it doesn't pan out in TV terms, it'll end up as a 30-second reader instead of a 2-minute report. One way or another, it gets on the air. Whether it gets on the air with the reporter's name on it is due partly to luck, but mostly to the reporter's own skill, drive, and hustle.

SHOOTING THE STORY

Technical matters such as camera operation, setups, shooting angles, and so on will be discussed in coming chapters. At this point, however, it should be noted that the reporter's and cameraman's overall approach to gathering story elements in the field is to get the job done quickly whenever possible. Only leading major market stations and networks can afford to allow reporters and cameras to linger on assignments. Much depends, of course, on the nature of a story. But overall, the approach is to get in and out quickly, to free up the camera for other assignments. In small and medium markets, reporters and cameramen routinely cover several stories a day, with cameramen shooting tape for more than one reporter. The quicker the tape is shot, the quicker a reporter writes and records his or her narration, the quicker the tape gets back to an editing room, the quicker the newscast can be assembled and the fewer the last-minute headaches for the producer.

Such speedy coverage in the field is sometimes referred to by TV journalists as "down and dirty" work. The term is pejorative—because reporters and cameramen would prefer to remain at a location long enough to get just the right picture and just the right content. Unfortunately, given the logistics of TV news gathering at most local stations, such an "artistic" approach is seldom possible.

COMPLETING THE STORY

While in the field, the reporter calls in periodically to discuss with the assignment editor and the producer the progress of the shooting. The producer wants to know if the story is working out and, if so, how much air time the reporter thinks it will require. They discuss the story briefly, and in the end it is the producer who decides whether the reporter will "package" the story as a self-contained report or whether the show will go merely with some AVO and perhaps a sound bite.

If the decision is for a package, the reporter will either write and record a narration in the field or come back to the station to do it. Naturally, it is more comfortable back at the station. More than likely, the camera will be wanted elsewhere, and the reporter will indeed be able to return to the newsroom, get some hot coffee, sit at a desk, compose his or her thoughts, and type out a nicely written track.

Often, however, that proves to be wishful thinking. The reporter may have to scribble out a narration in the field, perhaps leaning against a car fender or ensconced at a booth at a coffee shop, environments not conducive to creative thought. So be it.

Once the track is written, and before it is recorded, the reporter calls the producer to read the copy aloud for the producer's approval. At least, that's the way it's *supposed* to work. However, this simple measure of editorial "proofreading" is often lacking in actual practice. Time may be short, or the producer may be too busy with other matters. And this is how silly mistakes of grammar, not to mention errors of fact, get into what you sometimes hear on local TV newscasts. For once the narration is on tape and sent back to the station for editing along with the pictures, there is no way to change it. Thus, the producer is faced with a simple choice: use the narration complete with errors, or junk the report and substitute writer-written AVO. And producers in local TV are extremely reluctant to junk reports that have cost so much time and effort to obtain.

This lack of editorial control over reporters' copy recorded in the field is endemic in television at the local level. Regrettable but true. Reporters at

While WMAQ-TV videotape editor Bob Weiner monitors the sound level, reporter Otis Buchanan records the narration for a report scheduled for the Six O'Clock News. Buchanan will protect the story through the Ten O'Clock News, covering any developments that break between the two newscasts.

major-market stations and networks are expected not to make such errors as a condition of continuing employment. In other words, a reporter who consistently writes badly or whose narrations repeatedly contain factual errors is fired. Simple as that.

All of which provides me with another occasion to urge you to concentrate on your writing!

GOING LIVE

More and more, as the technology evolves and becomes affordable by more stations, the reporter stays in the field to go live during the news by minicam and microwave. Such coverage works best when an event is still going on at news time. More typical, however, is the situation where the story is basically over and the reporter is merely required to do a live tag or live open and tag. The reporter writes and records a *protected* narration for the pictures already shot. That much of the package is edited back at the station. The reporter then prepares opening and closing copy which he or she delivers live on cue, around the taped portion which is played from the station.

This sounds complicated—and, quite frankly, it *is* complicated technically, since the field reporter must be wired in not just to the newscast itself (Program Audio), but to the director's commands as well (via IFB—Internal Frequency Broadcast) and since precise roll cues must be exchanged well ahead of time.

Going Live

A van equipped for live remote transmission features, in addition to the normal recording and accessory gear, an adjustable microwave transmitter (powered by a gasoline-fed generator), heavy-duty cables, and two-way radio links to both the master control room at the station and the main transmitting tower which relays the minicam's signal.

WMAQ-TV, Chicago

Reporters going live from the field wear an earphone through which they can hear both the live program audio and the director's instructions. Usually the earphone wire is worn under the jacket or taped to the reporter's back so that the viewers can't see it.

WMAQ-TV, Chicago   WBBM-TV, Chicago

WRAPPING UP

The reporter's day is not finished after recording his or her narration or going live during the Early News. There's still the Late News. Whether in the field or back at the station, the reporter checks with the Late News producer to learn if the producer wants (1) a late angle for the show, or failing that (2) a shorter, rewritten version of the Early News story.

In the first case, the reporter will grab a sandwich (maybe, if there's time) and head back to the field along with a cameraman. Given the fierce competition in local news, reporters frequently must stick with their stories through the evening. In the second case, the reporter writes and records a *fresh* version of the package—a protected one that will stand up overnight for possible replay the next morning during a local news cut-in in the programming of the station's network.

Then the reporter can go to dinner and thence home. At least for a while. As I said at the start of this chapter, reporters are on call 24 hours a day.

INFLUENCING EVENTS

The presence of a camera of any kind causes people to alter their behavior. The changes may be subtle, as when people casually rearrange their hair or straighten their clothing, or they may be pronounced, as when attention-seekers wave and clamor "Me! Me!" This is a special problem for TV journalists, who can live with subtle changes in behavior but who abhor major ones that can influence the flow of news events.

Frequently, the camera's mere presence triggers an apparent reflex action among people, especially youngsters, to wave and shout. Some teenagers go so far as to walk to wherever the camera is pointed, plant themselves solidly in front of the lens, and yell "Hello" to the world. Such activity is annoying in the extreme. But reporters and cameramen must deal with it almost daily, not by threatening bodily harm to the perpetrators (who, in any event, outnumber the camera team), but by asking politely but firmly for their cooperation. If that doesn't work, then a camera position must be found that effectively blocks off the offenders' access to the shot.

All that is a minor problem next to the possibility of the camera causing distortion of events. Most people these days know the power of television. They presume—sometimes rightly—that pictures of their activities on the 6 o'clock or 11 o'clock news can lend credence and validation to those activities. Unfortunately, this leads many interested parties to stage "news events" *with the main intention* of getting TV coverage. This occurs frequently at political or issue-oriented rallies and demonstrations; a group of pickets or demonstrators may swing into action only when they see the camera approaching.

Experienced reporters and cameramen know how to deal with these situations, too. For one thing, they keep the camera out of sight until they have assessed the true nature of an event, to make sure that the scene is not being staged for their benefit alone. Since local TV reporters' faces quickly become known in their communities, it is sometimes best for *them* to stay out of sight, too.

Many times, in the end, the camera does roll on such events. In those cases, it is the reporter's duty to explain the circumstances in his or her narration: "In an event apparently staged more for the camera than for the public . . ." and so on. Admittedly, local reporters do not always do this, thus, in effect, bending themselves to the "newsmaker's" purpose. What it comes down to is a matter of journalistic ethics. At all times, the camera must remain *neutral*.

STAGING

"Staging" is a term widely misinterpreted by people who do not understand the technical requirements of television. Most people don't know the necessity for cutaways in the editing process (see Chapter 16). So, to them, such shots can seem to be a form of "staging."

What we're dealing with here is largely a semantic problem. In one sense, *all* TV news is "staged" to some degree. The camera lens does not see what the human eye sees. The camera's range, its focus, are much narrower. The TV picture is essentially the reporter's and cameraman's *interpretation* of reality, in the same sense that a newspaper story is the writer's interpretation of reality, not a verbatim record. The TV reporter, like the print reporter, is a trained professional and thus presumably a better judge of what is truly newsworthy than the average citizen. He or she decides what to show because that's the kind of decision that he or she has been trained to make.

That said, it is absolutely, positively unethical to re-create an event solely for the camera's benefit unless the viewing audience is expressly told of this fact. People must never be led to believe that they are seeing a real event when in fact it is a staged one. That's the true meaning of "staging."

There are, of course, degrees to this. Sometimes, for perceived purposes of tape editing, it may be necessary to ask someone to repeat a *minor* action that the camera missed, such as entering or leaving a building or vehicle, pointing to a document or object, and so on. Such "staged" shots are for the purpose of providing tape editors with what's known as "transportation," a visual method of getting from one place to another in a series of scenes. Whenever such shots are necessary, the reporter or cameraman should explain their purpose to the person or persons being taped, thus leaving no doubt in anyone's mind about so-called "staging."

THE RIGHT TO KNOW
VERSUS THE RIGHT TO PRIVACY

This is a real dilemma. On the one hand, the TV reporter is trying his or her best to get a story and the pictures to illustrate it. On the other hand, the newsmaker may not want to have his or her picture taken or may be emotionally ill-equipped to deal with the camera's presence.

Situation: A child is killed in a car accident. The mother is almost hysterical with grief. Should she be interviewed on camera, even with her consent?

Situation: A man is indicted for embezzlement. Although an indictment is merely an accusation, not a conviction, the man does not want to be photographed or interviewed. Should he be taped anyway, against his wishes?

Those situations are not hypothetical. The moral quandaries they cause among TV reporters and cameramen are faced day in, day out, in the normal course of news coverage. Which should prevail—the public's "right to know" (i.e., *see*) or the individual's "right to privacy"?

Reporters and jurists have been debating these issues since the establishment of a "free" press. But nowhere is the debate more intense than as it regards TV coverage—because *pictures carry emotional weight.* Somehow, the person refusing to defend himself on-camera against an accusation "looks guilty," even though he is merely exercising his constitutional right to remain silent so as not inadvertently to incriminate himself.

So what to do, given TV's intense, inescapable demand for pictures? I am not so foolish as to attempt definitive answers. Having myself faced such dilemmas on numerous occasions, I know that each case must be weighed on its own merits. However, I can and will offer broad guidelines:

1. The law says that you may take pictures of people in *public places,* with or without their consent. On *private* property, however, you may *not* take pictures without the owner's or proprietor's consent. However, if *you* are standing on public property, aiming your camera at private property, it is the property-owner's responsibility to protect his or her own privacy.

2. Even on public premises, secure permission from interviewees and participants whenever feasible. This is a matter of courtesy, if not common human decency. It also results in better interviews. A person's tacit or verbal consent puts him in a better frame of mind to handle your questions.

3. Refrain from attempting to interview emotionally overwrought people such as the grief-stricken mother. Never put yourself, by dint of your very presence, in a position of contributing to another person's pain or sorrow. Wait until such people have recovered their equilibrium. In any case, tape shot *from a distance* will adequately *show* a person's sorrow. What more could his or her words add in most cases?

4. Do not hound reluctant or reticent people with the camera. You can be forceful, even pushy, but don't be a bully. You have all seen shots where the camera is literally chasing someone down the street or has caught someone in ambush. Don't do it. So-called "ambush journalism" is frowned on, if not outright forbidden, in all reputable news departments.

Okay, having read all that, don't be surprised if your producer *insists* that you break one or more of those guidelines. The nature of competition is such that the producer is under enormous pressure to have pictures equal to if not "better" than those of other stations. And, of course, the producer is far removed from the anguished mother's tears and does not have to share the reporter's and cameraman's discomfort in facing her in person.

Most producers I have known are decent human beings who, especially in well-managed and journalistically sound news departments, see no need to include emotionally heavy videotape in their newscasts. But a few others, realizing that such tape has a very strong visual and emotional appeal for many viewers, insist you get it on occasion.

In the end, you yourself will define your own limits on this and other ethical matters.

19
REPORTING II: SHOOTING

"READY WHEN YOU ARE, MR. SPIELBERG"

One thing you'll quickly find if you spend time among TV reporters and cameramen: they love to go to movies. And after the film they discuss not only the plot but also how it was *shot*—what techniques and camera angles the movie's director used to show various scenes. They are merely engaging in a normal propensity to talk shop during nonworking hours.

Like it or not, a TV reporter is a kind of very junior Steven Spielberg, directing his or her own mini-miniversion of "Jaws" on every assignment. A TV report is a *story*. It has a beginning, a middle, and an ending, with a continuity to make it flow unbroken from first to last. While he or she may not take the pictures by holding the camera, the TV reporter must oversee those pictures at every step of the way, making sure each shows to best visual advantage the story element he or she wishes to describe.

By the time they reach college, some young people evince a well-developed "visual sense"; they are able, through coordination of hand, eye, and aesthetic values, to regard a scene and know innately how best to represent it on a stage, drawing board, or video screen. Such people are "naturals" for the theater, painting, photography, movies, TV—and TV news. Because their minds already hold the conceptual ability to assess a scene, they find that learning the formal descriptions—Long Shot, Closeup, and so on—comes easily.

Most young journalists, however, do not come by this visual sense so easily, either by birth or early training. Journalists deal by and large with ideas, both concrete and abstract, with issues, with thoughts, and with words. Those journalists wishing to enter TV news, if they don't possess an innate visual sense, must familiarize themselves with the camera angles and techniques that will enable them to illustrate the words and ideas they so cherish.

In other words, it is time to turn to nuts and bolts. But before proceeding, I suggest you review the material in Chapter 16 regarding the types of shots. Henceforth, we'll be using those terms often.

EQUIPMENT TESTING AND MAINTENANCE

In small markets, TV journalists operate the camera and recording equipment themselves. Elsewhere, from medium markets to networks and cable, they must at least be familiar with the equipment in order to know what it is capable of doing (or not doing).

Although most stations at all levels have a maintenance department to inspect and adjust equipment routinely, certain minor adjustments may be accomplished by comparative neophytes:

1. Test the camera and recorder *before* leaving the station. Is the camera battery fully charged? Is the *spare* battery fully charged? Is the tape *fresh*? (Overused tape deteriorates, resulting in streaks and sparkles that break up the picture.) Is the tape running smoothly in the recorder?
2. Test the microphone. Is the recorded sound clear and unmuffled? Or is there a "hum" or electronic buzz? If so, switch mikes. If the noise continues, switch mike *cables*. If the noise persists, the recorder needs skilled repairing.
3. Test the picture playback on a color monitor. Is the image sharp and true? Are the colors true? If not, take a new White Balance and try again. If the colors are still not true, skilled repairs are in order.
4. Last-minute checks: Did you pack the spare battery? Spare cassettes? Did you check the camera light? Have you got a spare bulb? Adhesive tape? Aspirin for when you get out in the field and realize you've forgotten any of the above?

CAMERA OPERATION

Each camera/recorder combination is slightly different when it comes to lenses, on-off switches, warning lights, and so on. In addition, professional gear does not have the same "bells and whistles" as does home consumer gear; there is no automatic focus or aperture setting. Each operation is by hand, *trained* hand, to yield a professional result.

There are certain procedures for shooting videotape (or film, for that matter), no matter what type or brand of equipment is used:

1. **HOLD THE CAMERA STEADY!!!**
Engrave that on your brain. The point is for the *subject* to move, *not* the camera. It's so fundamental that I'm going to say it another way: **Don't move the camera while shooting!!!**
Once you frame a shot, do *not* zoom in and out. What's that you say? The subject isn't *doing* anything? Maybe not. But remember this: movement is "added" to a piece *in editing*, not in shooting. This means you pick a shot, then hold it. If you want to change the shot, stop the camera, reframe the shot, then restart the camera. If you've got the shakes, use a tripod.
True, in the heat of the moment, you may have to zoom or pan with the camera rolling to keep the subject in view. Fine. But never zoom or pan unnecessarily, to be "artsy" or "creative" or whatever. Ultimately, it's the subject of the story that counts, not the camerawork.

2. **ALWAYS SHOOT WITH SOUND.**
No exclamation points here—but capital letters nonetheless. Anchor Voice Over stories are usually run with the natural sound under the anchor's voice. This natural sound, as in radio, lends presence. It's an easy matter to kill an unwanted sound track, but it can only die once. Therefore, always make sure the mike is plugged in and that the sound is being recorded along with the picture. No exceptions.

3. **MAKE SURE THERE IS ADEQUATE LIGHT.**
With modern, light-sensitive cameras, much less light is required than with older gear. Most outdoor locations, and many indoor locations, have enough ambient light for ordinary news coverage. However, at most indoor locations and even some outdoor ones, a camera-mounted light is a necessity. Much indoor lighting, especially overhead lighting, causes shadows in peoples' eye sockets. These shadows are emphasized on videotape, sometimes appearing as black holes. The camera-mounted light fills in these holes.
A well-equipped camera crew also carries a "fill light." This is a stand-mounted light used to fill in any dark areas of a scene, such as the space behind an interview subject. In most modern TV news photography, fill lights are not necessary, provided that the shot is framed correctly to begin with.

4. **KNOW HOW MUCH TAPE TIME IS LEFT ON A CASSETTE.**
Suppose that the governor is delivering an impromptu speech on a major issue or breaking news development. And suppose that the tape runs out just as he makes his most important remark. You can cry and you can curse, to no avail. But nine times out of ten you can avoid the mishap by making sure a fresh cassette has been inserted into the recorder ahead of time. So what if there was ten minutes' tape time left on the old cassette? Big deal. In a few days, the cassette will be degaussed (erased) for reuse anyway. Play it safe. Start with a fresh cassette, and change it *before* it runs out.

INTERVIEWS

Percentagewise, the one-on-one interview—or "talking head"—accounts for most of the tape shot in connection with a news story, not necessarily for most of the tape *used* in the final piece, but the most *shot*. It is well to remember while shooting an interview that the point of the exercise is to hear what the subject is *saying*. Thus, any distracting angles or camera movement are to be avoided.

There are a number of shots to any interview. Here they are, in order of importance:

Closeups

This is also known in interview situations as a "1-Shot" because it shows just one person, the subject being interviewed. The interview Closeup (CU) shows the subject's head and shoulders, framed in such a way that a lower-third electronic title can be laid in comfortably under the subject's chin during broadcast. Once found and framed, this basic shot should not—repeat, *not*—be changed during the *entire* interview proper. The reason (which should be obvious to you by now) is that you can't know till afterward which bite will be used. Most professional TV cameramen use a tripod for formal, sit-down interviews; even the best cameramen get tired after a while of holding the camera, and they know the greatest sin is not holding the camera steady.

Reaction Cutaways

As noted elsewhere, the cutaway enables the editor to edit remarks internally by covering a jump cut. The reaction cutaway is usually a CU of the reporter listening or pretending to take notes.

To take the reaction cutaway, the camera typically moves to the opposite side of the location in order to frame the shot from the interviewee's point of view. This is not as easy as it sounds. Pay attention here because this is very important.

Reverse Angles and Point of View (POV)

The camera does not see precisely what the reporter sees during an interview. The interviewee is looking directly at the reporter. But because the camera cannot occupy exactly the same space as the reporter, it will appear on the TV screen that the interviewee is looking either to the right or to the left. The way to see this most clearly is by looking at the interviewee's *eyes*. Are the eyes, from the camera's point of view (POV), looking to the right or to the left?

It is essential for the reporter and cameraman to know this precisely. Why? Because the reaction cutaway of the reporter listening must be in *exactly the opposite* direction, or the shot will not match. To appreciate this, it is best for you to see it demonstrated with recording and playback equipment. If from the camera's point of view the subject is looking to the left, then in the cutaway the reporter must be seen looking to the right, or the reporter will seem to be looking away from the subject instead of at him. Conversely, if the subject is looking to the right, the reporter must be shown looking to the left.

The matter of reverse angles is a phenomenon that is difficult to put in words. In fact, you probably won't believe me until you see it for yourself, perhaps by shooting enough wrong-angle cutaways to get disgusted with yourself.

Textbook writers have tried all sorts of formulas to make the phenom-

Shooting an Interview

1. WBBM-TV (Chicago) reporter Terry Savage, sound engineer Bob Gadbois, and cameraman Steve Lasker set up for a one-on-one interview. Both the reporter and the interviewee are wearing clip-on microphones.

2. The interview proceeds. Since the reporter is sitting slightly to the right of the camera, the interviewee will be seen looking slightly to the right.

3. The interview MS (2-shot) as seen through the camera lens.

4. The CU (1-shot) as seen through the camera lens. The cameraman holds this shot throughout the entire interview proper. Note the eye direction of the interviewee.

5. The interview proper now completed, the camera crew moves to the opposite side of the scene in order to shoot reverse angle cutaways and questions.

6. The reverse angle 2-shot as seen through the camera lens. Note that the reporter is seen looking to the left, where the interviewee is now sitting in relation to the camera.

7. The reaction cutaway in CU. It would have been possible to shoot this cutaway even without the interviewee's presence—but the eye direction must always match.

8. Conversely, an interviewee who is seen looking left . . .

9. . . . requires WBBM-TV reporter John Davis to be seen looking right in the reverse angle.

enon clear—drawing imaginary POV lines, designing graphs, and so on—all without success. At least half of you reading this book will, on your first field reporting assignment, come back with a wrong-angle cutaway (if you remember to shoot the cutaway at all). Well, given those odds, it can't hurt to try a formula of my own:

> Before shooting a cutaway, look at the subject's eyes from the camera's point of view. If the eyes were looking left, yours should be seen looking right. If the eyes were looking right, yours should be seen looking left. Thus, his left–yours right, his right–yours left.

What the heck, it was worth a try.

(While we are on the subject of reaction shots, there is some dispute over what the reporter should seem to be *doing*. *Listening*, yes. But should he also be *smiling* or *nodding*? Some news managements say no—that to smile or nod indicates agreement with what the interviewee is saying, and it's clearly not the reporter's role to agree or disagree. Other news managements scoff at this, saying a smile is only human and a nod merely means "I understand," without implying partiality. However, to be on the safe side, it's probably best not to smile or nod.)

Setup Shots

A setup shot (also called a "2-Shot"), which can be taken either before or after the interview proper, shows both the interviewee and the reporter as they appear to be in the midst of conversation. It's better visually if the interviewee is seen listening as the reporter asks a question. That way, a natural-looking edit can be made directly to the sound bite.

When are such shots used? Well, you see them all the time, perhaps not knowing that they are separate, formal shots. They allow a tape editor to provide visual apposition for the reporter's lead-in narration along the lines of

That's what I asked Widget President Oxnard Piltdown today. . .

or

Widget President Oxnard Piltdown disagrees. . .

In other words, the setup shot is for the few seconds of narration that set up the sound bite. It's the visual equivalent of a lead-in.

Reverse Questions

After the formal interview, at the same time as the reaction cutaway is taken, the reporter has the opportunity to ask the same questions he asked during the interview; this time, of course, his own face is on-camera. Such "Reverse Questions" can relieve some of the visual sameness of a long interview. However, there are very strict rules regarding them.

1. Any question asked in Reverse Angle must be *essentially the same question* asked during the actual interview. Obviously, by asking a slightly different question, the reporter, already knowing the answer, could seriously distort that answer. And that's clearly unethical.
2. Because the camera can tighten to a CU of the reporter, it isn't *technically* necessary for the interviewee to be present during the taping of reverse questions. However, most news departments require the interviewee's presence as an *ethical* necessity. The interviewee is advised to remain present to *ensure* that there can be no distortion of his remarks. It is thus necessary following an interview to explain to the subject the nature and purpose of any reverse questioning.

Frankly, some reporters use Reverse Questions as a means of clearing up any bobbles or poor choices of words in their original questions. Since TV is a medium where performance counts, such cosmetic use of the camera is permissible—as long as the end result is to clarify the content of a story rather than just an ego trip for the reporter.

In any case, on the matter of reverse questions, as with so many ethical matters, the reporter must learn his or her news department's policy before going on assignment.

Continuity

In TV news coverage, as in movie making, the term "continuity" refers to *visual* continuity. For example, you go to see a Burt Reynolds movie. In one scene, Burt's wearing a suit with a red handkerchief in the breast pocket. In the next scene, the handkerchief is powder blue. What happened? Well, the scenes were shot on different days, and somebody forgot to coordinate the colors.

That happens very rarely in Hollywood because people are hired for the express purpose of guarding against such visual anomalies. In TV news, the reporter and cameraman have to look out for them.

What could happen during an interview? Well, let's say you're interviewing Senator Piltdown in his office. The good senator is doing his blustering best to explain why he has been absent from the last 6,000 roll-call votes. Amid the blustering, a member of his staff interrupts the interview to deliver a written message. The camera stops rolling during this interlude, as Piltdown puts on his reading glasses to glance at the message. He chuckles, lays the message aside, and you resume the interview, complete with cutaways and setup shot.

Back at your station, playing back the tape, you decide that the best sound bite would entail a bit from the start of the interview plus a bit from the end, with one of those cutaways to cover the internal jump cut. Only you can't cut it that way after all because, as if by magic, Piltdown is suddenly wearing eyeglasses! Did he put them on during the 2 seconds we saw the reporter in the cutaway? Hey, maybe the guy's got quick hands. But if so, why? After all, he's not *reading* anything that we can see.

That is the sort of visual anomaly that can ruin continuity, and reporters and cameramen must be constantly on guard against them. In this example, either the reporter or the cameraman should have politely asked the senator to remove his glasses before taping was resumed.

Other things to watch out for include objects in people's hands (which can magically disappear or appear out of nowhere) and smokers (whose cigarettes can seem to burn out in a trice or whose pipes can be magically lit by unseen hands).

As we'll see in a few moments, there are certain "cover shots" that can be used to explain such mysteries visually, but they are a bother, and it's best to head them off at the pass.

"Things That Crop Up"

I didn't know what else to call this section, which deals with the most often asked technical questions about TV interviews:

Q: Where should the interviewee be looking, at the reporter or into the camera?

A: At the reporter. The camera is taping a conversation between two people who would normally be looking at each other, not at some piece of machinery. To look at the camera would be unnatural.

Q: How does the reporter know when the camera is rolling on the 1-Shot or the 2-Shot?

A: The cameraman tells him, usually just by saying "Okay, rolling." Nothing tricky.

Q: Should the reporter pause between the end of an interviewee's answer and the start of his or her next question, or should the reporter jump right in as fast as possible?

A: The reporter should pause slightly. The half-second or so of silence facilitates tape editing, reducing the likelihood of "up-cutting" either person's remarks.

Q: Should the reporter really be taking notes, or should the reporter maintain unbroken eye contact with the interviewee as in a "normal" conversation?

A: Pick your own method. But if you decide not to take notes, you may forget something important later when you write your narration. For this reason, some reporters carry a small audiocassette recorder as a handy way to keep a separate record of the interview, thus relieving themselves of having to take notes. The audiocassette can also be used to check the exact wording of questions to be repeated or re-asked during Reverse Angle shooting.

Q: What if the interviewee gets tongue-tied or says something inaccurate through oversight rather than by design? Should the reporter help him out?

A: Yes, by stopping the interview momentarily. He should say something like, "Hold on a second. You just said January Fourth, next Tuesday. But I thought the vote was set for next Monday, the Third." The interviewee, whose train of thought had caused the lapse, will be grateful. (If he wants to put his foot in his mouth about something important, fine and dandy. Don't help him in that case.) When the tape resumes rolling, the reporter should repeat the earlier question.

Q: Should a reporter ever suggest wording or substantive remarks to an interviewee?

A: No, never. That's staging. (At last—a short answer!)

Q: During the reaction cutaways, while the reporter is listening or pretending to listen, what should the interviewee be doing?

A: Talking, even though we see just the back of his head. The reporter should ask a question, then listen during the answer. The edited video will match the edited audio. The reporter may have to explain to the interviewee why the camera is now behind him instead of in front of him.

Q: Should the interviewee actually answer the Reverse Questions?

A: No, because the camera is now in the wrong place. On occasion, the second hearing of the question will cause the interviewee to recall some important (to him at least) point he forgot to make during the interview. In this case, when the reporter agrees that it's important, the camera should be set up anew in its former position. Taping can then proceed.

Q: Is one profile or eye direction better than the other?

A: No. However, when several interviews are done in connection with the same story, some interviewees should be looking right, others looking left. This provides a form of visual balance and is especially effective when the conflicting views of two people are edited together (face to face, as it were).

"Quickie" Interviews

Many of the sound bites used on the air result not from formal, sit-down interviews, but rather from the MOS approach discussed earlier, or from a hybrid sort of interview that barely qualifies for the name "interview." This so-called "quickie" interview results when both the reporter and the newsmaker are pressed for time. The interview is usually done standing up, the CU of the newsmaker hastily framed against a neutral background, and the reporter using a hand mike (instead of two lavalier or clasp mikes) which he aims back and forth at whichever mouth is speaking.

Typically, the interview is only two or three questions long, possibly even shorter if the newsmaker comes to the point without prodding. Even so, a reaction cutaway is necessary as an editing tool. And the newsmaker doesn't have time to stick around while the camera changes position. How to shoot the cutaway?

Here's where the limited view of the TV camera becomes a help instead of a hindrance. That's because the correct Reverse Angle CU of the reporter can be shot without the interviewee's presence and without moving the camera radically. The reporter has only to pivot in the correct direction for the camera to tape him in CU for a matching cutaway. Of course, the "correct" direction depends on the direction in which the interviewee was looking during the interview. Both the reporter and cameraman must pause to make sure the angles will match (according to the right-left, left-right rules described earlier).

One other thing when shooting such cutaways: the position of the microphone. If the mike is held differently in the cutaway than it was during the interview, the result will be a visual anomaly of the type mentioned earlier. It is thus best to frame the reaction cutaway close enough to cut the hand mike out of the picture. Otherwise, the reporter must pretend to thrust it back and forth as he or she did during the interview.

Interviewing Techniques

In terms of content and approach, the same questioning techniques apply in television as those discussed in Chapter 11 for radio. However, the TV camera with its big lens and attendant microphones and lights can be far more intimidating to an interviewee than a mere cassette audiotape recorder. There is nothing subtle about recording a TV interview, at least from the technical point of view. Put yourself in the shoes of the interviewee: there's a light shining into your eyes, you're facing two strangers, one of whom is pointing a microphone at you and the other of whom is aiming a fancy camera at you from a distance of only a few feet, and the one with the mike is trying to get you to address an issue about which you must carefully choose your words. I'd rather be the reporter any day than the interviewee.

Interviewing for television thus requires a special knack on the part of the reporter. He or she must be able to put the interviewee at ease, to somehow make him or her oblivious of all the electronic paraphernalia. This is all the more difficult in that the reporter himself or herself cannot be oblivious of it. The reporter, however, has the advantage of being used to it and thus able to cope with it as a matter of course. His or her task, then, is to project an aura of professionalism during the entire interview situation. Nothing makes an interviewee more ill at ease than a reporter who seems confused about what he or she is doing. The reporter should appear to be unconcerned about the camera's presence, even though he or she may secretly be worried about how it's all going to turn out in the editing room. Would *you* be calm around a doctor who fumbles a stethoscope or a nurse who hesitates while taking a blood sample?

Some people, of course, will be nervous, unresponsive, or both, no matter how professional the reporter. One of the cruel realities of television is that in practice it discriminates against such people, no matter how valid or valuable their opinions. TV news demands clarity of content from all concerned. But a person who trembles, who rambles, whose voice cracks or is very unpleasant, or who is physically grotesque, will rarely be shown on TV—not because of some half-baked notion of protecting viewers from unpleasantness, but rather because his or her voice, appearance, or manner of speaking detracts attention from what he has to say and thus from the story itself.

On the other side of the coin is the interviewee, usually a politician or public official, who is so accustomed to dealing with the media that he or she knows the requirements of television news as well as the reporter. Such people are adept not only at saying only what they want to say regardless of the reporter's questions, but also at placing themselves in positions, relative to the camera, that display their most "flattering" angles. Many office seekers actually hire "media consultants" to teach them how to do this. It can be amusing to watch such "media trainees" try to maneuver the news cameras into a position to capture their "good" profile. As in such interview situations in radio, it is well for the TV reporter to remember that he or she is the boss, *telling* the interviewee where to stand (but not, of course, what to say) and pressing for responsive answers. This often becomes a challenging battle of wits in which, most of the time, both sides retain their good humor.

INSERTS

As the name implies, an Insert is a shot, usually a CU or ECU, inserted into a sequence (series of scenes) to show in detail an object or process being described either by the reporter or by a speaker or interviewee.

Suppose that you are interviewing a home burglary victim who says,

> What they didn't steal, they broke. They smashed everything of value. That vase over there? It's been in the family for over a hundred years.

The shot of the victim, since this is during an interview, is in CU. It doesn't show the vase. But the reporter has pricked up his ears and made a note to shoot an Insert of the vase following the interview. The edited version can then start on the victim, and the tape editor can then lay in the B-roll (video only) of the vase at the precise time we hear the victim mention it. This makes not only for better video than just the talking head, it also permits the reporter to pack more details into his story; otherwise he might have to devote additional time in his script to a separate description of the broken vase.

Inserts are thus extremely valuable shots, and reporters must be constantly alert for them. In particular, they should watch out for

1. *Still photographs* of accident or murder victims, missing persons, and story principals who are out of town or otherwise unreachable by air time
2. *Documents* such as government reports, legal briefs, graphs, and diagrams
3. *Small objects* specifically referred to by speakers or interviewees which, in the reporter's opinion, may be used either in his or her own piece or as a still frame in an electronic graphic

Since such objects, documents, and still photos are usually very small and must thus be photographed in CU or ECU, they should not—repeat *not*—simply be hand-held close to the camera lens; the shot would be too shaky. Instead, they should be wall mounted (except, obviously, in the case of an object that isn't flat) and the camera mounted on a tripod. Such closeup photography is very difficult, and cameramen rarely do it hand-held or on a horizontal surface unless they are especially strong, steady-handed, and in a hurry.

Another type of Insert is the "cover shot" mentioned earlier. Let's return to the case of Senator Piltdown's eyeglasses: what's needed here (since the reporter forgot to ask the Senator to remove his glasses before resuming the interview) is a shot showing the senator putting on his glasses. It can't be face-on because the shot wouldn't match the rest of what we see. So it has to be from *behind* the senator, who must be shown *talking* to the reporter as he puts on his glasses. That Insert may then be used as a cutaway to bridge the two parts of

Inserts

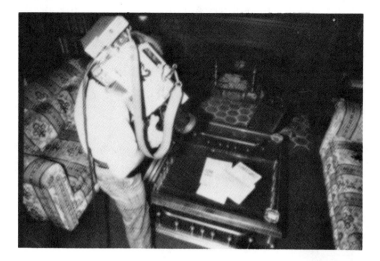

Although Inserts are normally shot with the camera mounted on a tripod and the insert material taped to a wall, WBBM-TV cameraman Steve Lasker was in a hurry (a normal state of affairs in TV news) and shot an Insert the hard way.

Lasker's Insert shot as it appeared on the air during a WBBM-TV newscast. Since Inserts are of material meant to be read by viewers, the camera must be absolutely steady during photography.

the edited sound bite. Similarly, an interviewee may be shown lighting a pipe, dashing out a cigarette, placing an object on a desk, or picking the object up. But to repeat: shooting such cover shots is time-consuming, and it is better to avoid them by being alert for visual anomalies during the main setup.

GROUP INTERVIEWS

Very often, a reporter must interview more than one person at a time: the family of a missing child, the co-winners of a prize, the co-inventors of a new widget, and so on.

Although each member of the group can be interviewed separately in the manner described earlier, the very fact of their being a group sharing an interest in the matter at hand may make it desirable to show them together in the same picture. This causes a few technical problems.

First, there won't be enough microphones to wire each participant. The mikes will thus have to be positioned to capture sound from different directions. This means the shooting location must be especially quiet.

Second, the camera may not always be precisely on the specific interviewee who spontaneously pops up with the response, forcing the cameraman to adjust his shot, which may result in a jarring movement or brief loss of focus. Thus, an array of cutaways is necessary, in addition to the standard reaction shot of the reporter, to cover the momentary loss of good video. Separate cutaways should be shot of:

> The reporter in CU looking *in each direction.* (Remember, some members of the group were looking right, others looking left.)
>
> Each member of the group, in CU, listening silently to the other members of the group.
>
> The entire group, *from behind,* as the reporter listens, first turning his or her attention from left to right, holding for a moment, then turning from right to left. (The camera does not move—just the reporter.)

These shots enable the tape editor to cover any jarring video from any direction.

The same types of shots should be taken in the case of stand-up interviews of two or more persons where the reporter is holding a hand mike. The reporter should be seen turning not just his or her attention, *but also the microphone,* in each direction.

DOPE SHEETS

Before we go any farther, let's regroup for a moment. We've seen how reporters hustle hither and yon, shooting tape here, interviewing people there, and so forth, collecting a mass of raw visual and informational material—so much material, in fact, that it's hard to remember it all. And indeed, memory alone is insufficient. A reporter should keep an accurate record of all persons and locations of which he or she has tape. That record is commonly called a "dope sheet."

If for no other purpose, an accurate dope sheet will allow a reporter to recall and organize story elements in the likely event that he or she will have to write a narration in the field, where there will not be an opportunity to view the tape first.

But there's another purpose, too. Suppose that you have just shot your group interview with those famous widget experts, John Doe and Richard Roe. Nice fellows, you thought, especially that Richard Roe with his handlebar mustache. You ship the tape back to the station and proceed to your next assignment, the bubblegum blowing semifinals. Well, there you are, camera poised to see whose face and hair get enveloped in bubble gum, when suddenly your beeper goes off or you get an order to call in via two-way car radio. It's the writer handling the widget story. Which, he wants to know urgently, is Doe and which Roe?

If you'd sent along a dope sheet, or at least scribbled a note, the writer wouldn't be bugging you or, more important, losing valuable editing and writing time because of your failure to provide basic information on the tape. Roe has a mustache? Then say so on the dope sheet. If nobody has a characteristic readily distinguishable from other persons in the group, what are their positions in the picture—right, left, or center? Or who spoke first—Doe or Roe?

This sort of information is *basic* to accurate TV coverage. The reporter is the only member of the team in a position to collect accurate identifications. He must make sure that the right information gets to the other members of the team.

Some reporters verbally identify all interview subjects on the tape sound track, spelling out names where necessary. But a written record in the form of a dope sheet to accompany the tape is the better method.

And while we're touching on the matter of reporters writing narration in the field without a chance to view the tape; I mention again that small audiotape recorder with which reporters can record the interviews they are simultaneously shooting on videotape. Thus, they can tailor their lead-ins to specific sound bites, resulting all around in a more cogent report. In those markets where union membership is closed and compulsory, however, technical crews may forbid reporters from operating their own gear, even so much as a microcassette recorder. In non-union markets, such strict job delimitations do not exist. (Then again, the pay in non-union markets also tends to be lower.)

WRITING AND RECORDING NARRATION (TRACK)

Writing the narration for a field report is the culmination of the reporter's craft. Often, the writing comes at the end of a long, frustrating day spent in gathering the right pictures. Thus, the writing can be somewhat anticlimactic. But it is precisely at this level, where the creative juices must be made to flow, that careers are made or broken. For only those reporters whose writing proves day in and day out that they can transcend the banality and pedestrianism that permeates so much of local TV news broadcasting in the United States, only those reporters stand a chance of moving on to the major networks.

As noted elsewhere, the conditions under which a TV reporter may have to write his or her narration can be far from ideal. Time may be very short. A courier may be standing by, unable to depart for the station until the field reporter has recorded the narration for shipment along with the taped visuals. The reporter may have little physical comfort—no desk, no chair, no typewriter, maybe no roof over his head. Typically, he will scribble his track in a notebook while seated in the crew car or minicam van, where he'll remain to record his track as well.

A reporter under this kind of pressure needs a capacity for a sort of self-hypnosis; he must shut out the world while he concentrates on his writing. If you're the type of person who prefers to read with the radio blaring rather than in silence, you will probably have little trouble writing a narration in a battle zone. The rest of you will have to work at it—or stay away from battle zones.

As to *what* and *how* you should write—well, I like to think that's what most of this book has been about. Now, as we near page 300, it's a bit late in the day to repeat Chapters 1 through 18. There are still a lot of technical and procedural matters to be learned—so let's move right along . . .

STANDUPPERS

Many news departments like their reporters to appear on-camera, at least part of the time, in their reports from the field. Since each story is different, there can be no fixed rules about when a reporter should appear and precisely what he or she should say. As a *general* rule, however, reporters should write voice-over narration for all elements of which they have pictures, and they should appear on-camera when they must relate something for which they do not have pictures. In other words, whenever possible, people would rather see the event itself than the reporter's face.

On occasion, a field report will consist entirely of the reporter on-camera. Such a report is called a "standupper"—a term derived from the typical picture of the reporter at the scene—standing up, delivering his copy directly into the camera, either from memory or from notes. Even a report in which the reporter is sitting down (say, from the bleachers at a ball game) is called a standupper.

Full-length standuppers have become rare in TV news. Technology has so speeded up the ability to gather or create pictures that at least some visual elements can be found for almost any TV piece. Nowadays, full-length stand-uppers are used in only two main circumstances:

1. *Live reports via minicam and microwave.* On many late-breaking stories, the reporter and camera arrive on the scene without time to shoot and package a report by air time. They thus prepare to go live, the camera crew setting up the camera and microwave transmitter, and the reporter dashing off to gather whatever information he can. Then, properly wired in and on cue, the reporter, the scene of the story behind him, tells the story (or whatever bits of it he's been able to learn in a short time) into the camera.

2. *Analysis and commentary.* Analytical pieces, dealing mainly as they do with ideas and relationships, are much more the province of newspapers and radio than of television. Still, when analysis is required—the "why" element of a story—a standupper may be in order from the staffer who has the most expertise in the matter at hand. Such pieces are usually carefully memorized and taped in the field (teleprompters or "cue cards" are rarely if ever used in the field).

   Commentary, as opposed to analysis, inherently includes the reporter's own opinions. Usually, commentary is reserved for senior staff members whose names and faces have long been identified in their communities, in other words, staffers whose opinions are informed and carry weight. Commentary, as opposed to analysis, is always labeled as such either in the lead-in copy, or by electronic title, or both.

In the normal course of everyday reporting, standuppers are broken into elements that form only part of the finished package: as *openers, bridges,* or *closers.*

WMAQ-TV, Chicago   WBBM-TV, Chicago

Openers

An "opener"—also called a "standup open" or just plain "open"—is, as the name implies, a shot of the reporter on-camera at the very start of a report. Of all the standup elements, openers are the most rare. That's because most of the time what a reporter could say by way of scene setting is better accomplished in the lead-in read by the anchor. An opening picture of a location or an event is a much stronger visual way to begin a story. Still, in certain stories, such as features in which the reporter's presence plays an important part throughout, a stand-up open establishes that close relationship immediately.

Bridges

A "bridge"—or "standup bridge"—accomplishes much the same thing in television as it does in radio (see Chapter 9), by tying two story elements or locations together. The copy in a bridge typically begins with a reference to what we have just seen and, serving as a kind of transition, concludes with a reference to what we about about to see. The second paragraph of the report reproduced in Chapter 17 (page 249) is a good example of a bridge.

Closers

A "closer"—or "standup close" or just plain "close"—again as the name implies, comes at the tail end of a report and thus includes the reporter's sign-off. Closers are the most frequently used type of stand-up element for the simple reason that, once shooting is completed, the reporter has fitted together the pieces of his video jigsaw puzzle and can now offer a sentence or two of perspective.

Standup elements of all stripes share certain characteristics:

1. They are short, running no longer than 15 or 20 seconds.
2. Their subject matter is narrow, limited to one or two story elements.
3. They show the reporter not just on-camera but at a specific location. The shot is framed in such a way as to show the reporter's proximity to the story.

4. They should not—repeat *not*—repeat information told elsewhere in the report. They *add* information. We should not be seeing the reporter's face just for the sake of its beauty.
5. The background should not be so "busy" that it competes for attention with the reporter's words.
6. The reporter is dressed appropriately. He or she appears neat and well groomed—like someone you would not hesitate to allow into your home.

Beginning reporters are advised to stick to doing closers until they get their feet wet and feel adventurous. Then they should attempt bridges here and there. Bridges and openers are tricky in that the story might change between the time they are taped and the time the final package is assembled, potentially rendering the copy dated or incorrect, and therefore unusable. There is much less danger of this with closers, which are usually written and recorded at the end of story coverage. However, that should not stop reporters from doing bridges anyway, for they can always be junked if necessary, but never recreated once the camera has left the scene of the action. Experienced reporters shoot bridges "on spec," on the chance that they will hold up, because when they work, they tend to work well.

RECORDING TECHNIQUES

As in recording spots in radio, recording narration for TV reports is not simply a matter of grabbing a microphone and talking into it. For starters, you should always try to use the *same* type of microphone for your narration as you used in your interviews and standup element. Why? Because each type of microphone has its own sound quality, and the sound quality should be uniform throughout your piece.

Second, it is important to eliminate as much unwanted background noise as possible. Be aware that certain closed places indoors yield poorer sound quality than does standing in the great outdoors; small rooms with tiled surfaces—kitchens and bathrooms, for example—can make you sound as if you are standing in a fishbowl or echo chamber. For recording indoors, choose a room with carpeting or drapes, which absorb sound instead of bouncing it back into your mike.

Third, when recording outdoors in windy conditions, use a windscreen or wrap a handkerchief around the business end of the microphone. A gentle breeze blowing over a microphone can sound like a cyclone to the recording head.

And don't fidget with the mike cable during recording. Moving the cable produces popping and crackling on the tape.

Don't eat the mike, either. Follow the same distance guidelines as for radio: mouth 6 to 18 inches away from the mike, depending on the type of mike and the strength of your voice.

Take Identification and Counting Down

In television, many news departments use countdowns and take IDs before both on-camera and voice-over segments, although this is not as widespread as in recording radio spots. A "take" is synonymous with a "try." An on-camera closer, for example, is identified verbally by the reporter as "Closer, Take One." If he bobbles and must start over, the ID becomes "Closer, Take Two," and so on. He also counts down from five, same as in radio. So the whole sequence goes like this:

> "This is a closer, Take One. Five-four-three-two-one. (half beat) Still unknown is whether the suspect . . ."

Remember, if you bobble or make a factual error, you must do the whole thing over *from the top* (in a standup element). Videotape can't be patched together like audiotape to eliminate a bobble. A jump cut of *you* looks even worse than a jump cut of an interviewee.

A countdown should be delivered before voice-over narration, too. Only this time it is *not* necessary to repeat from the top in case of error. (In case you're wondering why—and I hope by now you're not—in the voice-over narration, the editor will be working with sound only.)

Some news departments like their reporters, in addition to verbally identifying each take, to hold up the equivalent number of fingers in front of the camera. This permits the tape editor to locate the correct take (which you've noted on your dope sheet) by picture only, on Fast Forward Scan, thus saving a few possibly critical minutes of editing time. Of course, if you mess up more than ten takes . . . .

Closing Pad

You'll recall that in radio it is necessary to remain silent for a few seconds after completing a voice feed to provide time for the recording engineer to turn off the circuitry and thus avoid unwanted noise—a sort of buffer of silence. Well, in television what is needed is a buffer of silence *and* picture. The reporter himself acts as the "pad" to "cover" any delayed roll cues.

Thus, at the end of any standup element, but especially after the sign-off in a closer, the reporter remains *motionless*, eyes still directed toward the camera, for approximately 5 seconds. This is true for live standup elements as well as taped ones.

This is necessary just in case there's a delay in punching up whatever picture is to follow that of the reporter looking into the camera; he mustn't inadvertently be seen scratching his nose—or worse.

20
REPORTING III: BASIC STORY COVERAGE

I've been referring to outside reporting as "field reporting," which, although technically correct, somehow has a relaxed, almost rural connotation. In practice, TV reporters are likely to refer to themselves as "street reporters," not only urbanizing the connotation, but also showing how they perceive themselves: street-smart.

Indeed, reporters do have to be street-smart to be successful, whether in print or broadcast. But being street-smart in TV also means knowing where to go to get a desired picture and how to shoot it once on the scene. No one is born street-smart. It comes with experience. In the beginning, newly hired reporters are likely to be overwhelmed by the technical aspects of the job, to the detriment of their substantive reporting. This chapter, therefore, is designed to help beginners sort out the technical and procedural matters that can at first seem confusing.

A word of caution: The suggestions that follow for specific shots and story coverage are just that—*suggestions*. No two stories, no two events, are identical. Indeed, it is the reporter's job to learn what makes each event unique. However, news events do tend to fall into general categories: fires, road accidents, trials, parades, and so on. I offer the following suggestions category by category to help those of you who may feel at sea, but also in the hope that many of you will quickly find you can do better on your own.

FIRES

Fires are a staple of local news. TV broadcasters have been accused of devoting too much coverage to fires. Critics say TV journalists have become overly enamored of the bright, dancing pictures that fires provide for the screen. I'll sidestep the criticism by stating one indisputable fact: no one can predict how much injury or damage a fire will do; a fire must first be brought under control. And since by then it may be too late to get good pictures, the assignment editor has no choice. When the police or fire radio signals a fire, he orders a crew to the scene *immediately*. (In large cities where arson and accidental fires are virtually hourly occurrences, some newsrooms hold off until a fire reaches the two-alarm stage. But everywhere else, the practice in case of a fire report is *Don't walk— run!*)

Upon arriving at a fire scene, the reporter and camera should stay well away in order, above all, not to be in a position to interfere with fire-fighting and rescue efforts. The camera has a telephoto zoom lens, enabling photography from a distance. Basic coverage from this distance includes:

1. Several sustained LS and MS of the fire and fire-fighting activities. (CUs of fires are usually wasted; they all look alike.)
2. CU and MS cutaways of victims, spectators, and fire equipment.

If it's a small fire, brought under control quickly without injuries (smoke inhalation is the most frequent injury in a fire), those pictures will suffice as visuals for whatever information the reporter proceeds to gather; the story, if used at all, will wind up as AVO.

But if it's a big fire, causing injuries and heavy property damage, you must shoot more footage:

3. Paramedics, ambulances, and injured people being helped or carried away.
4. CUs of the burning premises' owners and residents, shot from a respectable distance. Such people, especially if related to the victims, will probably be emotionally distraught; their faces, shot from a distance, should tell the story without interviewing them at this point.

Once the fire is under control, you can proceed with your interviews:

5. The ranking fireman, the shot framed against the smoldering scene or the fire-fighting equipment. What caused the fire? How many injured? How? Any special fire-fighting problems? Special equipment used? Was it arson? (Don't forget the reaction cutaway.)
6. The victims— those willing to talk and having pulled themselves together. Where were they when the fire started? And what did they do? (Remember to spell their names accurately in your notes and/or dope sheet. And you may need reaction cutaways here, too.)

After getting clearance from the ranking fireman, you can now move closer to the debris for

7. CUs of fire damage. Look for the telling detail: a clock face, a child's toy, a smoldering mattress.

Keep an eye out for an arson investigator. In many cities, an arson investigation is routine, an investigator being dispatched at first word of a fire. In other cities, the overworked Bomb and Arson Unit can't send an investigator until hours or days later. But if one arrives, you'll want a shot or two.

Okay, you've got your information, visuals, and interviews. The next step is to call the producer of the next newscast and fill him in. The producer will then decide if he (or she) wants you to package a report; that decision depends on how many other stories, and of what importance, are vying for air time.

If the decision is for you to do a package, you must at least organize it in your head *before leaving the scene.* Why? Because if you are going to do a standup element, *that* is the location for it. Once you leave the scene, you won't be returning. So although you may be able to write and record your narration back at the station, you must write and shoot your standup element immediately.

And remember, in writing both your standup element and narration, you should not—repeat *not*—mention the *total* number of injuries or the condition of anyone hospitalized; leave that for the writer-written lead-in to your report. Why? Go back and reread Chapter 10.

ROAD ACCIDENTS

In broadcasting, a bus is a bus, a truck is a truck, but an "auto" is a *car*—and never a "vehicle." Whenever any of the foregoing run into each other or something without wheels, the resulting road accident is another staple of local news, especially in smaller markets, where a high proportion of viewers will likely be personally acquainted with the victims.

As with covering fires, TV reporters and cameras must hurry to the scene of road accidents, to beat the tow trucks; an accident scene doesn't look like much when all that's left is an oil smudge on the pavement.

Here again, it is important upon arriving not to interfere with any efforts to rescue injured or trapped victims. Keep out of the way!

Important: Car crashes and other violent events can be bloody, grisly affairs. Each news department has a policy regarding the showing of blood and gore. The reporter and cameraman must know the station's policy. Many stations which broadcast news at the dinner hour forbid "shooting bloody" or "editing bloody"—showing closeups of mangled corpses, severed limbs, or gushing wounds. There are ways of shooting such scenes to minimize the gore; I include them among the following shot suggestions:

1. An LS of the accident scene—wide enough to show not only the accident but also its immediate environment, such as interstate highway, local expressway, or residential neighborhood.
2. Several MSs of the wrecked or damaged vehicles and property, from different angles.
3. Cutaways of spectators, police, and paramedics.
4. Any scenes showing corpses, severely injured victims, or excessive blood should be *double-shot*. That is, shots showing any of the foregoing should be matched

by alternative shots from angles that obscure most of the potentially offensive material.

5. Time permitting and story meriting, interviews of participants or witnesses. (Cutaways!)

The reporter, naturally, gathers factual information on the accident—names, circumstances, and so on. The story may turn out to be more than just this one accident: maybe one of the drivers was drunk and had a prior record of drunk driving; maybe the accident location was poorly lit or poorly marked—maybe the scene of a rash of accidents; maybe the state, city, or county is dragging its feet on correcting matters.

What I'm getting at here is that the visuals of the story are not necessarily *the* story. Beginners tend to forget this, neglecting the basic follow-up work incumbent on reporters in *all* media.

NEWS CONFERENCES

Broadcasters generally prefer to say "news conference" rather than "press conference" to stress that all media were present, not just print. However you call it, news conferences are not the formal, infrequent affairs they once were. Nowadays, whenever an official or office seeker has something to say (often self-serving, to be sure) and wants to avoid giving a dozen separate media interviews, he or she calls a news conference. It may be in an office, but more likely it's in a nearby conference room or small auditorium. The point is, it's indoors—and that means you'll need a light, a tripod, and two microphones (one for the podium or conference table and one for yourself).

For TV coverage of news conferences (and most other events planned and announced ahead of time), it is important to *arrive early*. It takes time to set up the light and podium mike, and it's a good idea to shoot a couple of cutaways *before* the newsmaker arrives—the reporter pretending to listen and take notes. You might not get a chance to take the cutaways later, since you can never be sure what the newsmaker will say or when. If he or she happens to say something important while the camera is busy shooting cutaways, well, you're out of luck.

Audio engineers from Chicago stations WGN-TV and WMAQ-TV setting up microphones well before the scheduled start of a news conference. Arriving early is standard procedure in TV news.

A standard face-on CU for news conferences.

NBC News

Time and context permitting, the camera moves behind and to one side of the newsmaker for a cutaway in which the newsmaker's lips are *not* fully shown.

NBC News

In actual practice, news conferences usually provide only one element of a package—perhaps a sound bite and a few seconds of setup footage. But they must not be shot that way. There must be enough footage to provide adequate visuals for an *entire package,* just in case the news conference alone yields major news.

So here are news conference shots to cover any eventuality:

1. Reaction cutaways of the reporter before the newsmaker arrives
2. Cutaways of other TV cameras, also before the newsmaker's arrival
3. From the main tripod position, a sustained MS of the newsmaker walking into the room and taking his or her place behind the microphones
4. A *continuous* roll, in CU, of the newsmaker's remarks, stopping only to change cassettes if necessary
5. Time and context permitting, an ELS of the overall scene (to serve as a cutaway or setup shot)
6. Again time and context permitting, a hand-held shot or two from *behind* the newsmaker that shows him or her talking but does *not* show the lips
7. Back at the tripod position, a sustained MS of the newsmaker leaving the table or podium and exiting the room

You now have enough footage from enough different angles to package a report on the news conference alone. The fact that much of that effort may never be used on the air is not important. Unused footage, known as "outtakes," has the same status as a reporter's unused notes. The rule in TV news is: Shoot the tape and decide later which of it to use.

SPEECHES

Technically, TV coverage of formal speeches or lectures is very similar to coverage of news conferences, requiring the same gear and shooting procedures. The difference from the reporter's point of view is that he or she may be able to obtain an advance text of the speaker's remarks and thus roll only on the desired remarks during the speech itself. The danger is that many experienced speakers sometimes depart from their prepared remarks, and such ad lib comments are often more newsworthy than the prepared ones. If a speaker departs from the prepared text, the reporter has no choice but to roll and to continue rolling even through the unwanted text, because you can't know if or when the speaker will do it again.

A second consideration in covering formal speaking or lecture engagements is this: controversial speakers and controversial subjects can draw unruly crowds. This may take the form of demonstrators or hecklers trying to shout down the speaker. Such behavior may be rude and uncivilized, but it happens. And because it happens, newsmen have an obligation to cover it.

For the TV reporter and cameraman, this means being prepared to go portable at a moment's notice. If the hecklers are hustled out of the hall, you'll want a shot of it.

PARADES AND MARCHES

Everybody loves a parade —except maybe TV cameramen who've lost track of how many they've covered. Bored by the proceedings as they may be, professional cameramen remain sufficiently alert to make their parade pictures "match" on the air, by providing two indispensable elements:

1. A consistent POV (point of view)
2. A master shot for sound

Each of these elements takes a bit of explaining, starting with POV. Let's say you're a spectator at a parade. You've staked out a nice spot along the parade route, right at the curb and offering an unobstructed view. Okay, here comes the parade, from your left, marching in front of you, passing you, and moving away to your right. All you have to do to see anything you want is to turn your head a little.

Now suppose you cross the street. The parade looks just as good from there, except, of course, that from your new point of view the parade is passing from your right to your left. In life this makes no difference because your senses, perceiving a vast area, allow you to reorient yourself automatically. But on television, with its narrow, boxed-in perception, it makes a world of difference. According to what the camera now sees, there are *two different parades* marching in opposite directions, either away from each other or about to trample each other.

Therefore, the first rule in covering parades, marches, or anything involving movement in a single direction is *don't cross the street*. Find a nice unobstructed spot and shoot *everything* from that side of the street, including the cutaways. Only that way will the shots look consistent, that is, *match*.

As for the second indispensable element, a master shot for sound—well, this is a bit trickier. What's the typical sound you hear at a march or parade? A band, right? Now the people in the parade are not just hearing this music, they are marching or stepping *in time to it*. Thus, the videotape editor has got double trouble. First, how is he or she going to edit the music? Music has a beat, a tempo. You can't cut part of the music, edit it together, without risking a major clash of sounds.

The editor's second problem is all those marching feet. How can both the sound and the picture be made to match? I mean, you don't want a bunch of feet in the air on a downbeat, do you? The marchers would look like uncoordinated clods. There is just no way to switch in midbeat from "She Wore a Yellow Ribbon" to the "Washington Post March" and at the same time make sure the marchers don't have two left feet. What to do?

Okay, puzzle fans, here's what happens:

1. The cameraman picks *one band* and shoots *uninterrupted* for at least 1 minute. During that time, of course, the band will have passed the camera and no longer be a very interesting picture. But it's the *sound* that matters most here. This will be the tape editor's master sound track, over which he will be able to lay in different pictures (B-roll), even of different bands, without viewers being the wiser. That's because . . .
2. The cameraman also shoots other bands and marchers *without showing their feet*. Nobody at home can tell if the marchers look out of step, because they won't see any steps except for those established in the master shot. The edited parade footage will all look and sound natural.

What the home viewer sees is thus a sort of optical illusion. But lest you somehow think this is fakery or staging, I challenge you to come up with some other way to show a 1-minute version of a 2-hour event. No way. The only "trick" is to make the edited version come as close as humanly possible to recapturing the flavor of the event as a whole.

Remember, on any shooting assignment where music is involved—a concert, a night club performance, whatever—a master shot for sound is essential. It may be necessary to do more than one, to give the tape editor a choice.

SINGING AND DANCING

To provide editing tools for coverage of a singing performance,

1. Shoot a master shot of one entire song, *face on.*
2. Then shoot all cutaways and reverse angles of the singer from behind or to the side, so as *not* to show the singer's mouth. There's no way to edit lips that are singing "I Left My Heart in San Francisco" with lips that are singing "New York, New York."

Dance performances, especially ballet, are virtually impossible to edit. After all, the essence of dance is coordination of feet and body with the music. Therefore, shots without feet don't work.

In Hollywood they may use several cameras in different positions rolling simultaneously to film a dance number, enabling the editor to intercut at will. A TV crew has just one camera—so the best the cameraman can do is to shoot several long takes, hoping that in at least one of them the sound and picture will both be good.

PUBLICITY STUNTS

In the television age, snake oil salesmen have grown sophisticated. Public relations (PR) people, many of them ex-journalists, devote considerable time and effort to getting the clients or products they represent onto TV newscasts, especially on the local level. If they succeed, they get what amounts to free advertising. Thus, they are often the enemies of responsible news gathering. Be forever on your guard.

Many an assignment editor, especially on a slow news day, has been lured into ordering coverage of a seemingly straightforward "event," only for the reporter and cameraman to discover on arrival that the whole thing is a publicity gimmick. Let's say you're assigned to cover a man attempting to set a new world's record for continuous trampoline jumping. You arrive to find the man wearing a jersey emblazoned "I took the Pepsi Challenge." A little digging (i.e., asking a few questions) turns up the information that the man is being paid by the Pepsi Cola Company, which also bought the trampoline and hired the PR firm that called your station. Thus, you conclude, the "event" would not be taking place were it not for the commercial underwriting. Do you still cover it?

Maybe yes, maybe no. It depends on how you handle it. The "event" may turn out to be interesting, especially as a lighter item at the end of a newscast. But whatever happens, you owe it to yourself and your viewers to make clear in your copy that the "event" is being sponsored and is thus not "spontaneous." Commercial sponsorship should always be labeled as such.

And there are ways to minimize the "free advertising:"

1. Choose Medium Shots that do not highlight commercial elements such as posters, banners, or painted vehicles.
2. Frame interviews close enough to cut out commercial messages on clothing.

In the case of our fictional trampoline jumper this would mean shooting from a side angle that doesn't show the lettering on his jersey. If this proves impossible, remember this guideline: news is news, and ads are ads, and if ever the twain shall meet, viewers must be told.

PUBLIC HEARINGS

Public hearings, although normally orderly, are difficult to shoot because of the multiplicity of sound sources. And when they turn *dis*orderly, coverage difficulties are compounded because of the sudden multiplicity of picture sources, as well. Sometimes the holders of public hearings organize things so that anyone asking a question must come up to a fixed position in the room, and anyone being questioned must reply from a different fixed position, such as the center of a conference table. In such a case, you know where to put your mikes and aim your camera.

Unfortunately, things are rarely that well organized. Questions are typically asked from the floor, at the questioner's seat. And the responder (at public hearings there are several officials present to hear questions) usually answers from wherever he or she happens to be sitting. This is a nightmare from a technical point of view because of all the possibilities and uncertainty of who's going to say what from where.

One partial solution is to use a *shotgun microphone,* so named for its ability to pick up sound from any source it's aimed at from a distance. However, shotgun mikes are not magic. They do not pick up clear audio from distances of more than about 10 feet. What they do mainly is increase the mobility of the camera crew.

The real problem remains: How do you cover a public hearing without the camera and reporter dashing thither and yon, chasing each new mouth that opens? The solution is pleasingly simple. And it involves not technical virtuosity or wizardry but, rather, journalistic know-how. The reporter must learn who will be present and what issues or complaints will be raised, and by whom, *before* the public hearing gets under way. By preparing himself and his cameraman for what is *likely* to happen, and where in the room, the reporter can cover the actual hearing with a minimum of surprises and technical mishaps.

This form of blocking out the action ahead of time is a good idea, if not essential, for many types of stories. The reporter should do whatever he or she can to *foresee* actions and events, in order to prevent the camera from being taken by surprise. It is customary for organizers of scheduled events to provide reporters with a detailed agenda of the proceedings; the agenda is *must* reading.

CRIMES

It is a sad fact of life in late twentieth-century America that crimes against persons and property are commonplace. In our major cities, so-called "routine" murders, rapes, and armed robberies are often buried deep in the inside pages of newspapers and perhaps not even mentioned on radio or television. There is, of course, nothing "routine" about a murder, rape, or robbery to the victim or the perpetrator. Yet the news media in large cities, like the police themselves, cannot possibly devote great attention to every crime that is committed, because of lack of space, time, and personnel. By definition, "news" is what's uncommon and unusual. If crime, even murder, becomes commonplace, it is no longer automatically news.

But, remember, I've been talking about big cities—i.e., broadcasting's major markets. That is *not* where most of you will begin your careers. Instead you are likely to start in a town where murder is extremely rare and the armed robbery of a 7-Eleven convenience store is a very big deal indeed. So a lot of what you will be doing will involve talking with the police and understanding police procedure.

In all crime coverage, reporters are heavily reliant on the police, both for accounts of the alleged circumstances and for permission to visit the crime scene while it is still fresh. This is the natural order of things, but it is not always easy for reporters to swallow. The police are naturally more interested in solving crimes than in assisting reporters; they also routinely withhold information of the sort that, if made public, could in their estimation jeopardize an investigation. Reporters, for their part, while not wanting to jeopardize police work, suspect that the police many times black out news coverage merely to mask their own incompetence.

Whatever the case, crime news is almost always secondhand information. But there are no such things as secondhand pictures, so TV reporters have an even tougher job in telling crime stories than their print and radio colleagues. TV attempts to "reconstruct" the crime, even murder, through relevant pictures. Needed are

1. Insert shots of recent still photos of the victims
2. Several angles of the crime scene itself, showing police technicians going about their business
3. An interview of the ranking detective at the scene or back at the station house
4. Interviews of witnesses
5. Interviews of friends and relatives of the victim(s)
6. The corpse

Actually, item 6, the body, is the most important shot of all, but it requires explaining. First, there's the potential blood and gore problem mentioned a few pages back. You should find a camera angle that doesn't show a dead face or a massive wound.

Second, you may not be allowed on the premises (crime scenes are off limits until the police say otherwise). The routine in homicide investigations is to close off the area until police specialists have combed it for evidence. The corpse may not be moved (by law) until it has been examined by the medical examiner (in some states called the coroner). However, anytime thereafter it must be transported to a morgue or other facility for further examination and autopsy. And *that* is the shot—the draped body being carried out on a stretcher— that producers want above all. Why? Because it is grisly without being *overtly* grisly, dramatic without being *sickeningly* dramatic. And it shows movement in a sequence that otherwise would have looked static.

Another sad fact about crimes in late twentieth-century America is that most of them are never solved. In the news business, there's a pattern to crime coverage. On day 1, the day of the crime, the story is news. On day 2, if the crime was truly major, there'll be a follow-up story. On day 3—well, in TV news there usually isn't a day 3—unless the crime 48 hours earlier was truly spectacular.

But here's a tip: Keep in touch with whoever is heading the investigation of a crime you've covered. Call him every week or two. You may wind up with a minor scoop.

TRIALS

By the mid-1980s, at least 40 states were allowing TV cameras into selected courtrooms on a permanent or experimental basis. The rules for TV coverage of trials varies widely, but typically the final say in the matter is up to the presiding judge. In the states barring TV cameras from courtrooms altogether, visuals are provided by courtroom artists either on a station's full-time payroll or hired on a per trial or per diem basis.

Since, from the technical and procedural point of view, TV reportage is very different depending on the type of visual coverage permitted, it is necessary to examine each system separately.

With Courtroom Camera

The presence of TV cameras in courtrooms is the result both of technical innovations and of a hard-fought battle by broadcast news organizations to win for themselves what they perceive to be the same rights to cover trials as the print media. Broadcasters argue that sound and picture coverage of trial testimony, decisions by judges, and verdicts by juries is inherently the nature of broadcast news and that to forbid it amounts to discrimination in favor of print reportage.

Opponents argue that TV cameras are disruptive and thus influence the course of a trial, and may result in the declaration of a mistrial or harm the rights of the accused. They also argue that television news, in its constant search for dramatic pictures, tends to favor emotional testimony rather than legally important testimony, and thus presents a distorted picture of a trial.

The debate will continue, but even as it does, technical innovations are providing short- and long-term tests of each side's contentions. The main innovation is, of course, the small videotape camera with an extremely light-sensitive tube, enabling the camera to be placed discreetly, and the shooting of tape by natural light. The camera allowed inside a courtroom is usually not a standard model used for everyday shooting but rather a smaller model placed in a fixed tripod position off to one side. Although it has a zoom lens and can swivel (pan) at the cameraman's discretion, it can neither take the quality of image ultimately desired nor be moved to frame the ultimately desired shot. Sound capability is limited also, since it would be clearly both disruptive and technically unfeasible to wire everyone with mikes. Thus, sound is taken either by plugging into the courtroom's internal audio system (usually limited to the judge and the witness box) or by a shotgun mike that must be aimed in the same discreet fashion as the camera itself. In the first system, the remarks of the opposing attornies may be inaudible since they move around a lot; and in the second system, all the audio tends to be echoey or muffled.

One other thing: the courtroom camera is a *pool* camera; its image is shared by all stations covering the trial. The obvious purpose of this procedure is to prevent the sort of disruption caused by the presence of numerous camera crews arriving and departing at different times, setting up or dismantling a welter of equipment. Indeed, the recorders taping the image of the sole courtroom camera are usually located outside the courtroom, alongside a monitor. The absolute rule is that courtroom decorum must be maintained by all parties at all times. And the presiding judge may decide to ban or limit taping at any time.

Even with these limitations, TV reporters are able to cover trials with a complete range of tools in the *technical* sense. There remains, however, the more important problem of *editorial judgment*. Will the reporter indeed choose the emotional sound bite over the legally important one? And since the use of such a sound bite will occupy a portion of the edited report that may be disproportional to its importance in the day's testimony as a whole, will the result be distorted coverage? And will coverage be weighted in favor of those trial participants who know how to "play" to the camera and thus provide more appealing tape?

I think you can see how heavy is the responsibility of the TV reporter to ensure fairness and balance both in content and choice of pictures. I know of no other reporting situation where the reporter must give more attention to the ramifications of his or her words and pictures, for at stake are not just the reporter's ability to condense reality, but also the effects of his or her choices on both the rights of the state and the rights of the accused.

Technically speaking, the courtroom camera has simplified the gathering of visuals as well as their editing. There is now sufficient tape to support visually virtually anything the reporter wishes to write. And the entire package can be written and recorded at the courthouse and then sent back to the station for editing. With live minicam capability, reporters can save for a live closer their account of any court proceedings that may have transpired since they shipped their tape.

Without Courtroom Camera

Working with courtroom artists is much more difficult, both technically and procedurally, because the reporter must first coordinate with the artist what he or she wishes a sketch to show, and then must guide, in person or by phone, the shooting of the sketches onto videotape.

Marci Danits, a staff courtroom artist for WBBM-TV, Chicago, touches up a sketch of a witness giving testimony. The sketches will either be mounted on an easel for live insertion during a newscast, or, more typically, be shot on videotape to permit editing along with the rest of the reporter's taped visuals.

Courtroom artists, armed with large folders of drawing paper and boxes of multicolored chalk, work for newspapers as well as for television. Although they work quickly, it is humanly impossible to draw more than just a few sketches of each courtroom session. Thus, each sketch must be representational of some major aspect of the trial. Although most courtroom artists are professionals, they of necessity pay attention mostly to the visual qualities of the courtroom scene instead of to the substance of the proceedings. So the reporter must make quick, firm decisions on what he or she wishes a sketch to show; and since one is forbidden to talk while court is in session, the decisions must be relayed by passing notes or by discreet hand signal.

Once a session has begun, although reporters may discreetly leave the courtroom in most trials, artists must remain seated; they can't carry out their materials without causing a disruption. Therefore, the reporter must arrange for a camera to be present outside the courtroom during a recess or meal period in order for the sketches to be shot once the artist has fleshed them out. The logistics can be nerve wracking.

The sketches, however well executed, are static, limited visuals. Thus, TV reporters need other visuals to flesh out their trial stories. Here are some of the shots to go for:

1. An LS exterior of the courthouse as an establishing scene-setter.
2. Shots of the plaintiffs and the defendants, as well as each side's attorneys, arriving and entering the courthouse. Although the principals will usually keep their lips buttoned, their lawyers may very well offer some self-serving remarks. These may be useful as sound bites if they tell what the day's court session will entail— which witnesses will be called and so on.
3. The same shots *after* the day's session, in which the lawyers may offer more self-serving remarks about how the trial's going. Since reporters will have their own ideas about this, they can decide whether or not such sound bites should be used.
4. Shots of the *jurors* arriving and/or leaving. Jurors are instructed not to discuss the trial while it is in progress, and reporters must not attempt to goad them into remarks that could conceivably result in a mistrial. After a verdict has been pronounced, however, jurors are not only fair game, they should be actively sought out for interviews.

    In major criminal trials, juries may be sequestered—in which cases the only shot of them may be in a chartered bus as they arrive or depart the courthouse. You *will* want such a shot.
5. A standup element. Visually, a report should not end with an artist's sketch. It is a weak closing picture. Much stronger is a cut to a reporter's on-camera bridge or closer as he or she sums up the progress of the trial or tells what testimony or court procedure is scheduled for the next day.

As you can see, TV trial coverage demands a high degree of journalistic and technical savvy. The first time that a reporter is assigned to cover a trial, he or she should take the trouble to go over in advance with the producer, in great detail, the visual elements the producer would like to see, with the assignment editor the precise availability of a camera and where it is to be located, and with the courtroom artist (that being the case) the kind of sketches the artist is good at. The aim is to reduce the logistics and the imponderables to a manageable minimum, to enable the reporter to concentrate on the substance of the trial.

SPORTS

Although sports is primarily entertainment rather than news, it has come to occupy large chunks of local TV newscasts and therefore deserves serious consideration in a book such as this. As noted in Chapter 13, sports writing and reporting are vast wastelands of cliché-ridden and colorless, empty prose. One reason is that sports reporting, by and large, does not attract young people who are intellectually inquisitive and who have a flair for words. This is less true in print than in broadcasting, perhaps because print affords inventive writers the space (calculated in numbers of words) to give their talents full vent. TV sports reporters must necessarily compress their efforts into short takes often confined to telling the scores and highlights.

But it need not be thus. In fact, local news executives almost everywhere bemoan the shortage of good sports reporters—those who are able to get beyond "Hey, Coach, are ya gonna win on Saturday?" to the specific hows and whys of a team's strong points and shortcomings, and who can explain things in clear, grammatical English. In short, sports reporting in TV news is a wide-open area for newcomers with talent.

Modern TV sports reporting requires far more than a mere knowledge of the rules of the games and the names of the players and coaches; it requires as well a knowledge of the sports *industry*—the economics of ownership, player contracts, local tastes and income levels—as well as the history of games and athletic competition and the psychological role of sports in society. Young sports reporters should not accept the view that the "average" TV sports viewer is some hairy-chested, pot-bellied lump in a T-shirt whose only exercise is the beer run to the refrigerator. In fact, interest in sports cuts across all sectors of American society, and lively conversations about football or baseball can be heard in boardrooms as well as in bar rooms.

As for camera coverage: What is most important is showing *action,* even if such action is only practice. Sound bites of players and coaches can make for dull viewing, visually and intellectually. If during an interview a coach speaks of a particular player performing a particular action, then that player and action should be shot during practice, or the appropriate game file footage taken from the station's tape library, in order to lay the pictures over the coach's voice. In other words, the edited tape would show the coach just long enough to establish his identity, then cut to the action tape (B-roll) while the coach's remarks continue on audio. (This is a standard editing technique in much TV news presentation, as you've no doubt noticed.)

Another thing to remember about sports reporting is that teams are composed of individual players and that an effective method in TV coverage is to zero in on the efforts of just one or two of them. TV is inherently more effective in showing individuals than in showing groups. It's not enough to say "The *team* played well." You should tell who, how, and why.

In short, in sports reporting the accent is on *reporting*.

"CHECKBOOK JOURNALISM"

As we've seen repeatedly in these pages, much of news reporting, especially in television, comes down to a matter of ethics. So it is with the question of paying news sources for providing information and/or visual material.

The practice of, in effect, paying for the news has come to be known as "checkbook journalism." The term is pejorative, for the very idea of paying for information is repulsive to most reporters and their editors, who would like in all cases to uncover the news by their own efforts rather than reward interested third parties. Indeed there are some news departments that issue a stringent edict to all personnel: "Thou shalt not grease palms."

Unfortunately, however, the matter is not always clear-cut. As noted elsewhere, the competition in daily news-gathering is fierce, and it is a rare competitive news department that will not allow its reporters some leeway in cornering exclusive use of potentially newsworthy material. Even CBS News, which has strict prohibitions against staging of any kind, recently paid a reported $500,000 for exclusive broadcast rights to taped interviews of former President Richard Nixon, even though CBS News itself did not conduct the interviews, and even though some of the money was going indirectly into Mr. Nixon's pocket.

Obviously, the station you first go to work for won't have half a million dollars lying around. It may not even have fifty. So why have I bothered to bring up the subject?

Here's why: Suppose a small aircraft crashes on landing at your local airport. You and your camera are the first TV news crew to arrive at the scene. You busily go about your work of shooting tape and interviewing witnesses. And one of those witnesses, it turns out, had the presence of mind to aim his or her still camera at the plane and click away as it came in and belly-flopped. Or, better yet, was armed with a Beta, VHS or 8mm camera and captured the crash sequence on videotape. And the witness, naturally quite aware of the value of the property, offers to *sell* it to you.

I am willing to bet that this is a case (and not an unusual one) where any policy against "paying for the news" would go straight out the newsroom window. *Of course* you want that tape. (In fact, you're probably drooling over it.) The only questions are, How much will it cost? and, Will the owner sell it to your station exclusively?

Given that you probably didn't go into the news business in order to haggle over such matters, and given that you do not control the purse-strings of your news department, the first thing you must do is to stall the seller until you have contacted your news director. You must act without delay; you must not allow time for a competing station to "steal" this visual material from you without a fight.

The practice of paying for information, especially visual material, began long before the invention of television. It's a good idea to make sure you know your own station's policy on the matter long before it ever comes up in the field. And while you're at it, you should ask about a whole range of news-gathering methods that are tinged with ethical considerations: Does "cultivating a news source" include taking that source out to lunch at company expense? May you pay money to informants who call you with inside information or advance word of an upcoming event? May you "borrow" a document from someone's private files long enough to shoot insert tape of it? Should you respect someone's request *not* to use his or her picture?

And the other side of the coin: Should you, the reporter, accept a free meal while on assignment if the provider is a principal in the story? By the same token, should you accept free or discounted merchandise or services from such a person or organization?

Many news departments have policies regarding these and related matters. Many others do not. The way *you* answer those questions has a lot to say about what kind of person you are and what kind of journalist you will become.

ECONOMICS AND MEDICINE

I have lumped these two broad categories together not because they are related in subject matter—they aren't—but because they often lend themselves to similar treatment in TV reporting. An economic policy decided in Washington, and a medical treatment developed at, say, Johns Hopkins, will affect large numbers of people. But on television, you can't *show* large numbers of people; if you try, you find yourself uttering broad generalities which are uninteresting to hear or watch, as well as quickly forgotten.

A television report works best when it is *specific*, when it shows how a policy, issue, or event affects one or two individuals. You can't show 10 million unemployed people, but you can show how unemployment affects one family. You can't show how a new treatment affects 100,000 diabetics, but you can how it affects one or two of them.

The same is true of natural disaster stories. A tornado may destroy an entire town (a shot that can be taken from the air), but what viewers will remember is how it affected one or two families. The home screen is small. So should be the scope of a TV report.

There are several story categories—features, hostage situations, and so on—which by their very nature defy specification. So I will not even try. However, there at least two areas—investigative reporting and documentaries—that deserve special attention.

INVESTIGATIVE REPORTING

Author and broadcaster Edwin Newman, in his novel *Sunday Punch,* has his protagonist, a former editorial writer, describe how he came to learn the events he relates in the book: "At some of the events to be described, I was present. Some I was told about. Some I was told about only after asking—this is now called investigative journalism." Newman's point is that *all* journalism is to some degree "investigative." You don't get answers to unasked questions.

In today's broadcast news departments, the term "investigative reporting" has taken on the special meaning of uncovering heretofore unreported developments, mostly of an illegal or unethical nature. Such reportage is rarer in broadcasting than in newspapers for financial rather than philosophical reasons. Only a small percentage of TV stations can afford to remove a reporter, producer, and camera from the daily production pool. (Or at least they *profess* not to be able to afford it.) It takes weeks or months to investigate a story possibility, and in the end the story may not pan out either in content or visually; in effect, the effort may go for naught. That's the risk of investigative reporting, and precious few stations are willing to run it.

Where they do exist, Investigative Units (IUs) generally consist of a unit producer, a field producer, and one or two researchers. A reporter and cameraman usually step into the process only after the story has been firmed up through initial research and the on-camera work is ready to begin. At a few places, a reporter and/or camera are assigned to the IU exclusively, right from the start. As at newspapers and magazines, investigative reporting for TV involves great secrecy; therefore, as few staffers as possible are told of the proceedings, and all are sworn to keep their mouths shut at all stages of the investigation.

Preliminary Research

Obviously, what's necessary at this stage is to learn if there is indeed a story. But hand in hand, even at this early date, *two* investigations proceed simultaneously. The first seeks to learn if the story is true and can be documented; the second considers the visual possibilities: Can the story be *shown* as well as told? It isn't sufficient to learn the location of incriminating documents if the camera can't get to them for Insert taping. If the story comes from a tipster, will the tipster agree to go on-camera? If not full face, then in silhouette? Must his or her voice be distorted?

Although you probably won't be able to get a news director to admit it, stories which might reach fruition in print might be killed at an early stage in TV if there are no decent visual possibilities. However, with advances in electronic graphics, it is becoming possible to create visuals for virtually anything.

Preliminary Execution

This stage roughly corresponds with the stage in which a print reporter could begin to write his main article: the facts are firm, and only details need to be added here and there. In TV, it's just the beginning of the production process.

A reporter and cameraman are called in, briefed, and sent into action taping Insert material, stealthily taping interviews and exterior locations. To protect secrecy, this work is done swiftly, over as short a period as possible. As we've seen, there's nothing subtle about the presence of a TV camera. People begin to wonder, "Hey, what's this all about?" Taping continues until all the basic visuals are "in the can."

Final Execution

This is the stage, in practice perhaps only hours before the broadcast, where anyone incriminated or accused is informed *in general terms* of what the IU is about to report and given a chance to tell his side. Specific allegations or findings are *not* mentioned over the phone. Instead, that is done in person, and sometimes saved for revelation on-camera *during* the interview, because the best shot of all may be the interviewee's initial reaction to the allegations. This may seem unfair, a sort of springing of a trap on the unwary. But remember, an interview can always be declined. Furthermore, the surprised party can always say, "Now hold on here, give me a chance to check that out before I answer." As a general rule, an innocent party will bend over backward to cooperate. If the IU has done its work thoroughly, honestly, and ethically, innocent parties have nothing to fear from such tactics. And I would be less than honest if I did not say that the most dramatic footage possible is the surprised or angered face of a guilty party. The station wants it, not badly enough to be sneaky or unethical, but badly enough to want it through meticulous investigation.

Follow-up

Even before the report is aired, the IU has thought out what the possible reactions will be and has alerted the assignment desk to the potential need for reporters and camera crews to follow up the story. That's because competing stations and other media will be doing their best to find their own angles on the story once you've broken it. And as we've seen throughout this book, the news business involves staying on top of the news every step of the way. How embarrassing it would be for a competing station to beat you on reaction to your own story!

There's no rule on who gets assigned to an Investigative Unit. It could be long-time staffers who've proved their mettle in day-to-day General Assignment work. Or it could be specialists hired away from newspapers or magazines, because daily General Assignment reporting does not teach investigatory skills. However, if it is your goal to be a part of a TV Investigative Unit, you would do well to begin to specialize *now* in research techniques and the gathering of legal evidence.

DOCUMENTARIES AND "MINI-SERIES"

Like Investigative Units, Documentary Units are rare birds in local television— and for the same reason: money (or, rather, lack of profitability). Management in general perceives news documentaries as costly frills.

In recent years, however, there has developed a quasi-documentary form called a "series" or "mini-series." As the name implies, this is a series of reports on a single subject, reported in installments on successive evenings. A series broadcast over five evenings covers roughly the same ground as a half-hour documentary—and in fact may be rescripted, reedited, and rebroadcast in that form if the subject matter and its treatment are truly superior.

Mini-series production usually involves far fewer staff than Investigative Unit production. In fact, the entire series may be the work of a single reporter and videotape editor, calling on the services of different cameramen as they become available. Obviously, what a documentary or mini-series accomplishes is to treat an important story in far greater depth than would otherwise be possible. In terms of planning and production, this means that interviews run longer to allow the reporter to probe more deeply, and the chosen sound bites run longer, too. In a way, a documentary simply makes greater use of the same visual elements that are gathered for a one-time report, going over the same ground but lingering longer at each stop along the way.

But a documentary can also have a point of view. A reporter assigned to a documentary or mini-series reaches certain conclusions somewhere along the way, and in general he or she is allowed to express those views under the heading "analysis" or "commentary" at the end of the program (or in the last installment of the mini-series).

Because a mini-series is spread over several evenings, it cannot be presumed that all viewers will be watching each installment. Therefore, each installment must be written to stand on its own, so that viewers who missed preceding installments will not be left in the dark, coming in in the middle of the movie, so to speak. This entails a certain amount of repetition, usually accomplished by the anchor's lead-in plus opening copy along the lines of, "Last night, we saw how . . ." and so on.

In well-managed news departments, reporters are encouraged to propose stories for eventual mini-series. In television, a reporter's story or mini-series proposals should include ideas for *visual* content as well as for informational content.

PANEL AND MAGAZINE SHOWS

Until the explosion of local news programming in the 1970s, stations everywhere used to produce a variety of local programming: children's shows, cooking shows, and so on. Nowadays, such local programming tends to be issue oriented and is thus produced by the news department or by production units which draw on news department personnel, especially reporters and anchors.

Typically, such shows are broadcast weekly on Saturday or Sunday. Their formats vary widely, but two are pretty much standard: panel shows and "magazine" shows.

Panel shows are single set interview programs in which the guest is a local official or newsmaker who is asked a barrage of questions by one or two of the station's own reporters and one or two "guest" reporters from local newspapers (never from competing stations). A staff reporter may be assigned permanently to the weekly panel or be asked to step in at the last moment. Either way, the only way the show can shed light or make news is for the panelists to have boned up on the issues, following up on their colleagues' questions instead of striking out helter-skelter.

"Magazine" shows get their name from their typical format, which is to treat just two or three stories per program, the way a magazine would present two or three major articles per issue. Magazine shows were introduced on many local stations following the huge success of "60 Minutes" on CBS. And the local shows often emulate "60 Minutes'" mix of hard reporting, human interest, celebrity profiles, and off-beat locations.

Such shows are considered plum jobs in both local and network television, and appointment to them is generally won only after long, successful work as a General Assignment or feature reporter. On the local level, many such shows lean squarely toward entertainment rather than important issues; thus, much emphasis may be placed on a reporter's on-camera personality rather than on his or her reporting abilities. Either way, skill in interviewing is a prime asset.

21
PERFORMING

As stated in the introduction to this book, you do not have to look like a movie star to be a TV anchor or reporter. However, you can't look like the Hunchback of Nôtre Dame or the Wicked Witch of the West either. A certain modicum of appearance and performing ability is required.

No matter what TV journalists would *like* to call it, a newscast is a *show*, a "performance" by news professionals. That much is inescapable in a mass medium overwhelmingly dedicated to the proposition that an audience of 2 million and 1 is better than an audience of 2 million. Public television, too, requires performing ability inasmuch as it competes in the same commercial environment, trying to attract a share of the same audience as commercial stations.

So performing is a fact of life in television, even more so than in radio, because people can see you as well as hear you. This chapter, while it can't magically change you from a frog into a prince or princess, is designed to familiarize you with some of the cosmetic aspects of television that you will confront sooner or later.

VOICE AND POSTURE

Before continuing, reread, if necessary, the last part of Chapter 13 on performing in radio news. I am assuming that you now have reached the level of constant practice with a tape recorder or of delivering regular newscasts on your campus or corporate closed-circuit radio station.

The next step is to start practicing delivering the news in front of a mirror. We're not looking yet at the way you comb your hair or wear your lipstick. We're looking just at the way you move your head. You should *not* be moving it. In an effort to give their copy the right stress, the right intonation, the right "feel," many radio newscasters use a sort of body English. They hunch their shoulders and bob their heads up and down and from side to side. If you find yourself doing this, you must break the habit for television.

On TV, such body movements are distracting to say the least. And in closeups, both on the set and in taped standup elements, a bobbing head moves in and out of the frame. So a delivery must be attained that relies overwhelmingly on voice inflection and facial expression.

Nor is it desirable to sit there like a lump. A "dynamic attitude" can be created: shoulders erect (but not stiff) and one shoulder turned slightly into the camera, creating a "dynamic" pose. Try a number of poses, first left, then right. Now run through them again, closing one eye as you do so in order to see yourself as the camera does, in two dimensions instead of three, until you find a pose that is comfortable for you.

Ideally, your school or company should have some sort of studio camera or videotape camera by means of which you can see what you actually look like on television. Don't be surprised if you look far different from in real life. The TV camera doesn't show the true depth of your facial features; it squashes you into a flat image. It therefore tends to make people look fleshier than they really are; the camera makes many people look like they have fat faces. So in TV, thin is in.

As you practice delivering news copy into the mirror or camera, it is natural to feel uneasy or unnatural at first. That's because it *is* unnatural. It's a form of posing. You'll get used to it.

PERSONAL APPEARANCE

On-camera news personnel are expected to be well groomed at all times. For men this means a shaved face (unless you've already got a mustache or full beard) and a good haircut, the hair neatly combed. For women this means moderate makeup and a conservative hair style—no pigtails, frizzes, or cutie-pie curls.

As for wardrobe, men are expected to wear a jacket and tie and women to wear simple, tasteful clothing—no trendy army fatigues, low-cut dresses, or jerseys. Where appropriate, on field assignment, reporters may wear clothing suitable to the circumstances. Both sexes should avoid loud colors and bold checks or stripes that "bleed" on television; that is, they cause an electronic sparkle that plays havoc with video tubes.

Since the lower half of the body is seldom seen on-camera, it is possible to wear blue jeans and scuffed shoes without the viewers being the wiser. However, reporters daily confront a host of people while out on assignment, and such get-up creates a bad impression.

At a number of local stations, anchormen and women go to extremes to "improve" their appearances, spending small fortunes on cosmetics and hair styling. Such people are often deservedly the butt of their colleagues' derision, and critics sometimes refer to them as practitioners of "blow-dry news." There is absolutely no reason for reporters to go overboard in this manner.

MAKEUP

Thanks to today's light-sensitive cameras, it is almost never necessary for most reporters to wear special makeup in the field. On the studio set, however, where reporters appear frequently and anchors appear daily, the lighting can be harsh, giving light-complexioned faces a washed-out look. This is true of black and oriental skin tones, as well as of caucasian ones.

The problem can be corrected by applying a thin layer of pancake makeup around the eyes, nose, mouth, and chin. You will have to experiment, not only because each face is different, but also because lighting conditions are different at each station. Anchors with extremely fair skin may also have to apply makeup to the backs of their hands, or to cover skin blemishes. All such makeup should be water- rather than oil-based, so that it can be washed off easily.

Understandably, men may feel sheepish at first about wearing makeup. But they soon come to regard it as one of the occasional necessities of working in TV news.

CAMERA ANGLES

How you appear on-camera depends not just on your posture in facing the camera but also on the camera's location. If the camera is set high, forcing you to look up as you talk into it, different aspects of your face will be emphasized than when the camera is low, forcing you to look down. After a while, you will learn which angles and positions work best for you, and, circumstances permitting, you will be able to consult with camermen accordingly. But watch out you don't become a prima donna about it!

PERSONAL HABITS

I wish I didn't have to mention this, but a fact of life in TV reporting is that, in a modest way, reporters lead a public existence. Viewers stop them on the street to say hello or ask for an autograph. They are solicited by organizations to help in fund drives or to act as guest speakers. In short, apart from having their egos fed, they act as representatives of their stations in ways never demanded of print or radio journalists. Their personal lives and habits are thus more open than they might like to public scrutiny. Need I say more?

One other thing while we're on the subject of public attitudes: in any mass audience there will always be a certain number of cranks and a number of the outright mentally ill; they react more strongly to television news than to newspapers, perhaps because TV news is delivered directly by visibly flesh-and-blood human beings. At any rate, TV news anchors and reporters receive an alarming number of crank or perverted calls and letters. Mostly, the letters are in the nature of this one, which, typically, was handwritten and unsigned:

> Good bye Channel ————. I am also writing all your advertisers.
>   Television is a media [sic] for Education & Entertainment—not a forced doctrine of Liberal Communism. Mr. Watts [apparently referring to former Interior Secretary James Watt] is a very fine person—compared to Joan Rivers & her trashy friends—Why don't you get Ed Asner, Jane Fonda & her filthy friends all on one program—Then all the liberals & Commies can be entertained in one nite—
> Good bye
> P.S. I am 84 yrs. old. Ratings on your station can only go down.

The only unusual thing about that letter is that most of the words were spelled right. And, if anything, its tone was mild.

Unfortunately, there are some people who may try to harm TV journalists physically or who at least threaten to do so. In one case, a young woman anchor in a small market in a Western state was threatened at knifepoint by a would-be suitor, a total stranger. Although such overt violence is extremely rare, the threat of it is not, and TV news personnel, because of the public nature of their work, are frequently the targets. So it's best to be cautious in dealing with complete strangers.

TALKING TO THE CAMERA

Let's get back to matters of performance. As noted, delivering news copy into a camera lens is a kind of pose, which makes it difficult to remember that you're really addressing people at home. And in the studio there are other distractions: camera operators wheeling equipment into various positions, a floor director (TD) giving finger countdowns on tape roll cues, and so forth. It's hard to concentrate, much less sound relaxed. (You begin to appreciate why anchors are so highly paid.)

Each performer eventually hits on a technique that allows him or her to communicate through the unblinking camera eye. Some TV reporters and anchors pretend, while delivering copy, to be addressing a close friend or loved one instead of cold machinery. Others prefer to imagine a roomful of strangers who must be compelled to pay attention. And still others, the very few, take to it like ducks to water, indeed seeming to come more alive in the TV studio than in person.

WMAQ-TV (Chicago) studio engineer Dale Schaeffer loads script pages into a teleprompter machine and coordinates its speed with the reading speed of the anchors and reporters appearing on the set.

The teleprompter-projected script permits WMAQ-TV anchor Linda Yu to read the news copy fluently as she looks into the camera. The script she holds in her hands is merely a backup, in case the teleprompter fails.

TELEPROMPTER

Part of the showmanship of anchoring is in using a teleprompter correctly. The teleprompter is, in effect, a projector that throws the audio portion of the script across the camera lens; the projection is done with mirrors, creating a sort of optical illusion that enables the anchor to appear to be looking into the camera when he is in fact reading the script verbatim. Although he holds a copy of the script in his hands and appears to be glancing at it from time to time, the downward glance is a practiced pose. The only time an anchor truly reads his hand-held script is when the teleprompter jams temporarily. Otherwise, he's reading when he looks up, not down.

As you might imagine, it takes skill and practice to use a teleprompter effectively. Most beginners either wear a glassy stare, mesmerized by the projected words, or move their eyes jerkily back and forth, line by line, thereby destroying the illusion of fluency that the teleprompter is designed to create.

Very few stations nowadays are without a studio teleprompter. In larger markets, a full-time operator runs the machine to make sure the script pages are inserted in the right order and that the crawl speed corresponds precisely with the anchor's reading speed. Many smaller market stations use a self-operated teleprompter, the speed of which is controlled by the anchor himself by a remote-control device.

Either way, using a teleprompter is a learned skill, and job applicants who have never used it before should request either that it be turned off during their on-camera auditions or that they be given time to practice with it before taping. When a job is at stake, a newcomer may be better off relying on his or her hand-held script, looking up from it as often as possible to maintain eye contact with the camera. But it is far, far preferable to use the teleprompter if you at all can.

On, yes: There may be anywhere from two to four cameras on a studio news set. The one whose red light is on is the one you should be talking into.

22
THE FUTURE

THE COMPUTERS ARE COMING

Broadcast journalists have become accustomed to technological change. They have accommodated their working habits and techniques to suit, successively, the switch from black and white to color, the switch from film to videotape, the arrival of live minicam transmission, and the advent of computer-assisted electronic graphics and titles.

But none of these technological advances encompasses such thoroughgoing changes of environment and procedure as the coming computerization of newsrooms, the so-called "electronic newsroom." Computers bring a fundamental change to the very atmosphere of a newsroom and the interplay among journalists. They take considerable getting used to.

But get used to them we must, for they are not only coming—in some cases they are already here. At this writing, a handful of radio and TV news departments, sprinkled far and wide across the country, are almost completely computerized on an experimental basis. The experiment is not to decide *whether* to keep the computers but, rather, *to what extent* to use them.

According to estimates by a cross-section of news management personnel, computerized news operations will be standard in major markets by 1990 and in small and medium markets by 1995 (give or take a couple of years). In other words, *your* generation will witness their introduction and deployment.

The few computerized newsrooms already in operation permit rather precise predictions about the nature of broadcast news as it will soon be gathered and prepared just about everywhere. To people who have virtually grown up with computers and word processing programs, computerized newsrooms will seem normal and natural. To others, accustomed to the *feel* of pen and paper and to the palpable interaction of human beings from beginning to end, computerization presents a challenge that must be met and mastered.

HARDWARE AND SOFTWARE

As we've seen, broadcast newsrooms currently use typewriters, wire service teletype machines (either normal speed or high speed), and countless reams of teletype paper, copy paper, script paper, carbon paper, thermal paper, and various order forms. Say goodbye to all that when the computers arrive. In place of all these are video display terminals (VDTs) with attendant keyboards and memory storage units, plus a high-speed printer for the final script or whatever hard-copy production may be desired.

The "electronic newsroom" at WGN-TV, Chicago. Gone are the typewriters, teletype machines, wire copy, and script paper. In their places are VDTs and computer keyboards.

Changes in working procedures are sweeping. Newsroom personnel

No longer receive or read wire service copy on paper but instead scan the material on their VDTs

No longer type scripts or order forms on paper but rather on their keyboards for storage or further routing to whoever else must see the content

No longer update or substitute pages by hand but rather via their VDT keyboards

No longer recalculate cumulative cue times but rather reprogram the computer to do it

No longer have to keep an eye peeled on the (now non-existent) wire machines but instead on their VDTs, which flash for "bulletin" or "urgent" material

No longer *hand* material to anybody but rather "send" it to the desired party or parties through the computer

Will eventually not even prepare a hard copy of the newscast script, which instead will appear on VDTs in the control room and directly on the news set tele-prompter for live broadcast

Thus, computerization changes even the fundamental quality of *reading* and the attendant journalistic habit of *taking notes*. No longer can a writer or producer routinely tear off and save a piece of wire copy on which to make notes or underline key portions. Instead, he or she must either store it in a separate "file" in the computer's memory or else order the computer to print a hard copy of it. Since, as a practical matter, the printer, being the slowest part of the system (next to the human beings, of course), can quickly become over-loaded with simultaneous requests from other personnel, the usual practice is to use the electronic filing system. And since there is thus no permanent visual reminder of its existence, no piece of paper cluttering the employee's desk, it is regrettably easy to forget all about it; the employee has to *remember* to recall his or her "file."

Over the short term, computers can (and do) cause journalistic laziness or forgetfulness. They are intimidating to the uninitiated; a lazy or forgetful writer can neglect to recheck important details or deliberately write a "copy cat" version of whatever wire service story happens to appear on his or her VDT.

It is no wonder, then, that computerization is not done overnight. At the handful of stations where experimental systems are in use, the elements of writing and preparing newscasts "the computer's way" were being introduced slowly, step by step, to enable employees to retain their wits and creative instincts.

Psychologically, one of the effects of newsroom computerization is a vast decrease in the level of human contact. No longer do employees conduct all normal business face to face. Even though a writer and producer may be sitting within a few feet of one another, the producer does not assign a story to a writer by hand. Instead, the producer "sends" the story to the writer via the computer. And no longer does the writer hand the written story to the producer for proofreading and correction but, rather, "sends" it to him or her. The producer then keys it into the "script file" where the computer places it in the desired order among other finished stories, automatically recalculating roll cues and cue times in the process.

The WGN, Chicago, radio newsroom is completely computerized. By the time this book is published, there will no longer be any hard copy scripts; instead, newscasts will be announced directly off VDTs.

WGN-TV Midday News producer Forrest Respess proofreads a story "sent" to him by a newswriter. The "electronic newsroom" pictured in these pages is a system called "Newstar" and was designed by a division of the Dynatech Corporation. Competing systems have been designed both in the U.S. and abroad.

During a visit to computerized radio and television newsrooms in Chicago (at WGN-AM and TV), I was struck by the general level of *quiet.* There was, of course, no clattering of typewriters or teletype machines. But there was also a startling (to me, at least) lack of human concourse; the general hubbub of a newsroom—the shouted instructions, the verbal give and take of journalists discussing story content and handling, the rush of bodies to and fro—was eerily low-level. Still, the production of newcasts—the writing and assembling—was accomplished smoothly and seemingly effortlessly.

Because of the danger of power surges that can cause computers to "lose" their memories, newsrooms will for some time continue to print hard copies of newscast scripts. But once those "bugs" are eliminated through electronic safeguards, there may no longer be any need for paper in a broadcast newsroom, except for rundowns and casual note taking. Both in radio and in television, the already electronic existence of the newscasts themselves—the sounds and pictures—may at last be matched by total electronic preparation as well.

And, as ever more sophisticated, miniaturized components are invented and produced, the more newsroom computers will offer further uses. For example, portable VDT/keyboard units will enable producers and other employees to plug into the system from their homes or other locations, permitting them to keep up on the news and to monitor newscast production at any time. Reporters at outlying bureaus will be able to do background research in the field and program their narration copy directly into the system. Using VDTs, it will be possible to *originate* entire newscasts from the field; the anchors will no longer be set bound.

It would be incorrect to call newsroom computers "the wave of the future." They are very much the wave of the *present.* Station managements are asking not *if* they should computerize, but *when.* Some managements are even offering to pay part of the cost of home computers purchased by their employees, as well as to reimburse them for connection and transmission expenses.

Some TV news insiders fear that the new computer technology will have the same result, initially at least, as some of the preceding technological innovations, namely, to distract broadcast journalists from the main task of reporting the news clearly and accurately. That, of course, will depend on how well your and succeeding generations are able to cope with it all. In the meantime, it will be well to remember the classic caution regarding the use and value of computers: "garbage in, garbage out." In other words, the computer itself won't make an error, only its operator.

COMING TECHNOLOGY—RADIO

Radio news, I'm happy to report, will see very few technical innovations in the near future. Of course, there will be the major matter of computerization, which will eliminate scripts and teletype paper; entire newscasts, including tape cues, will be typed directly into the system, then read live off VDTs. But the techniques of field reporting will remain essentially unchanged, as indeed they have for nearly a decade now.

The chief difference in the field, experts report, will be the common use of cordless telephones and other radio-telephone devices over which to feed actualities and spots. In the mid-1980s, cordless telephones were essentially toys, of little use for professional purposes. The frequencies assigned to such phones were so limited that they were hopelessly overcrowded with would-be users, who found themselves unable to get dial tones or plugging into neighbors' conversations. Experts say that will eventually change as the FCC and private industry combine to find and regulate devices able to exploit frequencies that were heretofore inaccessible. In addition, so-called "cellular" carphones will relieve the current overcrowding of radio-telephone frequencies. In some cities, cellular systems are already in operation.

With a cordless phone in his gadget bag, the radio reporter of the future will be able to call in and feed tape from virtually anywhere. Editorially, his work will remain essentially the same, except, of course, that he'll have to be a little quicker to beat the competition.

COMING TECHNOLOGY—TELEVISION

In television, the story will be quite different from that in radio. Experts report that there will be three kinds of technological advances which, in greater or in lesser measure, will alter the nature of TV journalists' work, both in the studio and in the field.

Digitalization

The first advance, already nearing perfection, involves the changeover from the present analog system of television to the new digital system. The analog TV signal is produced by waves whose frequency and intensity re-create a picture *analogous* (similar but not an exact replica) to reality. The system entails a certain amount of distortion and picture loss, including the TV cutoff phenomenon discussed in Chapter 16.

The digital system, produced by, what else? computers, re-creates a picture *exactly* by breaking it down into digital information that is then reconstituted at the point of reception. No distortion, no picture loss—no more TV cutoff problem. Cameramen and tape editors will thus be sure that what they see will be the same as what home viewers see, and they will choose their shots accordingly.

Because analog and digital systems are incompatible (the home TV set has to be able to "read" the digital information), it will be many years before the new system completely displaces the old.

Miniaturization

The second predicted major technological advance is the perfection of a new generation of compact, lightweight videotape cameras and recorders.

Actually, advances in this field are being made all the time. But if TV stations were to adopt each one of them, they'd be buying new gear just about every year and going broke in the process. Generally, TV stations wait for some new "plateau" that promises both professional-quality pictures and a long-term reduction of costs. For example, only a handful of stations have adopted half-inch (Beta or VHS) tape formats both because stations only recently acquired three-quarter-inch (U-Matic) gear, and because half-inch yields only marginal economies.

According to TV technology experts, the next "plateau" will be the perfection of 8mm (also called "quarter-inch") videotape gear, with a cassette about the same size as a current audiocassette. Such small-format video gear already exists, but its quality at this writing was generally poor, not even good enough to satisfy most amateur enthusiasts. Inexorably, however, the technology will improve, and, the experts say, the day will come when both from the technical and financial viewpoints stations will no longer be able to resist—especially if, as seems likely, their three-quarter-inch gear is on its last legs at the time.

How will such miniaturization affect TV news reporters? For starters, surmise the experts, TV reporters will be able to easily carry and operate the gear themselves, much like radio reporters now do with audio gear. In short, stations could get rid of their staff cameramen and save a bundle in salary costs. Would TV news managements decide on such a course? The cynics say yes—anything to cut costs. The purists say no—a reporter can't be responsible for everything and still do a good job.

At this point, nobody knows. But if I were just starting out in TV news, I'd make it my business to know how to operate a camera and take decent moving pictures.

Minitransmitters

The third predicted advance in TV technology brings us into what only a few years ago was considered "Star Wars" territory. Today, however, we know not to scoff. I'm speaking about the development of powerful minitransmitters that will permit live remote broadcasting anywhere, anytime.

At this writing, the typical minicam transmitter mounted on a van has a maximum range of about 60 miles on a direct line (transmitter to tower). The quality of the picture depends greatly on atmospheric conditions and on the local topography, both natural and man-made. Although the public seldom realizes it, many live minicam reports fail to get on the air because of insufficient transmitting power to overcome atmospheric or topographical obstacles.

Soon, the experts predict, will come the day when a TV news reporter, a camera in one hand, a microphone in the other, and a minitransmitter strapped to his or her back, will be able to report live via satellite *from* anywhere in the world, *to* anywhere in the world, *anytime* day or night.

To tell you the truth, I wouldn't want to be the field reporter to come on the air after hearing the anchor say, "Our Joe Doaks is standing by live at that tank battle in Iraq. What's it look like, Joe?" No, sir, I wouldn't want to be "standing by" (or even sitting by) to report that story. But the point is it'll be technically possible. And in television news, what's technically possible sooner or later gets a tryout. It's in the nature of competition. One station wants to show it's the "news leader," and its competitors are forced to follow suit.

The other aspect of such transmitting capability of interest to field reporters is that it will make feeding video signals just as easy as feeding audio signals. The editorial choices won't change, but the working environment will. For, like radio reporters, TV reporters will have to work quicker—and so will the tape editors, writers, and producers back in the studio.

All things considered, the future demands of broadcast news gathering and presentation loom even heavier than the present ones.

23
JOB HUNTING

You should have a pretty good idea by now of the skills required nowadays of broadcast journalists. For those of you who may have conceived of broadcast news as a "glamor" profession, perhaps much of this book has come as a shock. If so, I've succeeding in painting a picture of broadcast news as it really is: a profession requiring highly honed verbal and technical skills, coupled with a ceaseless capacity for hard work. That's not exactly my definition of "glamor."

My objective has been to prepare you realistically for what to expect, not just on the job but also in seeking the job. For, in the real world of radio/TV news, people are not hired for what they *say* they can do, but rather for what they *show* they can do. Applicants at all levels must provide not just résumés outlining their experience; they must also furnish samples of their past work, either in the form of audio- or videotapes, in the case of on-air jobs, or written material in the form of scripts in the case of writing or producing jobs. Only *then*, having survived this initial elimination process, are applicants invited to take auditions which will finally determine their employability.

At the moment, and for the foreseeable future, broadcast news is and will remain a buyer's market; that is, employers can pick and choose from a large surplus of applicants. At the same time, there is a shortage of people who are truly qualified, people who not only *can* do the work but who continue to *want* the work long after they have discovered how demanding it is. The result is a rather steady turnover of personnel, some people moving on to bigger jobs in the business and others dropping out of it altogether. Those who can do the work and stick with it usually advance very quickly.

SALARIES

Starting salaries in all branches of journalism are usually very low. That's because unlike, say, medicine or the law, starting young journalists are, in effect, being paid while they learn. You'll hear a lot of numbers being thrown around about the "sky-high" salaries being paid to TV anchors at networks and major markets. Well, I suggest you keep your feet planted firmly on the ground. While it is true that *some* anchors and *some* correspondents do earn very high salaries indeed, *most* are within the so-called "moderate" income range. In other words, they earn enough to visit Hawaii, not buy it.

About those starting salaries: In 1984, journalists in both print and broadcast could expect to earn from about $12,000 to about $18,000 a year in their first jobs, depending on the locality and the news organization. Like the cost of living, salaries tend to go up every year, usually by an average of around 7 percent—so you should recalculate the foregoing figures according both to the year you read this book and to the year you begin your working career.

In both print and broadcast, salaries rise markedly as one both gains experience and moves to larger cities. However—and here comes the juicy part—salaries eventually become much higher in broadcasting than in print for people who either perform on the air or attain the upper levels of management.

Perhaps some actual salary figures will show the difference. The figures are for Chicago, the nation's #3 market, and compare the union-guaranteed minimum salaries (as of January 1, 1985) of two categories of editorial personnel: newswriters (called copy editors in print) and reporters.

PRINT

Copy Editor (starting)	$540/week
Copy Editor (after 5 years)	774/week
Reporter (starting)	497/week
Reporter (after 5 years)	748/week

(Source: Newspaper Guild of America)

BROADCASTING

TV Newswriter (starting)	$529/week
TV Newswriter (after 2 years)	735/week

(Source: NABET)

TV Reporter (starting)	629/week
TV Reporter (after 5 years)	930/week

(Source: AFTRA)

Remember, those are *minimum* salaries; in actual practice, many reporters earn much more than the minimum, especially in broadcasting. In addition, the foregoing figures are for a 40-hour week; overtime is paid at the rate of "time and a half," significantly raising earnings during periods of heavy work loads. Remember, also, that print and broadcast journalists do not start their careers at this level. They earn their way up from smaller cities and smaller news organizations. As a general rule (to which there are some exceptions), a minimum of 5 years' experience in journalism is required before an applicant will even be considered for a starting job in a major market.

Nevertheless, the figures do show vividly that the key to higher earnings in broadcasting is in appearing *on the air*. Of course, becoming a producer, executive producer, or news director also results in higher pay as compared with print. But the difference is not as marked as it is in the field of on-air reporting in radio and in television.

All of which, for the moment at least, is just pie in your professional sky. You haven't got that first job yet, and we all know that's the toughest one to find. So herewith are some pointers on where and how to look, and what to expect along the way.

WHERE TO LOOK

Small Markets

Unless you are exceptionally skilled, your first broadcasting job will not be in a major market or even a medium market. Instead, it will likely be in a small market or at a very small station in a fringe area of a larger market, the kind of place that can tolerate your mistakes because of the penurious wages it is paying you. Thus, while you should apply for jobs in larger markets, even in the almost certain expectation that you will be rejected, you should concentrate your realistic expectations on small market stations.

It used to be true that beginners had an advantage in their own hometowns. After all, it stood to reason (and still stands, in my opinion) that a hometowner's knowledge of the territory, his shared background with hometown listeners, and his ability to pronounce local names correctly would work to everyone's mutual advantage. But this is not necessarily the case nowadays. That's because there has been a sort of homogenization of America which has made one "hometown" very much like another, at least in terms of the types of local stories to be handled on a daily basis. And, employers as a general rule do not distinguish between "good newsmen here" and "good newsmen there." Rather, they believe, rightly or wrongly, that a good newsman is a good newsman *anywhere*.

That said, I still believe that your hometown stations, except for the big ones in major markets, should be your first stop.

Your second stop should be the stations in your "secondary" hometown, that is, the area where you have lived or studied away from your present home. There, too, you may be able to convince an employer to hire you over someone else because you know the territory better.

A third place to look, here at the very beginning of your job search, is at those stations with "special relations" with your school's journalism or communications department. Many schools have established "work-study" programs with nearby or regional stations, giving students a chance for on-the-job training and giving participating stations a chance to eyeball upcoming talent.

Internships

Still another way to begin is with a brief internship at a major station. Stations all across the country offer internships to newly graduated journalism majors. As noted elsewhere in this book, such jobs do not always afford newcomers an opportunity to do anything but menial chores. But at least they can open doors for opportunities elsewhere. After all, the people who work at a station as full-time employees had to come from *somewhere*—and usually they are happy to help interns seek jobs at those smaller "somewheres."

Trade Publications

It is important to understand that there are never a lot of *advertised* jobs in radio/TV news. That's because news directors at good stations are swamped with résumés and tapes from job seekers. Still, some stations do advertise, either because they're having trouble finding the type of people they want at the price they are willing to pay or because of a heartfelt desire to make sure through the broadest possible talent search that they hire the best people available.

There are two main sources for such Help Wanted ads. The first is *Broadcasting* magazine, which is the chief journal of the broadcasting industry as a whole. Published weekly, *Broadcasting*'s back pages contain job listings for both radio and TV, broken down into categories such as "newswriters," "producers," "anchors," and so on. *Broadcasting* is not available at your corner magazine stand. It is, however, subscribed to by almost every organization having anything to do with the broadcasting industry, including the radio/TV departments of schools and universities. If you do not have access to it, you may subscribe or purchase individual copies ($60 per year or $2 per issue) by writing to

Broadcasting Magazine
1735 DeSales Street, N.W.
Washington, D.C. 20036

The magazine also accepts "Situations Wanted" ads from jobseekers. Replies are channeled through blind "box" numbers so that both job hunters and employers can look to fill their needs without anyone being the wiser.

In addition, *Broadcasting* publishes an annual yearbook containing the names, addresses, and telephone numbers of all radio and TV stations with news departments, listing the names of executives, the size of news staffs, and each station's newscast format and programming schedule. The *Broadcasting* yearbook is expensive and, because of the heavy personnel turnover in broadcast news, tends to be slightly out of date by the time it's published. However, many schools and universities purchase it for their libraries. Or, if you're feeling flush, you can order your own copy by writing to the above address.

The other prime source of job listings is the placement service of the Radio-Television News Directors Association (RTNDA). The RTNDA placement service issues a job bulletin about twice a month. This can be obtained by writing directly to

Placement Chairman, RTNDA
c/o National Television News
6016 Fallbrook Avenue
Woodland Hills, Calif. 91367

There is a charge for the service (in 1984 and 1985 it was $8.00 for four issues), and a check accompanying the order should be made out to the RTNDA.

Job hunting, which tends to be a full-time job in itself, is also a matter of keeping an eye out for hirings and firings, both of which create job openings at one place or another. A good national source for such information (in addition to *Broadcasting* magazine) is the weekly journal of the entertainment industry, *Variety*. *Variety* always contains several pages of items about developments in radio and TV news—who's expanding, who's cutting back, and so on. *Variety* is published in midweek and usually reaches local markets by the weekend or the following Monday. It is available at large bookstores and at magazine concessions specializing in out-of-town newspapers.

HOW TO LOOK

Résumés

A résumé, or CV for "Curriculum Vitae," is the most important document a job seeker ever writes. A common mistake among beginners is to pad the résumé to make it look "more impressive." Believe me, employers are *not* impressed by a 22-year-old applicant whose résumé runs to two or three pages. Instead, they are likely to doubt the sender's common sense, not to mention his or her integrity and staying power.

Résumés should be *short* and *succinct*. They should be only *one page* long. They should begin with the applicant's name, age, address, and telephone number, then list briefly his or her experience, starting with last job first, then go on to state the details of his or her *higher* education (not high school), and conclude with a mention of a few references and any special talents (typing speed, foreign languages, awards won, etc.) And that's *it*. *No* long-winded statements about professional goals, attitudes toward journalism's role in society, how deep is the ocean, and so on. The only other thing you might include is a recent photograph if you're applying for an on-air position in television.

Okay, you say you don't have any professional experience; you're applying for your first professional job, and all you can list on your résumé is your amateur experience at school or office. What do you do? Well, incredible as this may sound to you, it is *better* to list no experience than to pad a résumé with phony experience. You're not fooling anyone but yourself. Small-market and small-station employers know full well that you're applying for your first job.

Heck, if you had experience you'd be applying elsewhere and for more money. What such employers want to see is your level of education and your cover letter, as well as you in person, to determine if you are the kind of go-getter who can deliver what you promise in return for the opportunity to get on with it.

Cover Letters

Next in importance to the résumé, and some say of equal importance, is the cover letter that accompanies it. The cover letter is a prospective employer's first inkling of both how you write and how you think. Therefore, it should be written just the way you'd write a broadcast news story: short and to the point. No frills, no detours, no gobbledygook.

The cover letter (and the envelope in which your mailing is sent) should be meticulous in spelling the news director's name right. I realize that seems obvious, but you'd be surprised how many applicants don't bother to do it. How do *you* feel about mail in which your name is misspelled? Chances are you don't have much respect for the sender. Well, news directors are no different.

The letter should be neatly typed on good stationery. Unlike the résumé, which may be mimeographed or photocopied, the cover letter is a personal sending. Even if the only thing you've changed about it is the name of the addressee and the station, it should at least appear to be the product of personal effort.

As for the writing: state what you want directly, namely, a job doing such and such; then, again briefly, state why you want it and how you are qualified for it. *Resist* all attempts at small talk, jocularity, and the same long-winded stuff you left out of your résumé. News directors are busy people. They don't have time for your small talk, and they don't give a damn about your long-range goals or theories about journalism. All they care about is if you're the kind of person who can cover or write a story about a school strike, city budget cut, or warehouse fire and get it on the air ahead of the competition. Period. And by the way, it helps if your signature is neat and clean instead of looking like a chicken came to roost on the paper.

Here's the text of a very poor cover letter received by a TV news executive:

Dear Mr. —————:

My career pursuit focuses on an enthusiastic challenge that will keep pace with the changing requirements of news broadcasting. I sincerely care about people as well as the community in which they live, and believe my mission is to present newsworthy events in a comprehensive and informative nature.

The ideal opportunity would involve active participation in the gathering and presentation of hard-news material. . . . By being in touch with the heartbeat of the community, I have developed a sixth sense that allows me to discern important facts, storylines and news events.

Please review my enclosed résumé. I feel my media skills and broadcast disciplines would be of value in meeting the needs of your major broadcasting accounts.

Sincerely Yours,

That letter, apart from its truly awful English and pretentious, nonsensical wording, touches on just about everything that employers do *not* want to hear. No responsible news broadcaster would trust such a poor writer and apparent fuzzy thinker to report or write the news for his station. (The applicant might, however, be considered for an *anchor* position if his or her tape showed superior performing ability.)

A newcomer's cover letter should go more or less like this:

Dear Mr. ————:

I'm looking for my first job in TV news. I'd like to be a reporter (writer, producer, etc.), but I'd welcome an opportunity in any area to show what I can do.

I haven't got a professional track record yet, so all I can offer is a readiness to work long and hard. I would very much like to discuss the matter with you in person, at your earliest convenience.

Sincerely,

Such a letter should be followed in two or three weeks by a phone call.

Testimony to the "equal employment" opportunities in modern broadcast news: WMAQ-TV (Chicago) assignment editor Angela Parker, 10 P.M. News producer Phyllis Schwartz, associate producer Karen Konyar (back to camera), and anchor/reporter Deborah Norville await late word on a breaking story from a field reporter. Sex and race are *not* factors in hiring practices. The only factor is ability to do the job, whether on the air or off.

Audition Tapes—Radio

Over the years, partly because of the relatively low cost of audiotape, it has become customary to submit a short tape to radio news directors along with the résumé and cover letter. For experienced applicants, the tape should include an air check of a recent newscast and a few voicers or wraps. For inexperienced applicants, the tape should be of a self-written newscast recorded in as professional a setting as possible; in other words, it shouldn't sound as if it was recorded in a dormitory clothes closet.

Whichever type of tape is submitted, it is well to include only your *best* effort. News directors have short attention spans because they're so busy. An audition tape has to "grab" them and not let go. Many news directors report that they make up their minds within 30 or 40 seconds whether to listen further.

For the few jobs in radio that do not require going on the air, professional writing samples should be sent.

Unfortunately, very few stations are decent about returning audition tapes. The feeling is apparently that since the tapes were unsolicited, there is no obligation to return them. Therefore, some job applicants withhold the tape, noting instead on their résumés or cover letters, "Tape on Request." Only if your credentials are strong to begin with should you not send a tape in radio.

Audition Tapes—TV

Given the higher cost of videotape cassettes and the greater difficulty in preparation, editing, and dubbing, you'd think it would be standard procedure *not* to send a tape in TV job hunting, except on request. Wrong. Indeed, sending a tape *is* standard procedure nowadays. And many prospective employers are no more decent about returning videocassettes than audiocassettes. So the job seeker's investment can add up.

On the plus side, although three-quarter-inch U-Matic tape remains the most standard format, more and more stations are equipping themselves with Beta or VHS (half-inch) tape gear for viewing material that does not have to be of broadcast quality. The cost of a Beta or VHS cassette is some 75 percent lower than a U-Matic cassette, and the postage to send it is a lot lower, too. Of course, you'll have to have to make sure in advance that the station is equipped to play the format you are sending. If you are short of tapes (or money) altogether, you might withhold the tape but note on your cover letter or résumé, "Tape on Request. Please specify U-Matic, Beta, or VHS."

With or without previous on-air experience, it is troublesome to prepare a TV audition tape. That's because, unlike radio, the tape may require sophisticated editing in order to include just those work samples you wish a prospective employer to see. Experienced applicants should include several reporting packages and, if available, an air-check of an anchor performance. Inexperienced applicants should go all-out to have themselves taped at university or corporate facilities, even if it's only of a self-written short newscast. Prospective employers *do* want to see what you look like on-camera, even if your anchoring or reporting is not as "slick" as you'd wish it to be. And remember, you can turn your lack of professional experience into an advantage of sorts: you can re-tape your anchor performance until you are satisfied with it.

Live Auditions—Radio

This is the real test of an applicant's qualifications. Up to now, the applicant has controlled the employer's view of his abilities. Now the employer finds out what the applicant *really* can do.

In radio, a more or less standard audition consists in being handed several hours' worth of wire service copy, given a time limit (usually 1 hour or 90 minutes), and told to write, and then read, a 5-minute newscast. A writer's audition would consist of the same test, minus the newscasting portion.

It is, of course, highly subjective who does well on such tests. One news director's criteria may be quite different from another's. What can be said with certainty, however, is that all such auditions are harder than the job itself. The applicant is perhaps in a strange town, is certainly in a strange environment, sitting in view of strangers, using an unfamiliar typewriter, and walking into an unfamiliar announcing studio, perhaps with his career on the line. He or she has every reason to be nervous.

But the employer knows for sure that if this young man or young woman can do a creditable job in *this* kind of situation, then he or she can certainly do it as part of the staff—and will probably be offered the job.

Although there are occasional exceptions, there are no distinct auditions for on-air radio reporting. Usually, all judgments are made on the basis of a newscasting audition. For example, a newsman who writes well but whose voice and delivery are deemed not "strong" enough to carry a full newscast may be offered a reporting position, provided that the staff is large enough to permit such specialization.

Live Auditions—TV

Writer. A writer's audition in TV may in practice not even be given, provided that the employer is satisfied with the applicant's job history and sample material. If an audition is given, it usually consists of rewriting a few minutes' worth of copy, incorporating graphics and titles where necessary.

Producer. Producers are generally promoted from the rank of writer. Producers hired from outside a shop do not take special auditions; their reputations usually precede them. But they may be asked to submit a detailed critique of a station's newscasts.

Assignment Editor. This is customarily another type of in-house promotion. However, there are cases where newcomers are hired directly as assignment desk trainees and then promoted to full rank if they quickly show a knack for the work.

Reporter. Reporters whose credentials and audition tapes pass muster are usually given a mock assignment, subject to the availability of a cameraman, which they cover and package as if it were for broadcast that day. Sometimes reporters are asked to rewrite a few wire service stories and deliver them on-camera from the anchor desk, merely to provide the news director with an idea of how the reporter looks and sounds in the station's particular environment.

Anchor. Since from the viewpoint of ratings and advertising revenue the anchor jobs are the most important (more so, even, than the news director), anchor auditions are very lengthy affairs. Competition for anchor jobs is extremely fierce.

By and large, anchors are hired on the basis of past performance and "ratings history." An employer wants to be as sure as possible (in a field where nothing is sure) that the anchor he or she hires will attract new viewers; and one way to narrow the choice is to hire someone with a proven record of increasing the ratings at his or her previous station. Thus, anchoring, while prominently associated in the public mind with the journalistic effectiveness of a station's news department, may in fact be the area at farthest remove from journalistic considerations.

This statement is not true at the networks, or at local stations where the anchors must really *be* first-rate newsmen and women, not just *appear* to be. Unfortunately, these stations do not abound. Many local stations will accept the appearance rather than the reality in their choice of anchors.

Hence, given the nature of things, if anchoring is what you aspire to—and why shouldn't you?—then you must start to do it whenever and wherever you can. In short, you must specialize in the performance aspect of television, perhaps foregoing journalistic opportunities in favor of performing opportunities. If you can do *both*, so much the better for you—and for television journalism as a whole.

ALTERNATIVE PATHS

Job hunting and career building defy the laws of geometry in that the shortest distance between two points is not always a straight line. Broadcast news is so vast and multifaceted an industry that it is impossible to make absolute declarations about what job seekers *must* do, what jobs they *must* have in order to get better ones. Life is too full of uncertainties.

For example, while the "typical" path to a major market or network job is first through small markets and then through medium ones, it is not the only path. Major market stations occasionally employ people as reporters or unit producers because of their expertise in a particular field such as law or medicine. Networks occasionally hire writers and reporters who have only newspaper experience. In other words, in some cases employers will go a long way to hire people with specialized knowledge, in the hope that they will quickly catch on to broadcast style and techniques.

Much depends, too, on the type of journalist *you* want to become. Unfortunately, small market and small station news departments do not provide the same sort of nuts-and-bolts *journalism* training as do most newspapers and news agencies. So if your goal is to be, say, a foreign correspondent or a specialist in business news, you would be wasting your time in a small market; you might be better off as a copy editor at a news agency or newspaper, or as a "stringer" in some foreign capital.

In the last analysis, no one controls your life but you yourself. Be wary of people who tell you there's only one way to skin a cat.

PERSISTENCE

When I was 21, (hey, it wasn't *that* long ago), time seemed to pass very slowly. My peers and I were impatient with the older generation. We were raring to get out and make our own marks on the world. Of course, you and your peers are now the impatient youngsters—I and mine the slow-moving oldsters you'd run right over given the chance.

I do have a point here . . . and it is this: If after six months of job hunting in broadcast news you have still not received an offer, do *not* become discouraged. Six months is *not* a long time to be job hunting in this field. Yes, it's discouraging, and, yes, it's demeaning—but, no, it is not unusual. A job seeker may send out 100 résumés and cover letters, may get answers to only 10, and may get serious consideration in only 2 or 3 cases. That's *normal* and in the nature of the beast. So get your second wind and try even harder.

Think of it this way: Is it reasonable to be any less persistent in landing that first job than in covering the news itself? Indeed, a few setbacks in finding work may be used as a positive guide for handling the things that happen once you do get the job. If a public official says "There's no story here," are you going to take his or her word for it, or are you going to press on?

And something about those busy news directors: just because they're busy, doesn't mean they won't talk to you or see you. You'll have to persist—just the way you would on a story. If a news director doesn't return your call, call him or her back. And call back again. Sooner or later you'll have his or her ear. Then, of course, you'd better have something to say. And I, for one, will be pulling for you.

SUPPLEMENTARY READING

Newswriting and Radio News

BLISS, EDWARD, AND JOHN PATTERSON; *Writing News for Broadcast;* New York: Columbia University Press, 1978.

CHANCELLOR, JOHN, AND WALTER MEARS; *The News Business;* New York, Harper & Row, 1983.

STEPHENS, MITCHELL; *Broadcast News: Radio Newswriting and an Introduction to Television;* New York: Holt, Rinehart and Winston, 1980.

Language and Usage

CLAIBORNE, ROBERT; *Our Marvelous Native Tongue: The Life and Times of the English Language;* New York: Times Books, 1983.

EHRLICH, EUGENE, AND RAYMOND HAND, eds.; *The NBC Handbook of Pronunciation*, Fourth Edition; New York: Harper & Row, 1984.

MITCHELL, RICHARD; *Less Than Words Can Say;* Boston: Little, Brown, 1979.

NEWMAN, EDWIN; *Strictly Speaking;* Indianapolis: Bobbs-Merrill, 1974; also, see his *A Civil Tongue;* Indianapolis: Bobbs-Merrill, 1976.

SAFIRE, WILLIAM; *On Language;* New York: Times Books, 1980.

ZINSSER, WILLIAM; *On Writing Well;* New York: Harper & Row, 1980.

History of Broadcasting

BARNOUW, ERIK; *A History of Broadcasting on the United States;* New York: Oxford University Press, 1966–70; also, see his *Tube of Plenty: The Evolution of American Television;* New York: Oxford University Press, 1975.

Biography and Autobiography

KENDRICK, ALEXANDER; *Prime Time: The Life of Edward R. Murrow;* Boston: Little, Brown, 1969.

Kurtis, Bill: *On Assignment;* New York: Rand McNally, 1983.

MACNEIL, ROBERT; *The Right Place at the Right Time;* Boston: Little, Brown, 1982

SHIRER, WILLIAM L.; *The Nightmare Years 1930-1940*; Boston: Little, Brown, 1984.

Collections of Broadcast Writing

KURALT, CHARLES; *Dateline America;* New York: Harcourt, Brace Jovanovich, 1979.

MURROW, EDWARD R.; *This Is London;* New York: Simon & Schuster, 1941.

OSGOOD, CHARLES; *Nothing Could Be Finer than a That Is Minor in the Morning;* New York: Holt, Rinehart and Winston, 1979; also, see his *There's Nothing I Wouldn't Do If You Would be My POSSLQ;* New York: Holt, Rinehart and Winston, 1981.

On Broadcast Journalism and Journalists

ARLEN, MICHAEL J.; *Living-Room War;* New York: Viking 1966–1969.

CROUSE, TIMOTHY; *The Boys on the Bus;* New York: Random House, 1972–1973.

FRIENDLY, FRED W.; *Due to Circumstances Beyond Our Control;* New York: Random House, 1967.

MACNEIL, ROBERT; *The People Machine;* New York: Harper & Row, 1968.

INDEX